RESTRUCTURING STRATEGY

Strategic Management Society Book Series

The Strategic Management Society Book Series is a cooperative effort between the Strategic Management Society and Blackwell Publishing. The purpose of the series is to present information on cutting-edge concepts and topics in strategic management theory and practice. The books emphasize building and maintaining bridges between strategic management theory and practice. The work published in these books generates and tests new theories of strategic management. Additionally, work published in this series demonstrates how to learn, understand, and apply these theories in practice. The content of the series represents the newest critical thinking in the field of strategic management. As a result, these books provide valuable knowledge for strategic management scholars, consultants, and executives.

Published

Strategic Entrepreneurship: Creating a New Mindset
Edited by Michael A. Hitt, R. Duane Ireland, S. Michael Camp, and Donald L. Sexton

Creating Value: Winners in the New Business Environment
Edited by Michael A. Hitt, Raphael Amit, Charles E. Lucier, and Robert D. Nixon

Strategy Process: Shaping the Contours of the Field
Edited by Bala Chakravarthy, Peter Lorange, Günter Müller-Stewens, and Christoph Lechner

The SMS Blackwell Handbook of Organizational Capabilities: Emergence, Development and Change
Edited by Constance E. Helfat

Mergers and Acquisitions: Creating Integrative Knowledge
Edited by Amy L. Pablo and Mansour Javidan

Strategy in Transition
Richard A. Bettis

Restructuring Strategy: New Networks and Industry Challenges
Edited by Karel O. Cool, James E. Henderson and René Abate

Innovating Strategy Process
Edited by Steven W. Floyd, Johan Roos, Claus D. Jacobs and Franz W. Kellermanns

Restructuring Strategy

New Networks and Industry Challenges

Edited by

Karel O. Cool, James E. Henderson, René Abate

Blackwell
Publishing

Learning Resources
Centre

12825700

BLACKWELL PUBLISHING
350 Main Street, Malden, MA 02148-5020, USA
108 Cowley Road, Oxford OX4 1JF, UK
550 Swanston Street, Carlton, Victoria 3053, Australia

First published 2005 by Blackwell Publishing Ltd

Library of Congress Cataloging-in-Publication Data

Restructuring strategy : new networks and industry challenges /
edited by Karel O. Cool, James E. Henderson, René Abate.
    p. cm.—(Strategic Management Society book series)
  Includes bibliographical references and index.
  ISBN 1–4051–2601–9 (hbk : alk. paper)
 1. Industries—Technological innovations. 2. Industrial management. 3. Strategic planning.
I. Cool, Karel O. II. Henderson, James E. III. Abate, René. IV. Series.
  HD45.R395 2005
  658.4′012—dc22

2004021406

A catalogue record for this title is available from the British Library.

Set in Galliard 10/12.
by Newgen Imaging Systems (P) Ltd, Chennai, India
Printed and bound in the United Kingdom
by T J International, Padstow, Cornwall

The publisher's policy is to use permanent paper from mills that operate a sustainable forestry policy, and which has been manufactured from pulp processed using acid-free and elementary chlorine-free practices. Furthermore, the publisher ensures that the text paper and cover board used have met acceptable environmental accreditation standards.

For further information on
Blackwell Publishing, visit our website:
www.blackwellpublishing.com

Contents

Contributors

Abate, René
Boston Consulting Group
e-mail: abate.rene@bcg.com

Blaxill, Mark
Boston Consulting Group
e-mail: blaxill.mark@bcg.com

Boutenko, Vladislav
Boston Consulting Group
e-mail: boutenko.vladislav@bcg.com

Cool, Karel O.
INSEAD
e-mail: karel.cool@insead.edu

Finkelstein, Sydney
Dartmouth College
e-mail: sydney.finkelstein@dartmouth.edu

Hansen, Mark H.
Brigham Young University
e-mail: mh_hansen@byu.edu

Henderson, James E.
Babson College
e-mail: henderson@babson.edu

Jensen, Robert
Wharton School, University of Pennsylvania
e-mail: jensen@management.wharton.upenn.edu

Jones, Neil
INSEAD
e-mail: neil.jones@insead.edu

Lévesque, Moren
Case Western Reserve University
e-mail: mxl101@cwru.edu

Lipparini, Andrea
Catholic University of Milan
e-mail: andrea.lipparini@unicatt.it

Lorenzoni, Gianni
University of Bologna
e-mail: lorenzon@economia.unibo.it

Mair, Johanna
IESE
e-mail: jmair@iese.edu

McEvily, Susan
University of Pittsburgh
e-mail: smcevily@katz.pitt.edu

Mooney, Ann C.
Stevens Institute of Technology
e-mail: amooney@stevens-tech.edu

Morieux, Yves
Boston Consulting Group
e-mail: morieux.yves@bcg.com

Nanda, Ashish
Harvard Business School
e-mail: ananda@hbs.edu

Nippa, Michael
Technische Universität Bergakademie Freiberg
e-mail: mnippa@marshall.usc.edu

Perry, Lee T.
Brigham Young University
e-mail: l_perry@byu.edu

Petzold, Kerstin
Technische Universität Bergakademie Freiberg
e-mail: kerstin.petzold@bwl.tu-freiberg.de

Prats, M. Julia
Harvard Business School
e-mail: mjprats@hbs.edu

Reese, C. Shane
Brigham Young University
e-mail: s_reese@statmail.byu.edu

Shepherd, Dean A.
University of Colorado
e-mail: dean.shepherd@colorado.edu

Szulanski, Gabriel
INSEAD
e-mail: gabriel.szulanski@insead.edu

Yao, Beiqing (Emery)
University of Pittsburgh
e-mail: bqyao@katz.pitt.edu

About the Editors

Karel O. Cool holds the BP Chair of European Competitiveness and a Professor of Strategic Management at INSEAD, based in Fontainebleau, France. His research interests include problems of industry and competitive analysis (e.g. industry overcapacity, profit dynamics, product standards, critical mass races, value creation, building unique resources). He has published in *Management Science*, the *Strategic Management Journal, Organization Science, Marketing Letters, Advances in Strategic Management*, etc., and has edited a book, *European Industrial Restructuring* in the 1990s. He is also the Associate Editor of the *Strategic Management Journal*. Professor Cool has consulted for many international companies on major problems of corporate and industry restructuring.

James E. Henderson is an Associate Professor of Strategic Management at Babson College based in Wellesley, MA. His research interests include industry competitiveness, and learning and strategic decisions (capacity expansion timing, supply chain management, and corporate venturing). He has published in several academic journals including *Strategic Management Journal, Academy of Management Best Paper Proceedings*, and *Frontiers of Entrepreneurship Research* and is also on the Editorial Board of the *Strategic Management Journal*. Professor Henderson has consulted for many international companies in the areas of business unit strategies formation, corporate venturing, and industry competitiveness.

René Abate is a Senior Vice President in the Paris office of the Boston Consulting Group. René Abate joined BCG in 1974. From January 1985 to December 1997 he was the Managing Director of the Paris office and Chairman of BCG Europe. He is now a member of the World Wide Executive Committee of the Boston Consulting Group. René Abate's professional practice focuses on assistance to large companies in strategy, new business development, acquisitions and organization. René Abate is a Civil Engineer from ENPC (Ecole Nationale des Ponts et Chaussées) in Paris. He received an MBA from Harvard Graduate School of Business Administration. He has recently published a book on the history of the largest French companies, entitled *Trajectoire d'Exception: à la découverte des plus grandes entreprises françaises*.

CHAPTER ONE

Restructuring Strategy

James Henderson, Karel Cool, and René Abate

Introduction

An industry consists of a complex web of rivals, customers, suppliers, providers of substitutes and complementary products (Rivkin and Porter, 2000). Typically industry structures or this web of relationships remain relatively stable over time. Change tends to remain incremental. For example, despite the bankruptcies, the US airline industry has been dominated by the trunks for the last 50 years. The soft drink industry has remained a comfortable duopoly between Pepsi and Coke. The automobile industry has remained a highly concentrated industry despite the inroads from the Japanese and Koreans. Industry structure historically has changed relatively slowly.

However, numerous triggers during the last decade including rapid globalization, technology jolts, shifts in consumers' needs, and regulatory changes have confronted a number of industries at an increasing rate. As a result, the environment has become increasingly volatile, turbulent, and uncertain. Hyper-competition has often been used to capture these new realities where companies face escalating competition from a number of fronts: from existing rivals, new players coming from different geographies, from substitute industries, or buyer or supplier industries. As a result, old barriers may crumble and in their place new ones may rise. Yet, the challenge for many incumbent industries, networks, companies, and management is to determine whether these changes are indeed "revolutionary" resulting in entirely new industries (e.g. the PC industry), "enabling" resulting in new end states for existing industries (such as Internet distribution of airline tickets, music, software etc.), or whether they are "complementary" resulting in small changes to the existing structure (such as physical distribution over the Internet). The test is to know which strategies and practices, regardless on what level of analysis (industry, network, or firm), are robust during these periods of potential industry restructuring.

This book provides a glimpse of successful strategies and management practices during periods of industry structuring and restructuring both from a theoretical and empirical perspective. At the end of the book the reader should have a better ability to answer the following questions. How is it that the Champagne industry still manages to earn significant above normal profits despite the change in the balance of power in the wine industry from the "old world" to the "new world?" How did the Italian motorcycle industry flourish (where in other countries it has failed) during the onslaught of the Japanese motorcycle manufacturers into Europe? How can pharmaceutical companies maximize their likelihood of drug leads when technology (e.g. genomics, biotechnology) is rapidly changing? Which e-consulting companies are most likely to survive an industry shake-out where demand plummeted due to the bursting of the Internet bubble? How should incumbents react in the face of a "disruptive" technological threat? How should companies expand overseas when the new country environments are radically different? What advice should we have for managers in these periods of industry structuring and restructuring? Finally, how should companies be governed during these periods of industry structuring and restructuring?

Industry Structuring and Restructuring Phases

Typically industries during periods of structuring or restructuring pass through several phases: an external triggering event, a period of experimentation or an era of ferment, and finally a movement back to the existing structure, or a shift to a new industry structure.

Triggers

What sparks the entry of new businesses, new business models, and/or new competitive positions prior to a system-wide industry restructuring is an external event or trigger. Typically this spark can come from changes in technology, changes in globalization, changes in consumer needs, or changes in regulations.

Changes in technology.   A change in technology may disrupt an industry in a number of ways. Christensen (1997) refers to technological disruptions because incumbents are wedded to their existing customer base, which would prefer to remain with existing rather than try new, often inferior, technologies. Yet, once the low-end technology gains hold in a smaller market segment, it is improved to the point that it satisfies the larger customer base. For example, he showed how the incumbents kept changing with each successive introduction of a new size in the disk drive industry resulting in a turbulent industry structure over time. The US steel industry has seen significant restructuring due to the introduction of minimills, or steel produced from recycled scrap. The minimill steel manufacturers, having first entered in the late 1960s, have evolved from low-end rebar manufacturers to high-end steel sheet manufacturers in the 1990s. Nucor, a minimill steel producer, rather than one of the traditional leading integrated manufacturers such as US Steel, Bethlehem etc. is now the largest steel manufacturer in the US.

New technologies can also disrupt industry structures because they render the existing incumbents' competencies obsolete (Tushman and Anderson, 1986). For example, the decline of Swiss watch manufacturers in the 1970s–1980s, the leaders in the global watch industry, could be traced to the commercialization of quartz technology by the Japanese. The new technology destroyed many of the existing watchmaking skills; employment in the industry dropped from 90,000 in 1970 to 32,000 in 1985. The global watch industry structure was dramatically altered.

Finally, new technological innovations may come from the altering of the product architecture or how the core and peripheral sub-systems interact. As Henderson and Clark (1990) argue, incumbents find it challenging to understand or comprehend new architectures because existing competencies may be structured around the existing product architecture. For example, Xerox, the pioneer of the plain paper copier, was unable to capture the lead in the small copier market despite the fact that architecture of the product was only altered in a seemingly minor way.

Yet these radical technological changes are infrequent. For example, Utterback (1994) was only able to collect a total of 22 such events over the last century. In many cases incumbents may possess complementary assets that allow them to weather the oncoming technological storm. For example, the introduction of the Internet, bar code scanners, radio frequency identification devices, satellite communications, and automatic distribution equipment only helped, not hindered, the dominance of such retailers as Wal-Mart in sustaining their cost advantages. Thus it is indeed a challenge for incumbents to determine how "disruptive" these new technological changes are going to be to their existing strategies and positions within their industry.

Changes in globalization.   In addition to changes in technology, we have witnessed over the last several years a relentless march towards a global economy. Liberalization of trade through the removal of tariff and non-tariff barriers has resulted in significant increased trade. The creation of regional trading blocs including the European Union (EU), the North American Free Trade Agreement (NAFTA), the Association of South East Asian Nations (ASEAN), and Mercosur has opened new markets for many different industries. For example, European insurance, banking, and airline industries have been significantly consolidated due to the reduction of regulations and non-tariff barriers. Regulations have been further and further standardized across these pan-regional blocs. For example, in the pharmaceutical industry, regulatory approval is now only required for the whole of Europe – previously it had to be done country by country. Even technologies and communications are spreading rapidly worldwide, allowing companies to extend their control farther distances. Finally, customer tastes are becoming more and more homogeneous as communications and companies have spread their messages and brands worldwide. What was once a formidable barrier to entry, distance, has increasingly been erased. The result has been a greater push toward global efficiency, and new global competitors. In some cases, it has meant significant change to existing domestic industry structures. For example, over the 1990s Toys 'R' Us redefined the Japanese toy retailing industry wiping out many of the small independent toy store owners that previously were able to survive in the highly regulated environment. However, in other cases, domestic incumbents are not only able to survive the globalization onslaught but also embrace it. For example, the structure of the sparkling wine industry still is dominated by Champagne producers despite the emergence and growth of the "new world" wines.

Changes in consumer and demographic needs.   Shifts in customer segments, needs, or wants may signal different ways to compete in an industry: either at a new cost level or providing differing drivers of perceived value. For example, as US households have become more affluent they continue to purchase second and third cars, larger homes, several golf sets, more clothes, more toys, etc. As a result, new industries have been spawned due to this continuous consumption of goods. For example, closet storage companies such as California Closets have flourished as households have had to cope with their increased amount of stuff. In the personal computer industry, as corporate purchasers and consumers became more at ease with the technology during the 1990s, handholding and expertise from resellers and computer salespeople became less important. This increase in experience fueled the success of the direct PC companies, Dell and Gateway, over the traditional incumbents, resulting in a changed industry structure. Yet not all changes in customer needs result in changes in industry structure. For example, the demand for increased consumer choice in cars has resulted in a proliferation of models and options. As Boston Consulting Group's Morieux, Blaxill, and Boutenko (this volume) explain, in 1950, Renault's range of passenger cars consisted of one model (the 4 CV) with two versions (*Normale* and *Luxe*) whereas today customers can choose from 14 Renault passenger car models, one with up to 39 different versions (Clio), up to 35 options, 17 exterior colors, 9 interior trims and two types of dashboards. While these combinations have increased 1,000-fold over the last 50 years due to this increased demand for choice, the global automobile industry has still remained reasonably stable over time.

Changes in regulations.   Many legislative and court decisions may change the nature of industry structuring and restructuring by changing the mix of buyer value and cost that companies are allowed to offer. For example, telecom deregulation in the 1990s led to a torrent of competitive local exchange carriers who were previously shut out; but their entry did not significantly alter the structure of the telecommunications industry dominated by the Regional Bell Operating Companies, AT&T, Sprint, and Worldcom. On the other hand, US banking deregulation has led to the creation of numerous universal banks that were previously non-existent. Breaking Napster's free distribution of music over the Internet gave the music industry some breathing room as it has been rapidly moving to another end state, music distribution over the Internet, to the detriment of the music retailers. The two-year unsuccessful battle to break up Microsoft ultimately left it, and consequently the personal computer industry, intact. However, numerous companies at the time were preparing for another potential industry structure.

There is evidence that the pace of these environmental changes or triggers has been increasing over time. For example, it took the telephone 35 years to get into 25 percent of all US households, the television 26 years, the radio 22 years, the PC 16 years and the Internet 7 years (Hammonds, 2001). Every region of the world has experienced dramatic increases in trade volumes in the 1990s (55 percent increase during 1990–8), achieving record levels prior to the Asian crisis. The proportion of mobile phones in the developing world has increased so quickly that they take up nearly one-third of mobile phone traffic. Migrant workers are more than ever looking for work outside their own countries. State governments in the developed and developing worlds have increasingly deregulated their industries including airlines, telecommunications, electricity, etc.

In summary, numerous external changes can trigger the entry of new businesses, the creation of new business models and competitive positions. Some of these changes will indeed result in the structuring of new industries or the restructuring of existing industries through changed power relationships between buyers and suppliers, unseating of incumbents or changes in concentration. Yet, in other situations, these changes may lead to a temporary jolt to the existing order. While incumbents may respond to the changes, they are not completely unseated from their positions of power.

Experimentation

An external trigger such as a change in technology, regulation, customer habits, usually leads to new trial and error search from both incumbents and entrants. New entrants may try out new business models, new positions, and different configurations of activities to deliver various combinations of price and perceived value to the customer. For example, numerous entrants into the Internet e-commerce world experimented with a number of different ways to earn revenues: referral fees, advertising revenue, product revenue, and information selling. Similarly with the advent of genomics, thousands of new companies have entered: those focusing on genomics technology building blocks, genomics information provision, those providing contract research services using their new search technologies, and finally those who were trying to become full-fledged bio-pharmaceutical players (e.g. Millennium Pharmaceutical and Human Genome Science).

Existing companies may modify their existing business, launch new internal ventures, or invest in external ventures as a way of shaping the future industry structure or of hedging bets should the final structure veer in another direction. For example, with the numerous technological and regulatory changes in the telecom industry, many incumbents established corporate venture capital funds to cope with the uncertainty, an amount of approximately $1.6 billion in 2001. Similarly US automobile companies have been investing in differing amounts in response to the advent of telematics or wireless services for the car. GM's response has been a full-fledged commitment in a new business unit called OnStar whereas Ford and DaimlerChrysler's responses have been more experimental, based on their differing views on the ultimate potential of the new opportunity.

The result of this increased activity and pace of change has certainly fueled more uncertainty and volatility. Between 1991 and 2001, the number of listed companies accounting for 80 percent of the world's market capitalization rose from 5,000 to 8,000. Furthermore, the number of listed companies comprising the remaining 20 percent rose from 3,000 to 13,000 over the same period (Morieux et al., this volume). The 120-month average of monthly amplitudes of the Dow Jones Industrial Average increased from 5.5 percent in 1947 to approximately 9 percent in 2001. The 36-month average of the NASDAQ composite index jumped from 6 percent in 1985 to 21 percent in 2001 (Morieux et al., this volume). Earnings have become more difficult to forecast. For example, the average absolute error on analysts' one-year forecasts has increased from 4 percent to 8 percent over the last 10 years (Morieux et al., this volume).

Often in response to this uncertainty and lack of information, entrants and incumbents seek to gain knowledge from others through alliances. Yet, these alliances can also be conduits for rampant imitation as new business models are quickly mimicked by others. As a result, too many companies may crowd into a new opportunity. For example, with the advent of the Internet, more than 100 e-consulting firms sprouted from 1995 to 2000, many seeking initial public offerings (IPOs) during the time and afterward (Prats and Nanda, this volume). Furthermore, capital providers such as venture capital companies can also get wrapped up in the mania as they are working with the same lack of information. For example, venture capital funding climbed from $13 to $93 billion from 1997 to 2000 during the Internet boom.

How these experiments play out ultimately affects the oncoming industry equilibrium. The challenge for incumbents is to determine how disruptive the changes may be, what actions they can take to shape the future of the industry into a new equilibrium or respond to them such that their existing positions of power remain intact.

Converging to new, shifting back to old

Many of the entrants during the experimentation phase will fail. For example, in the newly developed e-consulting industry, Prats and Nanda (this volume) show that of the 100+ firms that were in existence only 40 were still standing by December 2001. Numerous high profile e-commerce companies including Streamline, WebVan, Peapod (grocery delivery), Buy.com, Value America, and eToys (consumer goods), FreePC, and Gobi PC (free personal computers in return for Internet service provision fees) have all but disappeared. Yet, some remain standing and have ultimately redefined industry boundaries. For example, Cisco, a newcomer in the 1990s, has completely dominated the networking equipment industry putting enormous pressure on the previous incumbents Lucent and Nortel Networks. Dell, like many other entrants into the PC industry, started as a direct distributor of build-to-order machines for large customers. This distribution method ultimately dominated the industry by the late 1990s as Dell had become the undisputed industry leader. Yet in other situations, despite the vast increase in experimentation, the status quo remains. Often incumbent strategies are robust through these periods of turmoil. With the exception of Amazon.com, existing "bricks and mortar" players such as Wal-Mart and Toys 'R' Us remained on top of their respective retailing spheres despite the attempts of other pure Internet players including Buy.com, Value America and eToys. It was reasonably straightforward for incumbents such as Wal-Mart to incorporate the Internet into their existing way of competing in the industry. The Internet was simply another ordering option for customers who would prefer the convenience of purchasing while remaining at home. Wal-Mart could still leverage its enormous bargaining power, and logistics system from their existing businesses into this new distribution channel.

Yet, the key is to determine whether the changes and the ultimate increase in experimentation will in fact result in a convergence to a new industry order or a shift back to the existing status quo. What are industries, networks, companies, and management supposed to do during these periods of industry upheaval? We call it "restructuring strategy" and the following chapters provide a glimpse. We divide the book into three sections focusing on three different levels of analysis: the industry, the firm, and management. They are entitled Industry and Network Competitiveness, Successful Business Strategies during Periods of Industry Structuring and Restructuring, and Superior Management and Governance Practices.

Industry and Network Competitiveness

The first section of the book concerns industry and network competitiveness. Despite an environment of increasing volatility, complexity, and uncertainty, how do industries and networks of firms maintain and sustain their competitiveness? The chapters in this section build on the "relational based view of the firm" (Dyer and Singh, 2000) by illustrating the robust value of developing cooperative relations across firm boundaries in order to increase the benefit of the industry as a whole or of the network of firms allied together. Clearly, under increasing volatility, complexity, and uncertainty, mechanisms should be put in place to maximize interaction value rather than minimize interaction costs. Each chapter illustrates this important finding but from slightly different angles: understanding the mechanisms to avert opportunism in order to maximize benefits; determining the mechanisms to maximize relational benefits; optimizing the knowledge landscape in which the company is embedded; and finally reorienting the company to embrace rather than avoid complexity during periods of industry restructuring.

In the second chapter, Cool and Henderson build on a detailed case study of the French Champagne industry to develop a model of maintaining collective assets for supply chain performance. We have witnessed the dramatic restructuring of the global wine industry with the shift from the "old world" to the "new world." Interestingly, one old world industry, Champagne, has been somewhat immune to this dynamic. Rather than suffering dramatically, it has consistently outperformed other supply chains in the industry, for example Bordeaux. The authors argue that the Champagne supply chain has consistently been able to profit from its "collective asset," the reputation and quality of the Champagne name, despite the fact that it is owned by no one and accessed by everyone. Theory would suggest that this common asset should be subject to a "tragedy of the commons" through non-contribution, over use and hold-up. However, based on the study of the functioning of the Champagne supply chain, the authors identify nine drivers that affect the nurturing of the common asset. These drivers include self-regulation which lowers governance costs and enables five mechanisms that avert hold up, underinvestment, and overuse: restricted access to the Champagne common (defined boundaries); full contribution to the common asset (through a common fee imposed on the growers and producers of Champagne); multiple issues in negotiations (to ensure a higher likelihood of a cooperative solution); transparency in the use of the common (through the availability of statistics); and the establishment of formal and informal enforcement mechanisms. However, they also argue that opportunistic behavior is conditioned by the number of investment options; the level of the discount rate; and the track record of cooperation as a benchmark and signal.

While the second chapter focuses on the mechanisms to avert opportunistic behavior in order to sustain a common asset, in the third chapter, the authors discuss the mechanisms to maximize relational capital. Based on extensive fieldwork conducted on the Italian motorcycle industry, Lipparini and Lorenzoni document a number of managerial actions aimed at leveraging the knowledge generated, accumulated, and transferred across a network of suppliers. For example, the design of relational structures supporting and fostering reciprocal learning processes, the creation of a trust-based relational environment, the early involvement of suppliers in knowledge generation activities, and the development of relational capabilities are deliberately designed management practices with positive effects on product innovation, therefore increasing both the lead firm's and its network's competitiveness. Their findings support the idea that in industries where know-how is broadly dispersed, a strategy aimed at maximizing a firm's relational capital and creating a fertile environment for joint learning, efficiency, and flexibility can be a source of competitiveness despite industry restructuring threats. Indeed, this "relational capital" may be one reason why Italian motorcycle companies such as Ducati, Piaggio, and Aprilia have thrived despite the entry of the Japanese producers, Yamaha, Kawasaki, and Honda, whereas others in Europe (e.g. France and UK) have not.

While the previous chapter focuses on the mechanisms to maximize relational capital to maintain industry and network competitiveness, the fourth chapter discusses the importance of the content behind those relationship ties. Yao and McEvily introduce the concept of "knowledge landscape" to describe the distribution of knowledge in alliance networks. This landscape can be evaluated by mapping the size of a company's knowledge stock, the Euclidean distance between the firm's and its partner's knowledge stocks and finally the Euclidean distance among its partners' knowledge stocks. The authors suggest that a firm's position in its knowledge landscape affects the quality and diversity of the information and knowledge it is exposed to, and thereby its innovation performance. They indeed find empirical support for these assertions from studying over 150 alliances based in the global pharmaceutical industry. The results suggest that despite the decreasing trend for new drug approvals, increasing research and development budgets, and an ever consolidating pharmaceutical industry, those companies could improve their innovative outcomes by optimizing the knowledge landscape in which they are embedded.

The final chapter in the Industry and Network Competitiveness section concerns the changes that companies must embrace as they are increasingly faced with an environment of increasing complexity. Historically, companies attempted to avoid complexity and concentrate on strong environmental signals through organizational streamlining and simplification. However, in this chapter, the authors, Morieux, Blaxill, and Boutenko skillfully show through signal theory, network topology, and organizational sociology, the implications of the rising supply and demand for interactions: noise. They suggest that organization structures that "face" complexity and "leverage" weak signals will succeed in maximizing interaction value. The authors argue that organizations such as Cisco, which "face" complexity, have built up very successful and dense horizontal communities of practice where customer ideas and problems can be quickly solved through internal networks of contacts. They also argue that incentives should be designed to increase interactions rather than avoid them and that information and communication technologies should be focused on increasing effectiveness (value-generating ideas) rather than improving organizational efficiency.

In summary, those companies that can use mechanisms to avert opportunism and maximize relational capital, optimize their knowledge landscapes across organizational boundaries and organize their structures to embrace complexity, are likely to perform better individually and collectively, as a network of partners or as an industry as a whole, during periods of industry structuring and restructuring – as we have witnessed throughout these past couple of years. However, there may be strategies that entrants and incumbents can still deploy that position them particularly well during these tumultuous periods. It is to these individual company strategies, we now turn.

Successful Business Strategies in Industry Structuring and Restructuring

The second section of the book concerns successful business strategies during periods of industry structuring and restructuring. In an environment of increasing volatility, complexity, and uncertainty, how do new industry participants survive? How do incumbents respond? The following chapters emphasize a similar theme: the importance of strategy. Each chapter highlights this theme from a slightly different perspective. For example, the sixth chapter suggests that small companies entering into a new rapidly growing industry should focus on a particular area of expertise and should not grow too quickly (especially through acquisitions). The seventh and eight chapters argue that incumbents need not immediately enter into new arenas despite being potentially disrupted by upstarts. They can delay entry as they have the requisite complementary assets or robust product development capabilities, which may take entrants several years to develop. Finally, when faced with transferring competitive advantage, incumbents seem to be better off copying exactly their existing practices rather than adapting to local circumstances.

The sixth chapter illustrates a period of industry structuring in its purest form. E-consulting, the industry under study, experienced a dramatic rise in demand triggered by the introduction of the Internet. As a result of the many changes the Internet created, many company executives began assessing their own business and technology strategies, their marketing, sales, and pricing activities, their operations and organizational structures, and their relationships with customers, suppliers, alliance partners, and employees. Many "old economy" firms felt at a significant disadvantage (rightly or wrongly) to their "new economy" start-ups. E-consulting became a booming industry as old and new economy companies looked for help to navigate through the complexity. Yet, as Prats and Nanda show, the e-consulting party did not last particularly long, a phenomenon they refer to as "an entrepreneurial bubble." Through an exploratory cluster analysis of the performance drivers for 31 newly formed e-consulting firms over the period January 1998 through December 2001, the authors determined that those competitors who stuck to their strategies were most likely to survive through both periods. They found that those firms which sustained superior performance throughout the mania and shakeout periods of the bubble did not get embroiled in the rapidity of change. Rather they focused on a narrow rather than broad portfolio of skills, expanded organically rather than through acquisition, and finally grew less rapidly than those companies which only succeeded during the expansionary period of the industry.

While the previous chapter focused on robust strategies for entrant firms in a newly forming industry, Chapters 7 and 8 focus on optimal response strategies for incumbents facing a potentially disruptive technology. In Chapter 7, the authors, Lévesque and Shepherd, propose a theoretical model that determines an incumbent's optimal time of entry. Their model takes into consideration (1) the possible tradeoff between profit potential and mortality risk in early entry, (2) the incumbent's stock of resources and the value of those resources relative to those of the pioneer(s), and (3) any changes in the external environment that may affect entry timing. Lévesque and Shepherd provide a very useful example of their model using a "bricks and mortar" retail firm entering the "virtual" grocery market place. In Chapter 8, the author, Neil Jones, empirically examines one of the previous model's effects: the incumbent's stock and value of resources compared to the entrants', in particular "robust" product development capabilities. Jones develops and tests the impact of such capabilities following radical competence-destroying technological change, in this case, the switch from electromechanical to semiconductor component systems in the telephone switching industry. Using data drawn from 39 product development projects over a 16-year period, Jones found that while entrant firms initially possessed superior capabilities in the new technology, over the medium and longer term incumbent firms through their robust product development capabilities improved more rapidly and eventually outperformed entrants. This finding suggests that incumbent product development capabilities may be positive or negative depending on the time frame considered. Furthermore, incumbent firms may manage technological transitions more effectively in the long run than has been contemplated by the recent literature.

While Chapter 6 examined the robustness of entrants' strategies in periods of industry restructuring or industry shakeouts and Chapters 7 and 8 showed how important the existing incumbent firm resource base is in surviving and indeed thriving during industry turmoil, Chapter 9 focuses on another critical area of complexity: how assets should be configured in different environments. How robust is a business model across borders? In particular, Szulanski and Jensen examine how the internal transfer of knowledge assets should be adapted to fit local conditions in a host environment. Given that the ex-ante understanding of a host environment, even for the host, is limited, the configuration of knowledge assets when adaptation begins may differ from the final form when adaptation efforts abate. In this chapter the authors explore the impact of one possible adaptation mode, an initial adaptation based on a presumed understanding of the host environment. Through an in-depth field investigation of an international expansion of a franchise organization, Mail Box etc., Szulanski and Jensen explore how adherence or non-adherence to recommended franchise expansion practices affects the rate of network growth in the host country, in this case, Israel. The authors find, contrary to received wisdom, that initial changes or presumptive adaptation causes poor network growth, while closely following the original practice results in rapid network growth. Thus, similar to the previous chapters, successful strategies can be robust across several different environments and that adaptation based on presumed understanding of the environment can ultimately be detrimental to performance.

In summary, we see from these brief chapter summaries that successful companies faced with tremendous environmental change whether it comes from severe demand decline, technology shifts or geographic differences can rely on robust strategies. Rather than immediately shifting according to the environmental change, collectively these chapters suggest that relying on the qualities of the existing strategy – focus, use of complementary assets, and well-honed routines and capabilities – can often enhance not only the company's survival but also performance. Yet, ultimately it is the quality of management and corporate governance which translates this focus, use of complementary assets, and well-honed routines and capabilities into actions that will allow companies to successfully navigate through these tumultuous periods, the subject of the last section of the book.

Superior Management and Governance Practices

The last section of this book concerns how companies can be steered in the proper directions through management or corporate governance practices. In an environment of increasing volatility, complexity, and uncertainty, what should management do? How important are top and/or middle management's actions? How much should they be constrained by corporate governance practices? What corporate measures work during these periods of industry structuring and restructuring? Each chapter in this section provides a glimpse of the newest thinking on managerial and corporate governance practices especially during these periods. For example, the tenth chapter suggests that managerial actions rather than resource heterogeneity explain performance differences across companies within a similar industry. The eleventh chapter indeed illustrates how managerial actions, in this case, middle manager entrepreneurial behavior, can be so performance enhancing. Finally, the last two chapters argue the importance of the process rather than structure of corporate governance in enhancing decision quality and ultimately corporate performance.

The tenth chapter shows that the current thinking behind the source and sustainability of competitive advantage, the resource-based view, requires reconsideration. The authors indeed provide a telling example of one reason why. The resource-based logic would suggest that no Idaho farmer who grows potatoes and has access to essentially the same resources – seed potatoes, fertilizers, equipment, and labor, weather, air, water and soil quality – would realize a competitive advantage vis-à-vis other farmers in the region. Yet, some farmers clearly enjoy a competitive advantage as evidenced by their survival, expansion, and wealth relative to their neighbors, some of whom are forced into bankruptcy. Hansen, Perry, and Reese argue that these gaps between theoretical and practical utility of the resource-based view come from the overgeneralization and vagueness in the specification of the relationship between resources and competitive advantage. However, the authors suggest that the gap can be narrowed in two ways. First, the connection between resources and competitive advantage may be enhanced by the explicit recognition of Penrose's (1959) distinction between resources and services. This distinction suggests how important managerial actions are in converting resources into valuable services. Second, Hansen, Perry, and Reese argue that the statistical techniques should reflect that the resource-based view is a theory about extraordinary performers or outliers rather than means. The authors use a novel Bayesian Hierarchical methodology to examine actions taken by new CEOs that allows one to make meaningful probability statements about individual rather than groups of firms.

While the authors in the tenth chapter argue how important managerial action is to transform resources into services, the eleventh chapter provides some empirical support. Mair argues that despite prior research on middle management, we still do not know whether and how their behavior translates into superior performance. This chapter thus examines whether and how middle manager entrepreneurial behavior within the same corporate context affects profitable growth at the sub-unit level. Empirical analysis on 118 middle managers of a large Dutch financial services firm suggests that entrepreneurial behavior does trigger profitable growth at the sub-unit level through the innovative use of resource combinations to explore and exploit opportunities. Furthermore, the results reveal that personal and unit-specific characteristics are significantly related to superior performance.

Even if the quality of management is at the heart of making good strategic decisions especially during periods of industry structuring and restructuring, their actions still need to be checked and monitored to ensure that those decisions are indeed in the best interests of the shareholders. In fact, the response to many of the latest corporate governance scandals – Tyco, Enron, Adelphia Communications, etc. – has been to increase the degree of monitoring through newly enacted laws such as the Sarbannes–Oxley Act in the US and *KonTraG* in Germany. Yet, as the authors, Nippa and Petzold, argue in Chapter 12, increased uncertainty coupled with bolstered external monitoring and pressure can trigger managerial reaction and ultimately costly justification behavior in the form of modifications to previously made decisions, decision-making processes or interactions between shareholders and management. Under increasing justification pressure, top management may deviate from their intended decision and conform to the shareholder view, which may not necessarily be economically favorable. For example, Kodak may cave in to the demands of shareholders to reinstate its dividend rather than spend it on digital photography pursuits to enhance the survival of the company. Furthermore, justification pressures may make top management spend more resources on evaluation, information gathering and selection issues resulting in decision delays, extra time, and cost. Finally, managers may increase their reporting to shareholders through investor relations, improve the translation of their actions into shareholder friendly terms, may spend effort obtaining outside certification of their decisions by well-known consultants and/or further educate shareholders through investor conferences. All of these efforts also take time and cost money. Indeed, the authors are the first to show the importance and cost of this phenomenon "justification" in strategic decision making that may limit the perceived benefits of increasing corporate governance pressure.

In addition to increasing monitoring, the received view in corporate governance has been to focus on board structure and independence as mechanisms to improve strategic decision making and ultimately corporate performance. However, in the final chapter, authors Mooney and Finkelstein argue that these "usual suspects" concerning board structure and independence – the number of outside board directors, director shareholdings, board size, and whether the chief executive officer (CEO) also holds the Chair position – do not always ensure a board is truly effective. Rather, they argue that board process is the key to making boards work better. Based on structured interviews with members of corporate boards, the authors suggest a number of process mechanisms that may improve the effectiveness of boards on strategic decision making. Constructive or cognitive conflict allows the members to debate the specific decision at hand without members feeling threatened through affective conflict. Building an integrated team enables easy information exchange and joint decision making. Finding the right degree of decision involvement ensures that the board is not micro-managing. The importance of decision comprehensiveness ensures that the board is drilling down to understand the specific issues of each decision. Finally, the authors provide some suggestions as to how boards could improve these process mechanisms, thus enhancing their effectiveness overall and the quality of a company's strategic decisions.

In summary, we find from these brief chapter summaries that above all it is the quality of management, and corporate governance practices that will navigate incumbents and entrants through these periods of industry structuring and restructuring. Personal characteristics and entrepreneurial behavior, especially at the middle management level, allow an incumbent to maintain its position while exploring new opportunities at a local level. Finally, corporate governance processes where there is a healthy, informative, constructive dialogue between management and shareholders will likely result in superior decisions and ultimately improved corporate performance.

Conclusion

A common reaction to the increased pace of change that may result in radically altered industry structures has been to postpone strategy setting or abandon it. Many have argued that incumbents have to remain flexible. With the influx of so many companies during the Internet bubble, for example, the general conclusion was that companies had to be ready to change their goals and strategies virtually overnight. Some have argued that establishing a strategy is fruitless as it would be rendered obsolete immediately to the pace of environmental change (Stepanek, 1999). Thus, rather than focus on strategies and efforts that are robust through these periods of turmoil, companies would be better off learning, executing, refining etc.

Yet, strategy and uncertainty resolution go hand in hand. Strategies can shape the very industries that companies are trying to understand. Rather than being obsolete, the explicit setting of strategy, and the underlying factors that improve existing industry orders, network competitiveness, and incumbents' positions, are in fact more important than ever. Qualities of the existing strategies – relational capital built through strong networks, focus, use of complementary assets and well-honed routines and capabilities – do seem to matter. Furthermore, the role of management and corporate governance is crucial in understanding how these strategies can be set and executed during these periods. This book thus sheds new light on this very important topic of restructuring strategy or how new and existing industries, firms, and management can best take advantage of the increasing pace of change that is facing them.

References

Christensen, C. 1997: *The Innovator's Dilemma: When New Technologies Cause Great Firms to Fail*. Boston, MA: Harvard Business School Press.

Dyer, J. and Singh, H. 2000: The relational view: Cooperative strategy and sources of inter-organizational competitive advantage. *Academy of Management Review*, 23, 660–679.

Hammonds, K. 2001: What is the state of the new economy? *Fast Company*, 50, 101–104.

Henderson, R. and Clark, K. 1990: Architectural innovation: The reconfiguration of existing product technologies and the failure of established firms. *Administrative Science Quarterly*, 35, 9–30.

Penrose, E.T. 1959: *The Theory of Growth of the Firm*. Oxford: Basil Blackwell.

Rivkin, J. and Porter, M. 2000: Industry transformation. Harvard Business School Case 701-008.

Stepanek, M. 1999: How fast is Net fast. *Business Week E.Biz*, November 1, 52–54.

Tushman, M. and Anderson, P. 1986: Technological discontinuities and organizational environments. *Administrative Science Quarterly*, 31, 439–465.

Utterback, J. 1994: *Mastering the Dynamics of Innovation: How Companies Can Seize Opportunities in the Face of Technological Change*. Cambridge, MA: Harvard Business School Press.

Industry and Network Competitiveness

Maintaining Collective Assets, the Tragedy of the Commons, and Supply Chain Performance: The Case of the Champagne Industry

Karel Cool and James Henderson

Introduction

The dominant view in supply chain management is that supply chain competitiveness comes from forging long-term recurrent bilateral relationships with a number of suppliers to maximize transaction value rather than minimizing transaction costs (see e.g. Dyer, 1997). Through exchange of information, coordinated decision-making, self-enforcing safeguards such as goodwill, and trust, hold up is minimized while suppliers make specific investments beneficial for the relationship (Dyer, 1997; Corbett et al., 1999). Yet this view and analysis of supply chain management under-estimates the importance of horizontal coordination among the various players within each stage of the supply chain (see e.g. Sako, 1996; Lazzarini et al., 2001). Indeed, an increasing number of longer-term supply chain initiatives involve a large number of players both along the supply chain (vertical) and within each stage (horizontal) in building common assets: setting up new distribution channels such as satellite systems; agreeing on product standards and guarantees; introducing new technical standards (e.g. GSM, Bluetooth); developing payment system (e.g. smart-cards); creating industry-based research and development centers (e.g. Sematech, National Oil Research Alliance), building information systems (e.g. EDI, B2B exchanges); ensuring a collective reputation for quality (e.g. Japanese automobile exports, Cognac, Port, Rioja); or environmental responsibility (e.g. Responsible Care Program of chemical manufacturers) or marketing a common brand name (e.g. milk, pork, oil, gas, etc.). In such cases, the players involved may not only be linked vertically as buyer and suppliers but also horizontally as competitors.

Supply chain competitiveness may increasingly be linked to the abilities of other firms both vertically and horizontally in managing and nurturing common assets built up over time. For example, the competitiveness of the Japanese automobile supply chain due to its common asset, the high quality and reliability of its cars, has been linked to not only well-known long-term vertical contracts with its suppliers (see e.g. Dyer, 1997) but also the horizontal coordination of its supplier associations (Sako, 1996; Hines and Rich, 1998). Given that networks of firms or supply chains are increasingly competing with each other (see e.g. Gomes-Casseres, 1994), the lack of research on this topic is surprising (cf. Monge et al., 1998).

We argue that establishing and maintaining collective assets may not only be subject to hold up along the vertical axis of a supply chain but also the "tragedy of the commons" along the horizontal axis (see e.g. Hardin, 1968). Hardin (1968) developed the tragedy metaphor to illustrate the problems of non-contribution to and over-use of common resources such as fisheries, common pastures, or forests that are accessed by similar players. Hardin asked the reader to imagine what would happen to a common pasture if each herder were to add a few sheep to his herd. Since each grazer would reap all the profits from these extra sheep but bear only a fraction of the cost of overgrazing, the result would be a tragic loss of common pasture for the entire community. His conclusion was that "freedom in the commons brings ruin to all" (Hardin, 1968: 1244).[1]

Supply chain competitiveness hinges upon the development and proper use of collective assets (e.g. standards, brand names, reputation for quality) such that firms' strategies are better coordinated, transaction costs are minimized; joint payoffs are increased, and all the players in the chain are better off. Yet these collective assets are prone to opportunistic behavior both vertically and horizontally: some firms may invest too little; others may abuse the collective assets, while others will hold out for higher profits. The purpose of this chapter, therefore, is to explore, to date, this under-researched topic: how collective assets are maintained and nurtured to improve supply chain performance while averting non-contribution, over-use and hold-up. The objective of this chapter is not to determine how a collective asset is established (see e.g. Monge et al., 1998 for propositions concerning the provision of public goods in alliances) but to explore how collective assets are maintained and nurtured in multi-firm partnerships (Dyer, 1997), networks (Sydow and Windeler, 1998) or constellations of firms (Jones et al., 1998) along a supply chain. We do so by exploring the mechanisms in which the French champagne supply chain has success-fully managed its common asset, the reputation of the Champagne brand. We focus on two stages of the champagne supply chain, namely the growers and the houses[2] and examine both their vertical and horizontal relations.

The chapter is thus organized as follows. We first highlight our research methods and describe the industry in which we carried out our field study. In the section thereafter, we build on an in-depth case study of the champagne industry to introduce a model for maintaining collective assets for supply chain performance. In so doing, we highlight the key drivers and how they may interact in nurturing a common asset. In the last section, we conclude by exploring the generalizability of this model.

Methods

We pursued our research by iterating inductive and deductive reasoning to develop our proposed model. While concerns for external validity and generalizability indeed remain, qualitative, historical research was chosen over pure deductive reasoning in order to gain greater insight into a phenomenon that has not been completely understood: the maintenance of collective assets through horizontal and vertical coordination (Yin, 1984; Eisenhardt, 1989). However, as we were studying the phenomenon, we compared our findings with transaction cost economics and public goods and commons literature. This way we were able to "infold the literature" on the topic (Eisenhardt, 1989).

Research setting

The model is based on 3 years of historical and field-based research on the functioning and dynamics of the French champagne supply chain, located southeast of Paris. The industry which represents approximately 7 percent of the total sales of sparkling wine worldwide, counts over 15,000 growers, 8,000 with less than one hectare (2.5 acres) of land; 4,500 grower-producers, 45 cooperatives and 260 champagne houses who grow approximately 10 percent of their own grapes. Champagne, similar to any wine, is an experience good such that the quality of the drink can only be ascertained after use. Thus, a consumer's willingness to pay may be related to the reputation or information of the past quality of the Champagne brand. Given the vast numbers of players in the champagne supply chain, we may assume that consumers may base their decisions on the "collective reputation" of champagne (e.g. its superior product quality and brand image with respect to other sparkling wines) rather than, or in addition to, the reputation of one particular firm, such as Moet et Chandon, Laurent Perrier, Mumms or any of the champagne coming from the grower-producers (see e.g. Sharp and Smith, 1991). Indeed, in their study on Bordeaux wine, Landon and Smith (1997) found that both the individual firm's quality and collective reputation of the regions (e.g. Medoc, Graves, Pauillac etc.) affected a consumer's willingness to pay for a bottle of Bordeaux.

However, the large number of parties and significant uncertainty surrounding the weather and the long time lags between production and sale suggests that managing the collective asset, the reputation of the "Champagne" name, would be subject to a tragedy because of non-contribution, over-use and hold-up (see e.g. Stigler, 1964; Olsen, 1965). In the absence of any established rules, what rational grower or house would help to contribute to the reputation of the Champagne name when non-contributors could benefit as much as the contributors? Furthermore, unless certain incentives are established, the payoffs to "over-fertilizing" to increase the yields, to pressing the grapes a few more times, or to fermenting champagne for less than one year, far outweigh a grower-producer's or house's share of a common cost shared by all, the depreciation of the collective reputation of Champagne. Finally, the growers and houses could hold each other up over the distribution of the benefits from the common asset thus tarnishing the industry's reputation. Yet, despite these incentives to behave opportunistically through non-contribution, over-use and hold-up, the supply chain has been remarkably successful at maintaining the reputation of the name, Champagne. Prior to exploring the factors that contributed to this success, we first present the historical context and the data collected for the study.

Industry background.   Grapes had been grown in the Champagne region for several millennia. However, it was not until the seventeenth century that local producers, including Dom Perignon and his Benedictine monks, developed a reliable method for the production of sparkling wine: "la méthode champenoise." The first champagne house, Ruinart, was founded in 1729 under royal permission.

From its earliest days, the production of champagne was divided between two different groups of firms: the *récoltants* who grew the grapes and the *négociants* who fabricated and sold the champagne. The growers formed an association to represent their collective interests, Syndicat Général des Vignerons de Champagne (SGV) in 1882, and the producers a similar association, the Syndicat du Commerce des Vins de Champagne (SCVC) in 1904. In 1911, the two groups organized their first joint meeting to discuss pricing of grapes. However, little success was made in establishing formal price agreements. The following 25 years would see the development of laws defining the production of champagne (*appelation d'origine contrôlée*). It was also during this period, in 1927, that the grape growing area in the Champagne region was defined.

The industry's first crisis occurred in the 1920s. Sales of champagne had peaked at 39 million bottles in 1910 but fell back to 12 million in 1921. In the same period, the Champagne region produced abundant harvests. Stocks reached 150 million bottles in 1934, over 5 years' supply; the price of grapes crashed. The growers were starving and showed their anger by rioting in the streets of Reims, the capital of the Champagne region. Action was taken by the government and professional bodies: a decree of September 28, 1935 limited the yield per hectare of vineyard and specified production quantities. The surplus began to reduce. Since then, annual meetings have been held between the growers, producers and the government to determine the amount of grapes (in kilos per hectare) that benefit from the appellation designation. Production above this amount was turned into wine, distilled or trashed.

After 6 years of successful negotiations, the growers and houses instituted a state-approved inter-industry body: the Comité Interprofessionel du Vin de Champagne (CIVC), which represented the interests of both parties. The organization defined its role quite broadly: to act as a forum for organizing the yearly negotiations, to act as a center of information and research on the industry, to conduct research and development on champagne growing and production methods, and to provide marketing assistance for the Champagne brand. Agreements covered a number of issues: price, yield, number of pressings, and the minimum alcohol quantity, for a period of up to 6 years. These agreements were the beginning of a new period of prosperity and stability that lasted approximately 30 years.

In 1971, the era of the multinational "luxury good" company arrived in Champagne when Moët et Chandon, then controlling 25 percent of the market, merged with the cognac firm, Hennessy, and later took over the House of Dior.

Other houses rushed to acquire perfume or similar luxury good producers. Moët-Hennessy itself embarked on a series of acquisitions of established champagne houses, such as Mercier and Ruinart. However, the industry adapted to the owner-ship changes and even held together during the economic downturn of the 1970s when grape prices and yields were drastically cut.

In 1989, champagne achieved record sales of 249 million bottles. During the same year, the mounting number of grower-producers saw an opportunity to capture more of the large retail margins for themselves by producing their own champagne. Given the limits on the land and the appellation decision, they kept more of the grape production for themselves. As a result, the growers were only prepared to supply 83 percent of the champagne houses' requirements. No collective agreement was struck and for the first time in over 40 years pricing was left to the free market. In the regulated market before 1989, growers would supply their grapes based on the negotiated price per kilo of grapes without knowing to whom they were supplying. Furthermore, each house was served with a quantity of grapes according to its sales in the previous year. After 1989 there were no such restrictions; the houses were left to negotiate with individual growers based on a "reference price" determined by the CIVC.

The negotiations in 1989 and 1990 were little short of chaotic. Few of the industry's players had any real experience of negotiating with one another. The large number of players compounded industry problems. Laurent-Perrier, for instance, found itself negotiating and signing contracts over a 2-week period with 1,200 individual grow-ers. Grape prices soared from around FF27 per kilo in 1989 to around FF60 per kilo in a few contracts in 1990 since there was little transparency regarding the individual contracts. At the same time, many growers, cooperatives and lesser-known houses continued to press forward with their plans to sell their own champagne with little regard to quality.

The houses reacted to increased grape costs by raising their prices by around 20 percent, just when the world economy was slipping into recession and military tensions in the Gulf started. Champagne consumption fell by 7 percent and grape prices decreased to FF30 per kilo in 1991. In spite of this demand decrease, the houses further raised prices by around 10 percent in 1991. Most houses saw this as the only way to maintain profitability and champagne's prestige position. As the demand for champagne continued to fall, stocks ballooned providing an opportunity for speculators to buy finished but non-labeled champagne (*vin sur lattes*).

Through the CIVC, however, the growers and houses searched for solutions to the crisis. By 1992, they agreed on improving the quality of the wines by reducing the yield per hectare (from 11,200 to 9,000 kg per hectare); reducing the number of pressings (from three to two leading to a ratio of 160 kg of grapes for each 100 liters of wine); pushing for longer fermentation times (from 12 to 15 months); introducing a *blocage* or reserve stock of champagne (2,900 kg per hectare that was pressed and made into wine, blocked in tanks at the champagne houses and financed by the grow-ers until officially released). Furthermore, they agreed on increasing the CIVC bud-get for promoting champagne worldwide. The effect of these agreements was to limit the production to 220 million bottles of champagne in 1992. However, despite the promotions, sales only reached 214 million bottles in 1992, equal to the previous year's sales.

Table 2.1   Prices and stocks in the champagne industry

	Average price/bottle (nominal)	Average price/bottle (real)	Price/kilo grapes (nominal)	Price/kilo grapes (real)	Stock/sales growers	Stock/sales producers	Stock/sales industry
1970	13.09	13.09	4.88	4.88	3.4	2.5	2.8
1971	13.84	13.12	5.42	5.14	3.4	2.8	3.0
1972	15.83	14.13	6.65	5.94	3.2	2.6	2.7
1973	19.08	15.87	8.37	6.96	3.3	2.7	2.8
1974	21.67	15.85	8.45	6.18	4.4	3.9	4.1
1975	18.80	12.30	6.10	3.99	4.4	3.8	4.0
1976	19.36	11.56	7.18	4.29	3.8	2.8	3.1
1977	21.02	11.47	7.98	4.36	4.4	2.8	3.3
1978	23.28	11.65	9.41	4.71	4.2	2.5	3.0
1979	28.79	13.01	11.56	5.22	2.9	2.2	2.4
1980	34.35	13.67	23.50	9.35	3.5	2.5	2.8
1981	42.48	14.91	20.00	7.02	3.4	2.5	2.8
1982	49.84	15.64	19.03	5.97	3.2	2.3	2.6
1983	51.05	14.61	15.53	4.45	4.5	2.8	3.3
1984	48.55	12.94	18.07	4.82	5.8	2.5	3.5
1985	54.33	13.68	23.03	5.80	5.3	2.4	3.4
1986	58.86	14.44	22.19	5.44	4.5	2.5	3.1
1987	57.81	13.75	21.77	5.18	4.3	2.8	3.3
1988	59.93	13.88	22.80	5.28	4.3	2.6	3.1
1989	66.34	14.83	27.00	6.03	3.7	2.4	2.8
1990	72.97	15.78	32.00*	6.92*	3.6	2.5	2.9
1991	78.31	16.46	30.00*	6.31*	4.3	3.4	3.7
1992	69.00	14.11	24.00*	4.91*	5.2	3.5	4.1
1993	60.19	12.06	20.50*	4.11*	6.1	3.3	4.2
1994	59.75	11.78	21.25*	4.19*	6.5	3.1	4.0
1995	60.00	11.74	22.25*	4.35*	6.3	2.8	3.8
1996	61.06	11.73	24.00*	4.61*	6.3	2.8	3.8
1997	62.26	11.80	24.00*	4.55*	6.5	2.8	3.8
1998	66.22	12.55	25.00*	4.74*	5.3	2.6	3.4
1999	73.58	13.77	25.50*	4.77*	4.7	2.5	3.2
2000	76.96	14.00	26.25	4.77	4.8	3.0	3.6

* Reference price.

Industry situation at the time of the field study.   Our initial contact with the CIVC and SGV and some of the major Champagne houses was in January 1994 when the industry was under significant pressure because of the growing stocks of champagne bottles, the decline in demand, plummeting prices for champagne bottles and the increasing financial burden to support the inventory. The evolution of the price of the grapes, the average price per bottle of champagne and the ratio of stocks to sales is shown in Table 2.1. Despite the efforts to resolve the crisis through the CIVC, tensions were still very high between the growers and houses.

Just prior to our visit, the Ministry of Agriculture encouraged the two parties to "hammer" out an agreement despite the ill will between the two parties. The appellation was reduced from 11,900 kg per hectare in 1992 to 10,400 kg per hectare in 1993. Other decisions were made as well: to maintain a reserve stock of 1,900 kg per hectare; to cancel the third pressing again; and to reduce the price of the grapes to FF20.5 (through arbitration). In spite of these efforts, there was still a massive supply–demand imbalance: the stocks were over four times annual sales. (Approximately 2.7 times annual sales were considered ideal.)

Yet, the growers and producers continued to come to agreements in the following years to solve their problems. Furthermore, renewed efforts by the CIVC were made in research and development through the Institut Technique de Champagne (ITC) and in promoting the collective brand. The industry appeared to have turned one of the worst pages in its history. While historic profitability levels had not been restored, the slow economic recovery and the new-found stability of 3-year supply contracts indicated that the industry was recovering.

This stability indeed was confirmed in the two following years. Refer to Table 2.2, which provides the performance of the houses of Champagne and Bordeaux. Industry observers gave a lot of credit to the inter-industry association, CIVC, and the way in which the industry had managed itself: "Industry associations are the only way for agricultural sectors to succeed. The CIVC is an obvious and envied proof. But success is never definitively achieved. It only continues so long as it is managed with a spirit of compromise and fairness."[3]

Data collection and analysis

Data were collected mainly from archives, interviews, and secondary sources to reconstruct the background and dynamics of the industry over the last 50 years. The primary sources included 25 individual interviews with 13 different people at various levels in their respective organizations including the Banque de France, the CIVC, SGV, Laurent Perrier, G.H. Mumm, LVMH, Association of Sparkling Wine Producers (Compagnie Française de Vin Mousseux), National Association of Inter-professional Wine Associations (OniVins), Association of Cava Producers (Union de Criadores Elaboradores de Vinos Espumosos), Association of Sekt Producers (Verband Deutscher Sektellereien), Comité Interprofessionel de Bordeaux (CIVB) and the EEC DGIV. In addition to the interviews, substantial archival sources from the CIVC, Banque de France and SGV on the Champagne supply chain were collected to gain a better historical understanding of the industry. Furthermore, more recent trade press articles were also collected to validate the content of the interviews.

Data analysis consisted of two different steps. During the first step, which lasted from January 1994 to September 1994, we collected and analyzed the data. During this stage the archives were reviewed; the interview notes were transcribed and categorized according to the topics describing the industry's history and the emergence of the CIVC, the drivers of its success and how the industry had managed an over-supply problem. The second part of the analysis started in September 1995 when we iterated back and forth from the description of the industry developed in the first stage and with the research on common resources (see e.g. Ostrom, 1990), and transaction cost economics (see e.g. Williamson, 1985). This process allowed us to

Table 2.2   Return on sales for producers in Champagne and wine merchants in Bordeaux

Year	Champagne	Bordeaux
1985	22.8	7.5
1986	24.3	7.4
1987	20.4	7.7
1988	20.9	5.9
1989	23.6	6.2
1990	23.7	7.1
1991	21.9	5.1
1992	12.5	4.6
1993	7.9	4.5
1994	10.5	4.6
1995	13.3	5.9
1996	14.0	6.9
1997	12.7	8.2
1998	14.9	9.3
1999	19.4	7.9
2000	20.1	7.4

Source: Banque de France, *Cahiers Régionaux*, various years.

compare and contrast with existing but separate theories to develop a model on the maintenance of common assets for supply chain performance.

A Model of Maintaining Collective Assets for Supply Chain Performance

The maintenance of the Champagne name has been obtained in spite of a number of factors that might have led to non-contribution, over-use and hold-up: a large number of parties in the chain, significant uncertainty in the weather, and long lags in the production process. Based on our observation of the champagne industry, we believe nine factors affect the maintenance of the common asset, the Champagne brand. These drivers include *self-regulation* which lowers governance costs and enables the following five mechanisms to avert a tragedy: *restricted access to the common asset; full contribution to the common asset; multiple issues in negotiations; transparency in the use of the common asset;* and the *establishment of formal and informal enforcement mechanisms.* However, opportunistic behavior is also conditioned by the *number of investment options; the level of the discount rate;* and the *track record of cooperation as a benchmark and signal.* Each driver is discussed in turn.

Lowering supply chain governance costs

Self-regulation.   Researchers from transaction cost economics argue that for a dyad, transactors employ specific governance mechanisms to protect themselves against the hazards of hold-up (Williamson, 1985). These governance mechanisms change and become more costly the more specific the assets become. They range from simple legal contracts to more complex contracts with contingency clauses. If asset specificity increases above a certain level then the costs of contracting become so high that the parties would begin to vertically integrate. Similar arguments have been made from the common resource literature. The traditional governance solutions to the commons dilemma have been either to fully integrate the property rights such that they can exclude others from its use or to have the government regulate it (Hardin, 1968). Most assumed that the appropriators of a common resource could not organize and set the rules or governance systems themselves because they faced another collective action problem, namely, who would provide the governance structure and rules; how could members credibly commit to those rules and who would monitor rule conformance (Bates, 1988; Elster, 1989).

Yet, researchers have shown other governance mechanisms at work. For example, relational-based transaction mechanisms, such as in the Japanese automobile industry, which rely neither on detailed contracts, nor on third party enforcement, can be used to safeguard transactions (Dyer, 1997). Typically referred to as self-enforcing agreements, or private ordering (Telser, 1980; Sako, 1996) transactors rely on trust, reputation, or investment hostages as a way to safeguard against opportunistic behavior. Furthermore, common property researchers have observed successful irrigation projects, common pastures and fishing grounds, where the appropriators of the resource self-regulate by creating their own forums to design and commit to their own rules of behavior (Ostrom, 1990).

Indeed, the champagne industry exhibits many of these same elements. The inter-industry organization, CIVC, the organization grouping the champagne houses (the SCVC), and the organization of the growers (the SGV), obtained a right to self-organize from the French Ministry of Agriculture in 1941. It consists of six representative growers and producers that discuss and negotiate the issues for the industry. This organization can be seen as lowering governance costs[4] for the supply chain. Since the annual negotiations regarding the harvest are completed once a year for all participants in the supply chain, search costs (i.e. finding the appropriate growers the houses would like to transact with) are minimized; contracting costs are lower since there is only one for the whole industry; and the monitoring and enforcement costs decline since there is only one agreement to adhere to. Furthermore, the CIVC is a forum that establishes rules to avert non-contribution, hold-up, and over-use. Each one is discussed in further detail.

Averting non-contribution

Restricted access to the common asset "champagne."   In a survey of 20 years of research on the incidence of the tragedy of the commons, Feeny et al. (1990: 6) concluded: "The evidence supports Hardin's argument concerning degradation due to the inability to regulate access to resources held as open access." That is, the tragedy of the commons is a regular occurrence when assets are used collectively and when the right of use is not properly defined. However, Feeny et al. (1990) also concluded that the tragedy is not necessarily due to the "common" nature of the asset, as Hardin implied, but to the absence of well-defined property rights to the common resource. If property rights are defined and enforced, collective assets may be sustainable.[5]

The champagne industry is a case in point. Prior to 1927, the rights to the use of the name "champagne" were not defined. Therefore, any producer selling sparkling wine could free ride on the reputation that growers and producers of the Champagne region had built in the previous two centuries. By 1927, however, after several years of fraudulent activity, the use of the champagne name became clearly regulated.[6] This was achieved by legally restricting the use of the champagne name to sparkling wine made from grapes grown in a region of 35,000 hectares in the Champagne region (in 1996, 30,700 hectares were in use). Thus, a geographic limit was established to demarcate champagne grapes from "regular" grapes. The original ruling did contain a provision that the total area could be increased if desired. Yet, to go into effect, the extension required the consent of the growers and producers in conjunction with the Ministry of Agriculture. This has turned out to be a major stumbling block; the area designated as "champagne land" has not expanded since 1927.

The original laws were intended to define the rightful users of the name "champagne" in France. The growers and producers also successfully broadened their claim beyond France when the CIVC established legal rights in the European Union (EU) to the name *la méthode champenoise*. It put significant pressure on the EU to have this right defended as widely as possible. For example, in 1993, the UK courts banned the sale of a sparkling alcoholic drink, called "elderflower champagne," made from flowers grown in the south of England, upholding the CIVC's case that the name "champagne" belonged exclusively to its members and the French region.[7] Protection of the name has also been sought beyond sparkling wine. When Yves Saint Laurent launched a new perfume in 1993 called "Champagne," it was immediately met with legal action by the houses, which succeeded in forcing the name to be removed in France. The above examples show that champagne growers and producers through the CIVC have been successful at defining and defending legal rights to the name "champagne." They turned what was once a common resource or asset with "open access" into a common asset with "restricted access." As a result of these laws, court rulings and administrative decisions, common property rights were established. These common property rights have enabled growers and producers of champagne to lawfully exclude firms from outside the defined area. The result is that the users can potentially appropriate the benefits from the common asset.[8]

Contribution to the common asset.   The exclusion of outsiders certainly increases the incentives of the rightful users to contribute to their common asset (Cornes and Sandler, 1996); however, contribution is certainly not guaranteed. Research in public good contribution experiments has in general confirmed Olson's (1965) arguments that with increasing group size there is either no voluntary provision of a public good (see e.g. Isaac and Walker, 1988) or sub-optimal voluntary contribution (Isaac and Walker, 1991). For example, for the last 6 years, in the US, the National Oil Research Alliance has "passed the hat" among the members (heating oil wholesalers and distributors) to pay for areas of common interest such as promotions for industry and research and development on oil burner technology. However, the total collections made were less than $500,000 showing the difficulty of gaining contributions even among the rightful users of the common asset. Similarly, in the absence of incentives, the various members in the champagne supply chain would likely rely on the others to contribute to the common asset. Indeed, many would likely look to LVMH, Seagram's, or Laurent Perrier for contributions. However, if all members of the supply chain thought similarly, efforts to collectively maintain the common asset would quickly unravel.

The majority of CIVC's budget comes from a state authorized mandatory transaction fee of 12 centimes per kilo of grapes transacted and 11 centimes per bottle sold. This budget then contributes to the common asset of Champagne: its quality and brand name reputation. The CIVC is able to fund research and development activities through its Institut Technique de Champagne (31 percent of the total budget), and protect the Champagne name, and promote it through organized tours of local facilities and the establishment of information bureaus in England, Switzerland, Australia, Japan, Belgium, Germany, and Italy (69 percent of total budget). Clearly, the common asset is also replenished through the independent marketing and research and development activities of the various players in the supply chain. However, full contribution to the CIVC, despite being small compared to the collective investments made by the houses and growers, still sends the signal that all participants are implicated.

Averting hold-up and over-use

Yet, even by excluding outsiders, and ensuring contribution from the rightful users of the common asset, hold-up and over-use may still occur. In the absence of mechanisms to reach an agreement, growers and houses in the supply chain may hold each other up on how the rents of the common resource should be divided. Furthermore, even if the benefits associated with the common resource were determined ex-ante, ex-post, in the absence of any credible monitoring and enforcement mechanisms, the players may try to over-appropriate its benefits.

A bargaining over multiple issues. In the champagne industry, bargaining could focus exclusively on a single issue and the source of significant value from the specific assets: the price of the grapes. Indeed, the price growers obtain for their grapes is the key driver of their profits and its appropriation of the common asset. Likewise, the cost of the grapes is the largest cost component for the producers in making a bottle of champagne; historically, it accounted for approximately 35 percent of the previous year's price of a bottle of champagne.

Yet, focusing on a single issue usually evolves into a tug-of-war between the negotiating parties (e.g. Dixit and Nalebuff, 1991; Bazerman, 1994) many times leading to no agreement at all. Moreover, in the event there is an agreement in a single-issue bargaining situation, it frequently is not Pareto efficient. The payoffs to both parties may be improved by extending the bargaining to multiple issues if the issues have different costs and benefits to the parties. A setting with multiple issues makes it more likely that an agreement will be reached given that each can obtain higher payoffs.

Negotiations between the champagne growers and houses have developed from a situation in the 1930s where price was the only negotiated issue to a setting after the establishment of the CIVC in 1941 where a variety of issues have been introduced and discussed. In addition to the price of the grapes, the other issues that are negotiated are: the maximum allowable yield of grapes per hectare (appellation); the percentage of the harvest that will be kept by the growers; the number of times the grapes will be pressed (up to three times, which can add 15 percent more juice than when pressed only once); the use of reserve stocks (*blocage*) which distinguishes the amount of wine from pressing that will be kept in casks (for up to 4 years) from the wine that will go immediately into second fermentation in the bottles; the financing of these stocks (who pays?), the length of time the wine has to be in bottles before it can be sold; the marketing investments for the Champagne region, etc.

Some issues are more important to one party than to the other. For example, growers typically want a high yield per hectare since this factor and the price of the grapes determine their income. The producers like to limit the yield per hectare since this driver reduces the output that will later hit the market. A compromise that has frequently been struck is to allow the yield per hectare to be slightly higher but to keep part of this in reserve stock (*blocage*). This amount is pressed at the cost of the producers but is financed by the growers. This way, both the growers and producers gain.

Negotiations also are conducted with a maximum amount of available information. For example, production rules are negotiated in September just before the harvest. Information concerning the quality of the crop and its size in the various areas becomes increasingly more accurate closer to the harvest date. Uncertain events such as hail storms, frosts, etc. can be taken into account. This "last minute" negotiating allows all parties to have as much information as possible about the costs and benefits of the issues that need to be negotiated.

Yet, even if the parties reach win–win solutions through the multiple issue negotiations, they may cheat on the agreement ex-post by over-appropriating the common asset. Indeed, the incentives are very high to do so. For example, growers have the choice of making vinegar or low quality, low priced table wine from the harvest above the official yield or "cheat" by trying to put a few more kilos into the system. Similar to the literature on the common property resources, we found that two mechanisms, transparency and enforcement, were in place to avert over-use.

Transparency in the use of the common asset.   Quite remarkable is the wealth of data that is collected formally and informally to monitor the use of the common asset. For example, at the time of the harvest, the growers must declare the crop to the town hall of their local community, to the *douanières* (tax officers) and to the CIVC. Once the harvest reaches the presses, the press operator in the *Carnet de Pressoir* (pressing booklet) records the amount. Both the agents of the CIVC and the government administrators regularly check this pressing booklet. The transactions between the houses and growers also are regularly checked by the CIVC. After each transaction, copies must be sent to all relevant parties: the government, the CIVC, and the town hall. Finally, government administrators regularly check the stocks of the growers and the houses to ensure the books match. Thus, there is formal, ongoing monitoring of the compliance of all parties by the local growers' office, the local town halls, the local agent of the CIVC, and government administrators.

The industry associations, the government, and the Banque de France provide additional, extensive information. For example, the stock of champagne bottles is very well tracked and published by the CIVC. In addition, the agencies of the Banque de France in Reims and Epernay, the capitals of the region, conduct regular surveys with a large number of growers and producers. These detailed studies document the investments and financial situation of the growers and producers: stocks, prices, working capital, etc. Further, government agencies make available price data regarding the sale of land, the rental price of land, etc.

More recently, the industry associations have set up an "economic observatory." The observatory collects information on the physical flow of materials (grapes, semi-finished and finished champagne in bottles) throughout the supply chain, that is, from the growers to the retail trade. The objective is to have the data necessary to establish whether all parties in the chain respect the collective agreements and to enable the CIVC to take corrective action if necessary.[9]

In addition to the formal data collection processes, there are informal ways of collecting information on the practices of growers and producers in Champagne. For example, the fact that there are over 15,000 growers on 30,000 hectares makes with spouses, children and workers more than one "policeman" per hectare to spot defectors! There is little chance a defection will not be noticed.

The average individual grower or producer would not significantly harm the collective interest if it were to over-appropriate the common asset. It therefore may be attractive to quietly harvest more grapes or produce more champagne than allowed. The payoffs to over-use would be particularly high if everybody else cooperated. However, if a large number of players were to do the same thing, cooperation could unravel very quickly; the common asset would depreciate rapidly and total supply chain payoffs would fall substantially. The high transparency in the supply chain, thus, is an "early warning system" on over-use; it helps to identify opportunistic players very quickly. As defectors can be easily spotted, they may not find defection attractive.

Enforcement of collective decisions. Yet, in a recent evolutionary game-theoretic study on the dynamic of social norms in the use of common property resources, Sethi and Somanathan (1996) show that the tragedy of the commons may be observed even if defectors are spotted. In a situation of industry self-regulation, industry participants must take it upon themselves to punish defectors. However, they also incur a cost and thus have a lower payoff than cooperators who free ride on the efforts of these enforcers. If there are too many defectors, the pay-off difference between enforcers and those who cooperate but do not enforce is too large, resulting in a decrease in the share of enforcers out of the total number of participants in the industry. This makes defection even more attractive, since the likelihood of being punished for over-appropriating the common asset would decrease. However, Sethi and Somanathan (1996: 774) also argue that: "With sufficiently few defectors, the payoff differential between cooperators (who free ride on the enforcement costs) and the enforcers is small (it costs little to sanction very few people), so the number of enforcers declines less rapidly. Consequently, defectors are eliminated before the enforcer share falls too much."

Transparency of transactions in a supply chain thus is a necessary but not a sufficient condition to obtain cooperation. Defectors may be detected but go unpunished if the enforcement cost is high. How is the enforcement cost to cooperators reduced while increasing the likelihood that over-use will be punished?

The onus of enforcement per individual may be reduced if the collective enforcement costs are shared through self-policing. Sometimes, this sharing is done on a spontaneous, informal basis. For example, groups of growers in Champagne have been observed to take the law into their own hands and burn down the vines of growers who ventured "on the other side of the hill" to increase their crop. Indeed, the "hands-on" approach of French farmers is legendary. Acheson (1993) has observed similar behavior in lobster fisheries. In Maine, territories are claimed by groups of fishermen and are not open to outsiders. Violators who trespass are warned. If violation continues, equipment is destroyed, usually secretly (and illegally).

However, Champagne also has developed formal procedures once again through the CIVC to reduce the punishment costs. As part of its charter, the CIVC has administrative authority to impose four sanctions. In increasing order of cost, there are fines of up to 10,000 times the price per kilo of grapes, confiscation of production and profits, the temporary closure of production facilities, and the withdrawal of professional licenses. When there is a transgression, the CIVC or its two constituencies typically quickly notify and warn the defector. If the violation persists, administrative action follows. While there has always been cheating, it has been kept to a minimum. The difference, for example, between the actual amount harvested from the negotiated amount has been 0.11 percent on average from 1986 to 1995. Thus far, the CIVC has not felt the need to revoke licenses. Transparency and self-enforcement have very likely been effective deterrents to over-consuming the common asset.

Importance of the future

The inter-industry association, CIVC, enabled the champagne industry to ward off the three forms of opportunism while minimizing governance costs associated with search, contracting, monitoring, and enforcement. The above arguments assume that growers and producers choose cooperative behavior because the expected benefits from non-contribution, hold-up and over-use (i.e. higher payoffs but potentially higher costs from punishment) are less than the benefits from continued cooperation. However, this also implies that parties in the chain had few options for seeking alternative rents, and did not "discount" expected benefits too heavily. Indeed, these contextual factors have gradually changed over time increasingly putting stress on the champagne common leading to the breakdown of the negotiations in 1989.

Number of options. Empirical research on the commons found that the tragedy sometimes was avoided in situations where the users of the common resource (e.g. inland fisheries) depended exclusively on that resource for their income (e.g. Ostrom, 1990). Given the absence of other options, users are forced to take a long-term view. It was also found that when some of the users had income opportunities outside the common resource, opportunistic behavior often developed (Feeny et al., 1990). In the 1950s and 1960s, both the growers and producers in Champagne depended for their income almost exclusively on their common asset. Furthermore, there was a clear separation of activities with the growers supplying grapes and the producers making the champagne, suggesting that hold-up, especially on the growers' side, was not an option. They did not have the assets in place to produce the champagne. Consequently, the 1950s and 1960s also turned out to be a period of high cooperation and prosperity for both parties.

Yet, two events occurred that changed the option horizon for the growers and producers. First, as tourism increased, the growers increasingly forward integrated into the production of champagne as they could easily sell their champagne on-site. The number of grower-producers increased from less than 2,500 in 1960 supplying 21 percent of total champagne sales, to over 4,500 in 1989 supplying 34 percent of champagne sales. While the vast majority of the grapes were still supplied to the houses, by being vertically integrated, the growers could hold-up the houses either by not providing enough grapes for the houses' needs or by asking for an unreasonable price per kilogram of grapes. If the parties came to no agreement, the growers could always resort to producing more champagne themselves, increasing their take from the commons but also putting the commons at risk often by producing lesser quality sparkling wine.

Secondly, the arrival of the conglomerates in the early 1970s was also the beginning of a period in which producers had different investment and user horizons. The president of one of the champagne houses, Bollinger, has been quoted as saying: "We are moving towards a Champagne of two speeds. On one side the Finance-Industrialists, for whom champagne is an investment like any other. On the other, the family houses with vineyards concerned about the image of the wine."[10] Multinational conglomerates (e.g. LVMH) have a much wider range of investment options than the smaller champagne houses and the individual growers. To the extent these other options yield a higher return than the champagne business, conglomerates have a higher opportunity cost for staying in Champagne. To meet the opportunity costs threshold, the conglomerates' champagne divisions may be driven to actions for short-term profits, which put maintenance of the common asset in the supply chain to the test. For example, the *Grand Marques* producers, or those of the financial conglomerates, have taken actions, which may be deemed as over-consuming the Champagne common. Since the early 1970s and particularly in the 1980s, they have invested significantly in vineyards outside France.[11] The stated reason was that grape growing in Champagne was reaching its capacity. This explanation is not quite credible in the face of the practice of excluding each year large quantities of grapes from entering champagne production through the yield per hectare decision. While the champagne houses have repeatedly stressed that sparkling wine from the new regions is not champagne (for example, they refer to the process as the *Methode Traditionelle*), they have chosen brands and labels that unmistakably associate the sparkling wine with their French champagne brands and hence the Champagne common (e.g. "Domaine Chandon" from LVMH or Mumm Napa from Mumm et Cie in the US).

The discount rate of future payoffs.   A zero discount rate implies that parties attach an equal importance to current and future payoffs such that opportunistic behavior would be unlikely (see e.g. Hill, 1990). Vice versa, a high discount rate leads parties to be more opportunistic, putting stress on the maintenance of the common. Indeed, when the discount rate is sufficiently high, multi-period cooperation turns into a one-period situation where opportunistic behavior by both parties then is a dominant strategy. What has been the situation with the champagne industry?

It is well known that a firm's cost of capital increases when its operating and financial leverage go up (Brealey and Myers, 1984). Trends in operating leverage may be assessed by tracking capital intensity and the importance of fixed costs in total costs. Financial leverage may be observed from the importance of debt financing. For the champagne producers, the percentage of fixed assets to total assets increased from 17.1 percent in 1985 to 32.2 percent by 1996. This resulted from increasing investments in new production equipment. Capital intensity has also been significant due to the fermentation and aging requirements in the production of champagne. In the decade 1985–94, the percentage of stocks to total assets never fell below 48 percent.[12] Most grape growers have not invested to the same extent as producers in new production equipment: the average fixed assets-to-sales ratio has remained at 17 percent. However, growers carry stock levels that often exceed those of the producers by 50 percent (see Table 2.1). In addition, surveys from the growers' association show that the ratio of fixed costs to total costs for growers typically varies around 75 percent. Thus, grape growing and champagne production are characterized by high operating leverage.

Also, financial leverage tends to be quite high. Table 2.3 indicates the importance of debt financing for producers. Data from the growers' association indicate that growers also use debt financing to a substantial degree: their average debt-to-equity ratio hovers around one. Furthermore, growers are unlikely to have access to finance at the same cost as the large, multinational champagne houses. Growers and producers thus may be considered to have a high discount rate.

The increase in options for the growers and houses and rising discount rate may have indeed led to the 1989 breakdown in negotiations between the growers and houses. The dramatic increase in search and contract costs with individual growers, and the significant amounts of low quality champagne produced by the growers could have resulted in a continued degradation of the common asset. Yet, through the CIVC, the champagne supply chain was still able to reverse course without experiencing an oncoming tragedy. We argue that two other factors may have been responsible for this reversed course: the feedback and signal from past cooperation and the complementarities of these factors discussed.

Track record of supply chain cooperation

The above arguments view the maintenance of a common asset from the self-interest of calculating individuals. This perspective is essentially forward looking and does not consider the possible influences of the history of cooperation. In Champagne, growers and producers most of the time supported the Champagne common and fairly appropriated its value. Does this track record of cooperation in and of itself contribute to the maintenance of the Champagne common in the future? The common resource literature in fact has frequently found that historical conditions play an important role in explaining cooperation (see e.g. Bardhan, 1993). Two reasons can be cited: the feedback it provides regarding previous payoffs to cooperation and the signal it provides the players when they are uncertain regarding how others will act.

Table 2.3   Indicators of financial leverage of Champagne producers

	1990 (%)	1992 (%)	1994 (%)	1996 (%)	1998 (%)	2000 (%)
Interest charges/Value added	15.5	23.5	30.9	11.8	6.4	7.3
Debt/Turnover	76.6	104.5	128.3	158.1	66.1	89.5
Short-term debt/All debt	24.1	33.0	31.2	25.3	31.6	11.4

Feedback from cooperation.   The track record of cooperation provides a consistent and regular link between actions and outcomes. Given the significant uncertainty and asymmetry regarding future payoffs, we would expect that the growers and houses would try to use their track record or the link between their past behavior and payoffs as a benchmark for their present and future behavior. Furthermore, the literature on decision-making biases (e.g. Tversky and Kahneman, 1974; Bazerman, 1994) has repeatedly found that people attach a disproportionate amount of importance to vivid events. The breakdown in negotiations in 1989 and the subsequent profit reversals for both the houses and the growers is very likely such a "vivid event."

As shown in Table 2.2, champagne has historically produced high payoffs. As noted in the introduction, the Bordeaux region never established the same degree of cooperation between the growers and producers as the Champagne region. While the difference in profitability is also affected by other factors (e.g. different product, growth in demand), we note that returns for the producers in Champagne have been much higher than their counterparts in Bordeaux. However, when the economic crisis in the early 1990s hit, the returns for Champagne producers dropped by 200 percent over 3 years compared to only 57 percent in Bordeaux. The different levels of profitability in the two regions and the different drops are consistent with the observation that maintenance of the common asset in Champagne has been more effective in Champagne: when supply chain cooperation breaks down, returns fall to a level which is much closer to the returns in Bordeaux.

The wine regions outside Champagne have acknowledged that the Champagne organization is an "envied proof" of inter-industry cooperation. Obviously, the champagne producers and growers are cognizant of this and know their high returns are dependent on continued cooperation in the chain. Hence, the vividness of the negotiation breakdown in 1989 and the profit reversal in the early 1990s compared to outcomes linked to their prior track record of cooperation most likely had an influence on orienting them back to cooperation.[13]

Signal for future behavior.   The track record is relevant not only because of the information it provides concerning actions and outcomes but also the signal it creates for future cooperation. If the payoffs to cooperation and opportunistic behavior are very similar, each needs to determine how the other will act. Certainly, if the payoffs from defection suddenly increase, parties will need to make a judgment whether the others will cooperate even if it is not in their interest to do so. In these situations, reputations established in past negotiations are relevant: they credibly signal whether each is a cooperator or defector (Kreps et al., 1982). Particularly the track record of moves in situations where there were only marginal incentives to cooperate will be a strong indicator of expected behavior.

An individual's track record or reputation for cooperation and defection may be viewed as a capital stock (e.g. Dierickx and Cool, 1989; Seabright, 1993). Similar to other stocks where investments over time build up capital, an individual's moves in a series of situations where s/he cooperates or defects may be taken to build a reputation stock of "cooperativeness." Yet, all capital stocks erode. Like a stock of customer goodwill that erodes when customers forget or are disappointed with new products, an individual's reputation for cooperativeness erodes when other parties forget about the individual's past behavior or when s/he defects.

The stream of cooperation and defection decisions from the past thus may be viewed as a determinant of an individual's reputation stock. The value of this stock is largely irrelevant when there are strong incentives to cooperate (or defect) since it will be in their self-interest to cooperate (or defect). However, this stock may influence the likelihood of cooperation in situations where the benefits from cooperation are marginal (or negative) (Seabright, 1993). A track record of cooperation therefore makes future cooperation more likely. On the other hand, a history of defections may lead to new defection if benefits from cooperation are marginal.[14]

The breakdown in cooperation in the late 1980s very likely drained the reputation stocks of both the growers and houses. One indeed may observe that growers and producers no longer automatically assume that a mutually beneficial outcome will result from negotiations. However, since the history of cooperative events dwarfs the history of opportunism, the collective reputation stocks of the two groups had likely not drained to the extent that an "integrative" outcome was not sought in the early 1990s. Indeed, in the official newsletter of Champagne, the president of the SGV commented on the 1993 decisions as follows:

> I remind all that every decision between growers and producers is the outcome of NEGOTIATION [no emphasis added]. And to arrive at a consensus, the representatives of the SGV and the producers have presented and debated their arguments. And that everyone, while defending their position, has preferred to arrive at a compromise solution rather than to let chaos settle in.[15]

Complementarities in maintaining common assets

We believe each of these nine drivers described has an independent effect on supply chain performance, either directly or indirectly through the maintenance of the common asset. *Self-regulation* through the CIVC lowers search, contracting, monitoring, and enforcement costs and enables mechanisms to lower the risk of opportunism. *Restricting access* to the commons excludes external free riders. *Full contribution* to the common asset ensures full participation. The negotiation setting with *multiple issues* makes agreements more likely, reducing the chance of hold-up. *Transparency* exposes over-appropriators and *enforcement* punishes or deters them; the *number of options* and *the discount rate* determines how relevant the future is. Finally, the *track record of cooperation* provides a benchmark of comparison or feedback should cooperation break down and a signal of future behavior should the difference in payoffs be small between cooperation and defection. These relationships are shown in Figure 2.1. These nine

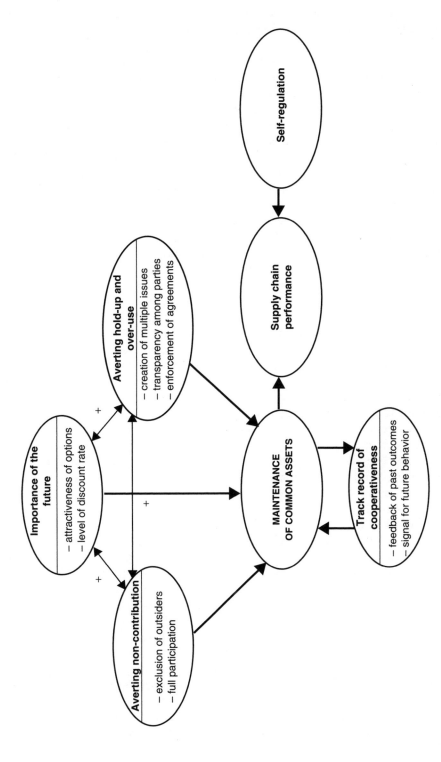

Figure 2.1 A model of maintaining collective assets for supply chain performance

drivers have been grouped into five factors: Self-regulation; Averting non-contribution; Averting hold-up and over-use; the Importance of the future; and the Track Record of Cooperativeness.

In addition to the independent effects of each of the drivers, we believe interactions among these drivers will also orient the industry towards maintaining the common asset. Complementarity among drivers exists when the level of one factor positively influences the level of another factor (Dierickx and Cool, 1989). These interactions are shown in Figure 2.1 by the arrows that are drawn between the factors. For example, if outsiders can be excluded, the attractiveness of investing in the common asset increases, which improves the attractiveness of the option and therefore the importance of its future. Furthermore, it is more worthwhile to invest in transparency mechanisms, which makes investments in enforcement mechanisms more worthwhile (lower cost and higher effectiveness). Negotiating with multiple issues makes contributions to the common asset more worthwhile. A negotiation in multiple issues also allows all parties to gain, which makes it less tempting for one party to defect, which in turn makes it more worthwhile to invest in expanding the range of issues that are examined. In sum, if drivers have such a relationship among themselves, then "early success breeds further success," since each reinforces the other.

The noted interactions among the drivers of maintaining common assets have two important effects. First, their complementarity leads to path dependency in nurturing and maintaining common assets. That is, initial successes set the stage for later successes. Vice versa, if the institutional mechanisms around managing the common assets are not well set up, it may quickly unravel or never commence. This implies that initial conditions in establishing common assets are of central importance. We can only speculate as to what the original driver was that created this success: exclusion of outsiders in 1927; creation of the CIVC in 1941; introduction of the transaction fee; multiple issue bargaining or the investment in transparency and enforcement mechanisms. However, the result of these initial conditions has led to a sustained track record of cooperativeness exemplifying the "success breeds success" phenomenon and reinforcing feedback and signaling from this capital stock.

Second, the maintenance of the common asset may be sustained, even if one or two drivers undermine cooperation, provided the other drivers sufficiently offset the negative effects of the one driver. We can use the breakdown in negotiations and the subsequent return to three-year contracts as an example. We already mentioned that the increasing options and discount rate led to the breakdown in negotiations in 1989. Hold-up by the growers led to a change in self-regulation from central management of the supply to individual contracts with the growers thus leading to significantly higher search and contracting costs for the supply chain. This new way of transacting for the industry lacked transparency on grape prices. It was not required before because there was only one price negotiated. Speculation around the grape prices in 1989 ran rampant leading to spot prices of double those in the previous year. These changes placed enormous stress on the houses regarding whether they should invest more in Champagne, or develop their sparkling wine holdings elsewhere. Indeed, this breakdown could have triggered a vicious "failure breeds failure" spiral. However, we argue that both the feedback and signaling of their track record of cooperation and the positive independent and interaction effects of the drivers that were not changed (i.e. exclusion of outsiders, contribution to the common asset, multiple issues) likely oriented the players to search for cooperative solutions.

For example, in 1990 the CIVC instituted a reference price mechanism, and invested in a new form of transparency to put an end to grape price speculation. The prices of the transactions were posted by the organization on the French teletext system, Minitel, removing the possibility of rumors developing around the prices paid. As a result of this action, the contract prices returned to the negotiated reference price. Furthermore, the multiple issues in their negotiations allowed the parties to come up with innovative solutions for subsequent harvests. For example, in 1992 and 1993, both parties agreed, as a compromise, to have a reasonably large harvest but have part of it pressed into a reserve stock financed by the grower. Also, the two parties agreed to eliminate a third pressing of the grapes thus reducing the output by approximately 5 percent and discussed lengthening the fermentation stage from 12 to 15 months with the intention of improving the quality of the wine. Finally, recognizing the importance of the common, they also agreed to increase their contribution by 2 centimes per kilo and per bottle sold to bolster the association's marketing budget. We, thus, believe that the complementarities among the drivers have shielded the players from a downward spiral of non-contribution, hold-up, or over-use.

Discussion and Conclusion

This chapter contributes further to our understanding of supply chain management by conceptualizing long-term supply chain initiatives as the provision and maintenance of common assets. This conceptualization requires that we go beyond viewing supply chain management in terms of mechanisms in improving bilateral vertical relations. We contend that providing and maintaining common assets requires mechanisms among players not only along the supply chain but also within each stage to avert a larger issue: the tragedy of the commons. In such cases, opportunism can come from not only hold-up or increasing the benefits in one stage over another in the supply chain, but also from increasing the benefits over others within each stage through non-contribution and over-use of the common asset. This view seems especially important, as supply chain competitiveness has become an increasingly more important driver of firm performance (see e.g. Gomes-Casseres, 1994; Dyer and Singh, 1998).

We believe that the maintenance of common assets in supply chains can be achieved largely because of rules, procedures and institutions that are established such that the payoffs to maintaining the common asset in the supply chain are larger than the payoffs to non-contribution, hold-up, and/or over-use. These mechanisms include: self-regulation, closed access to the common, full contribution to the common, creation of multiple issues, informal and formal enforcement of agreements, the number of options available to the parties, the level of the discount rate, and the track record of cooperation.

Many examples can be cited where these factors play a role: industry-based research and development (North America Oil Research Alliance); new payment systems (e.g. smartcards); regional identities (Chianti, Port, Camembert etc.); environmental responsibility (chemical industry's responsible care initiative); and quality standards (ISO). The Japanese automobile supply chain has been successful in maintaining its common asset, a strong reputation in quality and reliability, because of not only the vertical relationships with the individual suppliers but also the horizontal relationships among the suppliers themselves through supplier associations (see e.g. Sako, 1996). The issues facing these supplier associations are very similar to that of the Champagne industry: there are indeed incentives for individual suppliers to free ride on the research and development efforts of others in the industry. Yet the suppliers are self-regulated through the associations; access to the common comes from being a member; contribution comes from members' dues; transparency such as the grading of supplier performance is encouraged to not only monitor other players but also encourage greater learning; formal sanctions such as expulsion and informal social sanctions are also in place to punish free riders (Hagen and Choe, 1998); and finally multiple issues are discussed including quality, cost, health and safety.

The view we offer also extends the literature on alliances, supply chain management and the relational-based view where the level of analysis is typically the alliance, dyad, or network of alliances (see e.g. Dyer and Singh, 1998). From our case study, we would argue that the alliance is not the root unit of analysis for best understanding how to gain a supply chain advantage. As in the resource-based view, the firm is not the unit of analysis but rather the inimitable, non-substitutable, non-tradable resources possessed by the firm. Similarly, we would argue that at the level of the supply chain, it is not the members of the supply chain or the network as the unit of analysis but the common asset that the members can establish and maintain that leads to supply chain advantage.

Second, since the dyad, alliance, or network of alliances has been the unit of analysis, the focus has been on the vertical exchange or the transaction between the parties. Hence, significant attention has been paid to the mechanisms in which parties can make specific relationship-based investments without the fear of hold-up. Yet, by taking the perspective of building and maintaining common assets, the transaction may be a subset of a larger coordination problem. Mechanisms are required that avert not only hold-up but also other forms of opportunism such as non-contribution and over-use. Furthermore, this shifts the attention from simply minimizing transaction costs to not only maximizing transaction value in a bilateral relationship (see e.g. Zajac and Olsen, 1993; Dyer, 1997) but also maximizing the value of the common asset in a supply chain.

Third, since the common asset is an important unit of analysis, we echo other researchers in further applying the public goods, collective action and common property resource literature to the management and organization fields (see e.g. Monge et al., 1998). Lessons from non-traditional areas such as irrigation projects, fisheries, forestries, libraries, toll roads, etc., whereby members take it upon themselves to provide and maintain common assets, would be especially useful in better understanding how to manage collective assets within a supply chain.

Fourth, we extend Dyer and Singh's (1998) mechanisms that preserve rents in networks and supply chains. We argue that the complementarity of the mechanisms that avert opportunistic behavior can be added to causal ambiguity, time compression diseconomies, interorganizational asset interconnectedness, partner scarcity, resource indivisibility, and the institutional environment, as ways to sustain rents at the supply chain level. In other words, if outsiders can be excluded, then the attractiveness in contributing to the common asset, investing in transparency and enforcement mechanisms is more worthwhile (lower cost and higher effectiveness). Negotiating with multiple issues leading to higher payoffs for both parties makes contributions to the common asset more interesting. The complementarity of these mechanisms suggests institutional path dependence whereby initial successes can lead to further successes making imitation particularly difficult (Rivkin, 2000). Furthermore, a track record of success provides positive feedback and a signal for future behavior when some of the mechanisms may be negatively affected.

Finally, the findings from Champagne suggest some normative prescriptions for practicing managers. This view suggests that managers should take multiple perspectives on determining a company's success: industry structure and creation of market power (see e.g. Porter, 1980), unique inimitable resources within the firm for the creation of scarcity rents (see e.g. Wernerfelt, 1984), and more relevant for this chapter, unique, inimitable resources built through collective action for the creation of supply chain, relational, or association-based rents. Yet the achievement of these group-based rents is not easy to achieve. For example, Schmitz (1999) shows how the Brazilian footwear supply chain, located in Sinos Valley, failed to cooperate as a total supply chain despite the external incentives (significant competition from the Chinese) and the efforts among the trade associations to improve the region's overall reputation for quality and reliability. Even creating common assets in bilateral alliances is inherently difficult (see e.g. Das and Teng, 2000). Hence, understanding both how to establish and maintain common assets would be worthwhile for managers. This chapter provides only a glimpse of some of the mechanisms that are required to maintain and nurture these assets.

Yet, given the growing number of examples of establishing and maintaining common assets for supply chain performance, there is certainly a need for much more research in this area. What explains its creation in the first place? Are the mechanisms to encourage investment in the common assets the same as those that sustain its proper use? Who in the chain can credibly push the development of collective assets and how? Can a common asset be created if outsiders are not excluded? If a common asset is in place, there are other questions that need analysis: What mechanisms other than those raised in the chapter exist to exclude free riders and how can they be enforced? Are there ways other than creating full transparency among the parties in the chain to avoid free riding among them? Do we require the working of all factors in order to maintain the common asset? Given that discount rates depend on the financial and operating leverage of the players, does that imply that some supply chains are more prone to the tragedy of the commons than others? How fast does the capital stock of cooperativeness erode, i.e. what is its half-life? More generally, Figure 2.1 only lists the drivers and factors, which we believe are important to explain the sustained cooperation in Champagne. It does not indicate the relative importance of each factor and at this time, our qualitative analysis does not allow us to be more specific. While we believe all factors are necessary, more research certainly is required to establish the "weights" of each factor. Despite these limitations, we hope this chapter provides a glimpse on the key forces in maintaining common assets for supply chain performance.

Notes

1. Similar coordination problems had been pointed out by Olson (1965) regarding the collective provision of public goods. He stated that individuals do not have an incentive to contribute to the provision of public goods (e.g. education, security) since they cannot be excluded from their use. Free-riding ensues, undermining the provision of the goods (e.g. Cordell, 1978; Ostrom et al., 1994; Larson and Bromley, 1990). See also Gordon (1954) and Scott (1955).
2. While technically the supply chain of the French champagne industry would include the land owners, growers, brokers, houses, cooperatives, distributors, and retailers, we focus on the two most important links in the industry: the growers and houses.
3. Yves Bonnet, Government Commissioner.
4. We are using these terms more broadly than mere "transaction costs" since they also apply to the governance of the commons (e.g. costs associated with averting non-contribution and over-use).
5. Common resources with restricted access have been called "common property resources" (Seabright, 1993), "common pool resources" (Ostrom, 1990) or "communal property" (Feeny et al., 1990).
6. The farmers of the region were asked whether they would like to grow grapes or wheat. At that time, wheat was the more profitable crop. The land available for grapes thus ended up being much smaller than the total land available.
7. Also, in return for some agricultural import rights, Australia was convinced not to use the champagne label for their sparkling wines.
8. See Seabright (1993; 1997) for a further discussion of the importance of common property rights to avert the tragedy of the commons.
9. See the very interesting study of Soler and Tanguy (1998: 82).
10. *L'Expansion*, April 18, 1991.
11. The French champagne houses commenced production of sparkling wine at the beginning of the 1970s. Moët et Chandon was the first house to do so, acquiring a vineyard in California in 1976. Eight other champagne houses (Mumm, Roederer, Taittinger, Piper-Heidsieck, Deutz, Pommery, Bollinger and Laurent-Perrier) were to follow.
12. G. Besucco, "Bordeaux – Bourgogne – Champagne. Eléments de comparaison." *Cahiers Régionaux*, Champagne – Ardenne, Septembre 1995, No. 39.
13. In their discussion of the new contracts in Champagne, Soler and Tanguy (1998: 85) state that the long history management of the Champagne supply chain (and the prosperity associated with it), together with the most recent crisis, constitutes essential factors in the creation of a new organizational form (translated).
14. Seabright (1993: 123) states the impact of reputation stocks as follows: This stock is a "state variable whose value influences the probability of future cooperation independently of the direct payoffs associated with such cooperation."
15. M. Marc Brugnon in *La Champagne Viticole. Supplement*, No. 568, March 1993. In their analysis of the contract negotiations in Champagne, Soler and Tanguy (1998: 85) make the following observation: "Everything takes place as if the parties in Champagne have a capital of knowledge about each other's behavior established on the basis of many collective attempts to resolve problems. This is helped by the competence of the various representative organizations and the credibility they have with their constituencies . . ." (translated).

References

Acheson, J. 1993: Capturing the commons: Legal and illegal strategies. In T. Anderson and R. Simmons (eds.), *The Political Economy of Customs and Culture: Informal Solutions to the Commons Problem*. Lanhaw, UK: Rowman and Littlefield.

Bardhan, P. 1993: Symposium on management of local commons. *Journal of Economic Perspectives*, 7, 87–92.

Bates, R.H. 1988: Contra contractarianism: Some reflections on the new institutionalism. *Politics and Society*, 16, 387–401.

Bazerman, M. 1994: *Judgment in Managerial Decision Making*. New York: Wiley.

Besucco, G. 1995: Bordeaux – Bourgogne – Champagne. Eléments de comparaison. *Cahiers Régionaux*, Champagne-Ardenne No. 39.

Brealey, R. and Myers, S. 1984: *Principles of Corporate Finance*. London: McGraw Hill.

Corbett, C., Blackburn, J., and Van Wassenhove, L. 1999: Partnerships to improve supply chains. *Sloan Management Review*, 40, 71–82.

Cordell, J. 1978: Carrying capacity analysis of fixed territorial fishing. *Ethnology*, 18, 1–24.

Cornes, R. and Sandler, T. 1996: *The Theory of Externalities, Public Goods and Club Goods*, 2nd edition. Cambridge, UK: Cambridge University Press.

Das, T.K. and Teng, B. 2000: Instabilities of strategic alliances: An internal tensions perspective. *Organization Science*, 11, 77–101.

Dierickx, I. and Cool, K. 1989: Asset stock accumulation and the sustainability of competitive advantage. *Management Science*, 25, 1504–1515.

Dixit, A. and Nalebuff, B. 1991: *Thinking Strategically*. New York: W. W. Norton.

Dyer, J. 1997: Effective interfirm collaboration: How firms minimize transaction costs and maximize transaction value. *Strategic Management Journal*, 18, 535–556.

Dyer J. and Singh, H. 1998: The relational view: Cooperative strategy and sources of interorganizational competitive advantage. *Academy of Management Review*, 23, 660–679.

Eisenhardt, K. 1989: Building theories from case studies research. *Academy of Management Review*, 14, 532–550.

Elster, J. 1989: *The Cement of Society. A Study of Social Order*. Cambridge, UK: Cambridge University Press.

Feeny, D., Berkes, F., McCay, B., and Acheson, J. 1990: The tragedy of the commons: Twenty-two years later. *Human Ecology*, 18, 1–19.

Fudenberg, D. and Tirole, J. 1983: Capital as commitment: Strategic investment to deter mobility. *Journal of Economic Theory*, 75, 227–250.

Gomes-Casseres, B. 1994: Group versus group: How alliance networks compete. *Harvard Business Review*, 4, 4–11.

Gordon, J. 1954: The economic theory of a common property resource: The fishery. *Journal of Political Economy*, 72, 124–142.

Hagen, J. and Choe, S. 1998: Trust in Japanese interfirm relations: Institutional sanctions matter. *Academy of Management Review*, 23, 589–600.

Hardin, G. 1968: The tragedy of the commons. *Science*, 162, 1243–1248.

Hill, C. 1990: Cooperation, opportunism and the invisible hand: Implications for transaction cost theory. *Academy of Management Journal*, 15, 500–514.

Hines, P. and Rich, N. 1998: Outsourcing competitive advantage: The use of supplier associations. *International Journal of Physical Distribution and Logistics Management*, 28, 524–546.

Isaac, M. and Walker, J. 1988: Group size effects and public good provision: The voluntary contributions mechanism. *Quarterly Journal of Economics*, 103, 179–200.

Isaac, M and Walker, J. 1991: On the suboptimality of voluntary public goods provision: Further experimental evidence. In M. Isaac (ed.), *Research in Experimental Economics*. Greenwich, CO: JAI Press.

Jones, C., Hesterly, W., Fladmoe-Lindquist, K., and Borgatti, S. 1998: Professional service constellations: How strategies and capabilities influence stability and change. *Organization Science*, 9, 396–410.

Kreps, D. 1990: Corporate culture and economic theory. In J. Alt and K. Shepsle (eds.), *Perspectives on Positive Economic Theory*. Cambridge, UK: Cambridge University Press, 90–143.

Kreps, D., Milgrom, P., Roberts, J., and Wilson, R. 1982: Rational co-operation in the finitely repeated prisoners' dilemma. *Journal of Economic Theory*, 74, 245–252.

Landon, S. and Smith, C.E. 1997: The use of quality and reputation indicators by consumers: The case of Bordeaux wine. *Journal of Consumer Policy*, 20, 289–323.

Larson, B. and Bromley, D. 1990: Property rights, externalities and resource degradation: Locating the tragedy. *Journal of Development Economics*, 59, 235–262.

Lazzarini, S., Chaddad, F., and Cook, M. 2001: Integrating supply chain and network analysis: The study of netchains. *Journal on Chain and Network Science*, 1, 17–22.

Milgrom, P. and Roberts, J. 1995: Complementarities and fit: Strategy, structure and organizational change in manufacturing. *Journal of Accounting and Economics*, 27, 179–208.

Monge, P., Fulk, J., Kalman, M., Flanagin, A., Parnassa, C., and Rumsey, S. 1998: Production of collective action in alliance-based interorganizational communication and information systems. *Organization Science*, 9, 411–433.

Olson, M. 1965: *The Logic of Collective Action*. Cambridge, MA: Harvard University Press.

Ostrom, E. 1990: *Governing the Commons: The Evolution of Institutions for Collective Action*. New York: Cambridge University Press.

Ostrom, E., Gardner, R., and Walker, J. 1994: *Rules, Games and Common-Pool Resources*. Ann Arbor, MI: University of Michigan Press.

Porter, M. 1980: *Competitive Strategy*. New York: Free Press.

Rivkin, J. 2000: Imitation of complex strategies. *Management Science*, 46, 824–844.

Sako, M. 1996: Supplier associations in the Japanese automobile industry: Collective action for technology diffusion? *Cambridge Journal of Economics*, 20, 651–671.

Schmitz, H. 1999: Global competition and local cooperation: Success and failure in the Sinos Valley, Brazil. *World Development*, 27, 1627–1650.

Scott, A. 1955: The fishery: The objectives of sole ownership. *Journal of Political Economy*, 63, 116–124.

Seabright, P. 1993: Managing local commons: Theoretical issues in incentive design. *Journal of Economic Perspectives*, 7, 113–134.

Seabright, P. 1997: Local common property rights. In P. Newman (ed.), *The New Palgrave Dictionary of Economics and the Law*. London: Macmillan.

Sethi, R. and Somanathan, E. 1996: The evolution of social norms in common property resource use. *American Economic Review*, 766–788.

Sharp A. and Smith, J. 1991: Champagne's sparkling success. *International Marketing Review*, 8, 13–19.

Soler, L.-G. and Tanguy, H. 1998: Contrats et négotiations dans le secteur des vins de Champagne. *Annales des Mines*, 74–86.

Stigler, G. 1964: A theory of oligopoly. *Journal of Political Economy*, 72, 44–61.

Sydow, J. and Windeler, A. 1998: Organizing and evaluating interfirm networks: A structurationist perspective on network processes and effectiveness. *Organization Science*, 9, 265–284.

Telser, L. 1980: A theory of self-enforcing agreements. *Journal of Business*, 53, 27–44.

Tirole, J. 1993: A theory of collective reputations with applications to the persistence of corruption and to firm quality. IDEI, University of Toulouse, mimeo.

Tversky, A. and Kahneman, D. 1974: Judgment under uncertainty: Heuristics and biases. *Science*, 168, 1124–1131.

Wernerfelt, B. 1984: A resource based view of the firm. *Strategic Management Journal*, 5, 171–180.

Williamson, O. 1985: *The Economic Institutions of Capitalism*, New York: Free Press.

Yin, R. 1984: *Case Study Research: Design and Methods*, 2nd edition. Thousand Oaks, CA: Sage Publications.

Zajac, E.J. and Olsen, C. 1993: From transaction costs to transaction value analysis: Implications for the study of interorganizational strategies. *Journal of Management Studies*, 30, 130–146.

CHAPTER THREE

Organizing around Strategic Relationships: Networks of Suppliers as Knowledge Generators in the Italian Motorcycle Industry

Andrea Lipparini and Gianni Lorenzoni

Introduction

Firms are asked to learn and adapt to changing environmental conditions, but learning and adaptation cannot be enough. It is becoming increasingly evident that strategizing is not only about positioning a company or a product in a given industry structure; it is about positioning inter-firm networks. In fact, competition in many industries now extends beyond inter-firm competition to include networks of firms competing against other networks (Gomez-Casseres, 1984). Like corporations, networks are overlapped bundles of resources and competencies (Dierickx and Cool, 1989; Prahalad and Hamel, 1990; Teece et al., 1997) where unique sets of competencies are shared among competitors.

External linkages are both a means of gaining access to knowledge and resources to enhance product development and a way to test internal expertise and learning capability. Therefore, the management of these external sources of knowledge may emerge as a distinctive organizational capability, which may be critical to survival and sustained performance. However, despite the increasing attention to external knowledge as a strategic asset (Winter, 1987; Kogut and Zander, 1992; Nonaka, 1994; Van den Bosch et al., 1999), and to network forms as key drivers for flexibility and strategic focus, little systematic attention has been paid to the processes in which this organizational capability is developed or how external knowledge is generated, accumulated, transferred, and leveraged to enhance firm and network performance (Doz, 1996).

With the aid of data collected on the Italian motorcycle industry, we claim that competitive advantage comes not so much from within the firm, but more from the network, in which the lead firm is embedded. In particular, organizing and managing strategic relationships such that knowledge is generated, accumulated, transferred, and leveraged may render replication more difficult. How do competitors copy effective management routines such as the creation of a trust-based relational environment, the early involvement of suppliers in knowledge generation activities, and the design of relational structures supporting and fostering reciprocal learning processes? Furthermore, we claim that where knowledge generation and transfer occur among selected participants, peripheries not only constitute important sites for working and learning, (Lave and Wenger, 1990; Brown and Duguid, 1991) but also for *innovating* and *strategizing*.

This chapter is therefore organized as follows. The first section sets out briefly the theoretical background which informed our research. The second section presents the study, highlighting the industrial setting and the industry within which firms operate. The following section then focuses on the structuring and managing of inter-firm networks in the Italian motorcycle industry. Here we provide insights on processes of knowledge generation, accumulation, transfer, and leveraging occurring between lead manufacturers and key component suppliers that may lead to lead firm and network advantage. The final sections are reserved for discussion and conclusions, with implications for both further research and managerial behavior.

Theoretical Framework

The network as a knowledge-creating entity

Conceptualizing the firm and the network as knowledge-creating entities (Nonaka and Takeuchi, 1995), or as distributed knowledge systems (Tsoukas, 1996), requires a departure from the traditional explanation of company performance based on static theories. The basic assumptions of transaction costs economics (TCE) are inadequate for a clear understanding of either learning processes at the network level or the outsourcing trend affecting activities unrelated to manufacturing (Williamson, 1975).[1] The ability to experiment and innovate quickly is increasingly more important for competitive advantage. The problem here is not to integrate activities in order to lower transaction costs, but to organize a context that enables a better exploitation and management of knowledge and capabilities. In a similar vein, the assumptions of non-tradability and immobility of idiosyncratic resources as the base of the competitive advantage (Dierickx and Cool, 1989; Peteraf, 1993) make the resource-based view (RBV) inadequate for interpreting the dynamic nature of inter-firm networks (Hansen et al., 1997).

Although the TCE and RBV perspectives have contributed to managers' and academics' understanding of how firms obtain above-normal returns, they overlook the fact that a single firm is embedded in a network of relationships (Dyer and Singh, 1998). It is certainly true that capabilities are assets that are created over time through complex interactions among the firm's resources (Amit and Schoemaker, 1993); yet they are increasingly *network*-specific rather than *firm*-specific, sources of flexibility rather than rigidity and inertia (Hannan and Freeman, 1989). Consequently, some unique capabilities are more likely to be dynamic assets deriving from the interactions among network's resources.

Many contributions argue that the locus of innovative activities is the network of firms, not the single actor (Powell, 1990; Powell et al., 1996). The network is considered as a superior knowledge-transfer mechanism and may lead to greater innovation than is the case with the integrated firm (Von Hippel, 1988). Networks permit firms to enhance their ability to recognize the value of new, external information, assimilate it and apply it to commercial ends. The nexus of capabilities in the network makes the need for relational capabilities more pronounced. Among them, the most important are the selection of partners (Lorenzoni and Lipparini, 1999), the combination and coordination of diverse technologies and manufacturing processes of a large number of firms (Kogut and Zander, 1992), the ability to integrate these efforts with those of final assemblers or leading firms in the network (Lawrence and Lorsch, 1967; Helfat and Raubitschek, 2000); and the absorption of external knowledge, related to the absorptive capacity of the recipient (Cohen and Levinthal, 1990).

Relational and dynamic views of the firm

The focus on inter-firm networks has produced a proliferation of studies dealing with structure (Miles and Snow, 1986; Jarrillo, 1988), and to a lesser extent dynamics of inter-firm networks (Gulati, 1998). The *relational view* of the firm provided by Dyer and Singh (1998) suggests that a firm's critical resources may span firm boundaries and be associated with inter-firm resources and routines. This view proposes that the value of the network's resources may be enhanced by managerial actions, and that idiosyncratic inter-firm linkages may be a source of relational quasi-rents and competitive advantage. Inter-firm relationships generate competitive advantages if substantial knowledge exchange – including the exchange of knowledge that results in joint learning – occurs. Moreover, the combination of complementary resources or capabilities – by means of multiple functional interfaces – amplifies a firm's competitive effectiveness when appropriate governance mechanisms lower transaction costs.

In its present form, however, the relational view of the firm is not enough to fully understand lead firm and network advantage. In fact, this view falls short on truly understanding the processes by which knowledge is generated, accumulated, transferred, and leveraged within the network of firms. If the real long-term goal of management is to continually rebuild and expand the stock of strategic assets of the firm such that they continually create new sources of competitive advantage (Markides and Williamson, 1994), a dynamic rather than a cluster (Porter and Sölvell, 1998; Enright, 1998) or embeddedness view (Granovetter, 1985; Uzzi, 1997) of networks is required. Consequently, to better capture the role of suppliers in knowledge generation processes other perspectives should complement the relational view. In this sense, the dynamic capability approach (Lado and Wilson, 1994; Teece et al., 1997), and the knowledge-based view of the firm (Nonaka, 1994; Grant, 1996) reveal their usefulness in the analysis of a competitive advantage based on knowledge creation and transfer at the network level. The former view emphasizes mechanisms by which firms accumulate and disseminate new skills and capabilities despite conditions of path dependencies and core rigidities in technological and organizational processes.

The latter view emphasizes the importance of the firm's ability to integrate knowledge and to transform dispersed, tacit and explicit competencies into a wide body of organizational knowledge.

Two recent contributions could usefully complement the dynamic perspectives mentioned above. The first (Kogut, 2000) stresses the need for the development and application of generative rules that foster the cooperation and the formation of principles of coordination. These rules require capabilities that are not firm-specific, and that are leveraged upon the technological and social characteristics of the industry context. Outcomes generated by the application of these rules produce quasi-rents for both brokers – i.e. the leading firms – and the members of the network. An understanding of the nature and sources of generative rules is likely to be essential to understanding the fit between network-based strategies and network structures. The second contribution (Thomke, 2001) argues that networks can be the most important sources of ideas and information generated by experimentation. These experiments lead to superior inter-firm knowledge-sharing routines that are network-specific rather than firm-specific. These kinds of routines are a regular pattern of inter-firm interactions that permit the creation, transfer, or recombination of highly specialized knowledge (Grant, 1996). The network as a system for experimentation facilitates the unpacking of knowledge flowing from external component suppliers (Dyer, 1996), the assimilation of critical expertise, and the use of the "collective knowledge" (Spender, 1996) generated by the relational set as a whole. These two views provide interesting insights for our study. In fact, they stress: (1) the importance of the social dimension of competition and collaboration; (2) the need for a system of actions aimed at aligning the different partners in a network; and (3) planning and coordination mechanisms as essential requirements of an effective knowledge generation process.

The next section provides insights into the processes by which networks can generate, accumulate, transfer, and leverage knowledge for competitive advantage. The use of explanatory case studies can usefully complement the dynamic perspectives on the firms reported above. In this way, our perspective, which is also dynamic in nature, can extend the TCE, the RBV, and the relational views of the firm.

A Study of the Italian Motorcycle Industry

The need for an explanatory case study

The Italian motorcycle industry is an ideal context to deepen what is known regarding the benefits of collaboration in terms of knowledge generation, accumulation, transfer, and leveraging. First, Italy is the most relevant European market for scooters and one of the most important for motorcycles. The setting is hyper-competitive in nature, with domestic and Japanese producers competing to gain market share and to access best-in-class component suppliers.

Second, the industry is characterized by competing overlapping networks, with few large and medium-sized lead assemblers and their many small and medium-sized suppliers (Lipparini et al., 2001). This partially overlapped industry structure permits an analysis of network design effectiveness.

Third, in the motorcycle industry intense innovative activity is taking place, shaped by the introduction of electronics and the adoption of new materials such as titanium and plastics. The pace of technological progress and the rate of new models introduction would make an atomistic approach ineffective, either by the lead firm or the supplier, to the generation, accumulation, and transfer of knowledge.[2] Given this rapid technological progress, we can examine how management approaches carried out by lead manufacturers in supporting knowledge creation, accumulation, transfer, and leveraging may lead to lead firm and network success.

In sum, the focus on the Italian motorcycle industry provides evidence that networks are not only significant sites for manufacturing and innovating, but also for learning and strategizing. Inter-firm networks are recognized as an important source of differentiation and sustainability of a competitive advantage based on product innovation and reliability, as well as responsiveness to emerging market trends, customer needs, and environmental jolts (Lorenzoni and Lipparini, 1999).

Industry overview

Approximately 1.6 million motorcycles were sold around the world in 2000. Scooters and motorcycles with engine size under 500cc accounted for 40 percent of an industry that has grown consecutively in the decade 1990–2000. Europe is a prominent market, accounting for about 40 percent of sales in the heavyweight segment and for 60 percent in terms of scooters.[3] Sales of motorcycles and scooters in the Italian market totaled about 500,000 units in 2000, a growth of 30 percent over 1999. In 2000, registrations of motorcycles accounted for almost 30 percent of total industry sales in Europe (it was 17 percent in 1990). With a share of nearly 50 percent, Italy is the most important European market for scooters. In the last ten years, the scooter segment grew from 9 percent of all two-wheeled motor-vehicle sales, to 67 percent. It is no surprise that this market has been considered a tremendous opportunity for manufacturers, especially the Japanese. In 2000, Honda, Yamaha, Suzuki, and Kawasaki held 36 percent of the market – 41.8 percent if one considers Yamaha-owned MBK – while the Italians (Piaggio and the fully owned Gilera, Aprilia, Malaguti, Italjet, and Ducati) account for 41.6 percent of the market.[4]

The ranking of the top 20 motorcycles sold in Italy in 2000 confirms the strong penetration of Japanese companies, with only one Italian company (Ducati) within the first ten positions in term of sales. The situation is different when considering the absolute ranking of best-selling models, regardless of engine size category. Italian companies ranked at top with Piaggio – the well-known *Vespa* producer – and the Motorbike World Championships winner Aprilia. Such a strong presence of domestic manufacturers in terms of sales is unique in Europe. Even in France, with customer loyalty pushed up by a strong sense of identification with local brands, domestic manufacturers (Peugeot and MBK) sold only 27.4 percent of the overall marketed vehicles. In the UK, Japanese manufacturers dominate the market, controlling an estimated 70 percent by number of new registrations. However, their position, particularly in the scooter market, is being threatened by the re-emergence of Italian producers such as Piaggio, which have significantly increased their market presence over the past few years.

Data collection and analysis

We decided to focus on inter-firm networks whose "center" is represented by firms that are manufacturing their scooters and motorcycles in Italy, or that rely extensively on Italian suppliers or assembly facilities. With the aid of a questionnaire and interviews conducted in the period 1996–97, we collected data on 29 firms.[5] The first survey, exclusively based on lead assemblers, was aimed at: (1) gathering information on each company's history, products, and markets from open-ended interviews; and (2) mapping relationships with each company's component suppliers. The second survey was conducted in the period 1998–99 and extended also to the component suppliers.

In total, 58 companies (16 lead manufacturers and 42 suppliers of components) contributed to our comprehension of the connections and content of the relationships among the participants in the value system. Our third survey, conducted in 2001 and 2002 was aimed at exploring the dynamics related to network knowledge. We focused on two partially overlapped networks, both comprised of a lead manufacturer of scooters and ten component suppliers, different for their performance in terms of new models introduced in 2001. For these networks, we collected data on patent activity, dominant design, and product modularity with the aid of questionnaires, extensive interviews, and analysis of company reports. To provide further insights of the functioning of a knowledge network, we interviewed 14 of the most important suppliers of components,[6] derived from the previous survey as those recognized by the lead manufacturers as directly involved in practices of knowledge generation, accumulation, and transfer. They were asked to report on interaction modes and management practices used by lead manufacturers in leveraging their network resources. This data was collected in 1999–2000 and comprised 76 hours of direct interviews.

Knowledge Dynamics and Inter-firm Networks

Knowledge leveraging and product innovation

In contexts where product innovation is a crucial competitive weapon, dynamics related to knowledge are of utmost importance. New knowledge may turn into new products, making possible a strategy of permanent innovation. At the same time, knowledge generation is a precondition for knowledge accumulation, a source of sustainable competitive advantage. In the motorcycle industry, advances at the product level have ranged from significant innovations to stylistic features introduced at little cost by combining modified components from old models. Ducati's Desmodromic valve management system and L-Twin engine, or BMW's anti-lock braking system are examples of the former type of innovation. Improvements such as paint, trim, chrome, and exhaust pipe shaping have also been necessary to appeal to modern bikers. Nevertheless, deference to the company's styling tradition often causes innovation to occur incrementally. Starting in the mid-1970s, the most important trend in the industry has been the introduction of electronic components. More recently, companies introduced composites, such as carbonium, titanium, and magnesium to make their bikes lighter and more reliable.

Table 3.1 The hyper-competitive setting: versions of motorcycles and scooters introduced in the Italian market, 1975–2000

	Versions of motorcycles and scooters	
Manufacturers	1975–2000	Product portfolio (2000)
Aprilia	170	66
Benelli	78	24
Italjet	63	27
Malaguti	76	26
Piaggio	188	54
Gilera	131	28
Ducati	88	30
Total	*794*	*255*
Honda	252	102
Suzuki	179	53
Kawasaki	98	32
Yamaha	197	69
Total	*726*	*256*
Peugeot	86	32
BMW	93	36
MBK	35	24
Kymco	39	33
Sym	19	19
Total	*272*	*144*
Total	1,792	655
Others	1,417	484
All versions	3,209	1,139

Source: Adapted from Lorenzoni and Lipparini (2001).

Technological improvements in motorcycles have stemmed from different sources. Over the years manufacturers have concentrated on optimizing engine performance, reducing noise, decreasing motorcycle weight, and improving aerodynamics to lower fuel consumption and toxic emissions. Moreover, they have further promoted R&D and marketing collaboration. For example, a large number of technical improvements or innovations have come from market surveys or customer feedback. Yet, manufacturers have also pushed suppliers to improve quality and technology on such components as anti-dive systems in the air-assisted forks, mono-shock rear suspensions, and front and rear disc brakes. Since the early 1980s, some companies such as Honda, Kawasaki, Yamaha, and Ducati have also used racing competitions to develop and test new materials and mechanics, where many have been transferred into mass production.

Table 3.1 reports data on new products introduced by major players in the Italian market in the period 1975–2000. Over these 25 years, 96 companies marketed more than 3,200 different versions of motorcycles and scooters in the Italian market (Lorenzoni and Lipparini, 2001), of which almost 1,800 related to scooters. In 2000, the Italian market accounted for 1,139 different vehicle versions, of which 697 were scooters, manufactured by 59 companies. Through a more detailed analysis, the 50cc segment is the one characterized by the fiercest competition with 1,033 models introduced (Lorenzoni and Lipparini, 2001).

Knowledge generation

Inter-firm networks in the motorcycle industry demonstrated their usefulness in terms of fast learning and flexibility; they permitted a more focused development of internal expertise while maintaining collaboration with external sources of knowledge. As a consequence, the network approach has emerged as the most supportive to the lead manufacturers' strategy of rapid and reliable product innovation. Similar to the biotechnology industry (Powell et al., 1996), where learning mainly occurs through networks, in the motorcycle industry firms are willing to pursue a strategy of networking to benefit from unexpected discoveries stemming from tacit knowledge and technical interdependencies (Nelson and Winter, 1982). To highlight the importance of suppliers as knowledge generators in the motorcycle industry, we compared two inter-firm networks, comprised each of a lead manufacturer of scooters and ten component suppliers. The two networks have a different performance measured by the number of new model of scooters that have been introduced in the Italian market in 2001. To capture the potential of suppliers as knowledge generators, we used three parameters: patenting, incidence of employees related to knowledge-based activities, and experience as dominant designers.

In the motorcycle industry, both manufacturers and suppliers are active in patenting. The latter are providing an extension of the lead manufacturer's design capabilities. Preliminary data (Lipparini et al., 2001) highlighted the alignment of the innovative potential of the different partners in the network. For example, the most prominent supplier of frames to the industry holds 6 patents; the leaders in forks and brakes registered 39 and 34 patents respectively. The oldest companies supplying carburetors and engines recorded 45 and 38 respectively. Sometimes, the supplier patenting activity is more pronounced than the one observed at the lead manufacturer side.

A second measure of the potential for knowledge generation is the "knowledge worker index," or a ratio of the number of employees in knowledge activities to the number of total employees. Core activities such as R&D and engineering are increasingly organized around a network of external specialized suppliers. For example, lead manufacturers and their partners are employing computer aided design (CAD) and computer numerical control (CNC) technologies. Furthermore styling, product and process feasibility, surfacing, prototyping, structural analysis, and prototype engineering are now shared in the network.

Knowledge generation potential is not only related to patenting and knowledge workers but also to a history of developing dominant designs. The motorcycle industry has witnessed quite interesting dynamics; data from the scooter segment reveal that both lead manufacturers and component suppliers are responsible for significant innovations in the industry (Table 3.2). In particular, such dominant designs as wheels, suspensions, engine lubrication, and innovative ignition systems are examples

Table 3.2 Dominant design in the 50 cc scooter industry[a]

Main components	Dominant design	Introduction[b]	Period of affirmation	Old technology	Innovator (s)	Manufacturer/ supplier	Users
Frame	Single tubular steel frame reinforced with sheet metal	1950	1990s	Tubular steel frame (simple or double) and sheet metal	Innocenti (Lambretta C)	Manufacturer	All manufacturers of 50cc scooters
Main body	Injected and moulded plastic body	Late 1980s	1990s	Weight-bearing structures (Piaggio Vespa e Ducati Cruiser) or metal structures over the frame	Peugeot Honda Yamaha	Manufacturer Manufacturer Manufacturer	All manufacturers of 50cc scooters
Front suspension	Telescopic-hydraulic fork	Early 1980s	Mid 1990s	Front suspension with swinging levels; Telescopic fork with mechanical absorber	Paioli Marzocchi	Supplier Supplier	All manufacturers of 50cc scooters
Rear suspension	Rear suspension by swinging engine	1948	1948	Rigid rear suspension, or with elastic rubber support	Piaggio (Vespa)	Manufacturer	All manufacturers of 50cc scooters
Front brake	Hydraulic disc brake	Early 1990s	1995	Front brake with mechanical drive	Aprilia Malaguti Yamaha/MBK	Manufacturer Manufacturer Manufacturer	All manufacturers of 50cc scooters
Rear brake	Hydraulic disc brake	Mid 1990s	Late 1990s	Rear brake with mechanical drive	Italian and Japanese manufacturers of 50cc scooters	Manufacturer	All manufacturers of 50cc scooters
Wheel rims	Aluminium-alloy wheel rims	Early 1980s	1990s	Light alloy and metal wheel rims; printed steel wheel rims	Bassano-Grimeca	Supplier	All manufacturers of 50cc scooters

Clutch	Automatic centrifugal dry clutch	1955	1980s	Multiple disks – dry or in oil – with mechanical drive	Motobecane (Mobylette)	Manufacturer	All manufacturers of 50cc scooters
Tires	Tubeless tires	Mid 1980s	1990s	Traditional tires	All main tire producers	Supplier	All manufacturers of 50cc scooters
Engine	Single horizontal cylinder 2-stroke engine with controlled admission	1959	1980s	Piston-based system or piston-driven crossed lights	Piaggio-Vespa 150 Yamaha	Manufacturer Manufacturer	All manufacturers of 50cc scooters
Ignition	Electronic ignition Automatic choke	1970s	Early 1980s	Mechanical ignition	Bosch Lucas Marelli Motoplat	Supplier Supplier Supplier Supplier	All manufacturers of 50cc scooters
Starter	Electric and kick-start	1952	Late 1980s	Kick-start	Ducati (Cruiser scooter)	Manufacturer	All manufacturers of 50cc scooters
Engine cooling system	Forced liquid cooling system	1994	1994	Forced air cooling system	Yamaha	Manufacturer	All manufacturers of 50cc scooters
Engine lubrication	Lubrication by automatic mixing pump with separate oil tank	1970s	1970s	Lubrication in a fixed percentage	Mikuni	Supplier	All manufacturers of 50cc scooters

[a] For scooters larger than 50 cc, some dominant technologies are different. For example, the dominant design for engine is the four-stroke cycle; frames are not "tubular" but "a culla"; wheels have a larger size; suspensions are more sophisticated; brakes are even more integral or electronically controlled system (ABS).
[b] This refers to the first introduction of a technology in the 50 cc segment. Some of the dominant technologies entered the motorcycle market first.
Source: Authors' direct survey based on interviews and company archives.

Table 3.3   Knowledge generation factors in two differently performing networks[a]

Knowledge generation factors	High performing network (No. of brand new scooters introduced in 2001 > 10)	Low performing network (No. of brand new scooters introduced in 2001 ≤ 10)
Patent activity (avg)[b]	24.4	15.6
Knowledge workers index (%) (avg)[c]	21.5	13.1
Dominant design suppliers	5	5

[a] Data refer to two relational sets comprising a lead manufacturer and 10 component suppliers each. The suppliers considered are those providing lead manufacturer with: frames, forks, brakes, electronic ignition, carburetor, engine, tires, front and rear suspension, plastic and rubber, design and styling.
[b] Patents are only those related to the motorcycle industry. The survey compared the esp@cenet database with company data.
[c] KWI = (No. of employees in: product-process design; engineering and reverse engineering; prototype design; design of tools for machining; instrumentation and testing/Total employees.
Source: Interviews and company data.

of component supplier contributions. Indeed, dominant designs can be found in the network as a whole.[7] However, it was not always this way. During the industry's earlier history, lead manufacturers emerged as the developers of dominant designs. Pioneering firms, mainly the Italian and Japanese, introduced products developed in-house. A growing market began to take shape around that product; competitors either expanded the market further, or developed their own product version. Over time, lead manufacturers started to outsource the production of many of the dominant designs to specialized suppliers. These specialized suppliers through experimenting then created new dominant design components. The involvement of external suppliers in the innovative process has been critical. Thanks to their ability to improve existing components, no manufacturing firm has had a lock on the market. In sum, the ecology of competition has changed: from many firms and many unique designs, to fewer competitors with similar component designs.[8] As suppliers generated new knowledge they became involved at different stages of product development: sometimes in planning but more often in implementation and execution.[9]

While we have shown how these three criteria for knowledge generation have increasingly become dispersed in the motorcycle industry, we still need to show whether knowledge generation in the networks indeed leads to increasing product innovation, a leading measure of success in the industry. Table 3.3 shows the difference between a high and low performing network in the industry and tabulates the knowledge generation potential factors. As one can see from the table, the best performing network is comprised of suppliers with a higher patent activity (24.4) than the network with a minor impact in terms of brand new scooters introduced in 2001 (15.6). The number of workers carrying out activities related to knowledge generation is also higher in the high performing network (21.5 percent of the overall workforce). As to the third factor, the two relational sets see the presence of the same number of dominant designers (5).

In light of the previous discussion, we advance the following proposition:

Proposition 1:   The combination of the knowledge generated either by the lead firm or specialized component suppliers has a positive effect on product innovation, therefore increasing both the lead firm's and network's competitiveness.

Knowledge accumulation

Once generated, knowledge must be accumulated at the manufacturer and supplier level, in order to create a fertile and co-evolving environment. Accumulation occurs mainly by means of experimentation and modularity as a principle of design, the basis of the following discussion.

Lead manufacturers and their suppliers interact frequently, experimenting with diverse relational and strategic practices, either individually or collectively. For example, some manufacturers and suppliers experiment at the Superbike and Motorbike Championships. Furthermore, some are also active in the Formula 1 World Championships. For instance, the supplier of suspensions and forks for motorcycle supplies also provides Ferrari Formula 1 vehicles with suspensions and gas pumps. Brembo is another example of a specialist producer of brake systems for motorcycles, automobiles, and Formula 1 cars. Racing displays good product innovation conditions: rapid experimentation (as every race is a front load development giving quick feedback), the opportunity to fail early and often (early problem solving), and the chance to meld conventional with new technologies. These experimental fields enable early problem identification influencing the capability to introduce new models while reducing risk and time-to-market.

Knowledge can also accumulate more rapidly through the creation of an "experimentation center." These centers, often hosted at the supplier's plant, rely on physical proximity and day-to-day interaction to be effective. Technicians and engineers meet to exchange and develop new ideas, and assess the generative rules of their network. Here *learners* are not separated from *workers* (Lave and Wenger, 1990). Learning-in-working best represents the evolution of learning through practice. When shared and supported, generative rules govern the process of learning-in-working, foster interaction, and encourage joint-problem solving among participants. In many cases, the "experimentation center" represents the most appropriate organization for rapid experimentation of new products and new processes.

A third way to foster knowledge accumulation is through product modularity. Since the majority of components are produced by external partners, new version introduction speed is related to the lead firms' ability to coordinate in-house and outsourced design and manufacturing (Clark and Fujimoto, 1991). Firms use product modularity to permit experimentation and subsequent redesigning (Kogut and Bowman, 1995), as markets and capabilities evolve. One of the advantages is that incremental improvements do not have to be coordinated among other product modules. Furthermore, improvements are not locked into an integral design. Indeed this loosely coupled system of product modules not only enhances motorcycle performance through new combinations of modules but also accelerates new product introduction. While this

Table 3.4   Knowledge accumulation factors in two differently performing networks[a]

Knowledge accumulation factors	High performing network (No. of brand new scooters introduced in 2001 > 10)	Low performing network (No. of brand new scooters introduced in 2001 ≤ 10)
Suppliers involved in racing championships[b]	7	3
Experimentation center hosted at the supplier's plant[c]	9	5
Product modularity (%)[d]	60.3	41.2

[a] Data refer to two relational sets comprising a lead manufacturer and 10 component suppliers each. The suppliers considered are those providing lead manufacturer with: frames, forks, brakes, electronic ignition, carburetor, engine, tires, front and rear suspension, plastic and rubber, design and styling.
[b] Data refer to the number of suppliers whose components are equipping bikes participating at the Superbike and MotoGP Championships.
[c] An experimentation center exists when technicians and engineers of both lead manufacturer and supplier meet in a dedicated space to exchange and develop ideas.
[d] Number of components usable at least for two different products/Total number of components manufactured. Data reported are the average of the ten percentages relative to the component suppliers.
Source: Interviews and company data.

system flexibility lies in combinations of new modules, the network of suppliers remain established; each module can be replaced, strategic suppliers cannot.

Does knowledge accumulation in the networks indeed lead to increasing product innovation, a leading measure of success in the industry? Table 3.4 shows the difference between a high and low performing network in the industry and tabulates the knowledge accumulation factors. As one can see from the table, seven suppliers of the higher performing network are involved in racing, compared with the three of the low performing network. The knowledge accumulated through the interaction and joint experimentation with clients (in particular Ducati, Aprilia, Honda, and Yamaha), has a positive impact on knowledge and competencies required in the scooter segment. The high performing brakes and suspensions equipping the recent versions of scooters are derived from the supplier's racing experience. As to the second factor, almost all the suppliers (9) of the first network have an experimentation center, hosted at their plant, to facilitate interactions with the lead manufacturer and the accumulation of knowledge. This experiential field is present in five dyads in the second, low performing network. The codification and accumulation of knowledge are also promoted and fostered by the simultaneous presence of several manufacturers. It is not rare to observe, in the same space and in the same time, the interactions between the technicians of the supplying company and those from Aprilia, MBK, and Yamaha. Our measure of product modularity in Table 3.4 refers to the number of components that find application on at least two different products divided by the total number of components manufactured by the supplier. In the first network, the incidence is higher (60.3 percent) than in the lower performing network (41.2 percent). One explanation is that customers are willing to adopt reliable components, often developed with the contributions of their relevant competitors. The experimentation center, in this sense, facilitates the testing of solutions, often derived from the supplier's racing experience.

In light of the previous discussion, we advance the following proposition:

> *Proposition 2*:   Knowledge accumulation either by the lead firm or specialized component suppliers as measured by number of suppliers involved in racing championships, number of suppliers with experimentation centers, and the degree of product modularity, has a positive effect on product innovation, therefore increasing both the lead firm's and network's competitiveness.

Knowledge transfer

Once accumulated, knowledge needs to be transferred. The relationship between organizational knowledge and competitive advantage is moderated by the firm's ability in transferring knowledge within its boundaries and with its network of suppliers. Knowledge transfer occurs mainly through dense, frequent and long-lasting inter-firm relationships with specialized component suppliers. Yet, suppliers are shared with competitors. Italian and Japanese lead manufacturers alike use the suppliers of critical components, crucial for product differentiation and new model introduction: brakes, starters, suspensions, lights, forks, and frames. However, best-in-class suppliers allow all the industry members to benefit from learning processes related to an intense relational activity (Lorenzoni and Lipparini, 1999). Table 3.5 highlights how almost all the manufacturers of scooters and motorcycles in the Italian motorcycle industry share suppliers of key components.[10] The number of connections these component suppliers have reveals partial overlapping of inter-firm networks, accelerating the transfer of knowledge. Integration mechanisms are then necessary for the "recipient" to fuse the new knowledge with existing stocks of knowledge (Hamel, 1991). For example, concerns about benefits related to the sharing of component suppliers among competitors are reflected in the following quote provided by the famous *Vespa* producer:

> One of the most challenging initiatives faced by the company in the last ten years is the attempt to reorganize the supplier network at the local level. Dozens of suppliers were informed about our make-or-buy decisions for the future ... Some of them were asked to enter into a specific project called "grappolo" echoing the interrelation and reciprocal interdependence. These suppliers started to work with other companies in the motorcycle industry, some of whom are competitors to us. We agree, of course, 'cause they will come back with all their capabilities improved ... (former Piaggio's Head of Engineering Department, personal communication).

While these overlapping networks certainly enhance the industry's competitiveness, mechanisms still may differ within each network for enhancing knowledge transfer. We find that transfer is enhanced through network design, dense, frequent information exchange, commitment of the lead firm to frequent interactions, creation of generative rules to sustain supplier motivation, and the development of a relational capability. Each is discussed in turn.

First, in the Italian motorcycle industry, knowledge transfer can occur through network design. Two types can be developed: efficiency-driven, and knowledge-based (Lipparini et al., 2001). In the former assemblers rely on component manufacturers'

Table 3.5 The network of specialized component suppliers shared by lead manufacturers in the Italian motorcycle industry[a]

Manufacturers	Externally-manufactured key components										
	Brakes	Carburetor	Ignition system	Turn indicators	Forks	Plastics	Lights	Shock absorber	Front suspension	Tail lights, reflectors	Frames, footboards
Aprilia	■	■	■	■		■	■	■	■	■	■
Benelli	■	■	■	■		■					
BMW	■				■		■		■		■
Cagiva	■	■	■	■	■	■	■	■	■	■	■
Ducati	■	■	■	■	■	■	■	■	■	■	■
Harley Davidson					■		■			■	■
Honda	■	■	■	■		■	■	■	■	■	
Italjet	■		■	■		■	■	■	■	■	
Malaguti	■	■	■	■	■	■	■	■	■	■	
MBK		■	■	■	■	■	■	■	■	■	
Moto Guzzi	■	■	■	■		■	■	■	■	■	
Piaggio-Gilera		■	■	■	■	■	■	■	■	■	
Yamaha	■		■	■	■	■	■	■	■	■	■
Others[b]	3	10	8	9	6	11	11	7	6	9	3
Total relationships	13	19	19	20	14	22	23	17	17	20	9
Avg relat. duration (year)	12	16	9	6	12	17	16	8	8	10	16
Suppliers' age (years)	38	66	14	8	50	52	85	88	25	30	67

[a] Table refers to suppliers with the highest centrality indexes. These suppliers resulted as the most cited by lead manufacturers.
[b] Relationships with other firms producing scooters and motorcycles.
Source: Authors' direct survey on motorcycle industry.

capabilities, flexibility, and efficiency. In the latter, the lead assemblers rely on special-ized suppliers for their role in new product development.

Lead manufacturers can support a *dual network* strategy (Lipparini et al., 2001), where a knowledge-based network would include best-in-class suppliers that are extensively involved in co-design practices and strategic outsourcing activities. Intense relational activity results in increased specialization, larger volumes, and learning-by-interacting. In knowledge-based networks, specialized suppliers are mainly giving innovative ideas, while lead manufacturers show them the most appro-priate way of turning these ideas into value-added components. In knowledge-based networks, manufacturers and suppliers have a common vision, share goals, and their process and flows are interdependent. To remove a firm from this community would be to deprive it of important strategic capabilities that it could find difficult to recreate.

To the lead manufacturer, an efficiency-driven network is equally important; thanks to proximity and extensive use of subcontracting and outsourcing activities, minor modifications and adjustments at the process level (e.g. paint, testing, special, etc.), or at the product level can take place very rapidly. They guarantee their customers fre-quent and fast adaptation to market changes thanks to strong investment in design (e.g. CAD) and production (e.g. FMS – flexible manufacturing systems) technolo-gies, as well as management techniques aimed at improving efficiency (e.g. inventory control, quality management, logistics, and transportation).

A sustained network advantage is therefore the result of capabilities in building and governing both knowledge-based and efficiency-driven networks. Some of the most prominent examples of firms employing the dual network strategy in the Italian motorcycle industry include Honda's Supplier Consortium in Southern Italy, the C1 Project led by BMW in Turin, and the Network Project led by Piaggio in Pontedera. In particular, the Honda Consortium reflects an example of clustering around a cus-tomer's plant. Proximity makes possible communication mechanisms facilitating the flow of knowledge across firms (Almeida and Kogut, 1994), with positive benefits on the process of learning especially when technical information is exchanged (Sako, 1992). Due to the high level of automation and robotization of assembly lines, Honda needs a very close collaboration with external suppliers. All the local suppliers are working on the highest quality standards. They are connected via computer and everyone is informed about the stock levels and the work-in-progress of the others. Collaborative practices include quality circles, training, production scheduling, as well as marketing plans and engineering of new components.

Second, knowledge transfer through dense and frequent exchanges favors recipro-cal learning and the creation of a trusting environment; partners are encouraged to communicate their own requirements and be responsive to the needs of the other. As a consequence, the quality of design and manufacturing is enhanced and the parties are less likely to misread blueprints (Clark and Fujimoto, 1991). Feedback is more efficient with a positive effect on combinative (Kogut and Zander, 1992) and absorp-tive (Cohen and Levinthal, 1990) capabilities. Similar to what has been observed in the automobile industry, new model cycle time decreases as supplier-automakers engage in more frequent and face-to-face contacts (Dyer, 1996).

Third, the commitment of the most prominent firm in the network to those frequent interactions increases the chances for a "contagion" of ideas and information. Teams of engineers both from supplying and motorcycle companies repeatedly interact to solve problems. Within "customer trial centers," the parties accumulate specialized information that produces more efficient communication processes. "Situated learning" occurs, creating a kind of field for experimentation.

Fourth, the generative rules inspired by the lead firm sustain supplier motivation, identification, and alignment with the network. For instance, early participation of suppliers in the lead manufacturers' innovative process is a strong incentive to align their respective strategies. Along the same track is the creation by Honda of a buyer-supplier "council," or an increase in the level of *site asset specificity* driven by the need to improve coordination and lower inventory and transportation costs.[11] As a consequence, key suppliers are becoming even more involved in the lead assemblers' manufacturing strategy.

Fifth, the planning and execution of actions aimed at developing the relational capabilities of the lead firm (Lorenzoni and Lipparini, 1999) are necessary to exploit externally generated knowledge and to integrate different sources of innovation. The quest for quality, reduced costs, and responsiveness to market fluctuations is forcing final assemblers to forge strong commitments in favor of suppliers.[12] The adoption of modern manufacturing techniques and managerial philosophies like the Just-in-Time inventory and production-scheduling program suggests lead companies turn traditional arm's-length contracts into closer partnerships. Improvements in the relational capabilities of the network members benefit from day-to-day interactions to fit specific requirements: elimination of what does not add value to the product; upgrading of current systems for identifying manufacturing problems; realization of product-oriented layouts; quality control at source; preventative and production maintenance and set-up time reduction to increase flexibility. New systems of design and manufacturing are now relying on group effort, combination of talents, sharing of ideas, knowledge, and problem-solving skills. The management practices highlighted above should support joint learning and product innovation.

Table 3.6 compares the two inter-firm networks analyzed in previous sections. The data suggest that the high performing network turns managerial practices into effective learning by means of closer relationships with suppliers, their early involvement in new product development process, and the strong commitment to training delivered on issues related to product design and manufacturing. In particular, frequency of interaction in the high performing network is double that of the low performing one. Almost all the suppliers are involved in innovative activities in the high performing network compared to half the suppliers in the low performing one. Training hours (except those delivered on issues related to total quality management) are higher in number in the network with the best performance.

In light of the previous discussion, we offer the following proposition:

Proposition 3:   Appropriate managerial actions, such as: (1) the design of a relational structure supporting and fostering reciprocal learning processes; (2) the selection of specialized component suppliers, their early involvement in knowledge generation activities, and the creation of a trust-based environment; and (3) the development of a relational capability aimed at accessing and pooling specialized partners' knowledge, have a positive effect on product innovation, therefore increasing both the lead firm's and network competitiveness.

Table 3.6 Buyer-supplier relational practices and managerial actions in two differently performing networks[a]

	High performing network (No. of brand new scooters introduced in 2001 > 10)	Low performing network (No. of brand new scooters introduced in 2001 ≤ 10)
No. of buyer-supplier meetings (on avg. on a monthly basis)	10	5
No. of hours spent in co-design and engineering (on avg.)[b]	665	431
No. of suppliers involved at the concept stage of the lead manufacturer's NPD process	9	5
No. of suppliers adopting the same software package to manage relationships	7	5
No. of suppliers participating in joint testing activities with the leading firm	9	6
No. of training hours delivered on issues related to electronic interactions (on avg.)	261	229
No. of training hours delivered on issues related to product design (on avg.)	212	171
No. of training hours delivered on issues related to product manufacturing (on avg.)	333	234
No. of training hours delivered on issues related to total quality management (on avg.)	153	171
No. of training hours delivered on issues related to best practices (on avg.)	81	48

[a] Data refer to two relational sets comprising a lead manufacturer and 10 component suppliers each. The suppliers considered are those providing lead manufacturer with: frames, forks, brakes, electronic ignition, carburetor, engine, tires, front and rear suspension, plastic and rubber, design and styling.

[b] Data refers to the sum of the hours spent in co-design by the different members of the supplying company assigned to this activity.

Source: Direct interviews and company data.

Discussion and Conclusions

Diverse lessons are provided by a study of network dynamics within the Italian motorcycle industry. These lessons can have an impact on studies at business level strategy, knowledge management, and networks in general. From our study, we draw a number of conclusions. First, inter-firm networks can be a source of competitive advantage. They permit lead firms to combine different sources of external knowledge, partially embedded in components and partially embedded in social relationships among a large number of geographically dispersed firms (Uzzi, 1997). The extensive use of the "social" side of a relationship is critical to strategic flexibility and continuous learning. Within a strategy-making process aimed at exploiting network-specific advantages, a critical task is that of managing two simultaneous processes: (1) the ongoing relationships between the lead firms and each network member, and (2) the interdependencies between the different suppliers' network typologies.

Our data also reveal a different approach to strategic relationships. A strategic role of the central firm is its function as a triggering entity, engineering the design of each network and of the processes by which the learning and experimentation that occurs within the knowledge-based network is transferred via the central firm to individual firms within the adaptive network (Doz et al., 2000). A major implication of our work resides in a better understanding of the "loci of innovation" (Powell et al., 1996). In the motorcycle industry, improvements often originated at the supplier level, and the interaction with outside specialized firms helps lead firms to renew their competency base, thereby reducing resistance to change in hierarchical settings that appears to inhibit new product introductions (Helfat and Raubitschek, 2000). The technical and market evolutions of the motorcycle industry required significant improvements in electronics and new materials to lighten the products, as well as an evolution from single to group components. As we have argued, the new set of innovative sources and the ability to leverage these sources influenced actions and positioning of successful players.

This network-based approach has been experienced by other industries (i.e., civil aircraft and automobile), but in the motorcycle industry the product lifecycle is shorter and assemblers are mainly medium-sized companies, not large established firms. Despite these differences, Italian motorcycle manufacturers, like the Japanese ones in the automobile industry (Dyer, 1996), are enjoying the benefits of their suppliers' high levels of specialization in terms of productivity, modularity, product quality, and reliability. Specialized assets convey modularity but do not prevent the capability to customize the manufacturing tail. The active role of specialized suppliers, together with the deliberate support from assemblers, improves the absorptive capabilities of the whole network and fosters the adaptation of its participants. Our data suggest that important network-specific advantages persist even in the face of competitors attempting to imitate a company's network strategy, mainly because of significant causal ambiguity associated with the relational capabilities of the central firms. For a network to be efficient, external sources of knowledge need to be pooled and managed appropriately. Lead firms' relational capability is crucial in shaping network formation and development. Furthermore, it represents a structure-reinforcing competence difficult to imitate.

The distinctive governance pattern of inter-firm relationships has particular effects with regard to the quality and nature of knowledge flows between partners. Relational capability accounts for regulation and control of partnering firms (Lorenzoni and Baden Fuller, 1995), and is necessary to efficiently steer the process of boundary redefinition. In this industry, the ability to leverage multiple sources of learning is occurring with "strategic intent," and the functioning of the communities of cooperative strategic practices is governed by rules and principles generated by the lead firm

(Kogut, 2000) but continuously re-evaluated and re-adjusted by every participant in the network.

A key managerial implication lies in the need to ensure the competency convergence between lead firms and their networks of specialized suppliers. They need to be proactive with respect to the network as a whole, triggering entities working with autonomy but within a unique, complementary strategic plan. Their strategy-making process should comprise deliberate actions as well as initiatives aimed at supporting a learning process occurring incrementally. Their capabilities should be supported by managerial initiatives aimed at helping partnering suppliers to become component specialists (Kogut and Bowman, 1995). This would ensure a co-evolution of strategy and organization. Their ability not only to coordinate manufacturing efforts but also to integrate multiple sources of knowledge will turn into an important source of competitive differentiation. In all of the cases we studied, there was evidence that lead firms were very conscious of the need to act fairly in dealing with the diverse and competing demands of the members of their networks. We have described these efforts in more detail elsewhere (Lorenzoni and Lipparini, 2001). The data suggest to us that the managers of the lead firms were very much concerned about developing and sustaining high levels of relational quality (Ariño and de la Torre, 1998). In the course of interacting with their partners, managers of the lead firms appear to focus on issues related to both distributive and procedural justice, which Ariño et al. (2001) argue are important conditions for creating and maintaining high level of relational quality.

In conclusion, the results of our study of the Italian motorcycle industry suggest that for a strategy to be successful, a spirit of "openness to experimentation" among all of the players across the value system is critical. If managers can develop generative rules in different directions, it can be possible for them to employ a network strategy in which a community of cooperative practices flourishes. As with Italian motorcycle producers, such a community can be an important factor in a successful response to intense and intensifying competitive pressures.

Acknowledgments

We received helpful comments from Robert Grant, Elaine Romanelli, and Peter Smith Ring. We would also like to thank James Henderson and an anonymous reviewer for their insightful comments on a previous version of the manuscript. An early version of the chapter was presented at the 2002 SMS 22nd Annual International Conference, Paris, September 22–25. We are very grateful to the engineers and managers whose cooperation made this study possible. We alone are responsible for errors and omissions.

Notes

1. For a critique of the static analysis and normative assumptions underlying the TCE approach, see Ring and Van de Ven (1992) and Zajac and Olsen (1993).

2. At the same time, environmental constraints such as the introduction of the gas emission regulations ask the network to respond as a whole.

3. While in the past the term "scooter" was synonymous with small engines, limited speed, and transport orientation, overtime we observe 150cc, 250cc, even 500cc engine maxi-scooters emerging, blurring the distinction, previously clear enough, between bikes and scooters. At the same time, many scooter features became similar to motorbikes both in external design and, more importantly, in technology transfer.

4. In sum, Japanese and Italians represented 78 percent of the Italian market. It is interesting to note that the average scooter incidence in term of sales is 82 percent for the Italian players (98 percent without Ducati, which does not produce scooters), and 44 percent for the Japanese (59 percent without Kawasaki, which notably is not present in the scooter segment).

5. Among them were comprised all the notable Italian producers (Piaggio, Aprilia, Ducati, Malaguti, Italjet, Moto Guzzi, Benelli, Cagiva), the Japanese (Honda, Yamaka, Suzuki), other Europeans (MBK, BMW, Peugeot, Derbi), producers from other countries (Harley Davidson-Buell; Kymco, Sym).

6. The two networks have six suppliers in common.

7. Dominant design in a product class could be considered as the one that competitors and innovators must adhere to if they hope to command significant market following (Utterback, 1994).

8. The "dominant design effect" strongly reduces the number of requirements to be met by a scooter by making most of those requirements implicit in the design itself. For example, few knowledgeable customers today would ask if a 50cc scooter had an electric starter or a hydraulic disc brake. These features are not advertised as real advantages by any scooter manufacturer.

9. One example is the supplier specialized in high performing steel frames. Four years ago, the company opened two plants in southern Italy, to supply the Honda factory – its largest European plant – with high quality steel frames and components. The positive experience was replicated in 2000, with the opening of a new plant in Spain, close to the Honda factory in that country.

10. Data refer to 13 lead manufacturers and 11 suppliers; the latter have been selected on the basis of their network centrality indices based on customers' responses.

11. The Italian motorcycle industry is characterized by a very low level of *physical asset specificity*, as the parties are not making capital investments in customized machineries or other transaction-specific capital investments.

12. For instance, Harley has established a supplier advisory council (SAC), made up of 16 suppliers, to expose supplier executives to the best practices of other suppliers in the Harley-Davidson network. Furthermore, the Harley-Davidson's RIDE network (Rapid Information Delivery and Exchange) not only improves internal communication, but also serves to exchange information via the Internet with external suppliers.

References

Almeida, P. and Kogut, B. 1994: Technology, regions, and R&D spillovers: Knowledge diffusion in the semiconductor industry. The Wharton School, University of Pennsylvania Working Paper.

Amit, R.H. and Schoemaker, P. 1993: Strategic assets and organizational rent. *Strategic Management Journal*, 14, 33–46.

Ariño, A. and de la Torre, J. 1998: Learning from failure: Towards an evolutionary model of collaborative ventures. *Organization Science,* 9, 306–325.

Ariño, A., de la Torre, J., and Ring, P.S. 2001: Relational quality: Managing trust in corporate alliances. *California Management Review,* 44, 109–131.

Brown, J.S. and Duguid, P. 1991: Organizational learning and communities-of-practice. *Organization Science,* 2, 40–57.

Clark, K.B. and Fujimoto, T. 1991: *Product Development Performance.* Boston, MA: Harvard Business School Press.

Cohen, W. and Levinthal, D. 1990: Absorptive capacity: A new perspective on learning and innovation. *Administrative Science Quarterly,* 35, 128–152.

Dierickx, I. and Cool, K. 1989: Asset stock accumulation and sustainability of competitive advantage. *Management Science,* 35, 1504–1511.

Doz, Y. 1996: The evolution of cooperation in strategic alliances: Initial conditions or learning processes? *Strategic Management Journal Special Issue,* 17, 55–83.

Doz, Y., Olk, P., and Ring, P.S. 2000: Formation processes of R&D consortia: Which path to take? Where does it lead? *Strategic Management Journal Special Issue,* 21, 239–266.

Dyer, J. 1996: Specialized supplier networks as a source of competitive advantage: Evidence from the auto industry. *Strategic Management Journal,* 17, 271–291.

Dyer, J. and Singh, H. 1998: The relational view: Cooperative strategy and sources of interorganizational competitive advantage. *Academy of Management Review,* 23, 660–679.

Enright, M. 1998: Regional clusters and firm strategy. In A. Chandler Jr, Ö. Sölvell, and P. Hagström (eds.), *The Dynamic Firm: The Role of Technology, Strategy, Organization, and Regions.* Oxford: Oxford University Press, 315–342.

Gomez-Casseres, B. 1984: Group versus group: How alliance networks compete. *Harvard Business Review,* 72, 62–74.

Granovetter, M. 1985: Economic action and social structure: The problem of embeddedness. *American Journal of Sociology,* 91, 481–510.

Grant, R. 1996: Toward a knowledge-based theory of the firm. *Strategic Management Journal,* 17, 109–122.

Gulati, R. 1998: Alliances and networks. *Strategic Management Journal,* 19, 293–317.

Hamel, G. 1991: Competition for competence and interpartner learning within international strategic alliances. *Strategic Management Journal,* 12, 82–103.

Hannan, M. and Freeman, J. 1989: *Organizational Ecology.* Cambridge MA: Harvard University Press.

Hansen, M., Hoskisson, R., Lorenzoni, G., and Ring, P.S. 1997: Strategic capabilities of the transactionally-intense firm: Leveraging interfirm relationships. Texas A&M University Working Paper.

Helfat, C. and Raubitschek, R. 2000: Product sequencing: Co-evolution of knowledge, capabilities and products. *Strategic Management Journal,* 21, 961–979.

Jarrillo, J. 1988: On strategic networks. *Strategic Management Journal,* 9, 31–41.

Kogut, B. 2000: The network as knowledge: Generative rules and the emergence of structure. *Strategic Management Journal,* 21, 405–425.

Kogut, B. and Bowman, E. 1995: Modularity and permeability as principles of design. In E. Bowman and B. Kogut (eds.), *Redesigning the Firm.* New York: Oxford University Press, 243–260.

Kogut, B. and Zander, U. 1992: Knowledge of the firm, combinative capabilities, and the replication of technology. *Organization Science,* 3, 383–397.

Lado, A. and Wilson, M. 1994: Human resource systems and sustained competitive advantage: A competency-based perspective. *Academy of Management Review,* 19, 699–727.

Lave, J. and Wenger, E. 1990: *Situated Learning: Legitimate Peripheral Participation.* Institute for Research on Learning Report no. 90-0013, Palo Alto, CA.

Lawrence, P. and Lorsch, J. 1967: *Organization and Environment.* Boston, MA: Harvard University Press.

Lipparini, A., Lorenzoni, G., and Zollo, M. 2001: Dual network strategies: Managing knowledge-based and efficiency-based networks in the Italian motorcycle industry. Strategic Management Society 21st Annual International Conference, San Francisco, CA, October 21–24.

Lorenzoni, G. and Baden-Fuller, C. 1995: Creating a strategic center to manage a web of partners. *California Management Review,* 37, 146–163.

Lorenzoni, G. and Lipparini, A. 1999: The leveraging of interfirm relationships as a distinctive organizational capability: A longitudinal study. *Strategic Management Journal,* 20, 317–338.

Lorenzoni, G. and Lipparini, A. 2001: The Honda effect, part 3. Network-specific advantage in the Italian motorcycle industry. University of Bologna Working Paper.

Markides, C. and Williamson, P. 1994: Related diversification, core competences and corporate performance. *Strategic Management Journal,* 15, 149–166.

Miles, R. and Snow, C. 1986: Organization: New concepts for new forms. *California Management Review,* 3, 62–74.

Nelson, R. and Winter, S. 1982: *An Evolutionary Theory of Economic Change.* Cambridge, MA: Harvard University Press.

Nonaka, I. 1994: A dynamic theory of organizational knowledge creation. *Organization Science,* 5, 14–37.

Nonaka, I. and Takeuchi, H. 1995: *The Knowledge-Creating Company.* Oxford: Oxford University Press.

Peteraf, M. 1993: The cornerstone of competitive advantage: A resource-based view. *Strategic Management Journal,* 14, 179–191.

Porter, M. and Sölvell, Ö. 1998: The role of geography in the process of innovation and the sustainable competitive advantage of firms. In A. Chandler Jr, Ö. Sölvell, and P. Hagström (eds.), *The Dynamic Firm: The Role of Technology, Strategy, Organization, and Regions.* Oxford: Oxford University Press, 440–457.

Powell, W. 1990: Neither market nor hierarchy: Network forms of organization. In L. Cummings and B. Staw (eds.), *Research in Organizational Behavior.* Greenwich, CT: JAI Press; 295–336.

Powell, W., Koput, K., and Smith-Doerr, L. 1996: Interorganizational collaboration and the locus of innovation: Networks of learning in biotechnology. *Administrative Science Quarterly,* 41, 116–145.

Prahalad, C.K. and Hamel, G. 1990: The core competence of the corporation. *Harvard Business Review,* 68, 79–91.

Ring, P.S. and Van de Ven, A. 1992: Structuring cooperative relationships between organizations. *Strategic Management Journal,* 13, 483–498.

Sako, M. 1992: *Prices, Quality and Trust: Interfirm Relations in Britain and Japan.* Cambridge, UK: Cambridge University Press.

Spender, J.-C. 1996: Making knowledge the basis of a dynamic theory of the firm. *Strategic Management Journal,* 17, 45–62.

Teece, D., Pisano, G., and Shuen, A. 1997: Dynamic capabilities and strategic management. *Strategic Management Journal,* 18, 509–533.

Thomke, S. 2001: Enlightened experimentation: The new imperative for innovation. *Harvard Business Review,* 89, 67–75.

Tsoukas, H. 1996: The firm as a distributed knowledge system: A constructionist approach. *Strategic Management Journal,* 17, 11–25.

Utterback, J. 1994: *Mastering the Dynamics of Innovation*. Boston, MA: Harvard Business School Press.

Uzzi, B. 1997: Social structure and competition in interfirm networks: The paradox of embeddedness. *Administrative Science Quarterly*, 42, 35–67.

Van den Bosch, F., Volberda, H., and de Boer, M. 1999: Co-evolution of firm absorptive capacity and knowledge environment: Organizational forms and combinative capabilities. *Organization Science*, 10, 551–568.

Von Hippel, E. 1988: *The Sources of Innovation*. New York: Oxford University Press.

Williamson, O. 1975: *Markets and Hierarchies*. New York: The Free Press.

Winter, S. 1987: Knowledge and competence as strategic assets. In D. Teece (ed.), *The Competitive Challenge: Strategies for Industrial Innovation and Renewal*. Cambridge, MA: Ballinger, 159–184.

Zajac, E. and Olsen, C. 1993: From transaction cost to transaction value analysis: Implications for the study of interorganizational strategies. *Journal of Management Studies*, 30, 131–145.

CHAPTER FOUR

Assessing the Knowledge Landscape across Firms in Alliance Networks and its Impact on Organizational Innovation Performance

Beiqing (Emery) Yao and Susan McEvily

Introduction

The knowledge-based theory of the firm depicts organizations as repositories of knowledge and competencies (Kogut and Zander, 1996; Spender and Grant, 1996). Organizations exist because they are better able to create and transfer certain types of knowledge than the market (Kogut and Zander, 1996). However, firms also gain advantage by exploiting knowledge that resides beyond their organizational boundaries (Cohen and Levinthal, 1990; Powell, 1998). Alliance partners are an important source of such knowledge (Dyer and Singh, 1998; Gulati, 1998). They bring complementary expertise and diverse perspectives to bear on joint development activities, and provide opportunities for a firm to learn new skills and expand its competencies (Mowery et al., 1996). Alliance partners are especially valuable for accessing complementary assets, such as knowledge, that are idiosyncratic and indivisible, and thus not readily available in factor markets (Burgers et al., 1993).

Most firms engage in multiple alliances and authors have recently emphasized the need to examine the benefits associated with the whole set or network of alliance relationships a firm maintains (McEvily and Zaheer, 1999; Ahuja, 2000). In many cases, the network itself serves as a special form of resource, which firms use to conceive of and implement their strategies (Burt, 1990). Thus, competitive advantage derives not solely from firm level resources but also from the difficult-to-imitate capabilities embedded in dyadic and network relationships (Dyer and Singh, 1998; Lane and Lubatkin, 1998). In line with this, research on alliances and networks has revealed how various positional properties of firms, dyadic and subgroup characteristics, and overall network parameters affect knowledge transfer and value creation among firms (for example, Gulati and Gargiulo, 1999; Ahuja, 2000; Baum et al., 2000; Rowley et al., 2000, Yao and McEvily, 2001; Yao and Ge, 2002).

However, research in this stream tends to emphasize network characteristics and may underestimate the role of firm heterogeneity in influencing the value derived from alliance networks. We suggest that the distribution of knowledge within a network may be at least as important as network structure in shaping knowledge flows among organizations, as firms can only communicate about topics they understand. Specifically, network structure influences the pattern of knowledge exchange, while knowledge relation among firms affects the content of such exchange. The information exchanged through one network tie might be quite different in quantity and quality from that obtained through another tie, if those partners have heterogeneous expertise. If firm heterogeneity is important in shaping knowledge flows, predictions based solely on structural relations could be misleading. Prior work points to the need to integrate work on firm heterogeneity, particularly with respect to knowledge resources, with formal structural analysis of alliance networks (McEvily and Zaheer, 1999).

In this chapter we introduce the concept of knowledge landscape to evaluate firm-specific knowledge resources and inter-firm knowledge relations. The knowledge landscape across a group of related firms can be assessed through the size of an individual firm's knowledge stock, the distribution of a firm's knowledge across various technology domains as compared to its partners' knowledge, and relations among partners' knowledge. We apply this concept to the alliance context and propose that a firm's position and its relation to others in the knowledge landscape affect knowledge transfer and the firm's innovation performance. Findings from the alliance and patent profiles of global pharmaceutical firms support the proposed ideas. The results suggest that organizations could improve their alliance strategies by assessing the knowledge landscape they are embedded in. This study not only extends current research on alliance networks and knowledge transfer, but also contributes to knowledge-based study in general.

Assessing the Knowledge Landscape across Firms

Assessing the knowledge landscape across firms helps us to examine the "hidden" knowledge relations among a network of organizations, or the "hidden" structure based on the distribution of knowledge within the network. The two key elements of any structure are what actors are in the system and what relations exist among them (Dubin, 1978). Industrial organization theory explains industry structure as the number of firms in a market and the concentration of market share among them (Porter, 1980). Industry structure shapes firm conduct and thereby affects firm performance. Network theory defines a "network" as a set of actors and their connections among each other, and proposes that the structure of these relations

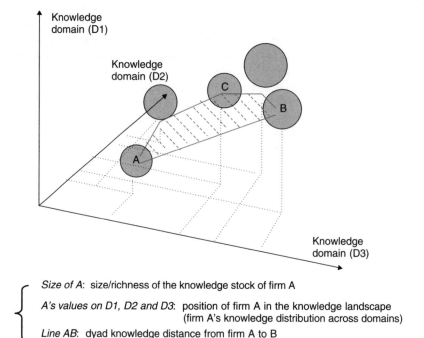

Size of A: size/richness of the knowledge stock of firm A

A's values on D1, D2 and D3: position of firm A in the knowledge landscape
(firm A's knowledge distribution across domains)

Line AB: dyad knowledge distance from firm A to B

Figure 4.1   An illustration of knowledge landscape across firms

affects firm actions and performance (Burt, 1990). Both theories suggest that firms gain individual power or status because of their positions within a system. In the case of industrial organization, a firm gains power through its market share and overlap in market participation (for example, degree of multi-market contact) with other firms in the industry. In network theory, a firm gains status, and hence the ability to influence others, through its network position and the structure of the connections among its ties.

Following a similar logic, we introduce the concept of knowledge landscape to describe a firm's position and relations to others in a knowledge space. A firm may derive status and influence if its position affords it privileged access to knowledge, and hence enables it to exploit or shape the direction of innovation opportunities ahead of others. A knowledge landscape can be assessed through the size of each firm's knowledge stock, the distribution of its expertise among various technology domains, and the relationship between a firm's knowledge and that possessed by others (knowledge distance/knowledge overlap).

In Figure 4.1 we use each axis to represent a knowledge domain/area. The illustration assumes there are three knowledge domains occupied by a set of firms. Each firm occupies a specific position in the knowledge space because of its value along each axis, which is determined by the unique distribution of its expertise across those knowledge domains. The size of each ball stands for the size or richness of a firm's overall knowledge stock. The line between any two firms shows the knowledge distance between them. The shadowed surface area within those inter-firm lines represents the knowledge landscape across those firms. Firms will occupy unique positions in such inter-organizational knowledge landscapes, according to their own expertise and the choices they make about which organizations to ally with. A firm that locates too close to its partners, or chooses partners with very similar knowledge, gains less novel insight from each partner and this may affect the type of advantage a firm attains from its knowledge position. In this study, we examine how a firm's knowledge position and its relations to others affect knowledge transfer and innovation performance in alliance networks. Specifically, we focus on the influence of alliance partners' knowledge stock, knowledge distance from the focal firm to its partners, and knowledge distance among its partners, on a firm's innovation performance.

From Knowledge Landscape across Firms in Alliance Networks to Organizational Innovation Performance

Size of alliance partners' knowledge stock

Several authors point out that we need to consider the characteristics of a firm's alliance partners in order to understand their contribution to a firm's success (Lane and Lubatkin, 1998; Stuart, 2000). Alliances are often formed specifically for the purpose of learning. To the extent that innovation and learning is the goal, more knowledgeable companies will make better partners, as they afford greater opportunities to learn new routines and extend existing competencies (Baum et al., 2000). Alliance partners can provide insight into which approaches have been tried and failed in the scientific and technological areas in which they have experience. The richer their experience, the better able they are to help their alliance partners select the most promising approaches. More innovative partners are familiar with the research process and may have better insight into how to carry out the various search and experimentation processes needed to find a solution. Thus, they not only bring a wealth of empirical data, problem-solving strategies, and partial solutions to a collaborative venture, they also contribute their adeptness at the process of doing research. Both types of knowledge should enhance a firm's ability to develop more effective solutions. Consistent with this, Stuart (2000) finds evidence that a firm that allies with more innovative partners experiences better innovative performance itself. Similarly, we predict:

> *Hypothesis 1:*   The size of the knowledge stock of alliance partners positively affects the focal firm's innovation performance.

Knowledge distance from the focal firm to its partners

Alliance networks may enhance the value of a firm's innovations to the extent they provide unique access to knowledge and information, or opportunities to combine their own distinctive competencies with complementary skills. Research on alliances has found that firms tend to partner with organizations that possess complementary resources and capabilities (Hamel et al., 1989; Nohria and Garcia-Pont, 1991). Such partners enable firms to leverage their distinctive competencies and to gain performance advantages more rapidly (Baum et al., 2000). Similarly, we expect that a firm can leverage what it knows, to create more valuable innovations, by allying with firms that understand phenomena it does not. We refer to the degree to which a firm's knowledge differs from that of its partners as the "knowledge distance" between them. "Distant" experiences can generate new perspectives or approaches to existing problems. This suggests:

Hypothesis 2: The knowledge distance between a firm and its alliance partners positively affects the focal firm's innovation performance.

Knowledge distance among alliance partners

The diversity of knowledge a firm obtains from its network depends not only on the distance between itself and its alliance partners, but also on the distinctiveness of each partner's expertise. The more heterogeneous the expertise a firm gets from its alliance partners, the more unique opportunities a firm has to combine its own knowledge with complementary scientific and technological expertise. Moreover, diversity among partners may also reduce conflicts that would inhibit them from sharing information (Baum et al., 2000). Nakamura et al. (1996) argue that the more heterogeneous partners are, the more information they will share with one another. This should enhance a firm's ability to develop useful and distinctive innovations because it suggests its R&D choices will be better informed. Therefore, we expect:

Hypothesis 3: The knowledge distance among a firm's alliance partners (excluding the focal firm) positively affects the focal firm's innovation performance.

Collectively, these hypotheses suggest that a firm can enhance its innovation performance by locating itself close to organizations that are highly innovative but in different scientific, technological, and/or application areas from itself. Further, the best partners are those that are themselves allied with firms that provide unique knowledge. We expect this position in a knowledge landscape to provide a firm with a greater volume of diverse and potentially complementary information and knowledge, and to thereby generate more numerous opportunities for innovation. To test these hypotheses, we require a setting in which innovation is an important focus of firms' activities, and where firms have a substantial number of potential alliance partners to choose from. The pharmaceutical industry seemed ideal, as innovation has always been central, and the increasingly complex body of knowledge firms must bring to bear on their research and development activities has increased reliance on alliances over the past few decades.

Research Design

Industry background and data collection

The pharmaceutical industry has experienced a series of fundamental shifts in technology and research approaches during its relatively short history, the development of

the germ theory of disease at the beginning of the twentieth century, the chemo-
therapeutic period of the 1930s and more recently the biotechnology revolution
bringing on breakthroughs in DNA technology and molecular genetics (Cockburn
and Henderson, 1996). To adapt to these changes, pharmaceutical firms have had to
develop new technological capabilities in research and development. At the same
time, the costs of innovation have risen dramatically, due to increased technological
complexity. To manage the expense, and keep pace with the expanding and diverse
body of scientific and technological knowledge, pharmaceutical firms have increasingly relied on networks of alliances with other organizations. These alliances take the
form of research cooperation, product co-development, technology licensing and
transfer, co-promotion, distribution and commercialization, and corporate joint ventures. Over the years, pharmaceutical alliances have shifted from downstream activities to a much greater emphasis on joint research, and very early stages of product
development (Yao and McEvily, 2001). However, little systematic evidence exists to
explain how and whether the knowledge properties of external alliances affect a firm's
innovation output.

We test the above hypotheses on firms in the global pharmaceutical industry, using
data from 1991 through 1996. Our focus is on firms that list their primary business
as pharmaceutical preparation (SIC code 2834). These designations are taken from
Compustat, and the Global Worldscope and Compact Disclosure databases. The
content of a network, that is, what is being exchanged or the reason for forming relations, can affect how network variables influence members' behaviors and hence performance outcomes (Gulati, 1998; Ahuja, 2000). We restrict our attention to
research and development alliances only, the focus of our study. Firms have ties with
one another if they are parties to a technology licensing or sharing agreement, are
engaged in a joint venture or R&D consortium to research a technology, or have
established other types of formal contracts for product development.

Information on alliance activities was gathered from a variety of sources:
Recombination Capital and Bioscan, which describe the alliance activities a firm has
engaged in since 1978 (Lerner, 1994; Lane and Lubatkin, 1998); US Securities and
Exchange Commission (SEC) filings; and a list of industrial newspapers and journals
that report pharmaceutical firms' activities, such as *Drug Store News, Healthcare
Financial Management, Health Industry Today, Natural Health, Pharmaceutical
Executive, Pharmaceutical Technology,* and *R & D Focus Drug News.*

Prior research on alliance networks has focused on leading companies, in order to
make the computation of the network measures tractable (Gulati, 1998; Madhavan
et al., 1998; Gulati and Gargiulo, 1999; Ahuja, 2000). We follow the same approach
by concentrating on companies that consistently reported R&D, total sales revenue,
and profitability during the 1990s. These firms generate the vast majority of patents
in the pharmaceutical industry. These criteria left us with a sample of 68 firms. Patent
data was collected from USPTO, the official US patent database containing the
searchable patent records of all firms since 1790.

Dependent variable

Innovation performance.   Patents have been widely used as a measure of innovative
performance, and, as they are used extensively to protect innovations in the

pharmaceutical industry, they are especially relevant for this study. However, not all patents are equal in impact, and we are particularly interested in how knowledge landscape affects a firm's ability to generate highly valued innovations. The number of citations a patent receives has been widely used as a measure of the value or quality of a firm's patents (Hall et al., 2000). Patents that receive a larger number of citations as prior art for subsequent patents are regarded as more important drivers of technological progress. Although not all patents are necessarily commercialized, there is evidence to suggest that highly cited patents contribute more to the economic value of a firm (Deng et al., 1999). Trajtenberg (1990) examined patents related to CT scanners and reported that there is high association between the citation weighted measure and the social value of patents in that technology field. Harhoff et al. (1999) conducted a large-scale survey study on highly cited patents and found that that "a single US citation implies on average more than $1 million of economic value." Firms that possess highly cited patents tend to be valued more by investors (Hall et al., 2000). To measure a firm's innovation performance, we collected the number of citations to a firm's patents during the 4 years after their issue. Thus, innovation performance in 1991 is the sum of all citations to patents granted in 1991, which were received during 1992, 1993, 1994, and 1995. Innovation performance in 1996 is the total citations to patents granted that year, which were received during 1997 through 2000.

Independent variables

Alliance knowledge stock.   Scholars have suggested that an organization's patent portfolio provides meaningful insight into an organization's knowledge base, since the patents a firm owns represent the types of phenomena it has learned about through its research and development activities (Jaffe et al., 1993; Ahuja and Katila, 2001). We measure the total amount of knowledge a firm's partners possess as the total number of patents that they have received. This variable is a sum of all the patents that a firm's alliance partners have received up to a given year. We measured this variable using all patents attained during a firm's lifetime, all patents received within a moving window of 6 years, and the cumulative number of patents attained within our sample period. Patent counts for the first two measures were taken from the National Bureau of Economic Research (NBER) patent database that covers a longer time frame than our study. However, the NBER database did not include all of the firms in our sample, so the results are reported with the third measure of patent stock; the results do not vary substantially.

Knowledge distance from a firm to it alliance partners.   The knowledge distance between a firm and its alliance partners was measured using Jaffee's (1986) approach. Each firm is given a vector to represent the distribution of its patents, each year, across the set of possible patent classes. The value in each cell for a firm is the proportion of its patent that falls within that class. Euclidean distance is used to calculate the technological distance between firms, according to variation in the distribution of their patents across these classes. The formula for the distance between any two firms, i and j, is:

$$DISTANCE_{ijt} = \sqrt{\frac{1}{C_t} \sum_{c=1}^{C_t} \left(\frac{N_{ict}}{\sum_{c=1}^{C_t} N_{ict}} - \frac{N_{jct}}{\sum_{c=1}^{C_t} N_{jct}} \right)^2} \qquad (4.1)$$

where i is the ith firm; j is the jth firm; t is the year; c is the cth patent class; C_t is the number of patent classes issued to the set of all sample firms in year t; N_{ict} is the number of patents in the cth class issued to the ith firm in year t; and N_{jct} is the number of patents in the cth class issued to the jth firm in year t.

To create the distance from a focal firm to its direct alliances, we average each dyadic distance from the firm to each of its alliances. In addition, each alliance partner may contribute a different amount to the total knowledge stock. The influence of each partner's knowledge on the average knowledge distance should reflect its contribution to this total patent stock. Therefore, we weight each dyad's knowledge distance by the proportion at which the alliance contributes to the total patent stock of alliance patents. The formula for this is:

$$DISTANCE\ to\ Partners_{it} = \sum_{p=1}^{P_{it}} \left(\frac{N_{pt}}{\sum_{p=1}^{P_t} N_{pt}} * DISTANCE_{ipt} \right)$$

$$= \sum_{p=1}^{P_{it}} \left(\frac{N_{pt}}{\sum_{p=1}^{P_t} N_{pt}} \sqrt{\frac{1}{C_t} \sum_{c=1}^{C_t} \left(\frac{N_{ict}}{\sum_{c=1}^{C_t} N_{ict}} - \frac{N_{pct}}{\sum_{c=1}^{C_t} N_{pct}} \right)^2} \right) \qquad (4.2)$$

where i is the ith firm; p is the pth partner; P_{it} is the number of partners the ith firm has in year t; C_t is the number of patent classes issued to the set of all sample firms in year t; N_{pt} is the number of patents issued to the pth partner in year t; N_{ict} is the number of patents in the cth patent class issued to the ith firm in year t; and N_{pct} is the number of patents in the cth patent class issued to partner p in year t.

Knowledge distance among a firm's alliances (excluding the firm itself). The knowledge distance among a firm's direct alliances (excluding the firm itself) is simply the average distance among those firms. We take the sum of each dyadic distance between a firm's direct contacts and divide the value by the total number of direct alliances of the firm. Since each pair of firms is counted twice, we also divide the value by 2 to get the final technology distance among a firm's alliance. The formula is shown as:

$$DISTANCE\ among\ Partners_{it} = \frac{1}{2 * P_{it}} \left[\sum_{j=1}^{P_{it}} \sum_{k=1}^{P_{it}} (DISTANCE_{jkt}) \right]$$

$$= \frac{1}{2 * P_{it}} \left[\sum_{j=1}^{P_{it}} \sum_{k=1}^{P_{it}} \left(\sqrt{\frac{1}{C_t} \sum_{c=1}^{C_t} \left(\frac{N_{jct}}{\sum_{c=1}^{C_t} N_{jct}} - \frac{N_{kct}}{\sum_{c=1}^{C_t} N_{kct}} \right)^2} \right) \right] \qquad (4.3)$$

where j is the jth partner; k is the kth partner; P_{it} is the number of partners the ith firm has in year t; C_t is the number of patent classes issued to the set of all sample firms in year t; N_{it} is the number of patents issued to the ith firm in year t; N_{jct} is the number of patents in the cth patent class issued to the jth partner in year t; and N_{kct} is the number of patents in the cth patent class issued to the kth partner in year t.

Control variables

Network size (firm degree centrality).   In this study we control for major firm network variables and focus on the roles of firm-partner knowledge relations. Firms embedded in larger networks may have access to a greater volume of knowledge, which could enhance innovation performance. The larger a network, however, the more costly it is to manage, and this could distract a firm and reduce its ability to effectively exploit the knowledge it has access to. To control for these forces, we include firm degree centrality, which counts the number of active alliances a firm has, in our models (Freeman, 1977; Wasserman and Faust, 1994; Ahuja, 2000).

For each year, we identify all active alliances for each firm in our sample, which pertain to research and development. To verify the dates that alliances are still active and when these relationships are terminated, we traced each alliance and its status every year since its formation, using the various information sources mentioned above. For example, in 1991 COR Therapeutics (NASDAQ: CORR) and Eli Lilly (NYSE: LLY), two global research-based corporations, initially set up a 4-year joint research agreement to discover and develop a class of new drug compounds that treat cardiovascular disorder, including myocardial infarction and angina. In this case, we treat the alliance as beginning in 1991. According to the initial terms of the agreement, it was to dissolve in 1995. In fact, in 1993 COR and Lilly decided to expand their original agreement to include the joint research, development and commercialization in North America, Europe and Japan of all intravenous and oral products resulting from their collaboration indefinitely. Therefore, we do not consider their alliance to have dissolved in 1995.

Network efficiency.   Firms embedded in more efficient networks have access to a greater diversity of information, which can expand opportunities for innovation (Burt, 1990). The fewer redundant contacts a firm has, the more efficient its network. Burt (1990) suggests that efficiency can be calculated based on cohesion relationships. Cohesion is the degree to which a firm's direct contacts are also connected to one another, whereas a contact is structurally equivalent if it connects a firm to a third actor that the firm already has a direct or indirect tie to. We use a measure of cohesion among a firm's direct alliance partners, as these contacts have the greatest influence on a firm's R&D activities (Burt, 1990). For each year, we identified active alliances for each firm in our sample, and constructed a matrix for each year to represent all connections among these firms. The matrix contains the ego networks for each firm by year. We compute the efficiencies of those ego networks using UCINET software (Borgatti et al., 1999). Following Rowley et al. (2000), we did not include firms that had no contacts during our sample period, as the concept of efficiency is only relevant to firms with at least one partner.

Firm's own past stock patent. We control for unobserved differences in a firm's ability and propensity to patent, the most pertinent fixed effects for our study, by including a firm's own stock of patents in the models. This is the cumulative count of a firm's patents, from the beginning of our sample period up to the year prior to the dependent variable. We again use the USPTO database to locate each firm's patent history.

Firm size. Previous literature suggests that a firm's size may affect its technology and innovation behavior. Authors have proposed that large organizations are often more bureaucratic and less entrepreneurial than small ones (Blau and Schoenherr, 1971; Abernathy and Utterback, 1978; Aldrich and Auster, 1986). Others postulate that firm size is associated with the rate of innovation as large firms usually generate a disproportionate quantity of innovations (Cohen and Klepper, 1992). Yin and Zuscovitch (1998) proposed that, because they invest in different types of innovation, large firms tend to remain dominant for the original product in the post innovation market, while small firms are more likely to lead in new product markets. We use the total number of employees a firm has in each year from the Compustat database to control for its size.

Firm tenure. Innovative capabilities of established organizations are generally better suited to producing incremental innovations along existing technological trajectories. Previous studies also demonstrate that innovations that spawn new technological fields often emerge from younger, entrepreneurial organizations (Tushman and Anderson, 1986; Christensen and Rosenbloom, 1995). Sørensen and Stuart (2000) suggest that aging has two seemingly contradictory consequences for innovation: on one hand as organizations age, the fit between organizational capabilities and environmental demands decreases; on the other hand, organizational competence to produce new innovations appears to grow with age. We control for a firm's tenure in the pharmaceutical preparation industry to capture these effects. We use the first date a firm appears in the pharmaceutical industry, subtracted from the current date, to calculate firm tenure.

Firm R&D intensity, year dummy, and number of patents issued to the firm in current year. R&D intensity, or the effort a firm puts into research and development, proportional to its sales volume, is an important determinant of innovative outputs. Cohen and Levinthal (1990) suggested that investment in R&D also enhances a firm's ability to innovate by augmenting the firm's capacity to assimilate and exploit external knowledge. We divide a firm's annual R&D investment by its annual sales in the same year to get yearly R&D intensity. We also include a year dummy to capture period effects. In addition we control for the number of new patents a firm obtained in the current year, since this may affect its opportunities to attract citations.

Model Estimation and Results

To test the hypothesized relationships, we estimate the model using a fixed effects Poisson regression, as the counts are constrained to non-negative integer values

Table 4.1 Means, standard deviations, and correlations

	Mean	S.D.	1	2	3	4	5	6	7	8	9	10	11	12	13	14	15
1 Citations	176.30	472.67															
2 Alliance knowledge stock	211.99	348.49	-0.15														
3 knowledge distance to alliances	0.481	0.86	-0.11	-0.12													
4 Knowledge distance among alliances	0.33	0.35	0.18	0.43	-0.16												
5 Degree centrality	2.32	2.97	0.12	0.67	-0.22	0.85											
6 Efficiency	0.59	0.43	0.13	-0.03	-0.01	0.02	0.05										
7 Own knowledge stock	31.49	80.61	0.35	0.19	-0.29	0.35	-0.23	0.34									
8 Firm size	8.45	18.31	0.37	0.09	-0.24	0.50	0.01	0.46	0.46								
9 Firm tenure	12.73	11.83	0.38	0.07	-0.12	0.55	-0.002	0.53	0.17	0.29							
10 R&D intensity	23.50	245.09	-0.06	-0.05	-0.05	-0.12	0.004	-0.14	-0.08	-0.10	-0.03						
11 New patents	7.65	18.29	0.404	0.132	-0.34	0.35	-0.194	0.33	0.80	0.49	0.19	-0.09					
12 Year 91	0.16	0.37	0.07	-0.22	-0.08	-0.05	0.02	-0.06	-0.12	0.10	0.07	-0.04	0.04				
13 Year 92	0.16	0.37	-0.03	-0.24	0.001	-0.07	-0.02	-0.07	-0.09	0.02	-0.03	-0.05	0.01	-0.12			
14 Year 93	0.16	0.37	-0.03	-0.16	0.27	0.16	0.04	-0.05	-0.05	-0.02	-0.04	-0.02	0.001	-0.13	-0.19		
15 Year 94	0.16	0.37	0.05	0.01	-0.08	-0.08	-0.03	-0.003	0.02	-0.02	-0.02	-0.06	-0.06	-0.13	-0.19	-0.21	
16 Year 95	0.16	0.37	-0.02	0.15	-0.14	-0.06	0.06	0.06	0.09	0.03	0.02	0.17	-0.01	-0.14	-0.20	-0.22	-0.22

(Hall et al., 1984). A fixed effects panel model with a robust variance estimator allows for multiple observations from the same firm, and builds serial correlation into the estimator (Hausman et al., 1984). We also estimate the same relationships using a random effects Poisson estimator. Since the results are similar, we only report the fixed effects regression in this chapter.

Each observation on the dependent variable was regressed against the values for the independent variable, lagged by a year. Thus, when the dependent variable captures the value of the innovations a firm produced in 1991, this is related to characteristics of its alliance network in 1990. We experimented with lag structures up to 3 years prior to the year a patent was received, and developed cumulative measures of the alliance and network variables during the $t-1$ to $t-3$ periods. Neither variation substantially altered the results. Research that investigates the influence of R&D investments on profitability or patenting also typically finds that alternative lag structures rarely improve upon one-year lag models (Griliches, 1984).

The results reported in the following tables support each of the hypotheses put forth in this chapter. Table 4.1 lists the basic statistics and simple correlations. As the correlation between degree centrality (number of alliance partners a firm has) and knowledge distance among those partners is fairly high at 0.85, we tested the hypotheses using a series of nested models. We are comfortable that multicollinearity does not affect our results because successive inclusion of the knowledge landscape variables with the network variables does not affect the signs, or substantially affect the significance, of these variables (Greene, 1993).

Table 4.2 lists the regression results. In general, we find support for all three hypotheses. Model 1 estimates the relationships between network variables, and control variables, and innovation performance. Both degree centrality and network efficiency negatively affect a firm's innovation performance, which is consistent with some prior research (Ahuja, 2000; Stuart, 2000). The finding for degree centrality is consistent with Stuart (2000), who suggests that the innovativeness of a firm's partners is more important than how many partners a firm has. The total stock of knowledge a firm has access to through its partners is what really matters. The greater the number of partners a firm must manage to access a given volume of knowledge, the less effective will be its innovation efforts. Firms may find it difficult, for instance, to combine the insights gained from a large network of partners, in order to discern especially valuable ways to recombine that knowledge.

Although the result for network efficiency departs from the theory of structural holes (Burt, 1990), it is more consistent with Granovetter's (1985) contention that in dense networks, firms may share information more freely because they are secure in the expectation that their efforts will be reciprocated and that "bad" behavior (e.g. misusing shared knowledge) will be punished in future interactions. In addition, this result may be sensitive to the treatment of firms with only one contact. According to the standard cohesion formula, these firms have maximum efficiency as this one contact is not redundant. Yet, a firm with one contact cannot span structural holes and thereby gain access to unique information ahead of other firms in its network. Hence, this measurement of network efficiency is not completely aligned with the theory of structural holes.

Model 1 also indicates that firms that have accumulated a larger stock of patents tend to produce more highly cited innovations. These firms may innovate more

Table 4.2   Regression results (fixed effect Poisson models)

Variables	Model 1	Model 2	Model 3	Model 4	Model 5
Alliance Knowledge stock		0.361***			0.356***
		(0.092)			(0.085)
Knowledge distance to alliances			0.293**		0.284**
			(0.051)		(0.048)
Knowledge distance among alliances				0.238***	0.243***
				(0.038)	(0.039)
Degree centrality	−0.414***	−0.401***	−0.411***	−0.405***	−0.399***
	(0.121)	(0.102)	(0.114)	(0.112)	(0.110)
Efficiency	−0.191**	−0.184**	−0.188**	−0.183**	−0.182**
	(0.063)	(0.059)	(0.061)	(0.058)	(0.056)
Own Knowledge stock	0.0381**	0.376**	0.380**	0.374**	0.373**
	(0.081)	(0.076)	(0.079)	(0.073)	(0.072)
Firm size	−0.624***	−0.620***	−0.622***	−0.619***	−0.620***
	(0.145)	(0.139)	(0.141)	(0.135)	(0.136)
Firm tenure	1.342	1.337*	1.340	1.341*	1.320*
	(0.894)	(0.153)	(0.0802)	(0.522)	(0.458)
R&D intensity	−0.118***	−0.115***	−0.117***	−0.114***	−0.115***
	(0.047)	(0.045)	(0.046)	(0.044)	(0.042)
New patents	−0.011***	−0.009***	−0.010***	−0.009***	−0.009***
	(0.003)	(0.002)	(0.003)	(0.002)	(0.002)
Year 91	1.743***	1.663***	1.687***	1.665***	1.657***
	(0.286)	(0.271)	(0.279)	(0.274)	(0.267)
Year 92	0.976***	0.971***	0.973***	0.970***	0.968***
	(0.230)	(0.227)	(0.229)	(0.227)	(0.225)
Year 93	0.604***	0.597***	0.601***	0.598***	0.596***
	(0.179)	(0.177)	(0.178)	(0.177)	(0.178)
Year 94	0.234	0.231	0.231	0.230	0.229
	(0.185)	(0.126)	(0.179)	(0.124)	(0.125)
Year 95	0.152	0.155	0.153	0.156	0.154
	(0.097)	(0.085)	(0.092)	(0.085)	(0.084)
Constant	2.999***	2.995***	2.987***	2.993***	2.991***
	(0.386)	(0.379)	(0.381)	(0.371)	(0.372)
Chi-square	176.31***	213.48***	208.93***	219.02***	239.81***

* $p < 0.05$, ** $p < 0.01$, *** $p < 0.001$.

consistently and hence be better able to discern which technological trajectories are the most promising. On the other hand, larger firms, firms that spend proportionately more on R&D, and firms that generate more patents in a given year seem to produce innovations of lower value. This is consistent with the idea that large firms innovate more intensively, but their efforts are concentrated on extracting marginal improvements from existing technologies (Cohen and Klepper, 1992).

In model 2 we test the main effect of alliance patents. We find support for hypothesis 1 or the more a firm's partners are innovative, i.e. the larger their cumulative stock of patents, the better is the firm's innovation performance. The coefficient of alliance patents is 0.361 and significant at $p = 0.001$ level. Innovative partners likely provide a firm with a richer experience base to draw on, and higher quality, leading edge information to inform its own innovation activities. In model 2, and again in model 5, firm tenure becomes significant. Firm age is believed to be associated with two effects: lower fit with the environment (e.g. engaging incremental innovation past the time when they are highly valued by customers or other firms) and improved ability to engage in innovation (e.g. moving candidate drug compounds through clinical trials) (Sørensen and Stuart, 2000). We expect the former effect is also largely captured by our firm size variables, and that the competence effect of age does not become significant until other age-related factors are captured. For example, older firms tend to maintain larger networks (the correlation between tenure and degree centrality is 0.53), which has a negative effect on innovation value in general. However, when we include the innovativeness of a firm's alliance network, this negative effect is not confounded with age. As a result, age reflects a firm's greater competence in carrying out innovation.

We test the main effect of knowledge distance from a firm to its partners in model 3, and find support for hypothesis 2. The coefficient of knowledge distance to alliances is 0.293 and significant at $p = 0.05$ level. This suggests that the focal firm benefits more from partnering with firms that have greater knowledge distance from a firm's own expertise, which is consistent with the idea that complementary knowledge enhances a firm's ability to generate valuable innovations.

In model 4, we test the main effect of knowledge distance among a firm's alliances. We also find support for hypothesis 3, as the coefficient of alliance patents is 0.238 and significant at $p = 0.001$ level. This suggests that the focal firm can enhance its innovation performance by maintaining diversified or heterogeneous alliance relations. Heterogeneous partners can provide the focal firm with more opportunities to access a variety of knowledge bases, which it may integrate with its own knowledge to produce valuable technology innovations.

In model 5, we pool the set of knowledge variables and controls together to run a full model. Again we find support for all of our hypotheses. Alliance knowledge stock has a positive effect on innovation performance as its coefficient is 0.356 and significant at $p = 0.001$ level. The contribution of "knowledge distance to alliances" is also positive. Its coefficient is 0.284 and significant at $p = 0.05$ level. Furthermore, we find that there is a significant relationship between "knowledge distance among alliances" and the focal firm's innovation performance, as the coefficient is 0.243 and significant at $p = 0.001$ level. In addition, comparing across the models, we detect that adding each knowledge variable to the baseline model significantly improves the chi-square value, and the full model shows the highest value and improvement. This again indicates the significance and the need to consider the contributions from the set of knowledge variables.

Discussion

This chapter serves as an extension and enrichment to the current research on alliance networks and technological innovation. Our study demonstrates that firm-specific knowledge positions and inter-firm knowledge relations play important roles in alliance knowledge transfer and value creation. We feel that the existing literature on alliance networks and innovation has not yet paid sufficient attention to the hetero-geneity of knowledge within the network. Network theory argues that the structure of relationships affects how information and knowledge is transferred among firms. Hence, the structure can provide insight into the diversity or timeliness of the knowl-edge a particular firm receives through its ties. However, the heterogeneity of what a firm's partners know likely has an equally, if not more, important influence on the char-acter of knowledge a firm is exposed to through its network. Firms can only understand and communicate about phenomena that they comprehend, such that two partners in equivalent structural positions are likely to convey unique ideas and opinions to a focal firm, if they possess distinctive expertise. Our results are consistent with this view.

The results for the knowledge landscape variables suggest that several factors are important for assessing the importance of alliance networks for innovation. Alliances are important knowledge sources, and innovative partners provide a firm with more valuable insight into the opportunities and direction of new research and product development. This appears to enable firms to select more promising technological trajectories, or more effective solutions to the problems that research seeks to address. In addition, a firm seems to benefit more from its alliance network when there is complementarity between its knowledge and that held by its partners. Further, the diversity of knowledge among a firm's alliance partners is important. Not only does it mean that a firm gains more distinctive knowledge from each partner, but communication among connected partners may also expand the variety of research approaches and opportunities for value creation, when partners are more heterogeneous. These results are robust to the inclusion of two important network structure variables: degree centrality and network efficiency, suggesting that network structure does not fully explain knowledge heterogeneity and transfer within a network. Taken together, our results reinforce Stuart's (2000) findings that the size and structure of a firm's alliance network may be less important than attributes of its partners. Both the inno-vativeness of a firm's partners and the uniqueness of the knowledge possessed by its alliances are positively associated with the value of a firm's patents.

Although we have applied the concept of knowledge landscape to understand how alliance networks facilitate innovation, the proposed 3-factor framework: knowledge size, knowledge distance to partners, and knowledge distance among partners has several other potential uses. It may be a helpful concept for advancing the resource-based view of the firm, which currently lacks a concrete and powerful analytic tool (Priem and Butler, 2001). It is difficult to measure many resources, particularly knowledge, which has received so much attention in this literature (Spender and Grant, 1996). The approach we adopt to analyze the knowledge landscape across firms could be used to assess the uniqueness of a firm's knowledge resources. In addi-tion, this approach can be extended to examine other resource relationships among firms. As Barney (2001) acknowledged, much of the research on the resource-based view has been static, but it is only through dynamic analysis that the full implications of resource-based logic for sustained advantages can be understood. Our approach could be used to track changes in the distinctiveness of firms' resources over time, and to relate this evolution to other trends in the industry.

This study also sheds new insight into alliance strategy regarding potential partner selection and alliance portfolio management. Practitioners have realized the contribution of alliance networking to organizational capability enhancement as evidenced by the recent rapid growth in cooperative technology development. In order to innovate and develop new competence, organizations have to renew and extend their existing core capabilities. Inter-organizational cooperation provides firms with exposure to new perspectives and skills, which may help them to overcome their own inertial forces within the organization. Nevertheless, each alliance relation requires long-term commitment and proportional resource allocation. Establishing and maintaining these relationships is a form of investment in "organizational capital," and the payoff is likely influenced by partner selection.

In this study, we have only focused on leading firms to make the alliance network computations more tractable. Doing so may neglect the influence of small firms in the industry. Our next step is to test our hypotheses on the total population of firms in SIC 2834 industry in order to capture more variety. In addition, the influence of network and knowledge landscape variables may be contingent upon certain industry contexts. Hence the findings may not be generalizable to industries with different innovation patterns than pharmaceuticals. For example, if we chose the steel industry as our context, we might find less knowledge heterogeneity and distance among firms, as it is more mature; product technologies are less complex, and there are economic pressures to adopt common process technologies. The pharmaceutical industry is representative of contexts characterized by complex product technologies and great variation in firms' approaches to research. Despite these limitations, based on our sample observations, we believe that our results illustrate that in technology-intensive industries, in which organizations increasingly rely on alliances to keep pace with scientific advances and to access complementary technologies, the distribution of expertise within alliance networks is crucial for understanding firms' innovation performance.

Acknowledgments

The research described here benefits from National Science Grant (SES-0217891) and two University of Pittsburgh Research Grants. The authors particularly thank John Prescott, Ravi Madhaven, Ray Reagans, Patrick Doreian, Wenpin Tsai, David Krackhardt, and James Henderson for their helpful comments. In addition the authors are grateful to Ronda Kopchak and Eric Larson for their generous research assistance. Please address questions and comments to Emery Yao.

References

Abernathy, W. and Utterback, J. 1978: Patterns of industrial innovation. *Technology Review*, 80, 2–9.

Ahuja, G. 2000: Collaboration networks, structural holes, and innovation: A longitudinal study. *Administrative Science Quarterly*, 45, 425–455.

Ahuja, G. and Katila, R. 2001: Technological acquisitions and the innovations performance of acquiring firms: A longitudinal study. *Strategic Management Journal*, 22, 197–220.

Aldrich, H. and Auster, E. 1986: Even dwarfs started small: Liabilities of age and size and their strategic implications. In B. Staw and L. Cummings (eds.), *Research in Organizational Behavior.* Greenwich, CT: JAI Press.

Barney, J. 1991: Firm resources and sustained competitive advantage. *Journal of Management*, 17, 99–111.

Barney, J. 2001: Is the resource-based "view" a useful perspective for strategic management research? Yes. *Academy of Management Review*, 26, 41–56.

Baum, J., Calabrese, C., and Silverman, B. 2000: Don't go it alone: Alliance network composition and startups' performance in Canadian biotechnology. *Strategic Management Journal*, 21, 267–294.

Blau, P. and Schoenherr, R. 1971: *The Structure of Organizations.* New York: Basic Books.

Borgatti, S., Everett, M., and Freeman, L. 1999: *Ucinet 5 for Windows: Software for Social Network Analysis.* Natick, MA: Analytic Technologies.

Burgers, W., Hill, C., and Kim, W. 1993: A theory of global strategic alliances: The case of the global automobile industry. *Strategic Management Journal*, 14, 419–433.

Burt, R. 1990: *Structure Holes.* Cambridge: MA, Harvard University Press.

Christensen, C. and Rosenbloom, R. 1995: Explaining the attacker's advantage: Technological paradigms, organizational dynamics, and the value network. *Research Policy*, 24, 233–257.

Cockburn, I. and Henderson, R. 1996: Scale, scope, and spillovers: The determinants of research productivity in drug discovery. *The Rand Journal of Economics*, 27, 32–60.

Cohen, W. and Klepper, S. 1992: The anatomy of industry R&D intensity distributions. *American Economic Review*, 82, 773–799.

Cohen, W. and Levinthal, D. 1990: Absorptive capacity: A new perspective on learning and innovation. *Administrative Science Quarterly*, 35, 128–152.

Deng, Z., Baruch, L., and Narin F. 1999: Science and technology as predictors of stock performance. *Financial Analysts Journal*, 55, 20–32.

Dubin, R. 1978: *Theory Building.* New York: Free Press.

Dyer, J. and Singh, H. 1998: The relational view: Cooperative strategy and sources of interorganizational competitive advantage. *Academy of Management Review*, 23, 660–679.

Freeman, L. 1977: A set of measures of centrality based on betweenness. *Sociometry*, 40, 35–41.

Granovetter, M. 1985: Economic action and social structure: The problem of embeddedness. *American Journal of Sociology*, 91, 481–510.

Greene, W. 1993: *Econometric Analysis*, 2nd edn. New York: Macmillan.

Griliches, Z. 1984: *R&D, Patents and Productivity.* Chicago, IL: Chicago Press.

Gulati, R. 1998: Alliance and networks. *Strategic Management Journal*, 19, 293–317.

Gulati, R. and Gargiulo, M. 1999: Where do networks come from? *American Journal of Sociology*, 104, 1439–1493.

Hall, B., Hausman, J., and Griliches, Z. 1984: Econometric models for count data with an application to the patents-R&D relationship. *Econometrica*, 52, 909–937.

Hall, B., Jaffe, A., and Trajtenberg, M. 2000: Market value and patent citations: A first look. NBER Working Paper.

Hamel, G., Doz, Y., and Prahalad, C. 1989: Collaborate with your competitors and win. *Harvard Business Review*, 67, 133–120.

Harhoff, D., Francis, N., Scherer, F., and Katrin, V. 1999: Citation frequency and the value of patented citations. *The Review of Economics and Statistics*, 81, 511–515.

Hausman, J., Hall, B.H. and Griliches, Z. 1984: Econometric models for count data with an application to the patents-R&D relationship. *Econometrica*, 52, 909–938.

Jaffee, A. 1986: Technological opportunity and spillovers of R&D: Evidence from firm's patents, profits, and market value. *American Economic Review*, 76, 984–1001.

Jaffe, A., Trajtenberg, M., and Henderson, R. 1993: Geographic localization of knowledge spillovers as evidenced by patent citations. *Quarterly Journal of Economics*, 108, 577–598.

Kogut, B. and Zander, U. 1996: What firms do? Coordination, identity, and learning. *Organization Science*, 7, 502–518.

Lane, P. and Lubatkin, M. 1998: Relative absorptive capacity and interorganizational learning. *Strategic Management Journal*, 19, 461–477.

Lerner, J. 1994: The importance of patent scope: An empirical analysis. *Rand Journal of Economics*, 25, 319–333.

Madhavan, R., Koka, B., and Prescott, J. 1998: Networks in transition: How industry events (re)shape interfirm relationships. *Strategic Management Journal*, 19, 439–459.

McEvily, B. and Zaheer, A. 1999: Bridging ties: A source of firm heterogeneity in competitive capabilities. *Strategic Management Journal*, 20, 1133–1156.

Mowery, D., Oxley, J., and Silverman, B. 1996: Strategic alliances and interfirm knowledge transfer. *Strategic Management Journal*, 17, 77–91.

Nakamura, M., Shaver, M., and Yeung, B. 1996: An empirical investigation of joint venture dynamics: Evidence from US–Japan joint ventures. *International Journal of Industrial Organization*, 14, 521–541.

Nohria, N. and Garcia-Pont, C. 1991: Global strategic linkages and industry structure. *Strategic Management Journal*, 12, 105–124.

Porter, M. 1980: *Competitive Strategy*. New York: Free Press.

Powell, W. 1998: Learning from collaboration: Knowledge and networks in the biotechnology and pharmaceutical industries. *California Management Review*, 40, 228–241.

Priem, R. and Butler, J. 2001: Is the resource-based "view" a useful perspective for strategic management research? *Academy of Management Review*, 26, 22–40.

Rowley, T., Behrens, D., and Krackhardt, D. 2000: Redundant governance structures: An analysis of structural and relational embeddedness in the steel and semiconductor industries. *Strategic Management Journal*, 21, 369–386.

Sørensen, J. and Stuart, T. 2000: Aging, obsolescence, and organizational innovation. *Administrative Science Quarterly*, 45, 81–112.

Spender, J. and Grant, R. 1996: Knowledge and the firm: Overview. *Strategic Management Journal*, winter special issue, 17, 5–9.

Stuart, T. 2000: Interorganizational alliances and the performance of firms: A study of growth and innovation rates in a high-technology industry. *Strategic Management Journal*, 21, 791–811.

Trajtenberg, M. 1990: A penny for your quotes: Patent citation and the value of innovations. *Rand Journal of Economics*, 21, 172–187.

Tushman, M. and Anderson, P. 1986: Technological discontinuities and organizational environments. *Administrative Science Quarterly*, 31, 439–465.

Wasserman, S. and Faust, K. 1994: *Social Network Analysis*. Cambridge, UK: Cambridge University Press.

Yao, B. and Ge, D. 2002: Value creation through "going together": An event study on market response to technology alliance formation. *Academy of Management Best Paper Proceedings*, BPS: W1-W6.

Yao, B. and McEvily, S. 2001: Absorptive capacity and alliance networks: Ability and opportunity to innovate. University of Pittsburgh Working Paper.

Yin, X. and Zuscovitch, E. 1998: Is firm size conducive to R&D choice? A strategic analysis of product and process innovations. *Journal of Economic Behavior and Organization*, 35, 243–262.

CHAPTER FIVE

Generative Interactions: The New Source of Competitive Advantage

Yves Morieux, Mark Blaxill, and Vladislav Boutenko

Introduction: The Rising Value of Interactions

Hyper-competition results in increased complexity and weaker signals for companies.[1] Typical responses are attempts to avoid complexity and to concentrate on strong signals. But alternative strategies that face and embrace complexity are emerging in organizations built around maximizing interaction value rather than minimizing interaction costs. This chapter shows how some functional properties can arise from rich interaction patterns and highlights the valuable role of such properties in dealing with complexity, in detecting, interpreting, and acting upon weak signals to achieve competitive advantage.

This chapter advances at the conceptual and practical levels the growing body of research on the role of interactions in the shaping of competitive advantage and wealth creation *within* (Rockart, 1998), *across* (Dyer and Singh, 1998) and *beyond* organizations (Johnson, 2002).[2]

The conceptual contribution is a better understanding of the causality relationship at the root of the so-called interaction revolution (Butler et al., 1997). Explanations of the growing role of interactions and network-related mechanisms in business have tended to focus on the fall of interaction costs, notably driven by advances in the information and communication technologies (ICTs). Our analysis shows that another causal mechanism is at work: the rise of interaction value, as a specific phenomenon relatively autonomous vis-à-vis the cost-related factor. Clearly a better understanding of this causality would make a difference for managerial implications. The analytical tools combine signal-processing theory and a framework that distinguishes between the generative and the allocative functions of interactions (Morieux, 2002). Interactions are generative to the extent that they allow for the emergence of new capabilities to handle complexity, notably the increased complexity of signal structure. Allocative interactions concern coordination, i.e. allocation of an order of some sort within a pre-existing set of resources or activities. The value of interactions is rising because their generative function has become the solution to increasingly challenging organizational problems that go far beyond coordination needs. One of these problems is that, despite the increased availability of information and knowledge management systems, there is a widening gap between (1) the capabilities organizations need to cope with the increased complexity of signal structure and (2) the capabilities resulting from their current organization forms – i.e., boundaries, internal design, and functioning. Bridging the gap calls for generative interactions, which in turn require new organizational forms. When the gap is not tackled, the organization's insight and impact deteriorate and its room of maneuver, notably its range of possible strategic moves, increasingly shrinks.

The practical contribution is to provide a managerially relevant framework drawn on network topology, organization sociology and signal processing theory that can help corporations change from complexity-avoiding strategy and reducing interaction costs to complexity-facing strategy maximizing interaction value. We expose the traps attached to "avoiding," versus the benefits and implications of "facing." With a complexity-avoiding strategy, interactions fulfill no generative role, and they ought to be minimized by containing coordination needs. A complexity-facing strategy, on the contrary, requires creating and animating generative interactions.

The chapter starts with an account of the evolving patterns and growing volume of interactions, analyzing the supply and demand factors that drive these changes. We apply signal processing theory to demonstrate that increased complexity of market signals exacerbates the cognitive challenges of corporations as measured by declining signal-to-noise ratios and that more of certain interactions solves this challenge, as shown by formal relationships between interaction patterns and the resulting organizational insight.[3] However, fostering more interactions and richer patterns of interactions is not trivial. In the second section, we contrast two typical strategic responses to complexity: those organizations that attempt to avoid complexity and concentrate on strong signals versus those companies that face complexity and appropriately exploit weak signals thanks to specific patterns of interactions. The final section discusses a resulting managerial agenda, for example new design rules, new management systems, and new use of ICTs, that fosters generative interactions.

Phenomenological Evidence of Changing Patterns of Interactions

The world's network of interactions has undergone several profound changes. First, the total volume of interactions has grown. The markets of "interaction enablers" (e.g. telecommunication services, Internet, and media) as well as "enablers of enablers" (e.g. telecommunication hardware and software, CRM, EDI, and e-procurement systems) have largely been outpacing GDP growth over the past few decades. For example, the share of IT spending in US GDP went from 2.5 percent in 1990 to nearly 6 percent in 2000.[4] Furthermore, the share of interaction-intensive, information-related employment in the US grew from 17 percent in 1900 to 62 percent in 1994 (Butler et al., 1997). Thus, interactive time is substituting non-interactive time.

Secondly, interaction patterns are tending to escape their historic boundaries. Personal interaction span, defined as the number of unique persons an individual interacts with over a one-year period, increased from approximately 25 in 1900 to about 90 in 1967 to almost 250 in 2000.[5] Of course, connections in 1900 were certainly different from those we have today through e-mail. Individual agents do not only interact more than in the past, but they also interact more outside their traditional scope of interactions. In network topology terms, the average span (i.e., the number of nodes a node is connected with) of interactions is widening, perhaps at the expense of interaction depth (e.g. amount of personal mutual knowledge involved in interactions, etc.).

Finally, a non-obvious implication of increased span is the decreased degree of separation, or the average number of links in the shortest path between two nodes (sometimes called geodesic distance or length). This correspondence can be shown using the following simplified relationship (Watts, 1998; Albert and Barabasi, 2002):

$$N \approx S^d$$

where N denotes the size of the network in terms of number of nodes, S its average span, and d the resulting degree of separation. As a matter of illustration, a well-known and controversial study (Milgram, 1967) estimated the degree of separation for the US population to be around 6 in 1967. With increased span, we calculated today's degree of separation to be approximately 4.6 despite a higher population.[6]

These three trends in interaction patterns – increased volume of interactions, increased span, and shortened degree – are occurring at the employee-to-employee level (more inter-individual activities); at the intra-company level, where there are more interactions between departments (more cross-functional activities or teams, more meeting attendees coming from different departments); and at the company-to-company level, (an increasing ratio of outside-facing employees to total employees due to an increase in dis-intermediation) (Slywotzky et al., 1999, Evans and Wurster, 2000). For example, a recent cross-industry survey by the Boston Consulting Group (BCG) has shown that purchasing as a percentage of company sales has increased on average from 41 percent in 1990 to 51 percent in 2000.[7]

These changes in interaction patterns can be explained by a shift in both interaction supply and demand.[8] The supply side analysis is rather straightforward. However, supply side factors alone are insufficient to explain interaction volume growth. Analysis of interaction demand is carried out in two steps: first, by describing the problems, and second, by showing how interactions help solve them.

"Supply" side factors

The supply side analysis is based on neo-classical economics. The supply curve for interactions has shifted toward more interactions as a result of plummeting interaction costs, i.e. the costs involved in exchanging information, goods or ideas (Hagel and Singer, 1999). For any type of interaction, three principal cost components can be determined: (1) the cost of searching for the party to interact with; (2) the cost of establishing a connection with the party; and (3) the cost of establishing understanding between the parties once they are connected. Each of these components is at work in selecting the party, and in specifying, controlling, and securing the desired outcome.

Costs for all three components have declined sharply. The main cost components of search are storage and processing of information. For example, to find an optimal overseas supplier for a specific product, a company needs to search a database of, strictly speaking, all companies in the world. This database needs to be created (information gathering and processing), maintained (information storage), and accessed/searched (information processing). The costs of storing one megabyte of information for one month declined by 25 percent per annum between 1969 and 1996; processing costs – e.g., the cost of one million floating point operations – declined by 30 percent per annum between 1946 and 1998 (Hayes, 1999). Clearly, while searching for an optimal overseas supplier was an expensive, time-consuming task for most small and medium-sized companies a couple of decades ago, it has now become a routine, almost cost free, activity thanks to search engines and databases such as Google.

Connection costs have also declined. For example, the price of an airline mile per passenger declined from $69 in 1930 to $11 in 1990. The cost to send a 42-page document from New York to Tokyo is about $7.50 by airmail versus less than $0.10 by Internet (Leijonhufvud, 1989); the bandwidth price index (Band-X, London to Paris) dropped from 100 in 1998 to 9 in 2000.[9]

The costs of establishing understanding, which are more difficult to quantify, have been decreasing as well, driven mainly by the emergence of various standards. Such standards include network interconnectivity protocols; the ubiquity of the Internet; common enterprise data structures (e.g. Web services-driven); common employee productivity software (e.g. Microsoft Office); common currencies (e.g. the Euro); and common languages (e.g. English), combined with increased globalization efforts by companies and the accessibility of translation services (IDC Website Globalization, 1999).

But the shift of the supply curve alone can only partially explain the observed increase in interactions. For example, the cost to provide a transatlantic telephone call declined by 40 percent per annum between 1983 and 2000 (Telegeography Research Group, 2001); yet the price to the consumer has decreased only by 10 percent per annum suggesting an increased demand for interactions (ITU, 2001). While consumed bandwidth volume has increased at a rate of about 60 percent per annum over the past few years, only half can be explained by falling bandwidth prices, once again suggesting an increased need for interactions.[10] In summary, the prices for interaction-enabling services have fallen much more slowly than their corresponding costs, suggesting an increased demand for interactions.

"Demand" side factors: problems triggered by the growing complexity of signals

We argue that hyper-competition has led to an increased complexity of signal structure. Signals are more uncertain, granular, and volatile and therefore more difficult to interpret. By using signal processing theory we illustrate how this growing complexity of signal structure results in interpretation problems for companies, as measured by declining signal-to-noise ratios. Through this analysis, which has received little attention in the field of strategic management, we can then illustrate how an increase in interactions (hence, the increase in interaction demand) can solve the interpretation problem or increase the signal-to-noise ratio.

Increasing signal uncertainty. Hyper-competition and increasingly diversified customer requirements have resulted in an extraordinary proliferation of products. For example, between 1980 and 1998, the number of skin care products introduced every year in the US increased from approximately 200 to around 1,200; the number of new vitamins and dietary supplements increased from approximately 70 to 1,300; the number of new varieties of ice cream and yogurt increased from 60 to 600.[11] Furthermore, the average number of stock keeping units (SKUs) at chain grocery stores increased from less than 100 in 1930 to more than 20,000 in 1995 (Matthews, 1998). In 1950, Renault's range for passenger cars consisted of one model (the "4 CV") that existed in two versions only (*Normale* and *Luxe*), with few options and seven available colors. Today, customers can choose from 14 Renault passenger car models, some existing in 39 versions (the Clio model), with up to 35 options, 17 exterior colors, 9 interior trims and 2 dashboards. Indeed, the number of different combinations the company offers has increased over 1,000-fold.

Yet, at the same time, product proliferation has increased signal uncertainty. Statistical estimation theory, based on the law of large numbers, shows that product proliferation makes understanding customers' responses and related needs through codified knowledge increasingly difficult or more uncertain.

Consider the following example. Suppose we want to codify customer satisfaction of a homogeneous market segment by surveying purchase and use of 400 units of a new product. We compare a standard offering (i.e. a single SKU) with a diverse offering (i.e. 100 different SKUs). Assume customer satisfaction for each product (SKU) is measured on a 1 to 5 scale; the segment's true value of customer satisfaction is 3 (i.e. "up to expectations") and its standard deviation is 2 due to differences between individual customers, inconsistencies between products, imperfect measurement methods and processing errors.

In the case of the standard offering, 400 units/SKU are sold and the feedback is gathered for each individual unit sold. An unbiased estimator of the true value of customer satisfaction is the simple average of the individual feedback values. According to the law of large numbers, the standard deviation of this estimator will be reduced by the square root of the number of samples averaged (e.g. 20). The standard deviation of the estimate would then be 0.1, and therefore customer satisfaction would be fairly accurately estimated as 3 ± 0.2 at a 95 percent confidence level. For a diverse offering, suppose only 4 units/SKU are sold. In this case, the standard deviation is only reduced by a factor of 2, or from 2 to 1, resulting in a customer satisfaction estimation of 3 ± 2 at a 95 percent confidence level. In this case, the estimation is uninterpretable since the only thing one knows is that customers rate the offering between terrible (1) and terrific (5).

The signal-to-noise ratio (SNR), defined as the mean divided by the standard deviation (Franks, 1969), is very high in the first case and very low in the second case. We can see that the SNR is a comfortable 30 for the standard offering and only 3 for the diverse offering. In summary, product proliferation results in increased signal uncertainty or an increased variance of codification-based estimation of important marketing parameters, as measured by a lower SNR.

Increased signal granularity. Increased granularity of signals has also lowered SNR. Evidence of increased granularity can be provided by the two following phenomena: increasing number of product characteristics and the increase in competition.

One can make a broad distinction between products defined by a small number of parameters, or commodities, and differentiated products, defined by a larger number of parameters. Typically, commodities are fully defined by their price only, or by some combination of variables leading to the overall price (e.g. oil). Differentiated products – such as luxury goods, software, or services – usually need a detailed description (or perception) of their functional parameters. The total GDP for a country can be broadly allocated to commodities or differentiated products. Our analysis shows that the share of commodity products in the US GDP fell by more than 50 percent between 1947 and 1997 (from approximately 34 percent to about 15 percent).[12] This finding implies that the total number of parameters that buyers evaluate has been increasing.

Increasing granularity has also come from the mushrooming of relevant signal sources to monitor due to an increase in competition. For example, between 1991 and 2001, the number of listed companies accounting for 80 percent of the world's market capitalization rose from 5,000 to 8,000. Furthermore, the number of listed companies comprising the remaining 20 percent rose from 3,000 to 13,000 over the same period.[13]

Increased signal volatility. Not only are signals more uncertain and granular but they are also changing in time more frequently, resulting in higher temporal frequency or signal volatility (Nelson and Winter, 1982). Evidence of increased volatility can be most easily seen in the stock markets. For example, the 120-month average of monthly amplitudes of the Dow Jones Industrial Average increased from 5.5 percent in 1947 to approximately 9 percent in 2001. The 36-month average of the NASDAQ composite index jumped from 6 percent in 1985 to 21 percent in 2001.[14] Increased signal volatility means that the currently known value of the signal will soon become inaccurate. Indeed, earnings have also become more difficult to forecast; the average absolute error on analysts' one-year forecasts has increased from 4 percent to 8 percent over the last 10 years.[15]

To summarize, we have witnessed an increasing complexity of the structure of relevant market signals as measured by declining signal-to-noise ratios due to (1) increasing signal uncertainty through product proliferation, (2) increasing granularity through a greater number of relevant signal sources to monitor, and (3) increasing signal volatility notably shown by the increasing amplitudes of the stock market indices. We refer to this problem as the weak-signal syndrome.

Derivation of interaction demand in dealing with signal complexity

How do companies cope with this increased cognitive complexity stemming from more uncertain, more granular, and more volatile signals? We show how increasing interactivity can overcome declining SNR by using two mathematical relationships: one concerns signal transmission within an organization and the other concerns signal detection and interpretation (detecting and receiving ends).

Signal transmission.   For signal transmission, we rely on the exponential SNR attenuation model. According to this model, each transmission of the signal from one
node to another attenuates the SNR by a factor A, less than, or equal to, 1. For
instance, suppose a manager called Adam communicates qualitative customer feedback (an impression, a customer "anecdote," etc.) to another manager, called Benito.
It is likely that Adam does not fully communicate all of the information he possesses
about the customer feedback (e.g. Adam may not fully describe the context within
which the anecdote took place, or may not fully remember the stream of "small" and
discrete events that triggered the "impression"). It is also likely that Benito does not
understand some of this information, and makes a biased interpretation of it or adds
other elements that were not present in the original signal. In any of these cases, the
SNR of customer feedback for Benito will be lower than the SNR for Adam. For
example, if Adam's SNR were 5 (e.g. a signal mean of 5 and noise standard deviation
of 1), the SNR received by Benito could be as low as 2 (i.e. a signal mean of 4 due to
the loss of some information and a signal noise of 2 due to a biased understanding or
an addition of irrelevant elements).

The exponential attenuation model estimates the potentially complex signal deterioration between two parties as follows:

$$SNR_{out} = SNR_{in} \, A^d.$$

where SNR_{out} or the output (received) SNR, is a function of SNR_{in}, the input
(exogenous) SNR, A, the attenuation factor, and d, the degree of separation. As the
degree of separation increases, the signal will deteriorate. If, for example, A were 0.8,
then after the first transmission SNR_{out} would deteriorate by a factor 0.8; after two
transmissions, by 0.64, etc. Since we have already shown that higher connectivity (i.e.
larger span) leads to a shorter degree of separation, then interaction-rich organizations should lead to lower attenuation of SNR, and therefore make better-informed
decisions with the same information.

An important assumption in this reasoning is that A remains unchanged regardless
of the individual span size. Arguments favor both a positive and negative effect of
increased span on A. A could decrease (stronger deterioration of the signal) if span
increases because of potential information overload. Assuming unchanged total interaction time, the time to process each interaction shortens in an organization with
greater span. However, A could remain constant if managers allocate more time for
interactions or even increase it if they learn to interact more effectively. In the remaining portion of this section, we assume that A is independent from span.

Signal detection and interpretation.   Another important mechanism is signal detection and interpretation (understanding). One of the ways to improve SNR is to trian-
gulate between several independent sources of the same noisy signal. For instance,
customer feedback can be independently gathered by two managers, and then discussed (triangulated). The consensus of this team of two managers should normally
lead to a better *SNR* than the opinion of a single manager. We use the linear filtering
model (Franks, 1969), where the output SNR is increased by a factor square root of
the number of independent sources of this same signal. Simply put, the linear filtering
model stipulates that the output signal is a simple sum, or average, of the input

signals. Since the noise components in these signals are independent, they add up "in quadratures," i.e., the standard deviation of the resulting noise is the square root of the sum of squares of the standard deviation of each noise component. At the same time, the averages (true value of the signal) add up linearly. As a result, the standard deviation over mean of the output signal is less than the standard deviation over mean of the input signals, i.e., SNR is improved. If one manager surveys their customers and finds their price elasticity is 1.3, and the other manager surveys a different set of customers from the same segments and concludes their price sensitivity is 1.5, they could agree, after discussion, on the price sensitivity of 1.4, which should statistically be closer to the true value of price sensitivity than the opinion of each individual manager.

Assuming that the number of independent sources of the same signal in a given point of an organizational network is equivalent to the number of non-overlapping (redundant) paths, we have:

$$SNR_{out} = SNR_{in}\sqrt{P}$$

where P denotes the number of redundant paths. The validity of this assumption depends on the exact topology of the network. In most networks, P is the upper bound of the number of independent sources, as there could be links between different independent sources making the signal propagation in one path somewhat polluted by the propagation in another path. However, it is intuitively clear that adding a new, non-overlapping path between a point X and a point Y in a network allows you to bring another nearly independent sample to Y, thus improving SNR according to the above equation.

To link the number of redundant paths with average individual span, we use a simple approximation that individual span is proportional to the number of redundant paths. Strictly speaking, the number of redundant paths can have a complex relationship with the individual span and depends on the topology of the network (Zykov, 1990). There appears to be no general analytical expression of this link. However, it is easy to understand that increasing the span by some factor will result in *at least the same increase* in the number of redundant paths.

Intuitively, the only way for a company to come up with a meaningful response to a complex environment is to correlate the signals from all sources. Increased interactions, then, lead to not only increased information collection from a larger number of sources, but also to correlation, or cross-fertilization of the different elements of information. In summary, with an increasingly complex environment, an increased number of interactions would allow for better-informed decisions (all other things being equal, notably possible cognitive biases).

In sum, the combination of the above two mechanisms, transmission and detection, gives

$$SNR_{out} = SNR_{in}\, A^d \sqrt{P} \quad \text{or}$$
$$SNR_{out} \approx SNR_{in}\, A^d \sqrt{S}$$

Given that degree is a decreasing function of span, we see that increased interactivity leads to better SNR as a result of both mechanisms. Figure 5.1 illustrates the concept.

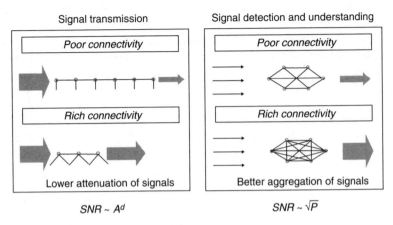

Figure 5.1   Impact of connectivity on insight

To give a numerical illustration of the above frameworks, suppose that a marketing manager in a medium-size organization ($N = 10{,}000$) has to make a decision based on the previous example on diverse customer offerings. In other words his received SNR of customer feedback would be 3 ± 2 at a 95 percent confidence or a unhelpful 1-to-5 estimate. Suppose this SNR_{out} of 3 is already the result of aggregating two signals transmitted through two paths, each one having a degree of separation of 4, and each node attenuating SNR_{in} by a factor of 0.8 (i.e. $A = 80$ percent). The original SNR was higher at the beginning of each path and was attenuated four times (once by each node) A-fold, resulting in a multiplication of SNR_{in} by ~0.41 (i.e. 0.8 to the power four). However, it was also improved through the averaging of the signals between the two paths, resulting in an additional multiplication of SNR by 1.41 (i.e., square root of 2). SNR_{out} would then be the multiplication of these two factors (i.e., $0.41*1.41 = 0.58$). Thus, SNR_{in} originally was 3/0.58 or 5.2. Clearly, the SNR_{out} of 3 is rather insufficient to make a well-informed decision.

Suppose organization connectivity doubles (i.e. doubling individual span via an increase in the number of cross-functional processes, participants in meetings, the creation of overlaps between teams, etc.). SNR_{out} would then increase because of two factors. First, the average length of transmission would decrease. As $d \sim \log N / \log S$, doubling S would result in a decrease of d from 4 to about 3 leading to a smaller attenuation of original SNR (i.e., 0.8^3 or 0.51). As a result, the SNR_{in} of 5.2 would be attenuated by only a factor of 0.51 instead of 0.41, improving SNR_{out} by a factor of 1.25. Secondly, the number of redundant paths would at least double, thereby increasing SNR_{in} by a factor square root of 4, instead of square root of 2. The total improvement of SNR_{out} would thus be the product of the two individual improvements (or $0.51*2$), or an increase of approximately 70 percent. Thus, the new received SNR would be about 5.30 (compared to the initial received SNR of 3).

In summary, we have formally shown that increasing interactions is a response to the problem of a lowering SNR, a measure of growing cognitive complexity. Given that the historical trend has been a lowering SNR, we have derived how explicit or implicit demand for interactions must have increased. Solutions to increasing complexity are rooted in interactions. Their value is rising. However, this shift in interaction value also sets new challenges for corporations, which have historically sought to spare interactions.

Interaction Strategy Models

Not all interactions are the same. Some are allocative and are used to coordinate events, functions, businesses, etc. such that these fit together and fit with a pre-existing scheme while minimizing the time, energy, etc. consumed to ensure the fit. Others are generative and are used to gain additional knowledge and insight. The generative function demands many more interactions, following different patterns (e.g. path redundancy as shown by the role of interactions in enhancing signal-to-noise ratios) than the allocative function, which, on the contrary, calls for interaction minimization.[16] Company strategies indeed reflect these two interaction types. Those companies that "avoid" complexity tend to stick with allocative interactions whereas those that "face" complexity tend to rely on generative interactions.

Avoid strategy

In the "avoid" strategy, corporations approach interactions from the traditional economics perspective of economizing on coordination, transaction, or information costs. Interactions are seen as distracting valuable resources (time, attention, energy, equipment, etc.) from productive use itself. Interactions embody some inescapable, yet cumbersome, coordination mechanism that ought to be minimized to the extent made possible by adequate combinations of hierarchies and markets. Indeed, the shaping of the modern corporation (i.e. separating it into as independent and self-sufficient parts as possible) reflects organizational solutions to the problem of achieving the gains of economies of scale while containing the cost of coordinating the processes required by such scale.[17] Removing interdependencies avoids the need for coordination between the parts. The need for interactions is thus contained, thereby efficiently minimizing their costs. When the function of interactions boils down to coordination, with no direct generative role, it is logical to approach them from the perspective of their cost and build organizations that minimize coordination needs thanks to an adequate partitioning design.

   For some companies, despite increasing environmental complexity, this avoid strategy can work. Some have the luxury to grow their narrow product line and related technological portfolio without diversifying, or multiplying their various distribution channels or geographic locations. However, these corporations will sooner or later be confronted with complexity if they want to keep growing (through diversified product ranges, new distribution channels, etc.). Savvier competitors could indeed start building competitive barriers against these players by learning how to face complexity.

   Other more diversified companies react to complexity by increasing their focus. They streamline activities, simplify product ranges, separate apparently conflicting customer demands (e.g. high quality and low prices) into different segments ascribed to different product lines, or mechanically enhance signal-to-noise ratios by aggregating market segments. Indeed, some major consumer goods companies shortened their US product roster by a third in the 1990s, cutting new product launches by as much as 20 percent on the grounds that "brand extensions had got out of hand." Furthermore, many major automotive players reduced their range by almost 20 percent.

However, these companies may have engaged in a dead-end simplification spiral. Simplification is path dependent. Each simplification move shows a positive contribution. However, a typical response to further pressure in complexity is yet another move in focus, resulting in even fewer degrees of freedom. In the end, these companies may be cornered into a commodity trap.

In summary, the "avoid" strategy relates to two kinds of situations: corporations that are still in the comfortable position of steering clear of complexity because their trajectory has allowed them that luxury, and corporations that have suffered from it but try to neutralize some of its sources (e.g. product proliferation).

Face strategy

A growing number of companies, notably in the high tech and consumer goods sectors, have deployed an alternative "face" strategy. This "face" strategy means embracing exogenous complexity and creating an interaction-rich organization (e.g. horizontal networks or communities). Specific features of such strategies include differentiating the offering and micro-segmenting the market, solving conflicting customer demands, and aggregating signals via human interactions. Two cases taken in very different industries illustrate these features.

The weak signals of Persian cats.   Royal Canin, acquired by Mars in 2001, is a major player in the pet food and animal health industry. Born in France, the company is now international and is notably commercially active in the US where it also operates production and R&D facilities. The company has enjoyed superior profitable growth compared to its competitors. The organization detects and serves many more market segments than its competitors, with an accompanying product portfolio of about 120, four times industry average. Royal Canin has developed an original "animal-centric" perspective by creating and exploiting a face strategy. Features of its face strategy include fluid and numerous interactions (high individual span) and partially overlapping functions (path redundancy) with relatively few procedures, resulting in a specific aptitude at detecting weak market signals and adapting its offering to the various stages (youth, pregnancy, etc.) and characteristics of its end-consumers. For example, in 1999, after recognizing that Persian cats have a peculiar way of catching food in their mouths and particular digestive constraints, Royal Canin designed a customized kind of meatball for this segment. More recently, the company created a specific product line adapted to the physiology and feeding preferences of another even more discrete segment of pedigree cats: the Maine coon. Such product proliferation allowed Royal Canin to enjoy over 20 percent sales and income growth between 1994 and 2001. Investors took notice. In 1997 the company's initial public offering was realized at a price-earnings ratio of 44, unusually high for a pet foods company.

According to CEO, Mr Henri Lagarde, the main reason for Royal Canin's profitable growth concerns its specific cognitive capability.[18] In this case, it seems that the

	Benchmark (Avoid)	Cisco (Face)
Strategy choices		
Number of customer accounts	80 000	350 000
Size of a customer account ('000)	~$250	~$60
Number of products [a]	~30	~70
Interaction choices		
Average span, ties	25	50
Internal degree of separation, ties	3.7	2.7
Distance to customer, ties	2.0	1.4

[a] Data networking products: optical, access, ethernet switches and routers

Figure 5.2   Illustration of "face" and "avoid" strategies and interaction choices of Cisco vs. industry benchmark

main driver of weak-signal acuity and the resulting competitive advantage in dealing with complexity is primarily based on specific organizational and managerial practices rather than on highly sophisticated use of ICTs.

Cisco: connectivity to adequately re-form around customer issues.   Cisco, the world-wide leader in data networking equipment, seems to have made the choice of an interaction-rich organization, allowing it to accurately listen to its customers and leverage the resulting complexity. This choice is described in Figure 5.2, which compares Cisco to another major industry player along usual complexity drivers and interaction topology metrics (average span, internal degree of separation), to which we have added the distance to customers (degree of separation from customers). Based on our interviews and data analysis, Cisco is able to handle much more complexity (large number of customer accounts, small size of customer accounts, and large number of products) and is much more connected both internally and with customers. At Cisco, the degree of separation from customers is only 1.4 ties (i.e. any employee is on average less than two ties away from a customer) resulting in better signal transmission. Many different functions are in touch with a given customer, contrary to the conventional wisdom that customers want one and only one point of contact with their supplier. Because these functions interact with one another, they are able to aggregate the specific knowledge they get on a given customer (each function, e.g. marketing, key account manager, technology, etc., knows a specific facet of the customer) so as to collectively obtain a very accurate understanding of the customer and act upon it. This path-redundancy enhances signal detection and interpretation and correspondingly increases the signal-to-noise ratios. Cisco leverages its knowledge in ICTs to support its interaction-rich organization.

Cisco employees have access to one of the most comprehensive Intranet sites. They spend about half their interactive time asking and answering questions on distribution lists (e.g., electronic lists of people that share some specific common interest and interact regularly), as knowledge is more up to date there. The dynamics of these distribution lists is very different from simple electronic redirection of questions. Some of Cisco's competitors have implemented these redirection tools. They complain that the system works well only "when you know who is supposed to answer the question." In this simple case, the asker will send the question to the person most knowledgeable on the topic (also copying management to ensure a proper response). However, many questions are so new that they "are not well formulated," which is an essential characteristic of weak signals. It is difficult for a sales person to formulate a precise question when it is based on customer "anecdotes and stories," even though such anecdotes often result in customer insights and improved sales force effectiveness. It is even more difficult to figure out who may have the answer to an unclear question. Cisco provides an interesting solution: the asker sends the question to several communities that seem close to the subject, and receives responses from the most relevant people. Interestingly, it is infrequent for answers to be contradictory or too numerous (in fact they are in the range of 5–10). People who are not knowledgeable on the topic will not waste two hours of their time trying to find something to say about it. Rather, only the most competent ones invest their time to answer the question.

Indeed, this distribution list connectivity relates to decision-making and innovation management. Sometimes the question does not even exist; the "asker" simply sends some "impressions" about the market to the communities. Often, several people respond with a more clear formulation of the question or pieces of context necessary to understand the question (effect of the triangulation and path redundancy). A fruitful discussion is started. In many cases, such discussions were followed by the formation of an exploration team, the creation of a successful product or service idea, and finally the formalization of a product development project by senior management. Without such discussion emerging out of weak signals, the idea would have never been submitted, as its generation required a combination of too much information from different and unknown sources. Combining them by systematic trial and error, without using the selective and self-organizing properties of such distribution lists would be possible, but would take incomparably longer. Using classical sequential hierarchy-based decision making, given all the attenuation that goes along the links (such as the regional sales manager who feels the need to discount for the "subjectivity" of the salesman, or the marketing manager who filtrates for the "commercial bias" of the regional sales manager, etc.), the initial signal would need to be quite strong to have a significant SNR left at the deciding end. But then, a strong signal would have been equally detected by most competitors.

In summary, the Royal Canin and Cisco cases illustrate how companies can embrace complexity. In the Royal Canin example, specific managerial practices allowed them to offer a much broader product portfolio than their competitors. In Cisco's case, by leveraging its ICT expertise, the company has been able to take advantage of weak signals much more quickly than its competitors. In total, the *face* is more appropriate than the *avoid* strategy when the demand for interaction is high, e.g., the signals to process by the company are complex. Secondly, interaction costs are low or can be lowered because of ICT technologies and/or particular features of inter-individual relationships (e.g., low risk of opportunism among participants, trust, shared mental models, etc.) Finally, drawbacks of interaction-rich mechanisms, such as slowness of top-down large-scale moves, are relatively not critical.

Achieving a Face Strategy: A Managerial Agenda

Since the business landscape is becoming increasingly complex, more and more value creating opportunities will present themselves for those companies deploying a "face" strategy. The challenge then is how to structure the organization and use management levers to maximize interaction value. We suggest using both network analysis and organizational sociology to help us in changing behavior, redesigning organizations, improving reward systems, and gaining maximum effectiveness out of ICT systems.

Understanding and selectively intervening on interaction patterns through the use of network topology and organization sociology

By fostering generative interactions, we need to consider interaction patterns, not just interaction costs. Two distinct organizational tools can be used: one that centers on the topology of interactions (nodes, graph of ties or links, degree of separation, individual span, density, etc.) and one that centers on the dynamics happening in that network. Structural (Burt, 1992) or descriptive (Wasserman and Faust, 1994) social network analysis and, more recently, statistical mechanics in physics (Albert and Barabasi, 2002) provide the tools to assess network topologies. The analysis of the dynamics requires an ad hoc combination of organizational sociology, system analysis, and game theory (Morieux, 1992). So far, these two analytical lenses have been kept separate. We use a real case to show how their combination leverages insight and impact.

Despite recent re-engineering of its operations, a hotel chain was still suffering from relatively poor operational effectiveness. Patrons were complaining about the lack of commercial attitudes of the customer-facing employees. Most complaints pointed to reception, the main contact point with customers. The department consistently suffered from high employee turnover. Receptionists were typically young, described as fragile and buckled under pressure. Furthermore, the high turnover rate ran against the usual employee learning curve, preventing receptionists from acquiring necessary customer-listening skills. The situation was made clear through a network analysis summarized in Figure 5.3. Receptionists appear as the central players of hotels, both as the key interface with customers and the "control tower" or orchestrator of internal operations towards customers, notably in dispatching customer demands to other functions (e.g., telling food production that a latecomer has called to require a kosher meal, etc.). However, since reception was apparently malfunctioning, the solution was to concentrate on this department. The thinking was that this function plays a central role; they are not good enough in that role. Let's improve the function. Commercial skills and customer service training programs were prepared for all reception departments throughout the chain.

For a variety of reasons (including the disappointing results of the programs), a deeper diagnostic was carried out a couple of years later. The diagnostic involved

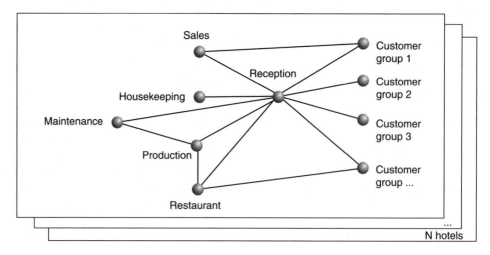

Figure 5.3   Topology: reception as central in the hotel net

a series of semi-structured one-on-one interviews and then an analysis of the dynamics of the network structure, focusing primarily on interdependencies, cooperation needs, the associated payoff matrices and resulting strategies of actors. This analysis put the functioning of hotel operations in a sharply different light. It showed that receptionists had to cope with customer dissatisfaction caused by other departments (e.g. heater or television remote control out of order because of maintenance; if housekeeping did something wrong, customers held reception responsible; if there was no kosher meal left for late room service, reception would get the customer's complaint in the morning, etc.). On a day-to-day basis, the main goal of the receptionist was, therefore, to avoid problems with customers, in front of whom they spent most of their time. Although other departments strongly influenced that goal, the receptionist had little leverage over the behavior of these departments to obtain their cooperation. These departments were much less dependent on the behavior of the reception department than it was dependent on them. Still, the reception department was bearing the cost of lack of cooperation from other departments through customer pressure and complaints. In fact, the receptionist was the weakest player in the game, bearing the consequences of the imperfect adjustments that took place between other players.

How did the reception department adjust? Depending on their relative resources they would resort to three different strategies. First, they would compensate for the failures of other departments: by going to a customer's room to fix a malfunctioning heater, or find a working television remote control, etc. The result was increased stress, burnout, and people eventually looking for another job. A second strategy was to retreat and protect behind formal procedures ("this is not our job"). The result of this strategy was angry customers and, often, a rebate to avoid a longer confrontation. Finally, reception would reject last minute reservations, despite occupancy rate-related incentives. Reception had discovered that one of the best ways to reduce

Table 5.1 Dynamics: Reception as dominated in the hotel "net game"

Actors	Goals/Problems	Resources	Constraints	Resulting strategy
Reception	Avoid problems with customers	Rules	Most exposed to customers Dependent on other functions No lever to foster the cooperation of other functions	(1) Over-invest • Compensating for other functions (2) Retreat – protecting behind rules (3) Fine-tune booking

the risks of service complaints was to make sure the hotel was not filled to capacity. The combination of these three strategies was a high turnover rate, customer dissatisfaction, weakening price points, and under-utilization of capacity. Dynamic analysis can be summarized as indicated by Table 5.1.

Although the drivers of poor operational effectiveness directly relate to reception, the real reasons had nothing to do with the visible surface of behaviors of that function. Rather, these behaviors were a result of the dynamics that went along the topological links. The key problem was that the (topologically) central function was (dynamically) dominated in the game and that the costs of uncooperative adjustments were not borne by those generating them. In fact these costs were externalized onto reception (foregone bonuses based on occupancy rate, loss of career opportunities because of turnover) and also on customers (dissatisfaction) and shareholders. The solution was, therefore, not to invest further in customer-facing techniques or skills, but to change the context such that cooperation occurred among backstage functions (e.g., making housekeeping check appliances in the rooms to anticipate preventive maintenance needs) and between them and reception. In the same way as the combination of topology and dynamics helped in the diagnosis by uncovering the system beyond the functions, it also helped in working out the solutions. New metrics and evaluation processes were installed. For example, part of the evaluation and therefore bonuses of backstage functions were determined by reception. This concerns what Axelrod (1984) calls the domain of reciprocity, a key driver of cooperation. But evaluation and bonuses occurred on a half-year basis. The network topology offered two important opportunities to initiate richer interactions on a day-to-day basis with snowballing effects. It was decided to enhance the "intensity" of interactions by setting up very frequent review meetings between all functions (when frequency goes up, the present cost of defection increases for those who do not cooperate, thus deterring defection) and to foster inversion (Axelrod, 1984) by implementing a rotation of employees between departments. In some larger hotels, the actual structure had to be modified (e.g., putting reception and housekeeping under the same hierarchy). In two years, operational effectiveness for the whole chain went up by 20 percent. This change reflects the power of generative interactions, even of a modest kind (e.g., diligent cooperation between the housekeeping and maintenance departments in preventive maintenance to ensure a faultless environment for customers; interactions between reception and sales to better understand and adapt to short cycle seasonality).

In summary, the combination of analysis of network topology and of social context dynamics to foster more generative interactions results in new ways to apply managerial levers and organizational design. Managing generative interactions is much less direct than managing allocative interactions. Managerial levers (metrics, incentives, rules, structure, etc.) cannot be chosen only on the basis of their direct impact on individual behaviors, but also on the basis of their emergent, or macro effects.

Dense topologies to foster motivation

Network topology cannot only be used to determine centrality of actors but also the density of the network. Density is measured by the total number of ties between nodes divided by the number of possible ties in a network regardless of number of links per tie. A typical low-density network is an assembly line or, trivially, a bucket-brigade. A very dense network is, for example, a distribution list where each agent can see the contribution of all. Let us consider the case of low-density networks. Where can one agent make a difference for the whole network? The answer to this question defines the negotiation-basis between the individual and the whole represented. In a low-density network, this critical area is below the standard contribution. At the extreme, the main difference a bucket-brigade node can make is to drop the bucket. For sure, it would have a greater impact on the whole than passing the bucket very quickly to the next node, given the non-zero probability that this next node could slow down the pace. In the terms of strategic analysis, as used in organization sociology, the "uncertainty" controlled by actors is – in that case – to do less than expected (Crozier and Friedberg, 1980). Hence, most incentives and control systems in low-density topologies (assembly line, hierarchy-based processes, etc.) are aimed at counter-balancing this inherent uncertainty controlled by individual workers.

Compare this situation with a very dense network, for example an active distribution list. Our analysis of distribution lists in the Cisco case shows that a question will typically get 5–10 answers. Suppose one node among the typical 50–100 members of the distribution list decides "to go on strike" and not to answer a question sent to the distribution list. Will this change even be noticed? The only way for an individual node to make a difference for the whole is to contribute faster and better than others. The negotiation basis between the individual and the whole – the uncertainty controlled by the individual – shifts from below to above the norm. Figure 5.4 illustrates this virtuous effect of dense topologies. Under some conditions, density drives motivation. Indeed, this phenomenon seems to explain the enigmatic high level of contributions in distribution lists and other dense networks usually explained tautologically: "culture" or "professionalism."

Of course, creating the right macro topology will also require interventions at the individual level. However, the point is no longer to take a global objective and then break it down into its individual objectives. Rather, the challenge is to create a "game" in which required behaviors constitute "winning strategies" for actors.

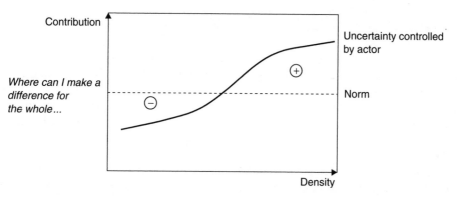

Figure 5.4   Virtuous effect of density

Instead of being managed, behaviors are "elicited" by means of a game that plays a selective role.

Interaction-based design versus partitioning and separation

Rules of organization design, which were meant to get rid of interaction needs, thanks to a specific partitioning of the firm, must be radically re-written. The classic rule of organizational design was to group activities, and then eventually define interaction patterns, i.e. linkages by means of hierarchical authority, functional coordination, or market mechanisms such as transfer prices. In following a "face" strategy, corporations will need to follow a sequence in reverse: define the capability or knowledge needs, work out the patterns (topology, dynamics) of generative interactions needed that would develop those capabilities, and eventually lay down the parts involved in such interactions. Such an approach to design is very different from the typical one derived from the cost perpective on interactions. Acknowledging the ICT-enabled fall of such costs, the typical approach is to replace hierarchies with as many market relationships as possible, including within organizations broken down into very small units. This approach views interactions only as allocative and keeps the cost perspective, as opposed to the one we advocate meant to harness the generative value of interactions.

Rewards and maneuvering room at middle and field management levels

The other consequence of such emergence-based management relates to rewards. The more interactions are used for their generative function the less trivial is the sharing of surplus among the interacting actors. In what proportion should rewards on the extra-productivity that emerges from generative interactions be distributed? Rewarding actors not so much according to their contribution to producing the composite quasi rent as according to the extent to which they are in demand on the job market would not work because the reward criterion would then implicitly switch from merit to mobility. Less mobile workers (those whose productivity is most dependent on the employing firm) would be handicapped. We argue that individual rewards will need to be granted on a more subjective and holistic basis, which would require greater maneuvering room for middle managers who assess performance and grant these rewards. Given their role in the detection, transmission, and interpretation of weak signals, middle and field managers' rewards and power should be reinforced. Years of de-layering and streamlining have considerably eroded their information role, which is increasingly performed by management information systems. However, such management information systems require codified knowledge, which is incompatible with the weak-signal syndrome described above (e.g., growing importance of qualitative judgments, stories, and anecdotes from the field). Middle management plays an important part in path redundancy (a driver of weak-signal acuity) and in relaying weak signals.

Information technology shifts from efficiency to effectiveness

Integrating ICTs into the formulation of business strategies has been a major advance (Morieux, 1991). Yet, at the interpersonal level, the main thrust of these systems is still efficiency over effectiveness. Consider employee portals, which attempt to harness the power of ICTs at the individual level. The main function of most employee portals is to cut the cost of allocative interactions, through efficiency: automation, service sharing, and outsourcing. On the generative side, employee portals, with a few exceptions, provide relief from space constraints (e.g., expert networks and databases in the knowledge management module) rather than enrich generative interactions.

As more companies deploy "face" strategies, we predict a proliferation of new enterprise software applications that will combine efficiency (cutting the cost of allocative interactions) with effectiveness by enriching generative interactions and enabling the management of complex interaction patterns. Examples could include software for managing intra-company distribution lists, vertical communication software, or company-wide meeting management software based on assessment of the needs for participants for each meeting. For example, eBay incorporates trust-ranking mechanisms that (1) reassure new entrants and help build traffic and (2) reward trusted sellers.[19] Such features could bear relationships with the classic drivers of cooperation, notably frequency, duration, inversion, and domain of reciprocity (Axelrod, 1984).

Table 5.2 summarizes the main elements of the managerial agenda, depending on interaction status.

Conclusions

The bases of selective advantage will move from sparing interactions to fostering interactions, not only because their costs are falling, but also, and more fundamentally, because interactions are solutions to new competitive challenges. Dealing with the complexity of signal structure is one of these fundamental challenges, conditioning

Table 5.2 Interaction status given competitive hurdles and resulting organizational thrust

Competitive hurdles	Organize for scale economics	Organize to handle increased complexity – weak signals
Relative knowledge status	Richness	Poorness
Main function of interactions	Allocative	Generative
Thrust of organization design	Minimize interaction costs – Partitioning	Maximize interaction value – Connecting
Thrust of information and communication technologies	Efficiency – cut cost of allocative interactions	Effectiveness – enrich generative interactions

a corporation's insight and impact from strategic to most operational matters. A complexity-facing strategy requires generative interactions, which in turn call for different analytical tools and managerial practices. At the analytical level, data about structures (organizational chart) and data about activities (process mapping) must be complemented with data about interaction topology (network analysis) and interaction dynamics (sociological analysis using system dynamics and game theory). As the hotel chain example shows, looking at the topology alone (e.g. centrality in interactions) may be misleading without careful understanding of what actually happens in the interactions (e.g. real power, i.e. control of uncertainty). In terms of management practices, organizational design must switch from partitioning to connecting. Organizational forms that provide a viable vehicle for maximizing generative interactions will benefit from a selective advantage in the current environment. Beyond a new design, such forms also require different use of managerial levers (e.g. objective setting, rewards, etc.). These levers will be used not so much to directly intervene on behaviors as to obtain the adequate interactions and, eventually, the desirable effects that emerge from these interactions. Such kinds of emergence include employee motivation. Beyond direct intervention on employees to "motivate" them, we have shown how dense topologies can indirectly, thanks to autonomous interaction-based properties, give rise to motivation. Cisco gives a clear example of the extent to which motivation can arise from specific interaction patterns without direct "motivating" intervention on individuals. Organizational forms that face complexity will also be characterized by a renewal of some functions. Middle management for example, almost suppressed in the complexity-avoiding and interaction-cost minimizing model, is likely to need reinforcing because of the role they play in generative interactions and in the assessment of contributions difficult to capture with management information systems that focus on quantitative outputs. A complexity-facing strategy also requires new use of information technologies, fostering effectiveness by enriching generative interactions rather than efficiency alone by cutting the cost of allocative interactions.

Acknowledgments

We would like to thank James Henderson of Babson College for his insightful suggestions, as well as the BCG team: Marc Benayoun, Laurent Blivet, Laurent Bourgoing, Ariane Gorin (now with Microsoft), Nicolas Meary and Bob Wolf for their contribution to the analyses reported in this chapter, and Philip Evans, Xavier Mosquet, Bob Shapiro, Armin Schmiedeberg and Dave Young for skillful steering of the discussion. Some issues also emerged in the course of previous joint work by one of the authors and Olivier Raiman, now at Agilence. We are also indebted to Jean-Marc Gottero and Nikolai Ermochkine of Cisco Systems for insightful discussions. All mistakes, of course, remain the authors' own responsibility.

Notes

1. The main reason for divergence among advocates (e.g., D'Aveni, 1994) and critiques of the concept of a general move toward hyper-competition seems to lie in different perspectives. For example, some critiques (e.g. McNamara et al., 2003) take instability in the factors that explain the variance in Returns on Assets over time as the main characteristic of hyper-competition. They observe that such instability has not significantly increased and thus question the concept. In this chapter we consider a different perspective, like that of Michaud and Thoenig (2003) for example, that centers on the cognitive implications of the multiplication of choices offered to customers and the resulting multiplication of sources of signals that firms must monitor.

2. This body of research is different from the classical stream that tends to explain the structure of markets and organizations in terms of choices and efforts to economize on interaction costs, e.g. Coase (1988), Williamson (1985), Hagel and Singer (1999).

3. Our definition of signals follows that used by Arrow (1974: 38) in his analysis of information and organization: "The concept of signal is to be interpreted broadly; some signals might inform the individual of the outcome of his decisions, some might be used as the basis of decisions, if only of implicit decisions not to act. A signal is then any event capable of altering the individual's probability distribution; in more technical language, the posterior distribution of signals conditional on the observation of one may, in general, differ from the prior. This transformation of probabilities is precisely what constitutes the acquisition of information." Arrow goes on to suggest that quantitative treatment of information is of poor practical interest on the ground that some signals may be worth the same amount of bytes from a quantitative information perspective whether the signals are useful or useless. Our quantitative treatment does not apply to signal content but to the topological mechanisms that condition their accuracy. Thus our approach does not fall into the trap rightly observed by Arrow. Indeed, it makes a practical difference whether we get useful signals accurately or fuzzily.

4. Source: BCG analysis of US Census Bureau data.

5. Source: BCG analysis of Stanford Internet Report and Pew Internet Life Report data (US figures). Interactions used to measure span are: person-to-person communications and post, email and other computer networks, and telephone and fax.

6. Assuming N was 200 million in 1967, the resulting 1967 span was about 25. This number is smaller than the above-mentioned span of 90 in 1967 because of the "tighter" definition of span used by Milgram. This difference shows the risk of mixing apples and oranges when performing network analysis. Rigor is needed in the definition of what a "connection" actually means. However, applying a proportional correction to today's span, one could expect today's degree of separation to be about 4.6 (for $N = 280$ million in 2000) in the terms of Milgram's study.

7. Source: BCG survey of 156 purchasing organizations.

8. Orthodox economists could question the use of concepts such as supply and demand for mechanisms such as interactions that have no obvious market to trade them. Strictly

speaking, the market is rather for devices or services that enable interactions. Still, interactions fulfill a need, so it makes practical sense to evoke a demand for them (in the same way as one can refer to value in use and value in exchange as discussed later in the chapter). The concept of "connections" that we sometimes use would better fit the idea of a "market" because of its technological (hardware or software bases) connotation. But, precisely because of this connotation, it may be too restrictive by not emphasizing enough the inter-individual and action content of "inter-actions." A connection tends to carry a notion of stock, a platform on which interesting things can be built; interaction is closer to a flow in which interesting things actually do happen (such as cross-fertilization, joint discovery, progressive building of trust, etc.).

9. Source: BCG analysis on Federal Communications Commission (FCC) data.
10. Indeed, our analysis has shown that price elasticity was approximately 2 (i.e. 2 percent increase in volume for a 1 percent decrease in prices) for US long-haul bandwidth over the same time period. Bandwidth prices have decreased by about 17 percent per annum over the same time period, which would explain an increase in volume of about 34 percent. The difference between 60 percent and 34 percent suggests that the demand for interactions has increased as well.
11. Source: BCG analysis of data from the Dallas Federal Reserve Board.
12. Source: BCG analysis of US Department of Commerce and Bureau of Economic Analysis data. The commodity share of GDP is different from the *rate of commoditization*. While the commodity share of GDP has decreased, the rate of commoditization has increased, i.e., a given product type, first introduced as a differentiated product, now quickly becomes a commodity. To offset price erosion usually accompanying commoditization, companies respond with increased innovation and introduce new product lines more often, resulting in lower overall share of commodities
13. Source: BCG Analysis of Compustat data from 1991 to 2001.
14. Source: BCG analysis of public data sources.
15. Average of top five US market caps: GE, Microsoft, Exxon Mobil, Wal-Mart, Pfizer.
16. In a knowledge-rich environment, interactions are mainly of the allocative kind. Indeed, when knowledge is not really the problem, generative interactions are superfluous, and organization designs that spare interaction needs are the right answer. The allocative function was predominant in most of the twentieth century when organizations were knowledge-rich relative to their needs – the extreme case being instanced by scientific management and Fordian organizations. By being sufficiently attentive to scientific management principles, organizations would obtain (despite poor individual knowledge at the worker level) the "one best way" of solving corporate problems. Relative knowledge-richness in the modern industrial corporation of the twentieth century can be explained, mainly, by the central function that the corporation played in the wake of the second industrial revolution: to create the conditions for mass production. The problem was the product – it was scarce relative to consumption needs – not the customer. When the problem is the product the solution rests on the producer's side. Required knowledge is endogenous. At the extreme – according to scientific management – internal "time and motion studies," i.e. some kind of organizational introspection, are enough to gather all the necessary and sufficient knowledge. The factors accounting for the relative knowledge-richness of organizations have gradually disappeared. In the simplest terms, the problem is not the product anymore – the problem is the customer. The pertinent uncertainty has changed side in the exchange relationship. Not only the pertinent objects of knowledge, but also the mechanisms to generate that knowledge are increasingly outside the corporation's full control. Corporations have become knowledge-poor relative to their needs. The generative function of interactions has thus become crucial.

17. Williamson (1985): "The modern corporation is mainly to be understood as the product of a series of organizational innovations that have had the purpose and effect of economizing on transaction costs" (p. 273). "The progressive evolution of the modern corporation records the inprint of transaction cost economizing at every stage" (p. 295). "Organizational variety arises primarily in the service of transaction cost economizing" (p. 387).
18. Source: Ecole de Paris du Management, meeting with Mr Henri Lagarde: "Royal Canin: market leader in the animal health sector," November 9, 2001.
19. There is a quantifiable economic value to trust. Our analysis of auctions on eBay shows that the 10 percent most trusted sellers can sell their goods at a price more than 50 percent higher than the 10 percent lowest trusted sellers. It is not that the most trusted sellers cheat on their buyers, but that the lowest trusted sellers have to pay for the cost of their previous defection or lack of visibility.

References

Albert, R. and Barabasi, A. 2002: Statistical mechanics of complex networks. *Reviews of Modern Physics*, 74, 47–97.

Arrow, K. 1974: *The Limits of Organizations*. New York: Norton.

Axelrod, R. 1984: *The Evolution of Cooperation*. New York: Basic Books.

Axelrod, R., Riolo, R., and Cohen, M. 2000: Beyond geography: Cooperation with persistent links in the absence of clustered neighborhoods. *Personality and Social Psychology Review*, 6, 341–346.

Barabasi, A. 2002: *Linked: The New Science of Networks*. Cambridge, MA: Perseus.

Bell, T.E. 1993: Bicycles on a personalized basis. *IEEE Spectrum*, 30, 32–35.

Burt, R. 1992: *Structural Holes: The Social Structure of Competition*. Cambridge, MA: Harvard University Press.

Butler, P., Hall, T., Hanna, A. et al. 1997: A revolution in interaction. *The McKinsey Quarterly*, 1, 4–23.

Chandler, A. 1990: *Scale and Scope: The Dynamics of Industrial Capitalism*. Cambridge, MA: Harvard University Press.

Coase, R. 1988: The nature of the firm. In *The Firm, the Market, and the Law*. Chicago, IL: University of Chicago Press (originally published 1937).

Crozier, M. and Friedberg, E. 1980: *Actors and Systems: The Politics of Collective Action*. Chicago, IL: University of Chicago Press (originally published 1977).

D'Aveni, R.A. 1994: *Hypercompetition: Managing the Dynamics of Strategic Maneuvering*. New York: Free Press.

Davenport, W. and Root, W. 1987: *An Introduction to the Theory of Random Signals and Noise*. New York: Wiley-IEEE Press.

Dyer, J. and Chu, W. 1996: The determinants and economic outcomes of trust in supplier-buyer relations. International Motor Vehicle Program Publications, MIT.

Dyer, J. and Singh, H. 1998: The relational view: Cooperative strategy and sources of inter-organizational competitive advantage. *Academy of Management Review*, 23, 660–679.

Ecole de Paris du Management 2001. Royal Canin: Market leader in the animal health sector. November 9th meeting with CEO Mr Henri Lagarde, notes by L. Claes.

Evans, P. and Wurster, T. 2000: *Blown to Bits*. Boston, MA: Harvard Business School Press.

Franks, L. 1969: *Signal Theory*. Englewood Cliffs, NJ: Prentice-Hall.

Hagel, J. and Singer, M. 1999: Unbundling the corporation. *Harvard Business Review*, 87, 133–141.

Hayes, F. 1999: 100 years of IT. *Computer World*, 33, 74–75.

International Telecommunications Union (ITU), 2001: *Telecommunication Indicator Handbook*. Geneva: Internation Telecommunications Union.

Johnson, J. 2002: Open source software: Private provision of a public good. *Journal of Economics and Management Strategy*, 4, 637–662.

Leijonhufvud, A. 1989: Information costs and the division of labor. *International Social Science Journal*, 120, 165–176.

Matthews, R. 1998: A look back over 90 years. *Progressive Grocer*, 77, 8–16.

McNamara, G., Vaaler, P., and Devers, C. 2003: Same as it ever was: The search for evidence of increasing hypercompetition. *Strategic Management Journal*, 24, 261–278.

Michaud, C. and Thoenig, J.C. 2003: *Making Strategy and Organization Compatible*. London: Palgrave MacMillan.

Milgram, S. 1967: The small world problem. *Psychology Today*, 2, 60–67.

Morieux, Y. 1991: Strategic analysis and information technology. In E. Sutherland and Y. Morieux (eds.), *Business Strategy and Information Technology*, London: Routledge, 26–34.

Morieux, Y. 1992: Managers, shareholders, organizations: What logic for action? *Revue Française de Gestion*, 87, 62–74.

Morieux, Y. 2002: Interaction-based competitive advantage. The Boston Consulting Group Working Paper.

Nelson, R. and Winter, S. 1982: *An Evolutionary Theory of Economic Change*. Cambridge, MA: Harvard University Press.

Rockart, J. 1998: Towards survivability of communication-intensive new organization forms. *The Journal of Management Studies*, 35, 417–420.

Shannon, C. 1948: A mathematical theory of communication. *Bell System Technical Journal*, 27, 379–423 and 623–656.

Slywotzky, A., Morrison, D., Ouella, J. et al. 1999: *Profit Patterns: 30 Ways to Capture Profit for Your Business*. New York: Times Business.

Teleography Research Group, 2001: *Teleography 2001*. Washington: Primetrica.

Wasserman, S. and Faust, K. 1994: *Social Network Analysis: Methods and Applications*. Cambridge: Cambridge University Press.

Watts, D. 1998: *Small Worlds: The Dynamics of Networks Between Order and Randomness*. Princeton, NJ: Princeton University Press.

Williamson, O. 1985: *The Economic Institutions of Capitalism*, New York: Free Press.

Zykov, A. 1990: *Fundamentals of Graph Theory*, Moscow: BCS Associates.

PART II

Successful Business Strategies during Periods of Industry Structuring and Restructuring

Sustaining Superior Performance through a Bubble: Inter-firm Differences in the e-Consulting Industry

M. Julia Prats and Ashish Nanda

Introduction

Empirical research has shown that many industries have undergone, soon after their inception, a cycle of rapid growth followed by severe contraction (Gort and Klepper, 1982; Hannan and Freeman, 1989; Klepper and Grady, 1990). This pattern has been observed in a wide range of industries, including newspapers (Delacroix and Carrol, 1983), operating railroads, scheduled air transportation operators, commercial banks (Carroll, 1984), disk drives (Sahlman and Stevenson, 1986; Lerner, 1997), savings and loan banks (Rao, 1989), the United States beer brewing industry between 1880 and 1890, and the US automobile and tire industries (Horvath et al., 2001). In a study of 46 new industries, Klepper and Grady (1990) found that the evolution of the number of firms in those new industries follows a similar pattern. Initially, the number of firms in an industry grows. At a later point there is a shakeout until the number finally stabilizes (Gort and Klepper, 1982; Klepper and Grady, 1990). The modal shakeout involved a decline of about 50 percent in the number of producers, and in extreme cases the number of firms declined by roughly 80 percent in 10–15 years (Klepper and Miller, 1995).

A variety of theories have been proposed to explain this pattern of rapid growth and shakeouts across industries. Some theories emphasize the role of precipitating events, such as major technological changes (Utterback and Suarez, 1993; Jovanovic and MacDonald, 1994), others interpret shakeouts as part of a gradual evolutionary process shaped by technological change (Klepper and Grady, 1990; Klepper and Miller, 1995), or determined by the carrying capacity of the environment (Brittain and Freeman, 1980; Carroll and Hannan, 1989). Institutional theory argues that this pattern exists because firms initially lack external legitimacy due to their small numbers (Scott and Meyer, 1983), whereas other theories posit a multiplicity of factors that may be at work (Aldrich, 1999). In his research on the origin and evolution of new businesses, Bhide (2000) found that turbulent markets, and especially new industries with unsettled market conditions, are common ground for "promising" start-ups. Some characteristics of this type of environment attract many entrepreneurs under the mirage of improving a startup's prospects in several ways. Entrepreneurs believe they have advantages that will help them exploit market failure for economic gain. However, these advantages tend to be small and transitory while start-up costs typically are prohibitive. Indeed, empirical evidence shows that a large proportion of new business organizations fail shortly after being formed (Freeman et al., 1983; Carroll, 1984; Singh et al., 1986), and a large fraction of surviving firms achieve only marginal performance (Cooper et al., 1991; Bhide, 2000).

Although considerable research has been conducted on why this boom-bust phenomenon exists, not much research has been done to identify the different strategies that new entrepreneurial firms pursue at industry inception (Teplensky et al., 1993), and few empirical studies have explored a model including the effects of factors on firm performance at more than one level of analysis (Romanelli, 1989; Eisenhardt and Schoonhoven, 1990; Teplensky et al., 1993; Baum et al., 2001). Furthermore, no known analysis has been conducted as to the effect of strategies, initial endowments, and founder's human capital on the performance of firms going through the boom and bust cycle of a new industry.

Using a multilevel model that identifies a typology of firm strategies, this chapter explores the effects of early strategies, initial organizational endowments, and environmental conditions on firm performance. Concretely, we answer the following research questions: *In the context of a cycle of boom and bust at industry inception, do distinct growth strategies exist among new ventures in the same industry? If so, what is the nature of each strategic archetype? Do they differ for each phase of the cycle? Does each archetype differ in its impact on firm performance?*

The rapid rise and sharp decline of the e-consulting industry in the US affords us an opportunity to study the varied strategies and performance of firms. The rapid rise and decline of the industry allows a careful study on drivers of entrepreneurial firms' performance as industry prospects change dramatically. Within this context, we focus on how the three potential drivers – founding team characteristics, organizational strategy, and environmental conditions – interact to determine the performance of entrepreneurial firms. For 31 e-consulting firms, we collected data on management team composition, firm organization, firm strategy, and firm performance.

The rest of the chapter is organized as follows: the next section discusses performance drivers for young entrepreneurial firms. The third section presents the methodology used in the analysis and describes the sample, the data set, and the variables. The following section reports the empirical results and the fifth section concludes with a discussion of results, limitations, and opportunities for future research.

Drivers of Performance in Young Entrepreneurial Firms

Although there is a long tradition of research investigating the factors that impact firms' chances of survival in their early years, results are inconclusive. First, researchers have used unclear definitions of business failure (Watson and Everett, 1993), making the interpretation of available statistics on firm mortality (Watson and Everett, 1996) and comparisons across studies problematic. Secondly, researchers have often relied on biased samples and questionable methodologies (Aldrich and Baker, 1997). Furthermore, previous studies have focused on varying levels of analysis failing to control for the omitted variables. As a result, previous empirical findings have been mutually inconsistent and sometimes contradictory (Aldrich and Baker, 1997). Nevertheless, prediction of success and failure remains relevant because it benefits would-be and current small business owners, along with those who assist, train, and advise them, those who provide capital for their ventures, their suppliers, and public policy makers (Reynolds and Miller, 1989).

The literature on performance of new firms has taken different approaches. Some authors have assumed that the founder is critical to organizational success.[1] Accumulating evidence suggests that founders with similar previous professional experience that enables them to understand how an industry works contribute to the success of new ventures (Timmons, 1999). A number of studies have confirmed that successful ventures are often established by groups of individuals rather than a single person (Eisenhardt and Schoonhoven, 1990; Kamm et al., 1990). The nature of the founding team (Eisenhardt and Schoonhoven, 1990), as well as previous joint work experience, is linked to successful venture creation because it leads to faster decision making, higher trust, and better communication (Stinchcombe, 1965; Eisenhardt and Schoonhoven, 1990; Roure and Keeley, 1990).

A second approach to understanding early performance emphasizes the characteristics and activities of organizations as determinants of young firms' performance.[2] For example, Abell (1980) suggested that a firm's strategy varies over the product life cycle in systematic ways; in the initial stages the primary choices focus on how strongly to enter the market and how broad a segment of the market to serve. Moreover, firms create value through their selection, development, and use of human resources (Hitt et al., 2001) where their portfolio of knowledge and skills can impact the quality of the services to clients resulting in higher performance.

Finally, other researchers have examined the effects of environmental conditions on failure rates among new organizations. Based on the observation that a firm's survival in a given population depends, in part, on endogenous conditions, population ecology studies focus on environmental factors at the time of founding, such as demand, population dynamics and population density (Carroll and Delacroix, 1982; Carroll, 1985; Aldrich, 1999).

These approaches together suggest – as has been pointed out by several authors (Schumpeter, 1934; Stevenson and Jarillo, 1991) – that the founders' human capital, the initial endowment of resources, along with the environmental characteristics in the firm's early years, should be explored jointly to account for differences in firm performance. Furthermore, a better understanding of how severe environmental shifts in an emerging phase of an industry affect newborn firms may lead to the development of a useful framework for understanding what causes what, why, and under what circumstances.

The Entrepreneurial Bubble Phenomenon

Previous research has found that environmental conditions in general, and economic conditions in particular, significantly influence new firms' survival prospects (Stinchcombe, 1965; Swaminathan, 1996). Predictably, economic expansion enhances probability of survival, while economic downturn increases the likelihood of failure (Carroll and Delacroix, 1982). This result has been proven true at any stage of industry evolution. However, a sudden shift on the environment entails unique challenges for new ventures.

Sharp environmental change at industry inception has been observed in a wide range of industries (Klepper and Grady, 1990; Geroski and Mazzucato, 2001). As Gompers and Lerner (2001) point out, the pattern of initial hype surrounding Internet companies during the late 1990s followed by disappointment in 2000–01 is far from unique. Further, a closer historical observation focusing exclusively on industry inceptions that have suffered acute changes early on in the number of participants – such as the disk drive, biotechnology, fiber optics, and video game industries – suggests a pattern of events that "arise because activity depends on the collective actions of entrepreneurs, venture capitalists, public capital markets, the media, lawyers, and industry professionals, who together actively create and sustain legitimate market space for new products, services, and technologies" (Schoonhoven and Romanelli, 2001: 384).

The cycle starts with an exogenous event – the commercialization of a new technology, industry deregulation, or the spread of a new business model – that triggers a new opportunity for profits. Initially the opportunity is identified and exploited by a few insightful entrepreneurs who are able to gather resources and, in many cases, start a new firm. Capital markets, potential entrepreneurs, and other constituencies observe the initial success of those individuals. Social construction mechanisms create a shared expectation that the opportunity will quickly expand. As projected growth triggers a racing behavior among entrepreneurs and investors, valuation of firms that are already exploiting the opportunity increases. The illusion of infinite availability of resources acts as an isolating mechanism helping new ventures – although only for a short period of time – to enjoy a protected prosperity. Furthermore, many firms push their expansion to unreasonable limits based on the sustainability of market expectations.

Even as many new projects are initiated and the valuation of existing businesses rises, new information about the size of the opportunity begins to set limits and provoke skepticism about the socially constructed enthusiasm. As expectations are revised and prospects for growth lowered, investors rush to cut financing and public markets hasten to trade down the valuations of existing companies. Firms then face a double challenge: on the one hand, a cutback in resources making it difficult to sustain previous commitments, and on the other hand, a decline in product/service demand. As a consequence, the industry experiences a shakeout with several of the entrepreneurial firms exiting the industry. In sum, the cycle may be characterized by two phases. First is the expansion phase, or period of mania, in which firms enjoy abundance of resources and the reinforcement of positive expectations about opportunity prospects. Then comes the contraction phase, or period of panic, where expectations fall and subsequently resources are reallocated to other opportunities. We have called this cycle "the entrepreneurial bubble phenomenon."[3]

Having defined and explained the entrepreneurial bubble phenomenon, in the rest of the chapter we explore the basic mechanisms that enable some firms to survive this environmental shift, contrasting them with unsuccessful strategies.

Methodology, the e-Consulting Industry, Sample, and Data Collection

The complexity of the cause-effect relationship of variables demands an exploratory analysis of the effects of strategy and organization characteristics on firm performance during such a tumultuous period. This exploratory analysis has two purposes. First, we will single out and describe the key factors that play a role in the development of the firm in both stages of the bubble. Second, we will generate the identification of distinct archetypes of firms in the context of the same industry and will link them to performance outcomes. This approach has been recommended for strategy research by numerous authors (Hambrick, 1980; Dess and Davis, 1984; McDougall and Robinson, 1990). Moreover, in using this method we are following the example of writers such as Glaser and Strauss (1967) who clearly stressed that practicing empirical research is the best way to discover tacit knowledge.

The e-consulting industry

To explore the effects on firm performance of new venture's early strategies, initial organizational endowments, and environmental conditions, we chose the e-consulting industry as a setting for our analysis. Because the e-consulting industry shifted from a dramatic growth to sudden collapse in a short window of time (1999–2001), it provides an opportunity to focus on a particularly intense bubble. Besides, the e-consulting industry is an attractive setting to study the phenomenon because not much research has been conducted on entrepreneurial professional service firms.[4]

The development of the Internet brought a unified protocol for communication among computers leading to an explosion in commercial applications. Following the introduction of Netscape in 1994, users were easily able to navigate among the myriad sites already on the World Wide Web. This new technology was expected to translate into greater productivity through the lowering of communication and transaction costs and the provision of a real-time channel to interact with suppliers and clients. Executives began rethinking their business and technology strategies, reformulating their marketing, sales, and pricing activities, revamping their operations and organizational structures, and changing their relationships with customers, suppliers, alliance partners, employees, and even competitors to take advantage of the new technology. Organizations felt themselves under pressure from "new economy" firms, new competitors exclusively based on the new technology, to reinvent themselves quickly so as not to lose their competitive edge.

A new consulting segment was born in the mid-1990s as firms began seeking management consulting advice to capitalize on the new business opportunities made possible by the Internet. This segment comprised the services provided by consulting firms to help conceive and launch e-commerce business models and integrate them, if necessary, with existing businesses.

The market opportunity attracted many different players to the arena. Between 1998 and 2000, strategy consultants, the Big Five accounting firms, software developers, hardware companies, systems integrators, advertising agencies, and professional service firms each claimed to be engaged in consulting with firms on their Internet strategy. Systems integrators and the Big Five consulting firms focused on technology implementation, management consultants on business strategy, and interactive strategists on web design.

The opportunity also led to the birth of numerous e-consultants, "pure play" firms, under the belief that traditional consulting would not be able to provide the desired services. The Internet was "too different," requiring a mix of skills, business models, and advice that were all distinct from those offered by traditional consulting firms. The new breed of consultants promised to develop deep and broad capabilities in technology, strategy, and creativity to offer clients "one stop shops" in strategy, implementation, and outsourcing consulting. Even more audaciously, several of the new e-consulting boutiques challenged the partnership model of traditional consulting firms by going public soon after incorporation.

The e-consulting companies were born and went public in a bull market. During the 1980s, and continuing into the 1990s, the management consulting industry as a whole was one of the fastest growing sectors of advanced economies. In 1980 worldwide industry revenues were estimated to be $3 billion. By 1999 this figure had grown to around $60 billion (Kennedy Information Research Group, 2000). With the commercial development of the Internet in the 1990s new business possibilities were discovered and developed. In 1999 Kennedy Information Group expected the global market for e-consulting to reach $37.5 billion by 2003; Forrester Research estimated that the US market alone would reach $47.7 billion in 2002; International Data Corporation estimated that within 4 years the worldwide market for e-consulting would grow 753 percent versus an increase of 83 percent in the traditional systems integration market.

Before 1991 there was only one firm – Cambridge Technology Partners (CTP) – that qualified as the seed for what would later become the e-consulting business model. Although some firms were started in the early 1990s, primarily by former CTP employees, the majority of e-consulting companies were founded after 1994. By January 2000 more than 100 companies were e-consultancies; of these 53 had gone public after 1996 and 18 more initial public offerings (IPOs) were scheduled during the second and third quarters of 2000.

To deliver the broad range of services they were expected to provide, e-consulting firms brought together creative, technology, and strategy consultants. The creative professionals in e-consulting firms included the graphic designers, marketers, copywriters, and informational designers who would work with clients to design the look of websites and develop Web brands for firms. On the technology side were professionals that developed web software applications, integrated them with other company operations, and ensured that they ran on the available hardware. Technology professionals included specialists in the back-end – software behind the site, such as customer databases, fulfillment systems, and visitor-tracking software – and in the front-end – design of the navigation and interactive elements of the websites experienced by visitors. Strategy consultants helped clients understand their e-business needs and helped develop e-business strategies to meet those needs.

Existing consulting organizations typically did not possess all the skills required to provide the entire range of e-consulting services. Most advertising and marketing communications agencies lacked the technical skills, such as application development and database integration, required to produce the increasingly complex yet functional solutions demanded by clients. Most large technology product and service vendors lacked the creative and marketing skills required to deliver unique and compelling content and were further constrained by their need to recommend proprietary brands. Internet access service providers, whose core strength lay in providing Internet access and site hosting rather than solution development, typically lacked both the necessary creative and application development skills.

The industry grew at an incredible rate (average of 200 percent per annum) from 1995 to 1999. However, on April 14, 2000 NASDAQ suffered its biggest point loss in history. From mid-March to late May 2000, the high technology sector experienced a substantial decline in market value, with the Nasdaq dropping 34.7 percent and the Internet Stock Index (ISDEX) falling 55.3 percent. The stock prices of most of the newly public e-consulting firms were grievously hurt by this correction in tech stocks.

The e-consultants had been capitalizing on the fear of the Internet among incumbent "bricks and mortar" firms, the chaos created by the frenzy to get on the Internet bandwagon, and the seemingly unlimited capital available to nurture that frenzy. Their sales teams did not need to be particularly strong because the demand for their services was so great. Once the market turned soft, demand for e-consulting services suddenly shrank as companies scaled back their Internet ambitions and decided that they could, after all, afford to take their time in implementing Internet strategies. Most e-consultants were ill-equipped to handle this tough new market and generate new business.

The difficult market conditions pushed several e-consultancies (including Marchfirst and Xpedior) into bankruptcy. Others (including Organic, Rare Medium Group, Razorfish, and Scient) watched their stocks trade below a dollar for weeks, putting them at risk of delisting from NASDAQ. Yet others were acquired (Mainspring by IBM, Proxicom by Dimension Data Holdings, Agency.com by Seneca Investments, Digital Island by Cable & Wireless, and Rare Medium by Motient). By December 2001, more than 60 percent of the e-consulting firms had disappeared.

Sample

Industry analysts have differed in their definitions of the e-consulting industry. Furthermore, this industry is different from the traditional industries. Firms identified by various observers as belonging to the e-consulting industry belong to as many as 13 four-digit SIC categories – 4813, 4899, 5961, 7311, 7371, 7372, 7373, 7374, 7375, 7379, 7389, 8711, 8742. Rather than following a pre-existing SIC category or adopting any one analyst's definition, we have proceeded as follows.

We define the e-consulting industry to be comprised of consulting firms that help conceive and launch an e-commerce business model and integrate it, if necessary, with an existing business. Thus, an e-consulting firm's main source of revenue comes from consulting services, including branding, information technology, and/or strategy oriented to the Internet.

To identify the industry participants, we reviewed the pronouncements of 12 different industry experts (Jupiter, KIRG, *Fortune, InfoTrends, Varbusiness, Upside, Red Herring*, Stephens Analysts, Forrester Inc., Morgan Stanley, Lehman Brothers, and *The Industry Standard*) over 4 years (1998, 1999, 2000, and 2001) to build a list of 269 firms that were cited at least once as e-consulting firms.

We narrowed this set by selecting firms that were cited as e-consulting firms by four or more source/year combinations. We eliminated firms for which the main source of revenue for the period studied was not a consulting mix of strategy, branding and information technology. Analysts from three investment banks following the e-consulting market, as well as five industry executives, were asked to review the selected set of companies to check for missing firms or inappropriate entries. This selection process produced a set of 51 firms.

Interviews with industry experts suggested that public firms had different evolution dynamics compared with private firms. Similarly, paralleling previous research (Biggadyke, 1979; Miller and Camp, 1985; McDougall and Robinson, 1990), a firm was considered a "new" venture if it was 8 years old or less at the beginning of the period considered in this study (1998). Thus we only included firms born after 1990. Applying this cut led us to the final population set of the sample for our study, comprised of 31 firms listed in Appendix 6.1.

Data collection

We gathered data on the history of each firm from birth (founding conditions) through December 2001 (or until the firm ceased to exist as an independent entity).[5] Quarterly data were recorded from 1997 to 2001 to capture the period of sharp industry expansion (from January 1998 to first quarter of year 2000) and the period of severe contraction (from second quarter of year 2000 to December of year 2001).[6]

Three levels of data were recorded: macroeconomic, firm-level, and founder-level. For the 31 companies we collected quarterly data on more than 20 different variables, such as firm economic and financial performance, amount of venture capital received, IPO data, headcount, organizational skill composition, geographical expansion, acquisitions, client concentration, mix of clients, founder and top team profiles, and macroeconomic conditions.[7] Several data sources were used, including Compustat, Datastream, Hoover's and Securities and Exchange Commission (SEC) filings; S-1, 10-K, and 10-Q forms; firm websites; firm press releases; analysts' and industry reports by brokerage and consulting firms (Investext-Thompson Financial); press articles (*Fortune, The Economist, Wall Street Journal*); specialized press (*Consulting*

News, Red Herring, The Standard, VARBusiness); and market-research reviews (Kennedy Information Research Group, IDC). The result is an unbalanced panel data set that encompasses quarterly data of 31 firms from 1998 to 2001. Appendix 6.2 presents summary statistics for the complete period.

Variables and data description

To describe and analyze the boom and bust that the e-consulting industry experienced from the last years of the 1990s to December 2001, we defined performance measures, strategy and organizational variables, and variables describing firms' founders.

Performance measures.   We use several performance measures. Survival, abnormal returns, and Tobin's q[8] are used as variables to reflect firm performance. To proxy for economic efficiency we define profitability and sales per employee.

Different definitions of business failure lead to different results (Watson and Everett, 1996). It is therefore important to define this variable in the way that best serves the purpose of the research. Entrepreneurship literature has used four alternative definitions of failure: (1) discontinuance of the business for any reason (Berryman, 1983, and Cochran, 1981); (2) bankruptcy and a resulting loss to creditors (Dun and Bradstreet); (3) disposal of the business to prevent further losses (Ulmer and Nielsen, 1947); and (4) failing to make a go of it (Cochran, 1981). Watson and Everett (1993) suggest four criteria for selecting a measure of failure: objectivity/verifiability, relevance/representational faithfulness, reliability/freedom from bias, and simplicity. Freeman et al. (1983) emphasize the importance of distinguishing between failure and acquisition of successful firms.

Taking the above cautions in mind, we decided to define two different variables to describe business failure and test both in our analysis. One defines failure as "discontinuance of the business for any reason," defined as either a change of ownership or closure of business, and another defines failure only in case the firm went bankrupt.

A firm was coded as surviving if it remained an independent organization. The variable $Survival_{i,t}$ is 1 if firm i survived in quarter t, 0 if the firm was acquired or went bankrupt. We define a variable that distinguishes among independent survival, acquisition by a competitor and bankruptcy. $MSurvival_{i,t}$ is a categorical variable that takes values 1, 2, and 3 for independent, acquired, and bankrupt, respectively. Both variables measure the firm's probability of survival in the next quarter $(t + 1)$.

To define abnormal returns we created an industry reference index for the e-consulting industry by using market value weighted stock price performance of all the firms in our sample.[9] Figure 6.1 presents a graphic of the evolution of the e-consulting Index in reference to the Nasdaq Index for the period explored. The *Abnormal returns*$_{i,t}$ variable is the abnormal return for firm i at the end of quarter t, with the e-consulting industry return as the baseline. *Market to book*$_{i,t}$ is Tobin's q for firm i at quarter t.

Finally, to proxy for economic efficiency, we define two variables. *Profitability*$_{i,t}$ is defined as profit of firm i in quarter t divided by sales of firm i during quarter t. The variable *Sales by employ*$_{i,t}$ is defined as sales of firm i in quarter t divided by firm i employees in quarter t.[10]

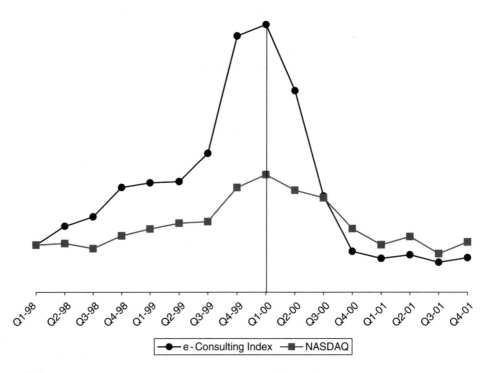

Figure 6.1   Indexes evolution for the boom and bust period

As of December 2001, of the 31 firms 14 were still independent (Answerthink, Braun Consulting, Cyberplex, Cysive, DiamondCluster, Digitas, Inforte, Predictive Systems, Navidec, Razorfish, Sapient, Scient, Tanning Technology and Viant), 11 had been acquired (Agency.com, Appnet, Cambridge Technology Partners, C-bridge, I-Cube, IXL, Mainspring, Organic, Primix, Proxicom, and USWeb/CKS), and six had gone bankrupt (Breakaway, Digitallighthouse, Luminant, Marchfirst, US Interactive and Xpedior). Total revenues of e-consulting firms grew from $2,445 million in 1998 to $5,728 million in 2000, almost a 135 percent increase. In December 2001 total sales were down to $2,237 million. Quarterly losses averaged $23 million per firm during the period from January 1998 to December 2001. The total market value of these firms rose from $5,543 million at the end of the first quarter of 1998 to $48,760 million in December 1999, a 780 percent growth over two years. From December 1999 to January 2001, however, the total market value decreased by 95 percent, from $48,760 million to $2,517 million. Market to book ratios suffered acute changes also. In March 1998, the quarterly average for the market to book ratio value was 99.4. In December 1999 it jumped to 208.8 and sank to 25.9 in December 2001. Abnormal returns were erratic, reflecting the volatility of the market. The efficiency ratio of sales per employ deteriorates from a quarterly average of $43,000 to $36,000 during the contraction period. Finally, profitability was on average negative with a quarterly average value of 81 percent for the whole period, although it went from 37 percent during expansion to 152 percent in the decline phase.

Strategy and organizational variables. Four different constructs are defined to describe the firm's strategy: rate and type of growth, international expansion, and client strategy. To characterize firm skills we define one variable: degree of focus.

Rate of growth is defined by two variables to differentiate between scale and scope. *Yearly employee growth*$_{i,t}$ is defined as the yearly rate of growth in employees of firm i in quarter t. *Yearly offices growth*$_{i,t}$ is defined as the yearly rate of growth in the number of offices of firm i in quarter t. Due to high correlation between these two variables, we ultimately use a composite of both variables derived through factor analysis. The type of growth indicates whether the firm grew mainly organically or by acquisitions. The variable *Acquisition last year*$_{i,t}$ describes for quarter t the number of acquisitions that firm i made during the previous year.

We use two proxies for international expansion. First the variable *Countries last year*$_{i,t}$ describes for quarter t the number of countries in which firm i opened offices during the previous year. Second, the variable *Employ by country*$_{i,t}$ is defined as the number of employees in quarter t divided by the number of countries where firm i owned offices. Finally, we define client strategy by two variables. *Client concentration*$_{i,t}$ is the percentage of revenue coming from the top 5 percent clients of firm i at quarter t. To identify the type of client, we define *Dot.com*$_{i,t}$ as the percentage of revenue coming from new pure Internet-based firms of firm i in quarter t.

Total headcounts in public e-consulting firms increased from 10,694 employees in March 1998 to a maximum of 38,835 in September 2000, a 265 percent growth. It had fallen to 10,197 by December 2001. The number of offices rose from 184 in January 1998 to 380 in June 2000, but then decreased to a total of 127 in December 2001. The average of total acquisitions performed by public e-consulting firms over the period January 1998 to December 2001 was 8.71 firms per company. However, the acquisition activity was clearly bimodal. Thirteen firms grew mainly by acquisitions. For example, US Web acquired 45 firms, IXL 38 firms. The other 18 grew organically, with selective acquisitions.

Twenty-five of the firms expanded internationally. Cambridge Technology Partners was the most international, with a presence in 18 different countries, followed by Marchfirst, which had a presence in 16 countries. On average, among the companies that went abroad, firms had a presence in three countries. The number of firms expanding internationally increased over time. In January 1998 only 16.67 percent of the existing firms were international compared to 81.48 percent in January 2001. The average client concentration was 46.7 percent. On average, in January 2000 firms in the sample had a 13 percent dot-com clientele.

E-consulting firms were created under the premise that to deliver value to customers three disciplines were needed in any given consulting team: strategy, information technology consultants, and branding or marketing advisors. We define the variable *Focusindex*$_{i,t}$ to describe the mix of professional skills in firm i during quarter t. The index is defined as

$$F_i = \sum_{j=1}^{4} p_{i,j}^2$$

that is, the focus index for firm i is the sum of the square of the proportion of employees that belong to each of the three disciplines, or a fourth category – other – that does not belong to any of these three. The focus index of a firm that is entirely focused on one capability is 1, and the focus index of a firm that is equally divided among four capabilities is 0.25. In our sample, we find that firms scored an average of 0.52 on this index.

Ownership and demographic variables.   At the firm level we define variables to describe ownership and demographic characteristics. *InsiderOwnershipIPO$_i$* measures the percentage of shares owned by firm's *i* insiders the day of the IPO as reported by the SEC. *VcBacked$_i$* is a dummy variable with a value of 1 if firm *i* received Venture Capital resources. The variable *Firmage$_{i,t}$* measures the number of quarters firm *i* has been in existence as of quarter *t*. Similarly, the variable *FirmageIPO$_i$* measures the number of quarters that firm *i* has been public.

Nine companies went public before January 1999; 21 were venture backed. On average, firms went public 13 quarters after founding. Luminant went public 2.75 quarters after being founded. Proxicom and Sapient took the longest to go public (25 quarters). At the time of the IPO, insiders held, on average, a 40 percent stake in their firms.

Founder variables.   To describe founder's characteristics we define four variables. *Founders$_i$* gives the number of founders for firm *i*. *Foundersage$_i$* is the average age of the founders for firm *i*. *ItFounder$_i$* is a dummy variable that takes the value of 1 if one of the founders of firm *i* had a background in the information technology industry, and 0 otherwise. Finally, *RepetEntrepreneurs$_i$* is a dummy variable that takes the value of 1 if one of the founders of firm *i* is a repeat entrepreneur.

On average, founders were 37 years old, the youngest being 26 and the oldest 57. In 16 of these firms, the founders were serial entrepreneurs. Thirteen firms had more than one founder, with founders coming from the same previous firm in seven of those cases. From a total of 52 founders, 34 came from IT consulting, 7 from strategic consulting, and 6 from marketing and advertising firms.

Macroeconomic variables.   Finally, to account for the environment we define the variable *Phase* as a dummy variable that takes the value 0 for the four quarters in years 1998 and 1999 and the first quarter of the year 2000, corresponding to the expansion phase of the bubble.[11] The variable takes the value of 1 for the declining phase, from the second quarter of 2000 to the last quarter of 2001.

Results

First we compared and contrasted averages and trends in expansion and decline phases respectively for each variable. Second, to explore a typology of strategies we conducted cluster analysis on the 31 firms. Cluster analysis groups firms with similar characteristics. We clustered our firms by the variables *Growth in scale*, *Growth in scope*, and number of employees. Hence, we seek to group observations into clusters such that each cluster is as homogeneous as possible with respect to three variables *Growth in scale*, *Growth in scope*, and *Employees*. We select the Euclidean distance as a similarity measure and the average-linkage method to obtain a hierarchical clustering.[12]

If we observe clustering, that suggests differential strategies by groups of firms within the industry. Finally, we relate these groups to firm performance.

Table 6.1 presents a summary of averages and trends for each one of the defined variables. Performance and growth strategy variables consistently show a significant difference in averages and trends for each period. Not surprisingly, firm performance was on average significantly better during the mania period than in the panic period. On average, firms were bigger in terms of sales, offices, and employees, and more international. However, although there are no significant differences between phases for client strategy, and organizational skills, a careful study of firm evolution unveils other dynamics. Client concentration shows that at the beginning of the period e-consulting firms had higher risk due to dependency on a small number of clients. Although they diversified during the expansion period they ended up in the same situation at the end of the contraction period. Similarly, the client mix between dot.com and traditional firms was fairly stable during the expansion phase, suggesting a conscious managerial decision regarding the quality and reliability of the client base. Finally, the evolution of the *focusindex* variable suggests what institutional theory calls isomorphism (DiMaggio and Powell, 1983). Clients in this market wanted end-to-end e-commerce packages that included strategy, marketing, design, and technology services combined. However, firms in this emergent industry had significant skill gaps that stemmed from their radically different origins. A close analysis of their growth strategies shows that firms followed explicit capability building strategies in order to conform to client demands in a similar fashion. For instance, Sapient has a history that follows the path of technology consulting in the 1990s. It began with client-server solutions, and then moved into enterprise resource planning (ERP) services and eventually Internet integration. The firm began pursuing a full-service strategy in earnest in 1998, picking up key skill sets like design and experience modeling through selected acquisitions.

Results from the cluster analysis show the existence of different archetypes of firms in the e-consulting industry. Figure 6.2 shows the clusters identified for the complete period. We observe three differentiated clusters and five firms that are very different from the others.

We can observe from Figure 6.2 one group of small firms composed by Braun Technologies, Inforte, Tanning technologies, Predictive Systems, C-Bridge, Cyberplex, Cysive, Navidec, Primix, and Mainspring. This cluster groups the smaller firms in the sample with an average size – measured in number of employees – of 316. These are firms that had a moderate average yearly growth (47 percent) compared to the other clusters. Sixty percent of them had, on average, positive abnormal returns (abnormal returns for the complete cluster averaged 3 percent), and the firms grew organically. Only two firms made more than 5 acquisitions in the whole period. In fact half of them never made an acquisition. All but one (Mainspring) were born in the first half of the 1990s before the mania period started. It is also interesting to notice that all but one (Mainspring was heavily oriented to strategic consulting) had a very strong technological orientation. At the end of the period of study, only two of these firms were acquired while the rest remained independent.

There is a second group of firms that may be classified as small/medium (on average the cluster has 515 employees). They exhibit huge variance in average growth rates during the period of study, although the overall average is the highest of the

Table 6.1 Variables evolution

Class	Variable[a]	Expansion phase		Contraction phase	
		Average	Trend	Average	Trend
Performance					
	Survival	0.993[a]	Decreasing	0.911	Decreasing
	Abnormal returns	0.109[a]	Increasing	−0.034	Decreasing
	Market value	1160.972[a]	Increasing	401.120	Decreasing
	Market to book	9.110[a]	Increasing	1.881	Decreasing
	Profit	−4.334[a]	Decreasing	−54.730	Decreasing
	Profitability	−0.374[a]	Stable	−1.521	Decreasing
	Sales by employee	46.839[a]	Stable	36.369	Decreasing
Strategy and organizational variables					
Size, scale, scope					
	Sales	28.678[a]	Increasing	39.673	Decreasing
	Employees	735.657[a]	Increasing	1092.775	Decreasing
	Number of offices	8.934[a]	Increasing	11.822	Decreasing
	Number of countries	2.715[a]	Increasing	4.195	Stable
	Number of acquisitions	0.832[a]	Stable	0.124	Decreasing
Growth					
	Yearly employee growth	5.205[a]	Increasing	0.355	Decreassing
	Yearly offices growth	1.016[a]	Increasing	0.418	Decreasing
	Acquisition last year	2.273[a]	Stable	1.290	Decreasing
Internationalization					
	Countries last year	1.018	Increasing	0.822	Decreasing
	Employ by country	281.078	Increasing	297.111	Stable
Clients					
	Client concentration	47.895	Decreasing	45.715	Increasing
	Dot.com	0.135	Stable	0.119	Decreasing
Organization					
	focusindex	0.530	Stable	0.507	Stable
Ownership and Demographics					
	InsiderOwnershipIpo	0.395	Invariant	0.395	Invariant
	VcBacked	0.656	Invariant	0.656	Invariant
	Firmage	17.917	Invariant	25.965	Invariant
	Firmageipo	17.018	Invariant	17.018	Invariant
Founder characteristics					
	Founders	1.611	Invariant	1.611	Invariant
	Foundersage	37.330	Invariant	37.330	Invariant
	ItFounder	0.636	Invariant	0.636	Invariant
	RepetEntrepreneurs	0.508	Invariant	0.508	Invariant

[a] Expansion and contraction phase have different means at 5 percent level of significance.

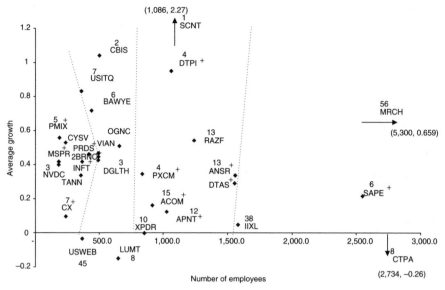

Figure 6.2   Cluster analysis: data for the complete period of study (1998–2001)

three groups (58 percent). These firms – Breakaway, Digitallighthouse, Viant, US Interactive, Luminant and Organic – all have very low abnormal returns on average (−12 percent). In fact, four of them (out of six) went bankrupt before December 2001. Those last firms grew mainly by acquisition. Only one firm in this cluster remained independent.

Although not all of them are in the same group, we consider a third cluster of firms: Agency.com, Proxicom, Razorfish, Scient, Xpedior, Answerthink, Digitas, DiamondCluster, and Appnet. These are bigger firms (average of 1,127 employees). On average, these firms had positive abnormal returns (an 8 percent average for the whole period). It is interesting to note that although half of the sample grew heavily by acquisition, on average growth was lower (by 34 percent) than in the other clusters. Half of them were still independent as of the end of the period.

Finally, we analyze the firms that were not assigned to any cluster. With the exception of US Web, these are the biggest firms in our sample. Interestingly, three of the firms were rollups. IXL acquired 38 firms in less than 3 years, US Web bought 45 firms and Marchfirst was the result of a merger between Wittman Hart Inc and US Web. Marchfirst went bankrupt and Scient acquired IXL in huge distress. All of them averaged negative abnormal returns for the whole period (7 percent for US Web, 0.08 percent for Cambridge Technology Partners, 5 percent for IXL and 19 percent for Marchfirst). Sapient is also a unique case, but for a different reason. It is one of the biggest firms, grew mainly organically and with some selective acquisitions, and had abnormal returns averaging 21 percent for the complete period of study.

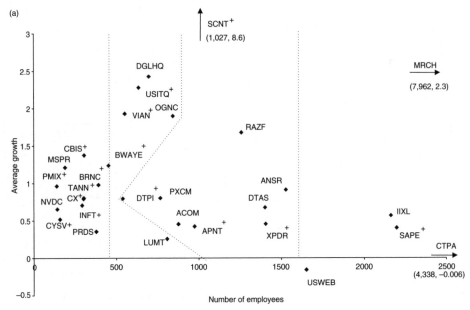

+ Indicates positive abnormal returns during the first period.

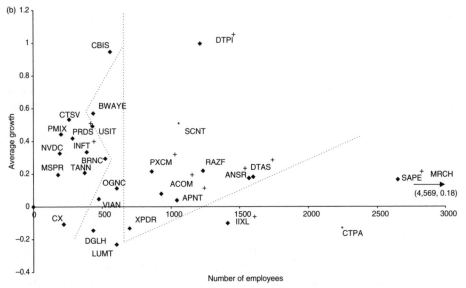

+ Indicates positive abnormal returns during the second period.

Figure 6.3 Cluster analysis for (a) mania phase, 1999–2000:Q1; (b) panic phase, 2000:Q2–2001

To understand the evolution of those firms during both periods – mania and panic – we performed cluster analysis for each one of the phases separately (see Figure 6.3a and b).

During the period of mania, we find the smaller firms growing at slower rates (83 percent) compared to the other clusters. On average, firms achieved positive abnormal returns (22 percent). During the panic phase, these firms maintained a relatively higher growth than the other groups (37 percent) and, although they were not able to achieve positive abnormal returns (−2 percent), they remained independent. In contrast, we find the second cluster – Breakaway, Digitallighthouse, Viant, US Interactive, Luminant and Organic – growing at the highest rates compared with all the other firms in our sample (167 percent). We see these small/medium size firms trying to reach scale very fast. In the second phase, however, we observe that the majority of these firms were not able to accomplish their purpose and performance suffered (abnormal returns for the first phase were − 3 percent and for the second phase − 15 percent). As a group, these firms experienced the lowest growth (13 percent) during the period of panic. Finally, the third group of firms resisted the downturn better without experiencing on average too many relative displacements (abnormal returns on average were positive, 27 percent in phase 1 and 3 percent in phase 2). The cluster's average growth for the mania period was 164 percent and 24 percent later on.

Summarizing, we observe three different strategies: (1) small firms growing slowly in the mania period and being able to sustain performance during the complete cycle; (2) small/medium firms trying to achieve scale rapidly during the first period and failing in their intent; and finally (3) bigger firms that were able to survive and achieve, on average, good performance.

Discussion, Limitations, and Future Research

This chapter has described a mechanism to account for severe changes in the environment that may affect patterns of firm entry and exit in a new industry. The mercurial rise and precipitous fall of the e-consulting industry has allowed us to explore which strategies entrepreneurs followed to cope with these circumstances and the consequences on firm performance. Findings presented above show that environmental conditions at founding and early organizational strategies jointly affect the survival likelihood of young firms. Surprisingly, we could not identify a founder's effect. We attribute this result to the preliminary stage of this analysis.

We find that size is an important variable for firm survival. It seems that small and "big enough" firms are more likely to survive independently. Although firm growth was positively related to the probability of staying in the market as an independent firm and to achieving higher abnormal returns in both phases, the type of growth affected survival. Firms that grew by acquisitions had lower probabilities of survival. Finally, although it did not have a significant effect on firm returns, professional skills defined as concentration of its personnel in each one of the three disciplines – strategy, branding, and information technology – had a significant and different impact on survival depending on the external environment.

In terms of industry formation, we have described the early years of an industry that was born in the mid-1990s under high expectations and that today may be considered history. The study of the evolution of the e-consulting industry as a whole is not the purpose of this chapter. We have only examined strategies of young entrepreneurial firms – the ones that spark the revolution in the consulting industry – to adapt to their environment. However, several factors, potentially affecting survival, and performance in general, will be addressed in future analysis. First, we plan to examine the evolution of client demands through the period of mania and panic. Some preliminary interviews with firm executives suggest that client engagements changed their nature over time. Second, the role of the incumbent firms in the evolution of the industry will be considered. Our current research on the interplay of incumbent and new ventures shows that in our industry incumbents had huge advantages in adapting. Reputation played a critical role in retaining and attracting new clients and therefore facilitating increased market share.

In terms of strategies and organizational characteristics our results are not surprising. Coinciding with previous research, we find that firm size is an important variable for firm survival and, in general, firm performance. Previous research has found that the likelihood of survival diminishes for small firms. However, in our study we differentiate the fates of small firms according to their growth strategies. On average, small firms that were growing too fast during the expansion period were the ones that suffered poorer performance and were unable to cope with environmental changes. Two alternative explanations are plausible. On the one hand, higher growth implies more potential coordination problems, increasing the risk to survival. On the other hand, empirical observation on the size of professional firms indicates that small and big firms coexist but medium-size firms are rare. We cannot unravel this complex issue in this study, but future research will address the concern.

Rollups and acquisitions in general have proven to be a tempting strategy to achieve fast growth and new skills, but often with negative results. However, some successes were observed. Our database allows us to distinguish between the different purposes of acquisitions (scale, geographical expansion or incorporation of new capabilities). We will include this in future analysis.

Our findings on the skills of organizations suggest that successful e-consulting firms during boom times were more focused on a specific skill. Firms with higher proportions of their teams under one discipline had higher probabilities of survival. Future research should identify how critically each skill – strategy, marketing, and information technology – affects survival. Previous research has found that successful entrepreneurs are usually niche-oriented (Bhide, 2000), because they serve markets with which they are better acquainted based on their skills. This is even truer of professional service firms. However, flexibility and adaptation in services appears to be critical in declining environments. Finally, analysis on clients should be incorporated in future work.

We plan to conduct more detailed analysis to confirm the robustness of our findings and to follow this study with in-depth case studies of the firms belonging to each of the clusters to identify management practices and work environments that might underlie the factors we identify here as determinants of firms' relative performance.

Acknowledgments

This research is funded in part by the Ewing Marion Kauffman Foundation. The contents of this chapter are solely the responsibility of the authors.

Notes

1. Research based on the idea that entrepreneurial status has a permanent nature embedded in individuals has failed to establish an empirical link between individual characteristics and organizational outcomes. Studies centered on the founders have described them by personality traits such as a high need for achievement and power (McClelland, 1961), or by functional roles such as a "coordinator," a "combiner of resources" (Say, 1830), an "innovator" (Schumpeter, 1934), or an "arbitrator" – an equilibrating agent in a world of imperfect information (Kirzner, 1973). Other characterizations define the entrepreneur as ultimate "decision-maker" under uncertainty (Knight, 1921) or as "speculator." More fruitful research has been developed using Human Capital Theory (Becker, 1975) as the basis to guide empirical research regarding the effects of founder characteristics on firm survival. In general, founder's education, career history, family background, and status have proven to affect firm survival. Similarly, founders' beliefs about information and the value of resources (Shane, 2000), different structural positions (Aldrich and Zimmer, 1986; Aldrich, 1999; Dunn and Holtz-Eakin, 2000) or different ties, social contacts, and prestige (Larson, 1992; Higgins and Gulati, 1999; Stuart et al., 1999; Lin et al., 2000; Hitt et al., 2001) also explain firm success.
2. Initial capital endowments (Evans and Leighton, 1989; Holtz-Eakin et al., 1994; Dunn and Holtz-Eakin, 2000), differentiation strategies (Sandberg and Hofer, 1987), earlier acquired legitimacy (Aldrich and Fiol, 1994), timing and scope of the firm's entry into the market (Teplensky et al., 1993), and environmentally adapted strategies (Romanelli, 1989) impact young firms' survival. Similarly, characteristics of the founding top-management team, strategy, and environment were related to sales growth of the newly founded firms (Eisenhardt and Schoonhoven, 1990; Baum et al., 2001).
3. This phenomenon belongs to a larger category of economic phenomena, collectively called speculative bubbles (Kindleberger, 1978; Stiglitz, 1990). Speculative bubbles have arisen numerous times in history across geographical borders. Underlying reasons put forward as causing the phenomenon are very diverse – i.e. lack of information about the underlying value of assets (tulip mania in the seventeenth century), uncertainty introduced by government manipulations (the Mississippi Bubble and the South Sea Bubble in 1720), new financial developments (the crisis of 1929), or major sectoral shifts. For a complete review see Kindleberger (1978). Theoretical models and empirical studies from finance (Minsky, 1977; Garber, 2000) as well as from sociology (Abolafia and Kilduff, 1988; Aldrich and Baker, 1997) has characterized this empirical regularity.
4. The subject has been explored previously only on related topics for physicians (Wholey et al., 1993), accountants (Pennings et al., 1998), and biotechnology scientists (Zucker et al., 1998). Wholey et al. (1993) study organization formation among physicians when interests of corporate clients are strong and professional diversity leads professional groups to expand their jurisdiction by organizing. Pennings et al. (1998) examine the effect of human and social capital upon firm dissolution with data from a population of Dutch accounting firms. Finally, Zucker et al. (1998) find that the timing and location of the birth of biotech enterprises is determined primarily by the local number of highly productive "star" scientists actively publishing genetic sequence discoveries.

5. The founding date corresponds to the initiation of formal operations and the establishment of a regular location of business. These dates were collected for all the firms from business press articles, 10-K's (annual reports supplied to the SEC) or prospectuses. Several firms changed their names during the course of the study. In those cases, we considered the date of founding to be that of the first organization. If the first organization was founded before 1990 the firm was discarded from the sample.

6. According to Lehman Brothers Global Equity research, April 9, 2002, the bottom of the market was September 21, 2001 and the end of the recession December 2001. Since the market trough on September 21, 2001, 68 percent of the S&P 500 industry groups are delivering the same relative performance that they have historically.

7. Quarterly data is necessary to capture sharp changes in a small time window. Imputation missing data methods are used when some data were missing.

8. Tobin's q is defined as the market value of the firm divided by the replacement value of assets (Montgomery and Wernerfelt, 1988).

9. The e-consulting Index represents companies that generate the majority of their revenues via e-consulting. To be eligible for the e-consulting Index, a stock issued through an initial public offering must have a minimum of 3 months' trading history, the company must be born after 1990 and its staff must be a combination of technical, creativity and strategy personnel (as of April 2000). The Index aims to consistently represent 90 percent of the float-adjusted e-consulting equity universe. It is a quarterly Index. At its inception in 1998:Q1, the e-consulting Index consisted of seven components. However, in order to meet the 90 percent float-adjusted market capitalization goal, other equities are added in increments of five. The e-consulting Index has been assigned a base value of 100 as of the close of trading in March 1998. If an Index constituent is delisted by its primary market, or enters bankruptcy proceedings, it will be deleted from the indexes immediately.

10. In a human capital intensive industry, variables defined per employee better reflect the economics of the firm.

11. We use expansion phase, mania period, or phase 1 interchangeably. Similarly, we referred to the contraction phase as the panic period or phase 2.

12. The distance between cluster k and cluster l is given by the average of the $(n_k * n_l)$ Euclidean distances, where n_k and n_l are the number of subjects in clusters k and l, respectively (Sharma, 1996).

References

Abell, D. 1980: *Defining the Business: The Starting Point of Strategic Planning.* Englewood Cliffs, NJ: Prentice-Hall.

Abolafia, M. and Kilduff, M. 1988: Enacting market crisis: The social construction of a speculative bubble. *Administrative Science Quarterly,* 33, 177–193.

Aldrich, H. 1979: *Organizations and Environments.* Englewood Cliffs, NJ: Prentice-Hall.

Aldrich, H. 1999: *Organizations Evolving.* London: Sage Publications.

Aldrich, H. and Baker, T. 1997: Blinded by the cites? Has there been progress in entrepreneurship research. In D.L. Sexton and R.W. Smilor (eds.), *Entrepreneurship 2000.* Chicago, IL: Upstar, 377–400.

Aldrich, H. and Fiol, C. 1994: Fools rush in? The institutional context of industry creation. *Academy of Management Review,* 19, 645–670.

Aldrich, H. and Zimmer, C. 1986: Entrepreneurship through social networks. In D.L. Sexton and R.W. Smilor (eds.), *The Art and Science of Entrepreneurship.* Cambridge, MA: Ballinger, 3–23.

Baum, J., Locke, E., and Smith, K.G. 2001: A multidimensional model of venture growth. *Academy of Management Journal*, 44, 292–303.

Becker, G. 1975: *Human Capital.* New York: Columbia University Press.

Berryman, J. 1983: Small business failure and bankruptcy: A survey of the literature. *European Small Business Journal*, 1, 47–59.

Bhide, A. 2000: *The Origin and Evolution of New Business.* Oxford: The Oxford University Press.

Biggadyke, R. 1979: The risky business of corporate diversification. *Harvard Business Review*, 103–111.

Brittain, J. and Freeman J. 1980: Organizational proliferation and density dependent selection. In J.R. Kimberly and R.H. Miles (eds.), *The Organizational Life.* San Francisco, CA: Jossey-Bass, 291–338.

Carroll, G. 1984: Organizational ecology. In R.H. Turner and J.F. Short (eds.), *Annual Review of Sociology.* Palo Alto, CA: Annual Reviews Inc., 71–79.

Carroll, G. 1985: Concentration and specialization: Dynamics of niche width in populations of organizations. *American Journal of Sociology*, 90, 1262–1283.

Carroll, G. and Delacroix, J. 1982: Organizational mortality in the newspaper industry of Argentina and Ireland. *Administrative Science Quarterly*, 27, 169–198.

Carroll, G. and Hannan, M. 1989: Density dependence in the evolution of populations of newspaper organizations. *American Sociological Review*, 54, 524–541.

Cochran, A. 1981: Small business mortality rates, a review of the literature. *Journal of Small Business Management*, 19, 50–59.

Cooper, A., Gascon, J., and Woo, C. 1991: A resource-based prediction of new venture survival and growth. *Academy of Management*, 113–119.

Delacroix, J. and Carrol, G. 1983: Organizational foundings: An ecological study of the newspaper industries of Argentina and Ireland. *Administrative Science Quarterly*, 28, 274–291.

Dess, G. and Davis, R. 1984: Porter's (1980) generic strategies as determinants of strategic group membership and organizational performance. *Academy of Management Journal*, 27, 467–488.

DiMaggio, P. and Powell, W. 1983: The iron cage revisited: Institutional isomorphism and collective rationality in organizational fields. *American Sociological Review*, 48, 147–160.

Dunn, T. and Holtz-Eakin, D. 2000: Financial capital, human capital, and the transition to self-employment: Evidence from intergenerational links. *Journal of Labor Economics*, 18, 282–305.

Eisenhardt, K. and Schoonhoven, C. 1990: Organizational growth-linking founding team, strategy, environment, and growth among United States semiconductors ventures, 1978–1988. *Administrative Science Quarterly*, 35, 504–529.

Evans, D. and Leighton, L. 1989: Some empirical aspects of entrepreneurship. *American Economic Review*, 79, 519–535.

Freeman, J., Carrol, G., and Hannan, M. 1983: The liability of newness: Age dependence in organizational death rates. *American Sociological Review*, 48, 692–710.

Garber, P. 2000: *Famous First Bubbles.* Cambridge, MA: MIT Press.

Geroski, P. and Mazzucato, M. 2001: Modeling the dynamics of industry populations. *International Journal of Industrial Organization*, 19, 1003–1022.

Glaser, B. and Strauss, A. 1967: *The Discovery of Grounded Theory: Strategies of Qualitative Research.* London: Wiedenfeld and Nicholson.

Gompers, P. and Lerner, J. 2001: *The Money of Invention.* Boston, MA: Harvard Business School Press.

Gort, M. and Klepper, S. 1982: Time paths in the diffusion of product innovations. *The Economic Journal*, 92, 630–653.

Hambrick, D. 1980: Operationalizing the concept of business-level strategy in research. *Academy of Management Review*, 5, 567–575.

Hannan, M. and Freeman, J. 1989: *Organizational Ecology*. Cambridge, MA: Harvard University Press.

Higgins, M. and Gulati, R. 1999: The effects of IPO team ties on investment bank affiliation and IPO success. Harvard Business School Working Paper no. 00-025.

Hitt, M., Bierman, L., Shimizu, K., and Kochhar, R. 2001: Direct and moderating effects of human capital on strategy and performance in professional service firms: A resource-based perspective. *Academy of Management Journal*, 44, 13–28.

Holtz-Eakin, D., Joulfaian, D., and Rosen, H. 1994: Entrepreneurial decisions and liquidity constraints. *Rand Journal of Economics*, 23, 340–347.

Horvath, M., Schivardi, F., and Woywode, M. 2001: On industry life-cycles: Delay, entry, and shakeout in beer brewing. *International Journal of Industrial Organization*, 19, 1023–1052.

Jovanovic, B. and MacDonald, G. 1994: The life cycle of a competitive industry. *Journal of Political Economy*, 102, 322–347.

Kamm, J., Shuman, J., Seeger, J., and Nurick, A. 1990: Entrepreneurial teams in new venture creation: A research agenda. *Entrepreneurship Theory and Practice*, 14, 7–17.

Kennedy Information Research Group 2000: The global information technology management consulting marketplace: Key data, forecasts, and trends.

Kindleberger, C. 1978: *Manias, Panics, and Crashes. A History of Financial Crises*. New York: John Wiley & Sons, Inc.

Kirzner, I. 1973: *Competition and Entrepreneurship*. Chicago, IL: University of Chicago Press.

Klepper, S. and Grady, E. 1990: The evolution of new industries and the determinants of market structure. *The RAND Journal of Economics*, 21, 27–44.

Klepper, S. and Miller, J. 1995: Entry, exit and shakeouts in the United States in new manufactured products. *International Journal of Industrial Organization*, 13, 567–591.

Knight, F. 1921: *Risk, Uncertainty and Profit*. New York: Harper & Row.

Larson, A. 1992: Networks dyads in entrepreneurial settings: A study of the governance of exchange relationships. *Administrative Science Quarterly*, 37, 76–104.

Lerner, J. 1997: An empirical exploration of a technology race. *Rand Journal of Economics*, 28, 228–247.

Lin, Z., Picot, G., and Compton, J. 2000: The entry and exit dynamics of self-employment in Canada. *Small Business Economics*, 15, 105–125.

McClelland, D. 1961: *The Achieving Society*. Princeton, NJ: D. van Nostrand Co, Inc.

McDougall, P. and Robinson, R. 1990: New venture strategies: An empirical identification of eight "archetypes" of competitive strategies for entry. *Strategic Management Journal*, 11, 447–467.

Miller, A. and Camp, B. 1985: Exploring determinants of success in corporate ventures. *Journal of Business Venturing*, 1, 87–105.

Minsky, H. 1977: A theory of systematic fragility. In E.I. Altman and A. Sametz (eds.), *Financial Crises: Institution and Markets in a Fragile Environment*. New York: Wiley, 138–152.

Montgomery, C. and Wernerfelt, B. 1988: Diversification, Ricardian rents, and Tobin's q. *Rand Journal of Economics*, 19, 623–632.

Pennings, J., Lee, K., and Wittelloostuijn, A. 1998: Human capital, social capital and firm dissolution. *Academy of Management Journal*, 41, 425–440.

Rao, H. 1989: The social organization of trust: The growth and decline of organizational forms in the savings and loan industry: 1960–1987. Weatherhead School of Management. Case Western Reserve University: Cleveland, OH.

Reynolds, P. and Miller, B. 1989: New firm survival: Analysis of a panel's fourth year. In R.H. Broackhaus, N.C. Churchill, J.A. Katz, B.A. Kirchoff, K.H. Vesper, and W.E. Wetzel (eds.), *Frontiers of Entrepreneurship Research*. Wellessley, MA: Babson College.

Romanelli, E. 1989: Environmental and strategies of organizations' start-ups. Effects on early survival. *Administrative Science Quarterly*, 34, 369–387.

Roure, J. and Keeley, R. 1990: Predictors of success in new technology based venture. *Journal of Business Venturing*, 5, 201–220.

Sahlman, W. and Stevenson, H. 1986. Capital market myopia. *Journal of Business Venturing*, 1, 7–30.

Sandberg, W. and Hofer, C. 1987: Improving new venture performance: The role of strategy, industry structure and the entrepreneur. *Journal of Business Venturing*, 2, 5–28.

Say, J. 1830: *A Treatise on Political Economy* (trans. C. R. Prinsep) 4th edn, Philadelphia, PA: John Grigg.

Schumpeter, J. 1934: *The Theory of Economic Development*. Cambridge, MA: Harvard University Press.

Scott, W. and Meyer, J. 1983: The organization of societal sectors. In J. Meyer and W.R. Scott (eds.), *Organizational Environments: Ritual and Rationality*, Beverly Hills, CA: Sage, 129–54.

Shane, S. 2000: Prior knowledge and discovery of entrepreneurial opportunities. *Organization Science*, 11, 448–69.

Sharma, S. 1996: *Applied Multivariate Techniques*. New York: John Wiley & Sons.

Schoonhoven, C.B. and Romanelli, E. 2001. Emergent themes and the next wave of entrepreneurship research. In C.B. Schoonhoven and E. Romanelli (eds.), *The Entrepreneurship Dynamic: Origins of Entrepreneurship and the Evolution of Industries*. Stanford CA. Stanford University Press, 383–409.

Singh, J., Tucker, D., and House, R. 1986: Organizational legitimacy and the liability of newness. *Administrative Science Quarterly*, 31, 171–193.

Stevenson, H. and Jarillo, J.C. 1991: A new entrepreneurial paradigm. In A. Etzioni and P.R. Lawrence (eds.), *Socioeconomics: Toward a New Synthesis*. Armonk, NY: ME Sharpe, Inc.

Stiglitz, J. 1990: Symposium on bubbles. *The Journal of Economic Perspectives*, 4, 13–18.

Stinchcombe, A. 1965: Social structure and organizations. In J. March (ed.), *Handbook of Organizations*. Chicago: Rand McNally. 142–193.

Stuart, T., Hoang, H., and Hybels, R. 1999: Interorganizational endorsements and the performance of entrepreneurial ventures. *Administrative Science Quarterly*, 44, 315–349.

Swaminathan, A. 1996: Environmental conditions at founding and organizational mortality: A trial-by-fire model. *Academy of Management Journal*, 39, 1350–1377.

Teplensky, J., Kimberly, J., Hillman, A., and Schwart, J. 1993: Scope, timing and strategic adjustment in emerging markets: Manufacturer strategies and the case of MRI. *Strategic Management Journal*, 14, 505–527.

Timmons, J. 1999: *New Venture Creation*. New York: McGraw Hill, Irwin.

Ulmer, M. and Nielsen, A. 1947: Business turn-over and causes of failure. *Survey of Current Business*, April, 10–16.

Utterback, J. and Suarez, F. 1993: Innovation, competition and industry structure. *Research Policy*, 22, 2–21.

Watson, J. and Everett, J. 1993: Defining small business failure. *International Small Business Journal*, 11, 35–48.

Watson, J. and Everett, J. 1996: Do small businesses have high failure rates? Evidence from Australian retailers. *Journal of Small Business Management*, 34, 45–62.

Wholey, D., Christianson, J., and Sanchez, S. 1993: The effect of physician and corporate interests on the formation of health maintenance organizations. *American Journal of Sociology*, 99, 164–200.

Zucker, L., Darby, M., and Brewer, M. 1998: Intellectual human capital and the birth of US biotechnology enterprises. *American Economic Review*, 88, 209–306.

Appendix 6.1: List of firms included in the sample

Company name	TICKER	Founded	IPO	Independent	Headquarters
1 AGENCY.COM LTD	ACOM	Feb-95	Dec-99	No	New York
2 ANSWER THINK INC	ANSR	Apr-97	May-98	Yes	Miami
3 APPNET INC	APNT	Nov-97	Jun-99	No	Bethesda/MD
4 BRAUN CONSULTING	BRNC	1993	Aug-99	Yes	Chicago
5 BREAKAWAY SOLUTIONS INC	BWAYE	1992	Oct-99	No	Boston
6 CAMBRIDGE TECHNOLOGY PARTNERS	CATP	1991	Sep-93	No	Cambridge
7 C-BRIDGE INTERNET SOLTNS INC	CBIS	Oct-96	Dec-99	No	Boston
8 CYBERPLEX	CX	1994	Apr-97	Yes	Toronto
9 CYSIVE	CYSV	Jan-93	Oct-99	Yes	Reston/VA
1 0 DIAMONDCLUSTER INTL	DTPI	Jan-94	Feb-97	Yes	Chicago
1 1 DIGITALLIGHTHOUSE	DGLHQ	Mar-96	Mar-00	No	Englewood, CO
1 2 DIGITAS INC	DTAS	Jan-95	Mar-00	Yes	Boston
1 3 I-CUBE	ICUB	Apr-92	Jun-98	No	Cambridge
1 4 INFORTE	INFT	Sep-93	Feb-00	Yes	Chicago
1 5 IXL ENTERPRISES INC	IIXL	Mar-96	Jun-99	No	Atlanta
1 6 LUMINANT WORLDWIDE CORP	LUMT	Aug-98	Sep-99	No	Dallas
1 7 MAINSPRING INC	MSPR	Jun-96	Jul-00	No	Cambridge
1 8 MARCHFIRST INC	MRCH	Jan-00		No	Chicago
1 9 NAVIDEC	NVDC	Jul-93	Feb-97	Yes	Greenwood/CO
2 0 ORGANIC INC	OGNC	Jan-95	Feb-00	No	San Francisco
2 1 PREDICTIVE SYSTEMS	PRDS	Jan-95	Oct-99	Yes	New York
2 2 PRIMIX SOLUTIONS INC	PMIX	Jan-94	Jul-96	No	Watertown
2 3 PROXICOM INC	PXCM	1991	Apr-99	No	Reston/VA
2 4 RAZORFISH INC	RAZF	Apr-95	Apr-99	Yes	New York
2 5 SAPIENT CORP	SAPE	Sep-91	Apr-96	Yes	Cambridge
2 6 SCIENT CORP	SCNT	Nov-97	May-99	Yes	San Francisco
2 7 TANNING TECHNOLOGY	TANN	Jan-93	Jul-99	Yes	Denver
2 8 U S INTERACTIVE INC	USITQ	May-94	Aug-99	No	Philadelphia
2 9 US WEB/CKS	USWB	Dec-95	Dec-97	No	Burlington/MA
3 0 VIANT CORP	VIAN	Apr-96	Jun-99	Yes	Boston
3 1 XPEDIOR INC	XPDR	Mar-97	Dec-99	No	Chicago

Appendix 6.2: Summary statistics: period from 1998:Q1 to December 2001

Class	Variable[a]	Number of Observations	Mean	Standard Deviation	Minimum	25th percentile	Median	75th percentile	Maximum
Performance									
	Survival	443	0.962	0.192	0				1
	Msurvival	443	1.052	0.277	1				3
	Abnormal returns	286	0.025	0.436	-0.992	-0.236	-0.036	0.214	2.323
	Market value ($ million)	310	746.730	1109.657	0.020	73.650	281.620	1021.280	7802.580
	Market to book	307	5.154	6.399	-2.839	0.953	2.996	7.370	64.101
	Profit ($ million)	439	-23.624	255.393	-5300.000	-9.499	-1.925	0.390	26.859
	Profitability	443	-0.811	2.822	-35.263	-0.633	-0.163	0.043	3.108
	Sales by employee	443	42.845	58.497	2.177	27.679	37.023	45.600	868.200
Strategy and organizational variables									
Size, scale, scope									
	Sales ($ million)	443	32.872	44.580	0.100	6.400	16.221	40.694	380.200
	Employees	443	871.894	1206.509	5	206	459	1048	9000
	Number of offices	443	10.036	10.716	1	4	8	12	70
	Number of countries	443	3.280	3.698	1	1	2	4	19
	Number of acquisitions	443	0.562	2.190	0	0	0	0	28
Growth									
	Yearly employee growth	443	3.355	16.798	-0.859	0.333	0.685	1.294	149.000
	Yearly offices growth	443	0.789	1.505	-0.813	0.000	0.345	1.000	9.000
	Acquisition last year	443	1.898	4.019	0	0	0	2	28
Internationalization									
	Countries last year	443	0.944	2.218	-6	0	0	2	18
	Employ by country	443	287.195	242.56	5.000	125.000	200.000	393.333	1449.500
Clients									
	Client concentration	443	46.744	16.071	6.000	35	45	60	84.8
	Dot.com	443	0.125	0.086	0.010	0.050	0.100	0.185	0.470
Organization									
	focusindex	443	0.522	0.196	0.268	0.375	0.474	0.640	1.000

Continued

Appendix 6.2 *Continued*

Class	Variable[a]	Number of Observations	Mean	Standard Deviation	Minimum	25th percentile	Median	75th percentile	Maximum
Ownership and Demographics									
	InsiderOwnershipIpo	443	0.395	0.239	0.010	0.140	0.370	0.609	0.780
	VcBacked	443	0.656	0.476	0				1
	Firmage (quarters)	443	20.973	9.208	0	14	21	28	42
	Firmageipo	443	17.018	7.364	6	10	15	22	32
Founder characteristics									
	Founders	443	1.611	0.944	1	1	1	2	4
	Foundersage	443	37.330	7.945	26	30	38	44	57
	ItFounder	443	0.636	0.482	0				1
	RepetEntrepreneurs	443	0.508	0.501	0				1
Macroeconomic performance									
	Phasedummy	443			0				1
	Yeardummy	443			1998				2001

[a] Variable values are by quarter unless otherwise indicated.

CHAPTER SEVEN

Delaying Market Entry: How Long Is Too Long?

Moren Lévesque and Dean A. Shepherd

Introduction

Most research on market entry indicates that timing of entry is a key factor for success (Golder and Tellis, 1993; Lambkin, 1988; Mitchell, 1991). Early entrants can often achieve higher profit potential than followers because early participation provides expertise (Feeser and Willard, 1990; Ghemawat, 1991); they find it easier to gain customers (Karakaya and Kobu, 1994; Robinson, 1988); and/or their market share gains are worth more (Carpenter and Nakamoto, 1989; Golder and Tellis, 1993). Also, early entrants can erect entry and mobility barriers to increase their advantage over later entrants: relationships with distributors and customers or other intangible factors, such as reputation or service, that raise buyer switching costs (Ghemawat, 1991; Huff and Robinson, 1994).

Pioneers in general, however, have a greater risk of mortality than do later entrants (Aaker and Day, 1986; Mitchell, 1991). The magnitude of a given firm's mortality risk depends, in part, on the management team's choice of when to enter. Waiting may lower the mortality risk, as the firm may be able to make use of early research at a lower cost (Mansfield et al., 1981). Waiting may also allow the firm to establish whether there is sufficient demand for the new product/service to sustain life (Aaker and Day, 1986; Williamson, 1975, 1988). Therefore, in deciding to enter a new market early managers must consider the possible tradeoff between increased profit potential and increased mortality risk.[1] But is the optimal time for entry the same for all firms?

There is considerable resource heterogeneity among potential entrants to a new market. An important distinction between firms is their access to resources. For example, greater legitimacy is attributed to firms that have considerable resources (DiMaggio and Powell, 1983; Haveman, 1993). The "deeper pockets" of a firm with more resources may also be necessary to survive environmental jolts (Venkataraman and Van de Ven, 1998) and thereby lower the firm's mortality risk. Incumbent firms typically have more resources than pioneers of new markets (e.g. Mitchell, 1991). As the pioneers accumulate resources to match those of the incumbent firm, this window will close. But because resources can be difficult for other firms to imitate/accumulate (Lippman and Rumelt, 1982), the period of opportunity for later entry may be considerable.

For example, the Reserve Fund of New York pioneered money market mutual funds in 1973 but incumbents entered soon after (Dreyfus Liquid Assets [1974], Fidelity Daily Income Trust [1974] and Merrill Lynch Ready Assets [1975]). "The tiny pioneer could not match the marketing, distribution, and financial advantages, as well as the reputation benefits, held by the imitators. Size mattered more than first entry" (Schnaars, 1994: 40). Another example is caffeine-free soft drinks. The pioneers (Canada Dry's "Sport" [1967] and Royal Crown's RC1000 [1980]) had a head start on Pepsi [1982] and Coke [1983] but were not able to match the distribution and promotional advantages of these giants (Schnaars, 1994: 39).

Scholars holding the resource-based view of the firm argue that firms differ in their stock of resources. If the stock of resources is highly related to the new market they are of greater value to the firm (Barney, 1991).[2] In this chapter we argue that an incumbent firm can effectively delay entry for a period of time and still achieve a long-term performance advantage over those that have already entered because the incumbent firm typically has a greater stock of resources than pioneers of that new field (Mitchell, 1991), even though those resources are likely to be less related to the new market as they were created for other purposes (they are less valuable).[3] When, then, should an incumbent firm enter the new market?

In addressing the above question, this chapter offers a model of entry timing that makes two important contributions to the entry strategy literature. First, most scholarly attention focuses on the relationship between timing of entry and performance, with little acknowledgment of "non-timing" related differences between firms. Mitchell's (1991) work, which represents a significant exception, introduces the concept of two clocks – one for incumbent firms and one for both incumbent and start-up firms (which are more likely to be pioneers). The present chapter makes a theoretical advance on Mitchell's work by explicitly modeling the impact of differences between incumbent firms and start-ups (in terms of their stock of resources and the value of those resources) on entry performance. Second, while there has been considerable research investigating the timing-of-entry decision, most scholars have used as their dependent variable either a measure of profit (Abell and Hammond, 1979; Schumpeter, 1975) or a measure of mortality (Aaker and Day, 1986; Mitchell, 1989; Wernerfelt and Karnani, 1987) – few studies have simultaneously investigated both. This is surprising, considering that the increased costs of mitigating these mortality risks may be acceptable if there is a corresponding increase in the probability of a high return (Bowman, 1982).

The chapter proceeds as follows. First, we develop a deterministic continuous-time mathematical formulation to derive a model of the time for market entry that maximizes overall firm performance. By selecting simple functional forms (e.g. linear and exponential) for the various performance measures we keep the model mathematically tractable, without (we argue) losing major insights into the entry decision phenomenon. The use of a mathematical approach is beneficial for theory development on the timing decision for an incumbent firm entering a new market because it identifies counter-intuitive propositions and offers a rationale for them. Second, to explore some of the possibilities of the model we use a worked example that restricts the dynamics of a firm's stock of resources and those aspects of profit potential and mortality risk that depend on the resources' characteristics. Third, we offer the contribution of our approach to the timing of entry literature.

Analytic Framework

Let t be the industry age when the incumbent firm is to enter. Let s_t (> 0) be the relative size of the incumbent firm's stock of resources over that of the pioneer(s) (relative resource stock) at t, which decreases over time at a non-decreasing rate reflecting the increasing ability for pioneers to improve their stock of resources. Formally, $ds_t/dt < 0$ and $d^2s_t/dt^2 \leq 0$. Let s_0 be the initial resource stock of the incumbent firm at the time of the pioneer's entry.[4]

Profit potential if the incumbent firm enters the market at t is denoted by p_t and decreases with t, the industry age, while increasing with the value of the resources, r. Valuable resources are those that enable a firm to formulate and implement strategies that create value for specific customers (Hitt et al., 1999).[5] Profit potential is the expected total return to stockholders during the life of the incumbent's firm, discounted at some rate (not accounting for risk as we attempt to treat risk separately, but accounting for the time value of money, such as in the calculation of an expected present value of future cash flows) – including both dividends and capital gain. Profit potential also increases with the firm's relative resource stock at a non-increasing rate (further increases will produce diminished returns), but at a steeper rate for high levels of resource value than for low levels. Formally, profit potential is expressed by $p_t = P_0 - \rho t + f(r, s_t)$, where P_0 is the incumbent's profit potential (not attributed to resource stock or value) if this incumbent were to enter the market initially (i.e. at $t = 0$) and be a pioneer too, ρ the direct marginal loss of profit potential due to delayed market entry (accounting for potential revenue loss and potential entry of other firms), and f a non-negative function with $\partial f/\partial r > 0$, $\partial f/\partial s_t > 0$, $\partial^2 f/\partial s_t^2 \leq 0$, and $\partial^2 f/\partial r \partial s_t > 0$.

Mortality risk if the incumbent firm enters the market at t is denoted by m_t. Mortality risk is the cost that arises due to uncertainty in demand and technology that leads to fluctuations in cash flows and may reduce stocks of resources below a sustainable level leading to bankruptcy.[6] Empirical evidence from evolutionary scholars (Freeman et al., 1983; Hannan and Freeman, 1984) and from the application of the learning curve to population level learning (Argote et al., 1990; Ingram and Baum, 1997) finds that mortality risk decreases with industry age, and at a rate η (> 0) well approximated by an exponential function. Mortality risk also decreases with resource value. Moreover, it decreases with a greater relative resource stock at a non-increasing rate, but at a steeper rate for high levels of resource value than for low levels. Formally, mortality risk is expressed by $m_t = \gamma e^{-\eta t} - g(r, s_t)$, where γ is a scaling parameter (large enough to keep mortality risk above zero) that controls for the direct effect of industry age as well as for an upper bound on mortality risk, and g a non-negative function with $\partial g/\partial r > 0$, $\partial g/\partial s_t > 0$, $\partial^2 g/\partial s_t^2 \leq 0$, and $\partial^2 g/\partial r \partial s_t > 0$. The function

$g(r,s_t)$ reflects the effect of resource value and an indirect effect of time due to changes in the relative advantage in the stock of resources that the incumbent firm has over the pioneer(s). Note that we choose to express mortality risk with an additive form – that separates the effect of resource characteristics (relative resource stock and resource value) and time – rather than its multiplicative counterpart (where, e.g., $m_t = e^{-\eta t}/g(r, s_t)$). We argue that the additive form is more appropriate because low levels of relative resource stock and resource value cause a high mortality risk, even when time becomes infinitely large. The industry age, t, thus has a direct effect on mortality risk, allowing it to decrease over time, but also an indirect effect (due to a decrease in the firm's relative resource stock), forcing it to increase over time.

The incumbent firm's objective is to enter the market so as to maximize expected total performance. Schoemaker and Amit (1994) indicate that new ventures' strategic actions constitute a tradeoff between maximizing expected returns for stockholders and maximizing survival chances. Radner and Shepp's (1996) analytical model proposes that corporate strategy should aim at maximizing a *linear combination* of profit (the expected total dividends paid out during the life of the new venture, discounted at some fixed rate) and bankruptcy (when the new venture's cash reserve falls to zero and it therefore ceases to operate). More recently, Archibald et al. (2002) compare inventory strategies that maximize survival to those that maximize average profit per time period. Hence, to exploit the tradeoff between profit potential and mortality risk we choose to model expected performance as a linear combination of profit potential and mortality risk, where the larger the profit potential but the smaller the mortality risk, the larger the expected performance. Inspired by the economics literature, performance is a risk-adjusted dollar value where expected profit potential (a function of firm outcomes) is linearly adjusted based on the risk propensity of a risk-averse decision-maker and the possibility of costs arising from variability in outcomes. Such a model allows us to keep the mathematics tractable, and, we believe, make some contributions to our understanding of market entry decisions. Formally, the incumbent firm's objective is:

$$\text{Max}_t\{p_t - \varepsilon m_t\} = \text{Max}_t\{[P_0 - \rho t + f(r,s_t)] - \varepsilon[\gamma e^{-\eta t} - g(r,s_t)]\} \quad (7.1)$$

where ε is the ratio of marginal performance loss from mortality risk to marginal performance gain from profit potential, that is, a conversion factor that transfers each unit of risk into a dollar value and therefore considers the strength of the tradeoff between profitability and mortality risk in the overall performance function.[7]

Optimal Timing of Market Entry

Necessary and sufficient conditions for optimality are provided by the first and second order derivatives of the objective function in Equation 7.1 with respect to t. These mathematical conditions are established in Appendix 7.1. The optimal timing of entry occurs at t^*, as Figure 7.1a illustrates (an explicit form for t^* cannot be provided unless functional forms for f and g are specified; this is done later in a hypothetical example). Figure 7.1a displays two performance curves labeled A and B.

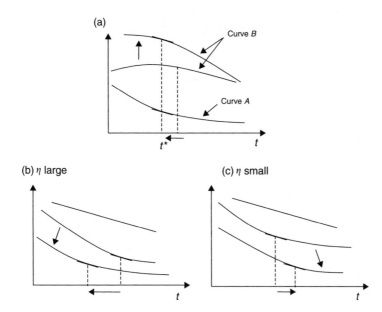

Figure 7.1   Performance curves A and B and some of their movements

Curve A represents the *reduction* in performance $(-\varepsilon\gamma e^{-\eta t}$, in Equation 7.1) over time that is due to the direct effect of time on mortality risk (i.e., the benefits to performance from reduced mortality risk decrease over time because of the decreasing slope of the mortality risk curve). Hence, the slope of curve A captures the marginal *gain* in performance that is due to the direct effect of time on mortality risk. Curve B (we offer two such curves for later usage) represents over time the sum of the performance due to the direct effect of time on profit potential, and the indirect effects of time (a decrease in the relative resource stock) on profit potential and mortality risk $([P_0 - \rho t] + f + g$, in Equation 7.1). The slope of curve B thus captures the sum of the marginal *loss* in performance due to the direct effect of time on profit potential, and the marginal *loss* in performance due to the indirect effects of time on profit potential and mortality risk. Curve A decreases over time at a decreasing rate while curve B decreases over time at an increasing rate.

The optimal time for the incumbent firm to enter the new market occurs when the slopes of A and B are equal (as expressed in the appendix by Equation A7.1). If the slope for A is larger than that for B, then the incumbent firm should delay entry; if the slope for A is less than that for B, then the incumbent firm should enter earlier. Moreover, changes in key model parameters move curves A and/or B, and as these curves change the optimal timing of entry is also likely to change (see Figure 7.1a). For instance, a comparative static analysis (e.g. Gravelle and Rees, 1992) suggests that the incumbent firm should enter sooner when there is an increase in the direct marginal loss of profit potential from delayed market entry (ρ) or greater resource value relative to pioneers (r), the latter prescription being consistent with Lambkin's (1988) finding that followers entering into a rapidly growing market typically had fewer related skills than pioneers.[8,9] Note that entry timing relates to the life cycle of the industry: "sooner" means earlier in the industry's life cycle; "later" means when the industry is more mature.

While these conclusions are self evident – higher valued resources relative to existing entrants and higher cost of waiting should encourage earlier entry – performing a comparative static analysis (or, equivalently, investigating the movements of curves A and B) on more puzzling parameters is not conclusive.[10] Therefore, in the next section we restrict our attention to specific forms for the dynamics of the firm's relative resource stock and for the portions of profit potential and mortality risk that depend on resource characteristics (the functions f and g).

A Hypothetical Example

Suppose that the incumbent firm's relative resource stock decreases over time at a constant rate and is given by $s_t = s_0 - \alpha t$. Also suppose that the portion of profit potential that depends on the resource characteristics (relative resource stock and resource value) is linear in its relative resource stock and is given by $f(r,s_t) = \beta_1(r) + \beta_2(r)s_t$. Similarly suppose that the portion of mortality risk that depends on resource characteristics is given by $g(r,s_t) = \theta_1(r) + \theta_2(r)s_t$. It is important to note that even when these relationships are not linear (e.g. the returns on an incumbent's profit potential from increases in the relative resource stock may decrease as at some point more and more resources provides limited benefits), these assumptions likely represent a good approximation in situations where these relationships are slightly curved. From solving Equation 7.1 we obtain an algebraic form for the optimal timing of market entry t^* (as given in the appendix by Equation A7.3) and derive the following propositions from taking the first order derivative of t^* with respect to each key parameter and deriving its sign (keeping all other parameters constant; proofs are offered in the appendix).

> *Proposition 1*:   The incumbent firm is encouraged to enter sooner when there is (a) a decrease in the ratio of marginal performance loss from mortality risk to marginal performance gain from profit potential (ε); (b) an increase in the rate at which the relative resource stock decreases over time (α); (c) an increase in the marginal gain in profit potential from an increased relative resource stock ($\beta_2(r)$); or (d) an increase in the marginal reduction in mortality risk from an increased relative resource stock ($\theta_2(r)$).

A decrease in the ratio of marginal performance loss from mortality risk to marginal performance gain from profit potential (Proposition 1a) has the effect of rotating both curves A and B counter-clockwise, and curve B is now linear because we chose linear forms for s_t, f, and g. These rotations decrease the steepness of the slope of A as well as that for B at any given time. For this hypothetical example, there has been a relative decrease in the costs of early entry (decreased mortality risk) that is less significant than the relative increase in the benefits of early entry (an increase in the increased profit potential), and therefore the change in the steepness of A is smaller than that for B. The slopes of A and B are equal earlier, and thus the incumbent firm should enter the market sooner.

Propositions 1b–1d are associated with the specific functional forms we chose for s_t, f and g and allow for both favorable and unfavorable changes to the external environment. Both types of changes, however, increase the steepness of the (constant) slope of B, which becomes equal with the slope of A earlier. Therefore the incumbent firm should enter the market sooner. In 1b, there is an unfavorable environment – an increase in the rate at which the incumbent firm loses its resource stock advantage. The incumbent firm must enter earlier. In 1c and 1d, there is a favorable environment – an increase in the marginal gain in profit potential (or the marginal reduction in mortality risk) from an increased relative resource stock. This favorable environment improves performance whether the incumbent firm decides to enter sooner or not. However, the relative resource stock is greater earlier, and earlier entry capitalizes on the increased benefits (or the reduced costs) arising from this advantage.

> *Proposition 2*:   The incumbent firm should enter sooner when there is an increase in the rate at which mortality risk declines over time (η) and that rate is larger than a critical value (as given by the right-hand side of Equation A7.6 in the appendix); but it should delay entry when there is an increase in the rate at which mortality risk declines over time and that rate is smaller than that critical value.

When there is an increase in the rate at which mortality risk declines over time should the incumbent firm enter earlier to capitalize on the reduced costs of this strategy or delay entry to benefit from the extra reduction in mortality risk? Interestingly, the answer appears to be both. The model suggests that the influence that this rate has on the incumbent firm's entry decision depends on the size of that rate relative to a critical value. This critical value represents the initial ($t = 0$) ratio of marginal lost to marginal gained performance from later entry. The lost performance is due to the direct effect of time on profit potential and the indirect effects of time (a decrease in the relative resource stock) on profit potential and mortality risk, and it equals the absolute value of the constant slope of curve B. The gained performance is due to the direct effect of time on mortality risk, and it equals the absolute value of the slope of curve A at $t = 0$.

When the rate at which mortality risk declines over time is relatively large, there is a pronounced curvature for curve A and no effect on curve B. We observe that an increase in this rate rotates curve A counter-clockwise. This decreases the steepness of the slope of A, which equals the slope of B earlier as shown in Figure 7.1b. Therefore the incumbent firm should enter the market earlier. In contrast, when the rate is relatively small, A will be relatively flat. Consequently even after an increase in the rate the slope of A still decreases relatively slowly, and as illustrated in Figure 7.1c the two slopes will become equal later, suggesting that the incumbent firm delay market entry.

That is, when the rate at which mortality risk declines over time is high (above the initial ratio of marginal loss to marginal gain in performance from later entry) and increasing, the environment is unfavorable to the incumbent firm and is deteriorating further as entry is delayed. Under these unfavorable conditions, performance lost (from the direct effect of time on profit potential and the indirect effects of time on profit potential and mortality risk) due to a delay in market entry increases so fast that the incumbent firm should enter earlier and gain greater profit potential at a lower mortality risk. When the rate is relatively small (below the initial ratio of marginal loss to marginal gain in performance from later entry), delaying entry yields only a minor reduction of mortality risk (from the direct effect of time) at the expense of forgone profit potential. However, under these conditions the lost performance from delaying market entry increases more slowly than the gained performance from decreased mortality risk, and hence, delaying entry becomes more attractive. This critical value is of primary importance in deciding on the optimal time to enter the new market.[11]

Numerical Analysis

We now offer a numerical example, not as an empirical test but to illustrate graphically some of our prescriptions. Consider a traditional grocery firm (e.g. Safeway, King Soopers, or Price Chopper) exploring the possibility of entering the "virtual" grocery market, which has recently been pioneered by a few independent start-ups (e.g. Peapod Inc. and NetGrocer Inc.). The incumbent grocery firm possesses a considerable stock of resources, including a chain of retail stores, quality sources of supply, and a high-technology inventory tracking and management system. While some of these resources are valuable to the "virtual" grocery market, others are less so. In comparison, the resources of the early entrants have greater value in the "virtual" grocery market (e.g. the independent pioneer Internet distribution system was specifically created to ship products efficiently from suppliers to customers in response to Internet orders). We will evaluate how long the incumbent grocery firm should delay entry into the "virtual" grocery market.

   We represent a time period as one month. Initial relative resource stock (at the time of the pioneer's entry) is $s_0 = 100$ units (the incumbent firm has twice the stock of resources possessed by the pioneer), and it decreases 5 units (5%) every month for which entry is delayed, i.e. $\alpha = 5$. Profit potential of the earliest entrants, P_0, is set to 4 (i.e., each unit represents $100 m$, and therefore the accumulated profit potential of the earliest entrant is set to $400 m$), whereas the direct marginal loss of profit potential due to delayed market entry, ρ, equals 0.4. The portion of profit potential that depends on the relative resource stock is represented by $f(r,s_t) = 0 + 0.002rs_t$, where the moderating effect of resource value on the relationship between the relative resource stock and profit potential is 0.002, and resource value is $r = 0.5$ (i.e., 50% of that for the pioneer[s]); hence the marginal profit potential from the relative resource stock is $0.002r = 0.001$. The scaling parameter for the direct effect of industry age on mortality risk is $\gamma = 1$, and the rate at which mortality risk decreases over time is $\eta = 0.1$. The portion of mortality risk that depends on the relative resource stock is given by $g(r,s_t) = 0.0005r + 0.0000996rs_t$; thus the marginal reduction in mortality risk from a greater resource stock advantage is $0.0000996r = 0.0000498$. These numerical values keep mortality risk between 0 and 1 on the planning horizon investigated. The ratio of marginal performance loss from mortality risk to marginal performance gain from profit potential is $\varepsilon = 5$.

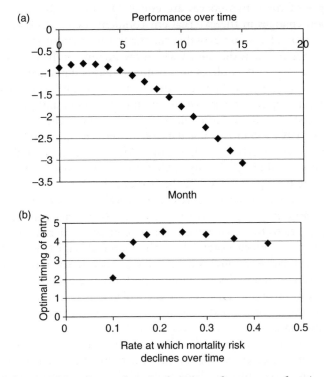

Figure 7.2 Performance function and optimal timing of entry as a function of the rate at which mortality risk declines over time (η) from the numerical analysis

Given these numerical values and over a period of 15 months, Figure 7.2a shows the performance function over time that must be maximized in Equation 7.1. The optimal timing of entry (Equation A7.3 in the appendix) corresponds to the month at which the slope of the performance function equals 0. Thus, the incumbent grocery firm is advised to delay entry into the "virtual" grocery market for two months ($t^* = 2.077$). Figure 7.2b demonstrates the optimal timing of entry (Equation A7.3) as a function of the declining rate of mortality risk due to time (η), and illustrates the implications presented in Proposition 2. In particular, when the rate is 0.1, as set in Figure 7.2a, the optimal timing of entry in Figure 7.2b also corresponds to 2 months. An increase in this rate encourages delayed entry as long as the rate does not exceed 0.207. When the rate exceeds 0.207, the optimal time to enter the "virtual" grocery market begins to decrease, although more slowly than it had increased at lower rates. The optimal entry time varies from approximately 2 to 4.5 months, with the rate varying from 0.100 to 0.430.

Discussion and Conclusion

We proposed an optimal time for an incumbent firm to enter a new market and illustrate the optimal strategy with reference to two curves: the optimal time to enter is when the slopes of these two curves are equal. Of course, the optimal strategy is dependent upon changes in the external environment – changes that may either be unfavorable or favorable. An unfavorable change to the environment that encourages earlier entry is an increase in the rate at which the incumbent firm's relative resource stock decreases (earlier entry utilizes an advantage that is diminishing more rapidly). Schoenecker and Cooper (1998) hypothesized that larger firms would be later entrants, but their empirical results (from the minicomputer and personal computer industries) suggest that these larger firms were actually earlier entrants. Similarly, Robinson et al. (1992) found (using data on manufacturing entrants) that greater parent corporation size discouraged late entry. While there are a number of potential explanations for these findings, we argue that it is not necessarily the size of the firm that influences the timing of entry, but the stock of the firm's resources (vis-à-vis the pioneer[s]), the rate at which the resource stock decreases over time (vis-à-vis the pioneer[s]), and the value of those resources to the market being entered.

Favorable changes to the environment that encourage earlier entry are an increase in the marginal gain in profit potential (or the marginal reduction in mortality risk) from an increased relative resource stock, and a decrease in the ratio of marginal performance loss from mortality risk to marginal performance gain from profit potential. For each of these favorable changes in the environment, performance improves whether the incumbent firm decides to enter sooner or not. However, when there is an increase in the marginal gain in profit potential (or the marginal reduction in mortality risk) from an increased relative resource stock, earlier entry capitalizes on this advantage when it is greater. As for the ratio, it represents a conversion factor that transfers each unit of risk into a dollar value and therefore considers the strength of the tradeoff between profitability and mortality risk in the overall performance function. When there is a decrease in this ratio, earlier entry capitalizes on reduced mortality risk and increased profit potential. The favorable changes in the environment should "pull" the incumbent firm into the market earlier.

We have focused on existing competitors within the targeted industry. An extension of the current model might include potential competitors. We argue that no changes to the model are required if those potential competitors are independent start-ups and/or incumbent firms with fewer resources. But if potential competitors are incumbent firms with more resources, then the strategist is at a potential relative resource stock disadvantage. Future research would extend our model to reflect the dynamic between the incumbent firm's relative resource stock (dis)advantage and industry age.

Notes

1. Schaffer (1989) argued that profit non-maximization may sometimes be associated with longer survival, and we assume that this tradeoff affects the decision of when to enter a new market. Such an assumption is consistent with Mitchell's (1991) finding of entry timing tradeoffs between market share and survival.
2. Resources and capabilities can also differ in the degree to which they are rare, costly to imitate, and non-substitutable. We focus on the resource value and hold constant the other qualities.

3. There are numerous examples of when an incumbent's stock of resources represents a lia-
    bility rather than an asset in entering a new market. For example, Henderson and Clark
    (1990) highlight those innovations that change the architecture of a product and, as a
    result, destroy the usefulness of the architectural knowledge of established firms.
    Tushman and Anderson (1986) also found that technological discontinuities can be com-
    petency destroying for the incumbent. For example, resources that are totally unrelated
    may represent a liability, tempting the firm to try to solve new problems with inappropri-
    ate methods (Nelson and Winter, 1982). Under these circumstances, the firm's stock of
    resources has no value (and possibly even negative value) for the market being considered
    for entry. Under such circumstances the optimal entry time is moot because the
    incumbent firm cannot catch up to the pioneers regardless of when it enters.
4. Resource advantage involves comparing the incumbent firm's resource stock with that of the
    pioneer(s). Measures of such an advantage could include the skills and experience of individ-
    ual employees, number and breadth of patents, cash and financial strength, and quality of the
    top management team as compared to those earlier entrants (adapted from Hitt et al., 1999).
5. Market surveys could determine whether customers perceive a firm's strategies as creating
    value for them. However, such market research is less effective for highly innovative prod-
    ucts because customers lack a frame of reference for evaluating such products (Slater,
    1993). Therefore assessing value *a priori* is a difficult task faced by strategists and
    resource-based scholars.
6. Profit potential is quite commonly operationalized in strategy research, whether by means
    of objective data from financial statements or by subjective assessments. Market research
    is well practiced in estimating profit potential (although with varying levels of success).
    Mortality has mostly been measured at the population level of analysis and in retrospect –
    the rate at which mortality occurred. This model requires an assessment of the costs of
    mortality risk in prospect for the individual firm. Such an assessment could use the mor-
    tality rate of firms within the industry to date to forecast future rates and/or use the
    mortality rate established in retrospect for a similar but more developed industry and
    then make an assessment of the costs of mitigating such risks.
7. ε can also be thought of as the risk propensity of a risk-averse incumbent, where the
    higher its value the more risk averse is the incumbent.
8. Both an increase in the marginal loss of profit potential (ρ) and greater resource value (r)
    have the effect of rotating curve B (in Figure 7.1a) clockwise. This increases the steepness
    of the slope of B, and the incumbent firm should enter the market earlier. Mathematically,
    we must have $dh_1(t^*,\rho) = h_{tt}(t^*,\rho)d\rho + h_{t\rho}(t^*,\rho)d\rho = 0$. This is equivalent to
    $dt^*/d\rho = 1/h_{tt}(t^*,\rho)$, which is negative for any t (and t^*). Similarly, we derive that

$$\frac{dt^*}{dr} = -\frac{ds_t}{dt}\left(\frac{\partial^2 f}{\partial r \partial s_t} + \varepsilon\frac{\partial^2 g}{\partial r \partial s_t}\right)/2h_{tt}(t^*,r) < 0$$

9. Moreover, the optimal entry timing of the incumbent firm is not affected by the initial
    environment, i.e. initial resource size advantage, s_0, and profit potential of earliest
    entrants, P_0, as these parameters are associated with a one-time gain or loss in perform-
    ance that is incurred independently of how long the incumbent firm delays entry into the
    new market.
10. E.g., a comparative static analysis on the ratio of marginal performance loss from mortality risk
    to marginal performance gain from profit potential (ε) and the rate at which mortality
    risk declines over time (η) is not conclusive, as the sign of the effect on timing of entry
    from a change in the corresponding parameter depends on a threshold condition on that
    parameter that cannot be established explicitly.

11. It may be more realistic to assume decreasing returns on performance from increased relative resource stock, i.e. f and g strictly concave in s_t. Hence, let f and g be increasing functions of the square root of s_t. Also, let the relative resource stock s_t be a generic function that decreases over time. Then, we can show that the results of Proposition 1c and 1d still hold. Proposition 1b will not be relevant since the rate α at which the relative resource stock decreases over time may vary. Proposition 1a may not hold, whereas Proposition 2 cannot be explicitly formulated as the existence of a critical value after which the relationship between market entry time and rate at which mortality decline over time shifts cannot be explicitly identified. A numerical analysis would be required in order to prescribe the missing relationships.

References

Aaker, D. and Day, G. 1986: The perils of high growth markets. *Strategic Management Journal*, 7, 409–421.

Abell, D. and Hammond, J. 1979: *Strategic Market Planning: Problems and Analytical Approaches*. Englewood Cliffs, NJ: Prentice Hall.

Archibald, T., Thomas, L., Betts, J., and Johnston, R. 2002: Should start-up companies be cautious? Inventory policies which maximize survival probabilities. *Management Science*, 48, 1161–1175.

Argote, L., Beckman, S., and Epple, D. 1990: The persistence and transfer of learning in industrial settings. *Management Science*, 36, 140–154.

Barney, J. 1991: Firm resources and sustained competitive advantage. *Journal of Management*, 17, 99–120.

Bowman, E. 1982: Risk seeking by troubled firms. *Sloan Management Review*, 23, 33–42.

Carpenter, G. and Nakamoto, K. 1989: Consumer preference formation and pioneering advantage. *Journal of Marketing Research*, 26, 285–298.

DiMaggio, P. and Powell, W. 1983: The iron cage revisited: Institutional isomorphism and collective rationality in organizational fields. *American Sociological Review*, 48, 147–160.

Feeser, H. and Willard, G. 1990: Founding strategy and performance: A comparison of high and low growth high tech firms. *Strategic Management Journal*, 11, 87–98.

Freeman, J., Carroll, G., and Hannan, M. 1983: The liabilities of newness: Age dependence in organizational death rates. *American Sociological Review*, 48, 692–710.

Ghemawat, P. 1991: Market incumbency and technological inertia. *Marketing Science*, 10, 161–171.

Golder, P. and Tellis, G. 1993: Pioneer advantage: Marketing logic or marketing legend. *Journal of Marketing Research*, 30, 158–170.

Gravelle, H. and Rees, R. 1992: *Micro economics* (2nd edn). London: Longman.

Hannan, M. and Freeman, J. 1984: Structural inertia and organizational change. *American Sociological Review*, 49, 149–164.

Haveman, H.A. 1993: Organizational size and change: Diversification in the savings and loan industry after deregulation. *Administrative Science Quarterly*, 38, 20–50.

Henderson, R. and Clark, K. 1990: The reconfiguration of existing product technologies and the failure of established firms. *Administrative Science Quarterly*, 35, 9–31.

Hitt, M., Ireland, R., and Hoskisson, R. 1999: *Strategic Management: Competitiveness and Globalization* (3rd edn). London: South-Western College Publications.

Huff, L. and Robinson, W. 1994: The impact of lead time and years of competitive rivalry on pioneer market share advantages. *Management Science*, 40, 1370–1377.

Ingram, P. and Baum, J. 1997: Chain affiliation and the failure of Manhattan hotels, 1898–1980. *Administrative Science Quarterly*, 42, 68–102.

Karakaya, F. and Kobu, B. 1994: New product development process: An investigation of success and failure in high technology firms. *Journal of Business Venturing*, 9, 49–66.

Lambkin, M. 1988: Order of entry and performance in new market. *Strategic Management Journal*, 9, 127–40.

Lippman, S. and Rumelt, R. 1982: Uncertain imitability: An analysis of interfirm differences in efficiency under competition. *Bell Journal of Economics*, 13, 418–438.

Mansfield, E., Schwartz, M., and Wagner, S. 1981: Imitation costs and patents: An empirical study. *The Economic Journal*, 91, 907–918.

Mitchell, W. 1989: Whether and when? Probability and timing of incumbents' entry into emerging technical subfields. *Administrative Science Quarterly*, 34, 208–230.

Mitchell, W. 1991: Dual clocks: Entry order influences and newcomer market share and survival when specialized assets retain their value. *Strategic Management Journal*, 12, 85–100.

Nelson, R. and Winter, S. 1982: *An Evolutionary Theory of Economic Change*. Cambridge, MA: Belknap Press.

Radner, R. and Shepp, L. 1996: Risk vs. profit potential: A model for corporate strategy. *Journal of Economic Dynamics and Control*, 20, 1373–1393.

Robinson, W. 1988: Sources of market pioneer advantages: The case of industrial goods industries. *Journal of Marketing Research*, 25, 87–94.

Robinson, W., Fornell, C., and Sullivan, M. 1992: Are market pioneers intrinsically stronger than later entrants? *Strategic Management Journal*, 13, 609–624.

Schaffer, M. 1989: Are profit-maximizers the best survivors? A Darwinian model of economic natural selection. *Journal of Economic Behavior and Organization*, 12, 29–45.

Schoemaker, P. and Amit, R. 1994: Investment in strategic assets: Industry and firm-level perspectives. *Advances in Strategic Management*, 10A, 3–33.

Schoenecker, T. and Cooper, A. 1998: The role of firm resources and organizational attributes in determining entry timing: A cross-industry study. *Strategic Management Journal*, 19, 1127–1143.

Schnaars, S. 1994: *Managing Imitation Strategies: How Later Entrants Seize Markets from Pioneers*. New York: Free Press.

Schumpeter, J. 1975: *Capitalism, Socialism and Democracy*. New York, NY: Harper and Row.

Slater, S.F. 1993: Competing in high velocity markets. *Industrial Marketing Management*, 24, 255–268.

Tushman, M. and Anderson, P. 1986: Technological discontinuities and organizational environments. *Administrative Science Quarterly*, 31, 439–466.

Venkataraman, S. and Van de Ven, A. 1998: Hostile environmental jolts, transaction set, and new business. *Journal of Business Venturing*, 13, 231–255.

Wernerfelt, B. and Karnani, A. 1987: Competitive strategy under uncertainty. *Strategic Management Journal*, 8, 187–194.

Williamson, O. 1975: *Markets and Hierarchies: Analysis and Antitrust Implications*. New York: Free Press.

Williamson, O. 1988: Corporate finance and corporate governance. *Journal of Financial Economics*, 43, 567–591.

Appendix 7.1: Mathematical Derivations

Optimal entry timing. The first order derivative of the objective function in Equation 7.1 with respect to t is equal to zero (a necessary condition) when

$$\varepsilon \eta \gamma e^{-\eta t} = \rho - \frac{ds_t}{dt}\left(\frac{\partial f}{\partial s_t} + \varepsilon \frac{\partial g}{\partial s_t}\right) \qquad (A7.1)$$

The second order derivative is

$$
\left(\frac{ds_t}{dt}\right)^2 \times \left(\frac{\partial^2 f}{\partial s_t^2} + \varepsilon\frac{\partial^2 g}{\partial s_t^2}\right) + \left(\frac{d^2 s_t}{dt^2}\right) \times \left(\frac{\partial f}{\partial s_t} + \varepsilon\frac{\partial g}{\partial s_t}\right) - \varepsilon\eta^2\gamma e^{-\eta t} \tag{A7.2}
$$

which is negative for any value of t, thus providing a sufficient condition for maximization. The optimal timing of entry occurs at t^* that solves Equation A7.1, and is illustrated in Figure 7.1.

Optimal entry timing for the hypothetical example. The first and second order derivate assumptions on the non-negative functions f and g now translate into

$$
\frac{d\beta_1}{dr} + s_t\frac{d\beta_2}{dr} > 0, \quad \beta_2(r) > 0, \quad \frac{d\beta_2}{dr} > 0, \quad \frac{d\theta_1}{dr} + s_t\frac{d\theta_2}{dr} > 0, \quad \theta_2(r) > 0 \quad \text{and} \quad \frac{d\theta_2}{dr} > 0
$$

From Equation A7.1,

$$
t^* = \frac{1}{\eta}\ln\left(\frac{\varepsilon\gamma\eta}{\varepsilon\alpha\theta_2(r) + \rho + \alpha\beta_2(r)}\right) \tag{A7.3}
$$

Proof of Proposition 1. For part (a) we have

$$
\frac{dt^*}{d\varepsilon} = \frac{\rho + \alpha\beta_2(r)}{\varepsilon\eta[\varepsilon\alpha\theta_2(r) + \rho + \alpha\beta_2(r)]} > 0 \tag{A7.4}
$$

For parts (b), (c) and (d), we easily verify that

$$
\frac{dt^*}{d\alpha} < 0, \quad \frac{dt^*}{d\beta_2} < 0, \quad \text{and} \quad \frac{dt^*}{d\theta_2} < 0
$$

Proof of Proposition 2. We investigate the entry strategy with respect to the rate at which mortality risk declines over time. We obtain

$$
\frac{dt^*}{d\eta} = \frac{1}{\eta}\left[\frac{1}{\eta} - t^*\right] = \frac{1}{\eta^2}\left[1 - \ln\left(\frac{\varepsilon\gamma\eta}{\varepsilon\alpha\theta_2(r) + \rho + \alpha\beta_2(r)}\right)\right] \tag{A7.5}
$$

which is negative if and only if (e is the base of the natural logarithm)

$$
\eta > \frac{\varepsilon\alpha\theta_2(r) + \rho + \alpha\beta_2(r)}{\varepsilon\gamma} \times e \tag{A7.6}
$$

Robust Capabilities? An Empirical Study of Incumbent–Entrant Product Development Capabilities after Radical Technological Change

Neil Jones

Introduction

The ability of firms to adapt to technological changes has been a topic of considerable debate since the time of Schumpeter. In environments of discontinuous and competence-destroying changes due to new product technologies, the value of existing capabilities of incumbent firms is partially erased and entry by firms new to the industry increases (Anderson and Tushman, 1990; Tushman and Anderson, 1986). In numerous industries, entrants have pioneered the new technologies and then dominated the industry at the expense of the formerly dominant incumbents (Henderson and Clark, 1990; Tushman and Anderson, 1986) as Utterback (1994) documents with some twenty apparent industry examples.

However, the reasons for the superior performance of entrants during and after such technological transitions remain a subject of debate. Sharply different theoretical assumptions concerning firm level differences in technological capabilities in technologies are prominent in the literature. In particular, the literature encompasses different assumptions about the sources of technological capabilities, how rapidly they may be changed, and how they are linked to overall firm performance. There are also apparent conflicts in the empirical results concerning relative incumbent and entrant capabilities.

For example, consider the research on the computer disk drive and typesetter industries which is examined in somewhat more detail later in the chapter. Analyzing a succession of new technology and market generations in the computer disk drive industry Christensen (1992) concludes that entrant firms outperformed incumbents primarily

because of their earlier introduction of technologies related to new drive sizes. He offers evidence that when incumbents did enter they were at least as technologically capable in the new technologies as entrants were. In contrast, in the typesetter industry, Tripsas (1997) offers evidence that new technologies created capability disadvantages for incumbents. Nevertheless, and unlike the disk drive industry, the product markets created by these new technologies were soon dominated by incumbents.

This chapter contributes to resolving the debate surrounding these issues by analyzing firms' responses to discontinuous technological change over time. More specifically, it focuses on incumbent product development capabilities relative to entrants, when new technological approaches undermine the relevance of incumbents' existing capabilities. Data from the Private Branch Exchange (PBX) industry, which underwent a discontinuous (radical) technological change from electromechanical to computer controlled products beginning in the early 1970s, are used to explore three related questions concerning incumbent-entrant capability differences and how they change over time: (1) Are incumbents initially less technologically capable than entrants after discontinuous technological change? (2) Over the longer term, should incumbents and entrants continue to differ in their relative capabilities following discontinuous technological change? (3) Are there differences among incumbents in their ability to adapt to discontinuous change? These questions motivate the literature review and hypothesis development section which follows immediately. Then the research methods are described. This section includes a characterization of the nature of technological changes in the PBX industry and the data employed. Following this, results are presented and then discussed in conclusion.

Literature Review and Hypothesis Development

Successful accommodation of technological changes requires strategic choices of when and how the new technology is to be introduced, as well as adequate capability in its application. However, theoretical explanations for the dominance of entrant firms following discontinuous technological change have tended to stress strategic choices as the root cause of incumbent failure. In particular, an extensive literature has argued that incumbents on average choose to introduce new technologies later than entrants. First mover advantages (Lieberman and Montgomery, 1988) gained by entrants then explain incumbent underperformance.

Three principal reasons for incumbents' choices of lagged entry have been proposed – cannibalization (Ghemawat, 1991; Reingenaum, 1989), biased choice (Christensen and Rosenbloom, 1995), and complementary assets (Teece, 1986). In the case of cannibalization, incumbents are understood to rationally choose later entry because entry timing is assumed to be a decreasing function of investment level in the new technology. That is, those who invest most, enter earliest. Since on average an incumbent's old products will have a decreased life when they are replaced by the new, they are assumed to invest less because the value to them of the new product is lower than it is to entrants who have no existing products.

The biased choice explanation proposes instead that incumbents tend to enter new technology markets late because existing customers for the old technology products tend not to be the early users of new technologies. The incumbent firm's existing customers, who prefer the old technology longer, therefore tend to create an impetus to maintain and improve the old technology for too long. Finally, Teece (1986) stresses that incumbents possess other assets, not tightly co-specialized to a given technology – such as those in sales and marketing – that can buffer them during times of technological transition. Therefore they may delay the introduction of new technologies because they wish to resolve uncertainty about their acceptance.

In arguing for the sufficiency of choices of timing differences resulting from a variety of sources to explain incumbent poor performance at points of technological transition, theoretical explanations in the literature have tended to minimize the potential for competitively significant capabilities differences in the new technologies to emerge at the firm level. Instead it has assumed that relevant technological capabilities may be assembled as quickly, effectively and efficiently by incumbent firms as by new entrants. A notable exception is Henderson and Clark (1990) who suggest a different reason than strategic decisions may lie at the root of incumbent poor performance. They suggest that discontinuous technological changes which alter the nature of the relationship between components in a technology are sufficient to render obsolete some of the organizational "capabilities" unconsciously utilized by incumbent firms in making technological choices. The argument suggests that incumbents misunderstand the implications of new technological capabilities and therefore make strategic choices to work on the wrong issues. In particular, they tend to apply their resources to solving technological problems in the existing architecture whose resolution is less valuable. Entrants then dominate incumbents despite incumbents' greater development spending (Henderson, 1993; Henderson and Clark, 1990).

Overall, in highlighting the potential impact of strategic choices, the theoretical literature has implicitly de-emphasized or explicitly discounted the potential for initially important capability differences among firms that might contribute to performance differences even among incumbents and entrants that had chosen *similar* strategies. This de-emphasis may be one reason why empirical work investigating capability differences even in the short term have been few and have so far produced ambiguous results using different measures. For example, as noted earlier Tripsas (1997) suggests that after a radical competence-destroying change in the typesetter industry, incumbents had lower capability. This conclusion is based upon the fact that incumbents' products, introduced later, were initially inferior to entrants'. However, Christensen (1992) shows that in the disk drive industry, while incumbents lagged in the introduction of new disk drive sizes when they entered, their technological capability, as measured by the level of key product attributes (capacity, overall size, and access time), was actually equal to or marginally *higher* than entrants.

While some work has raised, but not definitively answered, the question of initial incumbent–entrant capability differences after technological change, a second question of interest in settings of discontinuous competence-destroying change has not yet been addressed. Do incumbents and entrants differ in their relative capabilities in the new technologies over the longer term following discontinuous technological change? Studies of product development after competence-destroying technological change have focused on a relatively short five-year period after the disruption. While this five-year introductory phase may be competitively decisive in a number of industries (Christensen and Rosenbloom, 1995), in others many incumbents do survive if not flourish in the longer term. The relative capability of incumbent and entrant firms over such longer terms has not been adequately investigated. Moreover, while many incumbents differ along important dimensions, whether these give rise to significant capability differences among them has yet to be systematically assessed (Tripsas, 1997), giving rise to the third question for this research.

Hypotheses development

In addressing these three questions the chapter proposes that incumbent firms, who have adjusted to lower order technological changes in the past, possess "robust" capabilities whose value is preserved, in whole or in part even after radical technological change. There are at least two broad potential sources for such capabilities.

First, higher order or reliable knowledge (Constant, 1999) that is associated with the focal product market and system application undergoing change is likely to be preserved and to enable the development of competence in a new technology. For example, in the PBX industry, incumbent firms developed quite general high level theoretical knowledge concerning both components and systems that remained useful in system design, even after semiconductor components and new approaches such as time division were introduced. The development of information theory (Shannon, 1948) and systems engineering (Hughes, 1999) are two examples. They provided a basis for a formal methodology to use in understanding the implications of fundamental technological changes.

Second, incumbent firms also retain knowledge, experience, and know-how related to managing technology more broadly, for example in mobilizing and coordinating specialist knowledge to make complex system level tradeoffs that is largely complementary to any specific technology. Such management requires, for example, the location and hiring of appropriate specialists, mechanisms for planning, monitoring, and integrating component tasks. It also requires such organizational capabilities as being able to document and store earlier work to facilitate reuse or modification, such as software documentation, and the ability to increase process efficiency, for example through task specialization and refinement. Relevant coordination skills and experience typically extend beyond management of individual projects to management of multiple simultaneous projects that may leverage a common core. Overall, the relevance of some of these capabilities transcends the specific technologies that are employed at any one time. Moreover, they facilitate the ongoing introduction of (usually incremental) technological changes into existing processes that are of increasing importance as technologies mature.

In the short term, however, the performance-enhancing effects of "robust" capabilities based on these sources may be small compared with the negative impact of radical technological changes. By definition, radical technological changes introduce a greater change in techniques and skills in a shorter time than incumbent firms had been experiencing. As a result, radical changes are likely to demand more extensive modifications of organizational processes and procedures, i.e. their "routines."

Unless incumbent firms can set up entirely new organizations that eliminate ties to past organizational practices, they must separate those routines that are still relevant after the introduction of the new technology from those that are no longer relevant. In the short term, it is to be expected that many of an incumbent's routines associated with architectural and functional component knowledge will need to be modified or abandoned (Henderson and Clark, 1990), while others are still effective. Consequently, incumbents have the challenge of deciding which older practices to retain in addition to the challenge of building new component and architectural capabilities. Separating still appropriate from now inappropriate routines is likely to be error prone and time consuming, and some practices best dropped may be initially retained. Relative capabilities in the new technology are likely to be initially compromised by retention of such practices, since entrants, who need only to build relevant technological capabilities directly, do not have older routines to evaluate.

An initial disadvantage due to retaining no longer effective practices may be multiplied because of an additional complication facing incumbents. Capabilities which will be relevant to a radical technology as it matures may be less so during the technology's early stages. For example, initial development projects introducing radical technological changes are often small compared with mature technology projects, limiting or reversing the effectiveness of routines that presume the need to coordinate large numbers of specialists, such as those associated with extensive documentation and formal communications. Or, since early radical development projects are potentially successful as "one off" designs, completion may be slowed or otherwise hampered by reapplication of routines that plan and coordinate multiple related projects simultaneously. Therefore, the following baseline hypothesis is suggested.

Hypothesis 1: After a competence-destroying technological change, incumbents will initially exhibit lower capability in the new technology.

Over the long term however, robust capabilities can assert themselves and overcome an initial disadvantage relative to entrants. There are two main reasons. First, some incumbent capabilities may gain in value as the new technology matures. For example, some of the capabilities noted earlier, such as those associated with planning multiple products in a coordinated line, or those associated with integrating new people into coordinated development projects (which might confer a disadvantage initially if they were invoked), may provide an advantage later because competition in maturing technologies forces an emphasis on product development capacity, efficiency, and reliability. Since developing and integrating such capabilities is difficult and time consuming (Hannan and Freeman, 1989), retaining an existing and still appropriate routine is likely to be more efficient and effective than building a new one. Incumbents therefore gain an advantage over entrants who must build such capabilities from scratch, consuming time as well as resources.

The second reason to expect incumbents' robust capabilities to have an increased impact over time relates to incumbents' ability to modify their existing routines. Incumbents in general have more extensive experience in changing routines in response to both technological maturation and environmental changes. One aspect of modifying capabilities is simple elimination of some practices. Misapplication of pre-existing routines, a potentially major source of initial capability deficits, can be expected to decline over time as incumbents successfully identify and eliminate or change inappropriate routines. Such identification is increasingly likely as incumbents develop experience with the new technology, as they observe the products and practices of others, and as they gain more customer feedback.

In addition, over the longer term after radical technological changes, incumbents can call on two bases of experience that may enhance the facility with which new capabilities can be changed "dynamically." First, they will in general have introduced changes in routines before the technological discontinuity. Second, during the initial introductory period, they are forced to acquire still more recent and highly relevant experience in introducing changes to routines in their technological core. Such experience provides the basis for finding ad hoc practices for making improvements as well as more specific articulated and codified practices that systematize the accomplishment of changes in routine (Zollo and Winter, 2002). For example, Henderson and Cockburn (1994) argue that explicit science-based search for new drugs by some firms in the pharmaceuticals industry constituted a useful systematic knowledge base through which superior capabilities could be dynamically enhanced and maintained.

In contrast with incumbents, smaller or newly formed entrant firms may have few established reliable practices at the organizational level, and will have had little experience in modifying them. Yet, the number and variety of entrant routines that must be created and integrated typically grows rapidly during an entrant's early history – in response to increased product development opportunities and pressures (from customers and competitors). Increasing the reliability and efficiency of routines may thus be difficult and time-consuming for new firms (Hannan and Freeman, 1989), and there are internally (Henderson and Clark, 1990) and externally (Christensen and Rosenbloom, 1995) based tendencies for entrants to focus on refining existing capabilities rather than adding new ones. These factors create the potential for recent entrants to display greater inertia than more experienced firms during subsequent technological change which is incremental, but still rapid and competitively significant.

Therefore, since over time incumbents are expected to experience growth in the value of some of their robust capabilities, to have eliminated their initially ineffective routines and to have superior capabilities to change routines in response to changing conditions, the following hypothesis can be stated.

> *Hypothesis 2*:   After a competence-destroying technological change, incumbents will improve faster than entrants, and display greater product development performance over the longer term.

However, not all incumbent firms may adjust to a technological discontinuity equally well. In particular, three major factors are likely to influence the level of observed capability improvement exhibited by incumbents. First, incumbent firms differ in the ease with which under-performing routines can be identified. Larger firms are likely to face greater challenges. All else being equal, larger firms are more complex and must combine inputs from greater numbers of people within the organization. Therefore, they may require greater numbers of organizational routines or more complex ones. Consequently, organizational searches to identify and separate effective and non-effective routines may require greater effort and or last longer.

Secondly, a number of studies have suggested that the ability of firms to effect organizational changes is enhanced if performance threatens firm survival (Levinthal, 1992). Therefore, larger firms that can in general withstand financial losses more readily may be less effective in responding to the need for the development of new capabilities.

Thirdly, organizational routines are expected to become more ingrained and more difficult to identify as a firm ages. A number of studies suggest such firms are likely to exhibit lower levels of development productivity (Baron et al., 2001; Henderson, 1993).

In summary, it is expected that larger and older incumbent firms will have the largest initial capability deficits compared with entrants because they initially have to search through greater numbers of routines and are likely to have a greater number of routines that must be modified and re-integrated. These firms are also likely to experience fewer performance concerns and have more ingrained routines. Consequently, it is expected that these firms have the least effective robust capabilities. Indeed, these arguments suggest that robust capabilities may vary over a firm's life cycle; they may exhibit an inverted U-shaped relationship with size (Scherer, 1992). Using the above arguments the following two hypotheses can be provided:

> *Hypothesis 3a*: After a competence-destroying technological change, larger and older incumbents will initially exhibit the lowest capability in the new technology.

> *Hypothesis 3b*: After a competence-destroying technological change, larger and older incumbents will display less apparent capability improvement relative to entrants.

Research Method

I follow the example of several earlier studies in product development (see e.g. Clark et al., 1987; Iansiti, 1995), by measuring capabilities as the development resources required for equivalent development projects as the dependent variable or performance metric. This approach limits feasible data collection to a single industry because of the detailed historical market, firm, and technological information required. The PBX industry provides an appropriate setting since it underwent a radical competence-destroying technological change a sufficient number of years before the collection of data so that longer-term effects could be studied. The PBX industry has the additional advantage of allowing an unusually rich contrast between incumbents and entrants and among incumbents.

To understand industry technology changes and to gather more specific information on product development, approximately 120 interviews with industry participants, consultants and observers were conducted between 1993 and 1996. The study also used three leading industry reports as primary sources of archival information: Northern Business Information, the Marketing Programs and Systems Group

(MPSG) reports, and DataPro. Where necessary to corroborate information or resolve conflicts, a wide variety of other public sources such as trade journals were used.

Technological change in the PBX industry

PBXs are small telephone switches, usually privately owned. Beginning in 1972, semiconductor components were introduced in PBX products to replace older electromechanical components. The changes in PBX technology that resulted were competence destroying by virtually any standard and comparable to the replacement of electromechanical parts in cash registers and adding machines by modern semiconductor computer components. For example, as the logical processes for controlling calls were shifted from hardwired logic instantiated in electromechanical parts to software logic that ran on semiconductor-based microprocessors, the value of skills in electromechanical system and component design, fabrication, sourcing, assembly, testing, and maintenance were all deeply eroded, if not eliminated.

The technological changes in systems facilitated rapid entry by competing firms. Some 56 firms entered in total, 36 of whom were relatively small or de novo entrants with no experience in the industry. The PBX market grew rapidly in terms of both sales and the number of physical lines sold. By 1978 physical line sales had doubled over 1972 levels and by 1984 they had doubled again. By 1980 sales of the older electromechanical technology had virtually been eliminated.

However, there were rapid and ongoing incremental changes to PBX technology over the succeeding years that required continuous development of capabilities. Most fundamentally, new designs incorporated semiconductor components for which price performance was superior and growing very rapidly. The rising price-performance of microprocessors supplied by emerging specialist firms such as Intel and Motorola facilitated two important types of change. One was towards an expansion in functionality and features. The other was towards extension of the semiconductor designs into new line size segments. Through design architectures that coordinated across segments, many firms created product lines that shared a variety of physical components, software modules and user interfaces across market segments.

These two changes combined to create a third – the development of new system architectures that were much more complex and required large development teams. Initially, some systems had been designed within a year, employing in the case of some entrant firms only tens of man-years. By the early 1980s, even exceptionally lean development projects required hundreds of man-years, with many firms devoting several thousand man-years to development efforts. Large development efforts employed diverse and evolving technological skills such as software development management and system debugging.

A variety of firm types introduced the new products. Some, such as American Telephone & Telegraph (AT&T) and GTE, had long been incumbents in the US electromechanical PBX market. Others, such as Northern Telecom, NEC, and Ericsson, had experience developing and managing electromechanical equipment in their home markets, and had only recently entered the US market for electromechanical equipment, when the new semiconductor products were introduced. Still other firms were small new entrants who developed new semiconductor statistical process controlled (SPC) products. These firms included ROLM, Mitel and many others.

Sample

To identify candidate projects, interviews were initially conducted with industry consultants and with contacts at some of the incumbent firms. These contacts were used to identify an initial pool of product design engineers who had worked on some key projects. Press reports were also consulted and specific lead designers were traced in some instances through professional association contacts and trade journals. Each contact was asked for leads; further contacts evolved from these initial interviews until the full sample was obtained. Although product development samples were obtained partially opportunistically through suggestions from initial contacts, this does not introduce an evident sample bias. Projects came from multiple companies with no obvious relations among them. For example, even where a contact was identified because a designer had left one company and moved to another, interviews suggested that the projects were of different generations, employed substantially different architectures, and often were addressed to different market segments – limiting the potential for direct transfer of an organizational capability. One possible exception was the case of Intecom's initial development project. Intecom was successfully sued by Northern Telecom for using certain of Northern Telecom's technologies in the product.

Data

The overall sample includes data from 43 separate development projects. Projects in the sample range in introduction date from 1974 to 1991. The ultimate sample size reflected the practical limits for which reliable data could be obtained. For example, the level of technological maturity reached by the early 1990s meant few new platform projects were attempted. Furthermore, confidentiality concerns prevented additional data from being gathered.

The 43 development projects introduced products that attained roughly a 50 percent share of industry line sales over the sample period. They represent roughly 43 percent of the total development projects over the sample period. To mitigate potential bias, the sample was deliberately distributed along a number of dimensions that previous research suggested might influence results. The sample includes both incumbents and entrants, with 21 projects by entrants and 22 projects by incumbents. The sample consists of both first and subsequent projects for incumbents and entrants. Relatively successful and unsuccessful projects are also incorporated (as measured by total sales in proportion to development costs) from both successful (surviving) and less successful (exiting) firms. Projects also vary among market segments and include line sizes from small (under 200 lines) to very large (over 20,000 lines) and comprise products intended for niche markets in addition to those intended for sale in major market segments. Unavailability of control data for some projects reduced the useable sample to 39 projects.

Interviews for product development data typically lasted 1–2 hours and were, in most cases, conducted with the project leader. In a few cases, higher level management responsible for funding and oversight of the project supplied the estimates. First, the background context was obtained including the interviewee's professional experience, his role in the project, the project objectives, and the company's competitive situation at the time of the project. Then the scope of the design project was explored to determine which basic decisions about the project had substantial impact on the resources needed. This information was used to create the required control variables. The start time for the project and the date at which the initial design was completed were then established. Where possible, interviewees also provided dates of key milestones for staffing changes and the staffing levels during each time interval. Interviewees often retained key documents containing budgets and staffing levels. Detailed notes were taken for each interview.

The start of a product development project occurred when the decision was taken to begin detail specifications for a new product. Where there had been "forward looking" development research without a specific commercial product planned, the beginning was taken as the time when a formal proposal for a commercial product began. The end of the development project was the end of the "beta" test phase, i.e. after a full operational trial and system debug was completed and unrestricted commercial sale had begun.

The resources devoted to a project included all full and part time labor. Labor comprised all full and part time component, system, and software design people as well as draftspersons and other support function personnel. Resource estimates also included system test and debug, any manufacturing and marketing devoted to the project, field testers and documentation development. Respondents were asked to estimate full time equivalent (FTE) resources as the effective number of people devoted full-time to the project. Although all project leaders reported that teams often worked longer than 40-hour weeks, it was difficult to get good estimates of average hours worked. Hence, a bias could be introduced if some groups worked consistently different hours than others.

The decision to omit resources and time associated with "forward looking" work may mean incumbent resources and time are somewhat understated compared with entrants. However, the choice appears justified since, as many entrants hired personnel from incumbent firms, some of the benefits of forward looking research may have been captured "free" by entrants. Furthermore, much forward looking work had applications to many products, and a method for allocating costs or benefits to particular PBX systems was not evident. And, the most basic of forward-looking research was often the subject of conference presentations or publications in journals and hence publicly available, albeit with some restriction and time delay.

Wherever possible, independent estimates from two sources were obtained for each project. For the twelve projects where two estimates were available, the correlation was 0.995. To test if this level of agreement was disproportionately influenced by the high level of agreement between the two largest projects, these projects were eliminated, leaving ten points. The correlation was then 0.929. The average of the estimates was used when multiple estimates were available.

Explanatory Variables

Variables and their definitions are shown in Table 8.1. The dependent variable for the study is the natural logarithm of the development man-years employed on the development project. When project differences in scope and project design objectives are

Table 8.1   Basic measures and definitions

Variable	Measure	Definition
Product development performance	LnDManYr	Natural logarithm of the number of man years employed in the product development project.
Project design objectives	LnLines	Natural logarithm of the maximum number of lines a product could be used to switch.
	TotlFeat	Count of total software features available for the product at introduction
Project scope	Phones	Count of total software features available for the product at introduction
	IntSyst	Dummy variable equal to 1 if a development project included standards for international markets (in addition to US standards) and 0 otherwise.
	Chips	Dummy variable equal to 1 if a development project included custom chip design and 0 otherwise.
	DistProc	Dummy variable equal to 1 if a development project used a distributed architecture and 0 otherwise.
Relative incumbent capability	Incumb	Dummy variable equal to 1 if a firm had prior experience in electromechanical PBX technology and 0 otherwise.
	USTelco	Dummy variable equal to 1 if a firm had electromechanical designs for sale in the US before 1969 and 0 otherwise.
	TelcoInc	Dummy variable equal to 1 if a firm had electromechanical designs for sale in the US before 1972 and 0 otherwise.
	IEntYr	Variable equal to the number of years an entrant's product is introduced after its first product or zero for the first product
	IYrAftNt	Variable equal to the number of years an incumbent's product is introduced after its first product or zero for the first product
	USTelYrs	Variable equal to the number of years a USTelco's product is introduced after its first product or zero for the first product
	TIncYrs	Variable equal to the number of years a TelcoInc's product is introduced after its first product or zero for the first product
Other controls	LnDevTime	Natural logarithm of the product development time in years
	ATT	Dummy variable equal to 1 if a product was developed by AT&T and 0 otherwise.
	DLnSucc	Natural logarithm of the ratio of sales (in dollars) to development man years for the product

controlled, this measure reflects a key presumptive dimension of development capability – the resources required to develop comparable systems. The natural log was employed to make the data more closely approximate a normal distribution.

Relative capability variables

In order to test Hypotheses 1 and 2, an incumbent dummy (*Incumb*) is introduced to distinguish incumbents from entrants in the sample. Furthermore, two variables are constructed that contrast development capability over time. The variable *IYrAftNt* represents the interaction of the incumbent dummy and the elapsed time in years from the incumbent's entry to the new technology (initial product) to the completion of the focal development project. The variable *IEntYr* is the corresponding quantity for entrant development projects. Together, these three variables allow estimates of average initial differences between incumbents and entrants and direct interpretation of how incumbent and entrant projects change over time from their initial average levels.

Testing of Hypothesis 3 requires the introduction of a distinction among incumbents. *USTelco* is a dummy variable indicating incumbents with long participation in the US market. Together, the five *USTelco* firms held a market share that exceeded 85 percent of the US market for electromechanical systems in the late 1960s. Other telephone companies (*TelcoInc*) had entered the US market for electromechanical PBXs after the late 1960s but before the first introduction of a stored program control semiconductor switch in 1972. These firms had extensive electromechanical experience in their home markets, but relatively low US sales. Analogously with the variables introduced to test Hypotheses 1 and 2, the variables *USTelYrs* and *TIncYrs* represent the interaction of the elapsed time between the initial and focal development projects of a firm and the *USTelco* or *TelcoInc* dummy respectively

Control variables

Control variables were selected based on the interviews with product designers. I discuss these variables under two major headings: project design objectives and project scope.

Project design objectives.   Choices of design objectives were a major driver of design effort. One major dimension of choice was the intended market segment for the new product. Market segmentation was primarily by system size, with larger sites requiring a greater variety of features and a higher quality level than smaller ones. Larger systems, therefore, had much greater real-time processing demands (requiring complex multi-processor designs) and were much more complex to design. To illustrate, one aspect of higher quality was higher required reliability for large systems (necessitating the development of a "hot standby" redundant processor control), while another was richer feature content. The variable *LnLines* was introduced to control for this effect. *LnLines* was defined as the natural logarithm of the maximum design capacity of the system in lines.[1]

Within a given line size segment, customers also varied in the richness of the feature content needed. The major driver of this increase was an expanded software feature set. The variable *TotlFeat* controlled for this effect.

Project scope. Some projects included the design of customized or semi-customized hardware components, developed in-house, rather than purchased from standard commercial semiconductor suppliers. This activity was more common early in the second generation, when for example, Northern Telecom designed and developed its own chips to encode and decode Pulse Code Modulation (PCM) signals. Mitel, during this time developed its own gallium arsenide chip to implement its space division designs. In another example, the well-funded start-up CXC undertook many custom chip designs as part of its system development during the early 1980s. A dummy variable *Chips* was introduced to control for the effect of choosing to design chips in-house as part of a system design project.

Another important source of scope variation across projects was whether the project included design of a new telephone instrument or not. Some projects, often those introducing large numbers of new system features, included such design costs. Design of telephone instruments is a complex subtask. Their development increased complexity – originating chiefly from the needs to cheaply add functionality and to achieve ease of use for many complex features. Instrument design projects often involved multiple phone models, further increasing complexity. The dummy variable *Phones* distinguishes projects that included instrument design from other projects.

Discussions with project managers revealed an additional dimension that affected the resources and time required to complete design projects. Some systems were designed to meet international standards from their initial conception. In early designs, this dimension, for example, required substantial extra design work on the line cards to meet various international network interface standards. The variable *IntSyst* was a dummy variable introduced to control for such projects. In addition, designs that employed distributed architectures in which each processor makes independent decisions based upon common information were judged by designers to be the most complex to design and debug. Accordingly, the variable *DistProc* was introduced to control for these architectural choices.

Results

Table 8.2 presents descriptive statistics and correlations of the variables. As can be calculated, the average project in the sample took some 114 man-years and 3.3 years to complete. An average project had about 900 lines and 127 features. A relatively small proportion of projects employed technologically challenging distributed processing architectures and less than half of the projects involved new phone or specialized chip designs or required full international specifications. The average project in the sample was introduced 3.3 years after the firm's initial entry. The implications of a few highly correlated variables are discussed below in the context of specific regression results.

Ordinary least squares with the cluster option in STATA was conducted to test the hypotheses with the dependent variable, product development capability, measured as the product development effort. The results are presented in Table 8.3. Because the sample includes more then one development project from some firms, the cluster option in STATA was used to compensate for potential within cluster (i.e. company) error correlation.

Table 8.2 Descriptive statistics

	Obs	Mean	Std. Dev.	1	2	3	4	5	6	7	8	9	10	11	12	13	14	15	16	17
1 LnDManYr	43	4.74	1.44	1																
2 LnLines	43	6.82	1.23	0.51	1															
3 TotlFeat	39	1.27	67.9	0.54	0.42	1														
4 Phones	43	0.37	0.49	0.65	0.34	0.43	1													
5 IntSyst	43	0.35	0.48	0.31	0.12	-0.07	0.14	1												
6 Chips	43	0.26	0.44	0.34	0.12	-0.09	0.21	0.24	1											
7 DistProc	43	0.14	0.35	0.51	0.34	0.29	0.38	-0.15	0.23	1										
8 Incumb	43	0.51	0.51	0.25	0.16	-0.03	-0.02	0.42	0.15	0.12	1									
9 USTelco	43	0.26	0.44	0.12	0.10	-0.13	-0.12	-0.21	0.27	0.23	0.59	1								
10 TelcoInc	43	0.23	0.43	0.20	0.05	0.12	0.15	0.64	-0.07	-0.06	0.54	-0.32	1							
11 IentYr	43	1.14	2.49	0.11	0.01	0.18	0.03	-0.12	-0.01	-0.16	-0.47	-0.27	-0.25	1						
12 1yrAftNt	43	2.12	3.39	0.12	0.10	0.39	0.03	0.28	-0.13	0.11	0.62	0.20	0.47	-0.29	1					
13 1yrAftUS	43	0.84	2.28	0.20	0.07	0.22	0.08	-0.16	-0.01	0.39	0.36	0.63	-0.20	-0.17	0.53	1				
14 1yrAftTl	43	1.16	2.86	0.00	0.04	0.31	0.01	0.41	-0.13	-0.17	0.40	-0.24	0.75	-0.19	0.73	-0.15	1			
15 LNDevTim	43	1.19	0.64	0.63	0.22	0.39	0.53	0.29	0.28	0.12	0.15	-0.07	0.27	0.09	0.05	-0.02	0.09	1		
16 ATT	43	0.09	0.29	0.27	0.05	0.04	0.08	-0.23	0.36	0.56	0.31	0.55	-0.18	-0.15	0.23	0.52	-0.13	-0.02	1	
17 DlnSucc1	38	-0.39	2.01	-0.59	-0.47	-0.34	-0.54	-0.13	-0.03	-0.41	0.16	0.27	-0.06	-0.11	0.21	0.19	0.12	-0.47	0.23	1

Table 8.3 Ordinary least squares regression results (dependent variable: Product development performance)

Measure	1	2	3	4
LnLines	0.491***	0.357***	0.199**	0.225**
	(0.16)	(0.11)	(0.09)	(0.1)
TotlFeat	0.008**	0.013***	0.008**	0.009**
	(0.003)	(0.003)	(0.003)	(0.003)
Phones			0.968***	0.863***
			(0.29)	(0.29)
IntSyst			0.704***	0.867***
			(0.24)	(0.26)
Chips			0.344	0.338
			(0.23)	(0.23)
DistProc			1.149***	0.919**
			(0.34)	(0.33)
LnDevTime				
ATT				
DlnSucc				
Incumb		1.752***	1.228***	
		(0.38)	(0.28)	
1yrAftNt		−0.218*	−0.131**	
		(0.11)	(0.06)	
IEntYr		0.091	0.127**	0.116**
		(0.07)	(0.05)	(0.05)
USTelco				1.173***
				(0.29)
TelcoInc				1.245***
				(0.37)
USTelYrs				−0.069
				(0.05)
TIncYrs				−0.21***
				(0.07)
Constant	0.281	0.01	0.93	0.708
	(1.1)	(0.72)	(0.58)	(0.62)
N	39	39	39	39
R squared	0.416	0.5885	0.8475	0.8678

$* \ p < 0.1, ** \ p < 0.05, *** \ p < 0.001.$

Regression 1 provides a baseline model, controlling for major differences in project objectives largely associated with different market segments. Differences among projects are significant and of the expected sign. Larger systems and systems with greater numbers of features took greater efforts to develop.

Regression 2 introduces the explanatory variables to test Hypotheses 1 and 2. That is, it tests whether initial differences in product development capabilities exist and whether changes occur in relative development capability over time between incumbents and entrants. The model provides support for Hypothesis 1, which predicted that following a radical technological change, incumbents would initially exhibit inferior development capability. The *Incumb* dummy variable, representing an estimate of the manpower required for the initial projects of incumbents (i.e. when $t = 0 = IYrAftNt = IEntYr$), is positive and significant, indicating that incumbents initially required significantly greater development efforts (i.e. had lower development capability) than entrants while controlling for project design objectives.

Regression 2 also supports Hypothesis 2, which proposed that incumbents would improve capability more rapidly than entrants. The coefficient of *IYrAftNt* is negative and significant, while the sign of the variables *IEntYr* is positive (though not significant). Statistical tests of the differences in these coefficients are significant[2] and therefore support the conclusion that incumbents increase capability more rapidly than entrants over time after the introduction of a radical technological change.

Regression 3 explores whether the differences observed in Regression 2 can be explained by differences in the scope of the development projects undertaken by incumbents and entrants by adding controls for the scope of the development effort undertaken. If the observed differences in incumbent and entrant capability could be accounted for by choices in development scope, there are implications for the source of the observed capability differences. Specifically, this finding might suggest that capability differences in project execution may be ruled out and that the source of capability differences could be due to aspects related to choosing what to do rather than issues related to project execution. Choices related to the scope of product development add appreciable explanatory power. The control variables are each of the expected sign – i.e. development of systems that met a variety of international standards (*IntSyst*), or that encompassed custom designed phones (*Phones*) or semiconductor chips (*Chips*) increased required development resources, as does the adoption of distributed architectures in design (*DistProc*).

The effect of the additional controls for project scope variables is to lower the estimate of initial incumbent differences, indicating that differences in scope choice are responsible for part, but not all of the incumbent – entrant differences. Furthermore, even after controlling for scope differences, the coefficient for the *IEntYr* variable remains positive and is, compared to Model 2, significant. Overall, these results suggest that while initial difference between incumbents and entrants is partly due to development project scope, most is due to more deep-seated factors – those associated with the capacity to complete equivalent development projects with fewer resources.

Although the incumbent dummy is relatively highly correlated with the variables that record the elapsed time from the entry of each incumbent and entrants (0.62 and –0.47 respectively), further testing shows the robustness of the coefficient estimates. Indeed, splitting the sample into incumbent and entrant sub-samples and dropping the incumbent dummies – thus removing the multicollinearity in question – yields similar estimates of incumbent–entrant differences for both Regressions 2 and 3. While caution is perhaps still appropriate in interpretation, the coefficient estimates shown in Regression 3 suggest that within 5 years of developing the first product in the new technology, an average incumbent firm would have superior capability to an entrant with equivalent experience, despite being initially less capable. Or, seen differently, within 5 years incumbents on average appear to have *superior* development capability.

To test whether incumbents were merely converging to an industry standard level of capability, i.e. whether all firms in the sample were becoming more similar in development performance, perhaps through diffusion of best practices, the entire sample was tested for heteroskedasticity. The results provide no support that variance in the overall sample is decreasing.[3] In turn, this finding implies that diffusion processes did not cause convergence to a narrow range of "best practice" product development capabilities across all firms during the time period within the sample. Instead, perhaps because of the need to continue to add and modify capabilities dynamically, variance in product development capabilities among firms remained near the initial levels. This finding is consistent with other studies of product development in which significant differences among firms in product development capability are found even in relatively mature industries, such as in the automobile and mainframe computer industries (Clark et al., 1987; Iansiti, 1995).

Regression 4 tests Hypotheses 3a and 3b by examining whether there are product development capability differences among incumbents. For Regression 4, the incumbent variable is decomposed into two types of firms with electromechanical experience – firms with long tenure in the US market and with appreciable market shares (*USTelco*) and firms that had entered the US market a short time before the technological transition (*TelcoInc*). Further, it decomposes the *IYrAftNt*, the variable indexing changes in an incumbent's capability relative to entrants during the time after the introduction of the new technology, into two components. The component *USTelYrs* represents elapsed time between the introduction of the new technology and subsequent projects for *USTelco* firms while the component *TIncYrs* tracks the elapsed time for *TelcoInc* firms.

Regression 4 indicates that *TelcoIncs*, who had been in the US market for the shortest period and had lower market shares, developed capabilities significantly more rapidly than entrants. In contrast, *USTelcos*, that were initially larger and longer tenured in the US market, did not exhibit statistically significant superior capability over time relative to entrants, within the sample period. These results support Hypothesis 3b. Indeed, within 4 rather than 5 years, the average *TelcoInc* incumbents appear on average to have *superior* product development capabilities than the entrants. However, Regression 4 provides little support for Hypothesis 3a, since coefficient estimates for *TelcoIncs* are virtually identical to those for *USTelcos*.

As with Regression 3, the incumbent dummy variables are highly correlated with each other (0.63 for *USTelco* and *USTelYrs* and 0.75 for *TelcoInc* and *TIncYrs*), potentially inflating the estimated variance of the coefficients. This finding may be why the coefficient estimate for *USTelYrs* is not significant, although of the expected sign. Still, substituting the *Incumb* variable for *USTelco* and *TelcoInc*, which decreases the correlation among the independent variables, yields results essentially identical to Regression 4.

The total explanatory power of the results is comparable to those in other studies on product development capability (see, for example, Clark et al., 1987; Iansiti, 1995). More significantly, the results support Hypotheses 1, 2, and 3b. The weak support found for Hypothesis 3a is puzzling; it may be that the initial period of adjustment is so difficult for both types of incumbents that differences are negligible at that stage or that a larger customer base provides larger and more established incumbents with greater short-term adjustment pressures.

Tests of alternative explanations

Regressions 5–7 in Table 8.4 explore alternative explanations for these results. One possibility is that incumbents appear to have lower capability only because they chose to use shortened time-compressed development projects in an attempt to minimize any disadvantage associated with late entry. To test whether accelerated development programs might be responsible for the differences, Regression 5 controls for development time. The results suggest that the incumbent disadvantage is not due to accelerated development strategies. In fact, shorter development times are associated with lower product development resources, not higher, as increased spending to accelerate development would predict. Indeed, this finding is consistent with other studies which suggest that firms more capable in product development have both shorter development times *and* lower overall development expenditures (Clark et al., 1987; Iansiti, 1995). Here, longer development times appear to reflect lower development capability rather than a strategic choice. Consequently, this variable is omitted from subsequent regressions.

Regression 6 tests for a possible firm specific effect of AT&T, the single largest and dominant incumbent in the sample. Control for AT&T increases the estimate of the rate at which incumbents adjust relative to entrants. However, it provides no evidence that the basic results are biased by an AT&T specific effect. The variable was therefore dropped from subsequent regressions.

To test whether other important, but uncontrolled quality variables might be driving the results, Regression 7 controls for ultimate project performance. The variable *DlnSucc* is defined as the natural logarithm of the estimated dollar sales of a product divided by the number of development man-years employed. Although the coefficient estimate for the variable *IYrAftNt* dips just below significance, the test for a difference between it and *IEntYr* remains highly significant. The results indicate that differences between incumbents and entrants in product development capability are not due to uncontrolled differences in product price-performance as reflected in the ultimate financial performance achieved. This variable was therefore dropped from subsequent regressions.

A final possible counter-explanation for these results concerns a selection bias in the later years of the sample. Such a bias might arise if incumbent firms were eliminated from the industry more rapidly than entrant firms, leaving a higher performing subsample of incumbents in place to be compared with a less intensely selected subset of entrant firms. However, this potential bias does not appear to be the case here. First, statistical tests show that entrants do not survive longer than incumbents in this industry. Second, incumbent firms that subsequently left the industry are included in the latter part of the sample period.

Overall, the results indicate that controlled for strategy choices at the level of product development – in project objectives and project scope – incumbents exhibited lower initial development capability than entrants over the time period of study. However, also as hypothesized, incumbents exhibited superior rates of relative capability improvement. Not all incumbents performed equally well relative to entrants. Incumbents that were initially smaller and had less experience in the US market were most rapid in their adjustment to entrant product development capability levels.

Table 8.4 Alternative explanations (dependent variable: Product development performance)

Measure	5	6	7
LnLines	0.213**	0.226**	0.17
	(0.08)	(0.09)	(0.11)
TotlFeat	0.006**	0.009**	0.006*
	(0)	(0.003)	(0)
Phones	0.767**	0.966***	0.913**
	(0.29)	(0.3)	(0.33)
IntSyst	0.604**	0.936***	0.477*
	(0.23)	(0.28)	(0.23)
Chips	0.263	0.126	0.286
	(0.24)	(0.22)	(0.22)
DistProc	1.236***	0.796**	1.017**
	(0.35)	(0.38)	(0.36)
LnDevTime	0.379		
	(0.26)		
ATT		0.927**	
		(0.37)	
DLnSucc			−0.091
			(0.1)
Incumb	1.085***	1.078***	1.292***
	(0.27)	(0.31)	(0.3)
IYrAftNt	−0.114*	−0.156**	−0.104
	(0.06)	(0.06)	(0.07)
IEntYr	0.122**	0.114**	0.113**
	(0.05)	(0.05)	(0.05)
Constant	0.725	0.741	1.32*
	(0.51)	(0.62)	(0.7)
N	39	39	37
R squared	0.8619	0.8615	0.8523

* $p < 0.1$, ** $p < 0.05$, *** $p < 0.001$.

Discussion and Conclusions

The contribution of this work lies at the intersection of two important streams of research in strategic management – the literature on firm level capabilities within the resource-based view of the firm and the literature on discontinuous or competence-destroying technological change. In each stream, the scope of changes in capabilities that can be accomplished and the rate at which firms can change such capabilities has been a central concern. In the resource-based view of the firm, strategic options are constrained if capabilities cannot be transformed to match otherwise desirable changes in strategy. In the case of the literature on discontinuous technological change, the focus has been placed on whether incumbent firms can transform their capabilities in the short term to compete during rapid shifts in technological practices, products, and often customers. Empirical and theoretical investigations of these issues are still at an early stage and to date, they have not been satisfactorily resolved.

To contribute to this overall effort, the approach taken in this chapter has been to focus on a single, broad, but important aspect of capability – that of product development – and to analyze the differences among firms both in the short and long term, while controlling for the effects of the strategy chosen on the scope and design of the development project. In contrast to the dynamic capability view, the concept of "robust" capability focuses attention on the potential for existing firm capabilities to reassert their value as technologies mature. While the results suggest that the robust capabilities of incumbent firms are insufficient for them to adjust to radical competence-destroying change in the short term, longer term, incumbents appear to have advantages provided by robust capabilities; they are able to increase product development performance in the new technology at a rate faster than entrants and soon exceed them.

These results make sense in the context of the changes in this industry. Initially, low entry scale allowed small, focused teams of (often) elite engineers to create superior new product designs quickly and efficiently. However, increasing routinization of problem-solving, the need to involve specialists and then to coordinate large teams required additional organizational skills that were less easily acquired by entrants. For example, interviews at entrant firms suggest a number of instances where increases in development team sizes resulted in problems of coordinating design work, especially the negotiation and communication of changes that affected multiple workgroups. Organizational skills were further stressed by the need to work on multiple projects at once with decisions in one project impacting work on others. Further, the skills needed to track and integrate the many changes needed for different segments and make appropriate tradeoffs among an increasing number of experts in production, purchasing and other areas required still more skill development. In contrast, incumbent firms had encountered such challenges in the past, albeit in a somewhat different context, and had developed methods for coping with them. For example, their standards for documentation were much higher and finely articulated as were their procedures for testing and debugging systems. Project leaders in incumbent firms often pointed to precisely these factors when asked to explain initially poor relative performance. Observations from the field thus support the plausibility of the empirical findings that incumbent firms were able to improve their relative capability in product development more quickly.

Ultimately, these results suggest that the implications of prior experience in adapting and changing routines go beyond what a simple dichotomy of "core capabilities" or "core rigidities" can capture (Leonard-Barton, 1992). On the basis of the evidence presented here, previous capability both helps and hurts. In the short term, the need to locate, eliminate, replace and re-integrate routines appears to degrade capability. However, the potential reward for incumbent firms who do not merely begin de novo, but invest to adjust routines and retain those that are still effective, may have superior capabilities in the medium and long term. Therefore, which firms have an advantage may depend upon the type of advantage contemplated and the time-frame chosen for study. These considerations enrich strategic analysis and complicate prediction.

For practice, the results shown here suggest that issues associated with technological changes by incumbent firms cannot be quickly resolved through more informed strategic choice. That is, faster recognition of technological threats and choices to attempt earlier introductions, would be insufficient in and of themselves. Rather, requisite capabilities must be acquired partly by winnowing existing practices and partly developed or acquired. Attempts by incumbents to imitate entrants, perhaps by internally replicating a de novo environment, may be successful in the short term. However, longer term such attempts may obviate the value of precisely those robust capabilities that potentially form the basis of longer-term capability advantage. An intriguing implication for strategy that future research might usefully pursue is that capabilities complementarities between incumbent and entrant firms, often assumed in the acquisition literature, may be a chimera. Based on the evidence shown here the early merger of successful entrant firms and initially lagging incumbents may provide few benefits to the incumbent. This possibility warrants empirical test in light of the considerable number of small high technology firms that are purchased by larger ones in pursuit of the acquisition of capabilities that may prove illusory.

Notes

1. The logarithmic form was suggested by the skewed distribution of system sizes.
2. Testing the null hypothesis:
   $IYrAftNt - IEntYr = 0.0$ yields rejection at a greater than 5% level of confidence. Specifically: $F(1, 24) = 6.15$
   $Prob > F = 0.0206$
3. Cook–Weisberg test for heteroskedasticity (Null Hypothesis = No Heteroskedasticity) using ordinary least squares fit of Regression 3 yields:
   H_0: Constant variance
   $chi^2(1) = 0.07$
   $Prob > chi^2 = 0.7848$

References

Anderson, P. and Tushman, M. 1990: Technological discontinuities and dominant designs: A cyclical model of technological change. *Administrative Science Quarterly*, 35, 604–634.

Baron, J., Hannan, M., and Burton, M. 2001: Labor pains: Change in organizational models and employee turnover in young, high-tech firms. *American Journal of Sociology*, 106, 960–1013.

Christensen, C. 1992: The innovator's challenge: Understanding the influence of market environment on processes of technology development in the rigid disk drive industry. Unpublished Doctoral Dissertation Cambridge, MA: Harvard Business School.

Christensen, C. and Rosenbloom, R. 1995: Explaining the attacker's advantage: Technological paradigms, organizational dynamics, and the value network. *Research Policy*, 422, 233–257.

Clark, B., Chew, B., and Fujimoto, T. 1987: Product development in the world auto industry. *Brookings Papers on Economic Activity*, 3, 729–781.

Constant, E. 1980: *The Origins of the Turbojet Revolution*. Baltimore, MD: Johns Hopkins University Press.

Constant, E. 1999: Reliable knowledge and unreliable stuff: On the practical role of rational beliefs. *Technology and Culture*, 40, 324–357.

Cooper, A. and Schendel, D. 1976: Strategic responses to technological threats. *Business Horizons*, 19(1), 61–69.

Ghemawat, P. 1991: Market incumbency and technological inertia. *Marketing Science*, 10(2), 161–171.

Hannan, M. and Freeman, J. 1989: *Organizational Ecology*. Cambridge, MA: Harvard University Press.

Henderson, R. 1993: Underinvestment and incompetence as responses to radical innovation: Evidence from the photolithographic industry. *RAND Journal of Economics*, 24, 248–270.

Henderson, R. and Clark, K. 1990: Architectural innovation: The reconfiguration of existing product technologies and the failure of established firms. *Administrative Science Quarterly*, 35, 9–30.

Henderson, R. and Cockburn, I. 1994: Measuring competence? Exploring firm effects in pharmaceutical research. *Strategic Management Journal*, 15, 63–84.

Hughes, Thomas P. 1999: *Rescuing Prometheus*, New York: Pantheon/Random House.

Iansiti, M. 1995: Technology integration: Managing technological evolution in a complex environment. *Research Policy*, 24, 521–542.

Keister, W., Ritchie, A., and Washburn, S. 1951: *The Design of Switching Circuits*. New York: D. Van Nostrand Company Inc.

Leonard-Barton, D. 1992: Core capabilities and core rigidities: A paradox in managing new product development. *Strategic Management Journal*, 13, 111–125.

Levinthal, D. 1992: Surviving Schumpeterian environments: An evolutionary perspective. *Reginal H. Jones Center*, The Wharton School, University of Pennsylvania.

Lieberman, M. and Montgomery, D. 1988: First-mover advantages. *Strategic Management Journal*, 9, 41–58.

Nelson, R. and Winter, S. 1982: *An Evolutionary Theory of Economic Change*. Cambridge, MA: Belknap-Harvard Press.

Reingenaum, J. 1989: The timing of innovation: Research, development and diffusion. In R. Schmalensee and R. Willig (eds.), *Handbook of Industrial Organization*. Amsterdam: North-Holland, 849–908.

Rosenberg, N. 1982: *Inside the Black Box*. Cambridge, MA: Cambridge University Press.

Rumelt, R. 1991: How much does industry matter? *Strategic Management Journal*, 12, 167–186.

Scherer, F. 1992: *International High-Technology Competition*. Cambridge, MA: Harvard University Press.

Shannon, C. 1948: A mathematical theory of communication. *Bell System Technical Journal*, 27, 379–423 and 623–656.

Teece, D. 1986: Profiting from technological innovation: Implications for integration, collaboration, licensing and public policy. *Research Policy*, 15, 286–305.

Teece, D., Pisano, G., and Shuen, A. 1997: Dynamic capabilities and strategic management. *Strategic Management Journal*, 18, 509–533.

Tripsas, M. 1997: Unraveling the process of creative destruction: Complementary assets and incumbent survival in the typesetter industry. *Strategic Management Journal*, 18, 119–142.

Tushman, M. and Anderson, P. 1986: Technological discontinuities and organizational environments. *Administrative Science Quarterly*, 31, 439–465.

Utterback, J. 1994: *Mastering the Dynamics of Innovation: How Companies Can Seize Opportunities in the Face of Technological Change*. Boston, MA: Harvard Business School Press.

Zollo, M. and Winter, S. 2002: Deliberate learning and the evolution of dynamic capabilities. *Organization Science*, 13, 339–353.

CHAPTER NINE

The Form of Departure: The Consequences of Presumptive Adaptation of Franchising Knowledge for Local Network Growth

Gabriel Szulanski and Robert Jensen

Introduction

Scholars have theorized that the effective transfer of knowledge assets across national borders is a critical determinant of the success of multinational corporations (MNCs) (Anand and Kogut, 1997; Cantwell, 1989; Kogut and Zander, 1993; Teece, 1986). Traditionally, key issues in the transfer of firm specific assets across borders have been whether or not and to what extent an MNC should adapt core assets to fit local conditions. Empirical evidence (Onkvisit and Shaw, 1987) confirms that some degree of adaptation typically occurs. For example, human resource practices have been found to vary widely across national boundaries (Robert et al., 2000; Rosenzweig and Nohria, 1994) as have marketing practices (Douglas and Wind, 1987). Accordingly, much attention has been paid to the characteristics of the host environment that must be considered when crafting properly adapted practices (Lemak and Arunthanes, 1997; Yip, 1989).

However, research also suggests that the relevant environment for the purpose of adaptation typically turns out to be different from the one that is anticipated (Westney, 1987). Furthermore, Penrose (1959) argues that the relevant environment can only be fully determined ex-post. Thus, the final form of a transferred organizational practice will likely be different from the initial implementation in ways which cannot be completely specified ex-ante.

If the relevant environment cannot be specified ex-ante, the anticipated and the final form the practice takes may not fully correspond. If the initial form and the final form are different because the final form cannot be fully anticipated, the managerial challenge consists of choosing an initial form that would optimize the transfer effort. The practical problem of adaptation thus amounts to choosing the form of departure, or degree of initial adaptation when adaptation begins, that economizes on the effort necessary to arrive at the appropriate final form of the practice. Conventional wisdom seems to suggest that choosing such a form entails anticipating the relevant characteristics of the host environment and matching the form of departure to best accommodate those characteristics (Bartlett and Ghoshal, 1989; Prahalad and Doz, 1987), typically entailing a significant initial adaptation of the original practice. Much normative advice seems to assume that such a form, adapted to match the recipient environment, is most likely to be the optimal initial form (Griffith et al., 2000; Prahalad and Lieberthal, 1998). For example, Kostova and Roth (2002) argue that up-front adaptation matching the anticipated relevant aspects of the recipient environment enables the recipient site to accept and institutionalize the practice.

Yet accumulating evidence suggests that initial modifications to the original practice are often purposely postponed until adequate experience has been gained with the original practice in the host environment or until comparable results are obtained, with incremental adaptations of selected aspects of the practice occurring thereafter (*Financial Times*, 1997; Great Harvest Bread, 1999; McDonald, 1998). While not denying that the final form of the practice could differ from the original, this evidence does suggest that the optimal form of departure could closely resemble the original practice.

In this chapter we report a naturally occurring quasi-experiment that isolates the effect of the form of departure on performance. The setting is Mail Boxes, Etc. (MBE) in Israel. MBE is the largest non-food franchise organization in the world, with over 3,400 outlets in the US and over 1,100 outside of the US. The investigation covers the period from August 1995 when the MBE franchise network in Israel was established until July 2001. We systematically document how the Master Licensee's (ML's) choice of form of departure affects network growth.

The chapter begins by constructing competing hypotheses which flow from a theoretical treatment of the forms of departure at opposite ends of the spectrum, i.e., presumptively adapted (maximal fit with the presumed environment) versus as close as possible to the original practice. We then explain the setting and methodology as a preamble to an in-depth account of the form of departure and the observed level of growth of the MBE Israel network. Finally, we evaluate the data in terms of a naturally occurring quasi-experiment and conclude with a discussion of the implications of this research for the management of efforts to leverage knowledge assets.

Theory and Competing Hypotheses

Transfer of idiosyncratic firm resources across borders

Beginning with Hymer (1976), scholars in International Business have explained the existence of the MNCs in terms of leveraging superior idiosyncratic resources in different geographic locales (Caves, 1996; Teece, 1986). Dunning (1977) includes the "ownership advantage" of idiosyncratic resources as one of the pillars of his eclectic theory of foreign direct investment and Cantwell (1989) extends the concept of the ownership advantage by showing the strong geographic bias of transferred idiosyncratic resources. While the transfer of many different types of resources plays a role in establishing successful subsidiaries, knowledge assets have been argued by some to be the most critical assets transferred by MNCs (Anand and Kogut, 1997; Kogut and Zander, 1993).[1]

The need for adaptation

One of the central issues in the transfer of firm specific resources across borders, including knowledge resources (Kostova, 1999; Morosini et al., 1998), is whether or not and to what extent the firm should adapt the resource to fit local conditions (Bartlett and Ghoshal, 1989; Prahalad and Doz, 1987). Streams of literature in organizational theory (Kostova, 1999; Kostova and Zaheer, 1999; Scott, 2001), international business (Bartlett and Ghoshal, 1989; Griffith et al., 2000; Nohria and Ghoshal, 1997; Prahalad and Doz, 1987), and international marketing (Cui and Liu, 2001; Yan, 1994) have suggested that adaptation is necessary in order to ensure fit with the relevant characteristics of the local environment, which are typically different from those in the source environment along a number of critical institutional and market dimensions. Fit with the environment is argued to be essential not only for subsidiary success but also survival (Lawrence and Lorsch, 1967; Sorge, 1991). Some of the relevant environmental characteristics specified in the literature are culture (Buzzell, 1968; Hannon et al., 1995; Lemak and Arunthanes, 1997), basic market structures (Douglas and Wind, 1987; Kaufmann and Eroglu, 1998; Prahalad and Doz, 1987), distribution channels (Prahalad and Doz, 1987), marketing infrastructures (Douglas and Wind, 1987), regulatory, cognitive, and normative institutions (Kostova and Roth, 2002; Scott, 2001), consumer preferences and needs (Bartlett and Ghoshal, 1989; Cui and Liu, 2001; Douglas and Wind, 1987; Kashani, 1989; Lemak and Arunthanes, 1997; Prahalad and Doz, 1987), and labor practices (Rosenzweig and Nohria, 1994).

The form of departure

The form and the relevant environment.   While it seems sensible that the subsidiary must achieve fit with the local environment, research also suggests that the relevant environment for the purpose of adaptation typically turns out to be different from the one that is anticipated. For instance, in a study of transfers of organizational practices across countries Westney (1987) documents how the environment that was relevant for adaptation in Meiji, Japan, turned out to be qualitatively different than the anticipated one because of imperfect information on the environment and on the practice and unforeseen interactions between concurrently adopted practices. This point is also illustrated by Brannen and Wilson (1996) in their study of Disneyland Paris. In this case, market research led Disney to anticipate specific environmental characteristics that, in hindsight, were not the correct factors to base adaptations on.

In a point echoed by Burgelman (1983), Penrose (1959) argues that the relevant environment can only be fully determined ex-post. Until that environment is discovered through action it is in essence only the subjective expectations of the firm. Furthermore, Penrose (1959) argues that the relevant environment is subject to reciprocal influences from the actions taken by the firm, the same actions that uncover the true relevant environment. As Leonard-Barton (1988) suggests, the adaptation process involves mutual adaptation between the technology and the environment, implying that the final form of the practice cannot be adequately predicted ex-ante. Given host environment complexity and lack of previous experience with the practice being transferred it seems likely that the final form of a transferred organizational practice will be different from the initial implementation in ways that cannot be completely specified ex-ante.

While it may be beneficial to attempt to predict the relevant environment as accurately as possible it is quite likely that it will not be possible to specify it fully before the adaptation effort has begun. Thus, it would be safe to assume that the anticipated final form and the actual final form that a practice may take may not fully correspond. If these two forms are substantially different the managerial challenge consists of choosing a form that optimizes the transfer effort, i.e., that economizes on the effort necessary to arrive at the appropriate final form of the practice.

Optimal form as presumptive adaptation.   The literature on adaptation has traditionally overlooked the variance between initial and final forms and simply argued that adaptation, if appropriately matched to the relevant characteristics of the host environment, will enable successful transfers and hence, ceteris paribus, better performing subsidiaries. While not directly addressing the form of departure, the focus on relevant environmental characteristics seems to suggest that the optimal form of departure entails anticipating the relevant characteristics of the local environment and altering the organizational practice to best accommodate those characteristics (Bartlett and Ghoshal, 1989; Prahalad and Doz, 1987). The implicit assumption is that the practice will be adapted in a single effort, usually at the outset of the transfer. When this is the case, the adaptation of the practice is guided by presumed understanding of the relevant characteristics of the host environment, such as customer preferences and tastes.

This assumption is more explicit in recent work focusing specifically on the transfer of organizational practices. Concerning human resource practices, for instance, significant adaptation is explicitly argued to increase acceptance of the knowledge being transferred. A practice that is adapted comprehensively to match cognitive and normative institutions presumed relevant in the host environment becomes both more understandable and more acceptable to the local labor force responsible for its implementation (Griffith et al., 2000; Kirkman et al., 2001; Kostova and Roth, 2002; Luo, 2000; Morosini et al., 1998). In order for the practice to be understood and accepted, however, the adaptation must usually occur in a single step, or at least a series of rapid smaller ones. Progressive incremental adaptation leaves large portions of the practice less understandable and hence less acceptable (Tolbert and Zucker, 1983).

Thus, a form of departure adapted in a single step to be as close to the presumed final form as possible should lead to increased leveraging of the knowledge asset through increased implementation and hence, ceteris paribus, increased subsidiary performance.

> *Hypothesis 1:*   Ceteris paribus, presumptive adaptation of a transferred organizational practice to fit the local environment will result in enhanced subsidiary performance.

Optimal form as closest to the original practice.   Accumulating evidence from firms experienced in transferring organizational practices, however, indicates that these firms often postpone adaptation efforts and that they take mostly incremental steps when they do adapt (*Financial Times*, 1997; Great Harvest Bread, 1999; McDonald, 1998). Such anecdotal evidence raises questions about the validity of the traditional normative advice regarding the desirability of presumptive adaptation.

Indeed, presumptive adaptation makes heroic assumptions. First, it is assumed that the recipient of the organizational practice understands the local environment sufficiently well that appropriate adjustments to the transferred practice can be made. Business environments are complex and multifaceted (Sorge, 1991) and, as argued earlier, the anticipated and relevant environments often differ markedly (Westney, 1987). Even local, experienced managers may not fully comprehend their own environment (Burgelman, 1983; Penrose, 1959). In such a scenario significant adaptations made to match an uncertain environment can be risky and may or may not bring the practice closer to its optimal final form.

Second, conventional wisdom tends to assume that transferred practices are fully understood and transferred without difficulty. While this may be true of simple practices, many transferred knowledge assets may be at least moderately complex (Rivkin, 2000) and/or causally ambiguous (Lippman and Rumelt, 1982). As a result, neither the MNC nor the subsidiary may fully understand the practice nor be able to completely codify it. Such considerations only increase the already sticky nature of knowledge transfer (Szulanski, 1996; von Hippel, 1994).

In the case of difficult transfers, implementation at the recipient site is typically not a single event but rather it may require a prolonged iterative process where the implementation of the practice is compared with the original one in order to diagnose and solve problems that arise during transfer and implementation (Gielens and Dekimpe, 2001; Winter and Szulanski, 2001). Presumptive adaptation of the practice being transferred, however, may involve alterations of such magnitude as to make it incomparable with the original, precluding the use of the original practice as referent when diagnosing and solving problems in the new setting. Such a scenario would make successful implementation less likely.

When adaptation occurs after a period of time, comparison with the original may still be of use in diagnosing problems arising during the adaptation. When it entails the alteration of numerous facets of the practice prior to implementation, however, presumptive adaptation may hinder the ability to diagnose specific problems arising during implementation because the multiple possible combinations created by the interactions between the adapted facets of the practice, those that are left unadapted, and the environment create many alternative explanations that have to be ruled out.

Incremental adaptation, on the other hand, allows easier reversion to the original and much simpler classification and diagnosis of problems. Moreover, while experience with the practice in the local environment may increase the likelihood of understanding its relevant characteristics, a presumptive change may alter the practice sufficiently so that the interaction between the practice and the environment cannot be fully predicted ex-ante. As such the possibility of mis-adaptation may still be quite high. Given that presumptive adaptation requires significant time and resources, a series of smaller steps, with a correspondingly smaller chance of error and greater ease of recovery if an error is made, may lead to the appropriate final form of the practice with less effort.

Finally, even if the practice being transferred is simple and easily understood, significant adaptation of the practice may lead to incompatibilities with an overall system (Kaufmann and Eroglu, 1998). Depending on the nature of the systemic benefits, the loss of compatibility may offset presumed or actual benefits gained from a closer alignment with the environment.

> *Hypothesis 2*:   Ceteris paribus, presumptive adaptation of a transferred practice to fit the local environment will hamper subsidiary performance.

Methods

Setting

General setting: franchising.   The general setting for our study is multinational franchising. MNCs are particularly interesting settings to study the form of departure and presumptive adaptation as the transfer of knowledge across international borders increases the variance due to amplified isomorphic forces which increase the impetus to adapt (Sorge, 1991). In specific, multinational franchise organizations, as a subset of MNCs, are well suited for studying issues of organizational knowledge transfer (Nelson and Winter, 1982) in that they compete primarily through growth by first increasing the number of outlets during the expansion phase and later by managing same store revenue growth once the network reaches the carrying capacity of its environment. For both forms of growth, the transfer of know-how between geographic locations plays an important role. This allows us to more clearly observe the incidence of decisions concerning the form of departure. Franchises also tend to service individual consumers so that they are subject to strong pressures for local adaptation. Furthermore franchise organizations operate across an arm's length interface with their franchisees and cannot completely enforce how these franchisees receive and use the knowledge being transferred (Bradach, 1998; Kaufmann and Eroglu, 1998), with rescission of such agreements being a dramatic, costly, and undesirable event. Enforcement is even less likely between franchisors and individuals, often called Master Licensees (MLs), on whom they confer the right to grow their network in exclusive geographic territories (when such a system is used). That is because deviations from the type of knowledge transferred to MLs is often more tacit and less critical for the identity of the brand. Thus, there is likely to be greater variation in form of departure decisions for MLs than one might find in company owned stores or subsidiaries where the company can resort to fiat to enforce compliance with a particular set of practices (Williamson, 1975).

Specific setting: Mail Boxes Etc. in Israel.   The specific setting of our study is the Mail Boxes Etc. (MBE) franchise system in Israel. MBE is the largest non-food franchisor in the world. MBE in the United States was first launched in 1980 in San Diego, California, to fill a need for postal services. MBE specializes primarily in services for the small office and home office (SOHO) environments. These services include photocopying, color copying, packing and shipping, parcel and express courier, complete mailbox service, Internet access, and office and packing supplies. MBE quickly grew to 250 franchise outlets by 1986, when it went public, to over 1,000 centers in 1990, and to over 4,000 centers in 1999. After securing a strong foothold in the United States and building a strong foundation of experience, MBE decided, in 1989, to sell master franchise licenses abroad. MLs purchase the rights to build an MBE network in their country or defined, international territory. By 1999 MBE was operating, or had licensing agreements, in nearly 60 countries and had over 700 international outlets.

This study comprises the growth of the MBE network in Israel. MBE sold the rights to build the MBE network in Israel to Albert Alhadef in August of 1995. He opened his first store, the pilot store, in July 1996. As with other MLs, MBE provided Albert with substantial know-how on how to grow an MBE network. This chapter will focus exclusively on the transfer of knowledge concerning the task of building an MBE network rather than that of implementing the relatively more codified business concept within an MBE store.[2] The nature of the know-how for building a network will be detailed below.

In retrospect, the history of the MBE Israel network could be construed as a naturally occurring quasi-experiment which allows us to make inferences about the effect of presumptive adaptation on subsidiary performance, as measured by the growth in the number of stores in the network. Furthermore, because we were granted complete access to the ML management team, we could double check for emerging interpretations and thus rule out many potential threats to validity when drawing our conclusions. Moreover, focusing on a single network meant that we kept the environment constant, thus eliminating a large class of confounding factors that could cloud the effect of presumptive adaptation, further enhancing internal validity. Relying on a single case, however, substantially increases the challenge of establishing the generalizability of our findings, a challenge which we address in two steps. First, we rely on our broad exposure to the MBE internationalization experience to establish that the case of MBE Israel is indeed representative of, and applicable to, other contexts within MBE. Second, we argue that the case study serves as a potent counterexample to the seemingly pervasive conviction that presumptive adaptation is generally desirable. The lessons that we draw from this example about the possible ineffectiveness of presumptive adaptation cannot be easily dismissed, given the similarity of the knowledge transfer processes that we have studied at MBE with those occurring in other firms, and especially in franchise organizations.

Data collection

Following Yin (1989), we employed an explanatory case study methodology because we were examining a contemporaneous event in which the relevant actions could not

Table 9.1 Interviews

Persons interviewed, by job title	Number
MBE Headquarters, San Diego, CA, USA	
Chief Executive Officer	1
Executive Vice President in charge of Sales	1
Director of International Operations	1
Director of International Sales	1
Director of International Franchise Business Development	1
Director of International Training	1
MBE Israel Headquarters, Tel Aviv, Israel	
Chief Executive Officer	1
Chief Operations Officer	1
Director of Operations	1
Assistant Director of Operations	1
Director of Marketing	1
Franchisees in Israeli Network	4
Suppliers of Israeli Network	2

be manipulated and where the causal links were too complex to effectively study with only a survey instrument.

Data collection for this field investigation occurred primarily through a series of interviews with all of the relevant managers and employees at MBE headquarters and MBE Israel as well as extensive archival data gathering in both locations. After signing a comprehensive confidentiality agreement, we had complete access and cooperation in both locations. In all cases, the interviews were semi-structured with an aim of uncovering the role of the ML and the process and difficulties of expanding a franchise network overseas, specifically the balance between following the approach recommended by headquarters for growing a network versus developing one that is adapted to local needs. The interviews included are shown in Table 9.1.

The CEO at MBE Israel also completed a lengthy questionnaire as part of a wider, but connected study. Monthly e-mails and telephone conversations occurred prior to and following the on-site visits during the entire period of observation. The period of time tracked in the field investigation is 1995 to 2001. The data collection occurred in real time, negating any retrospective bias. To minimize observer effects we were careful not to intervene and offered no opinions or suggestions to the participants.

Data reduction

Following Miles and Huberman (1984), we approached the data collection step with prior theoretical constructs, allowing us to reduce the data to comprehensible proportions. This is reflected in the use of semi-structured interviews where we specifically sought to understand decisions concerning the form of departure. We validated our findings with the participants by contrasting our emerging understanding of the experience with their own. The following two sections detail how we measured the degree of presumptive adaptation and the growth of the network.

Presumptive adaptation.   We define presumptive adaptation as intended, a priori departure from a recommended approach, i.e., non-conformity with conventional ways of growing the franchise network. We operationalize presumptive adaptation as non-conformity to the standard approach, following a method pioneered by Westphal et al. (1997), as explained below. Westphal et al. (1997) measure qualitatively the intention to conform through a self-reported declaration of conformity to a "particular, standard ... model" (p. 378). Accordingly, we verify the existence of an intention to depart from the standard approach through interviews with the MBE Israel management team and external observers (e.g., corporate liaisons). We asked general questions about the process that MBE Israel was going through in establishing an MBE network in Israel. As the participants brought up issues of adaptation we probed the rationale underlying the adaptation and when and how the adaptation had occurred.

To establish the *degree* of conformity (or lack of it thereof) to the standard approach we adapted Westphal et al.'s quantitative measure of conformity. Their measure is computed by breaking up a policy (total quality management [TQM] in their case) into its constituent practices (twenty typical interventions in their case), and building a vector of implemented practices to determine the percentage of practices that are implemented. We utilize the same method, but rather than calculating the percentage in relation to the number of other units implementing the practices we compute the raw number of constituent practices implemented in comparison to the standard approach recommended by MBE headquarters. Our measure thus captures deviations from the standard rather than deviations from a norm, although, as will be shown in the section on establishing correlation, the standard and the norm are fairly similar.

In determining whether a deviation has occurred we utilize a cutoff point of one calendar year. One year is a long enough period to determine the vector of actions chosen by the ML but not yet sufficiently long to reveal fully the implication of the ML choices on the performance of the network in order to trigger corrective action.

Concerning how to grow an MBE network, MBE Headquarters provides recommendations to MLs on eight specific domains of activity that cover marketing the MBE franchise, selling the MBE franchise, training the franchisees, selecting sites, designing and constructing MBE centers, supporting the franchisee, developing infrastructure, and managing the franchisor/franchisee relationship. The eight domains can be considered "core" in the sense that nearly all potential elements of the system for network growth are interdependent with them (Hannan et al., 1996; Siggelkow, 2002) and they have a sizeable impact on the shape of future organizational elements (Baron et al., 1999).

The instructions for the first seven of these domains are organized in the form of a timeline known internally as the "52 week plan" that pertains to the initial year of the growth of the network.[3] The 52 week plan lists 330–335 actions (depending on whether the ML uses an area structure) to be taken by an ML, specifying their timing on a week by week basis. It is the number of specific actions taken in the 52 week plan that constitutes the raw score mentioned above.

It should be noted that the information contained in the 52 week plan, while codified, was still complex and somewhat ambiguous. The information represented a compilation of dozens of lessons learned through the building of the US and other international networks. When specific problems were encountered, the solution to those problems was incorporated as a task in the 52 week plan. For instance, experience revealed that it was desirable to delay some types of advertising until after the sixth week of network operation. Causal explanations of the mechanisms by which those moves affected growth were not, however, codified into the 52 week plan. Furthermore, the implications of advertising from day one or delaying it by six weeks were addressed haphazardly, if at all. Such knowledge, instead of being codified, was transferred predominantly through personal communications between MLs. Furthermore, the interrelationship between various parts of the 52 week plan and the plan's applicability to different environments was unknown, even by headquarters. The 52 week plan represented codified local learning and no-one had systematically mapped out the implications of altering or abandoning parts of that plan. While such learning was partially available in the larger MBE international network, again it was only transferred unsystematically via personal communication between MLs.

Instructions for the eighth domain, managing the franchisor/franchisee relationship, are, of necessity, less specific. They expected to align actions with the "Core Values" of MBE which are sometimes referred to as the "Family Principle" (see the appendix for further explanation). The essence of the principle hinges on the fact that the franchise contract is a blunt governance tool that is inadequate to rectify minor infringements. Termination of the franchise contract, which is normally granted for a period of ten years, is a costly and traumatic action that can be contemplated only in extreme situations. Thus, such a contract is of limited value to restrain undesirable minor deviations in the behavior of the franchisee. Moreover, the threat of termination provides, at best, a weak lever to induce franchisees to undertake specific actions, such as marketing their services locally ("farming"), investing in the remodeling of their store, or purchasing a new Point of Sales system. It certainly does not obligate them to provide positive referrals to prospective franchisees in order to help grow the network.

Because franchisees own their stores and the contract cannot be terminated easily, the franchiser cannot control franchisees as if they were salaried company employees. Rather, the key task of the ML consists in empowering the franchisees so that they succeed in the implementation of the franchise, as the success of the franchisee is a prerequisite for the success of the ML. It is for this reason that nurturing the franchisor/franchisee relationship means thinking of franchisees as if they were family members (such direct comparisons are often made in training meetings and materials) and the main means for effective governance is persuasion.[4]

In order to determine the boundaries of the family principle, as its application is not as clearly codified as the 52 week plan, we interviewed a number of employees in the international department at MBE headquarters and a sample of MBE MLs.[5] Along with a more general discussion of application of MBE's core values we specifically asked three questions: (1) how would you deal with late royalty payments; (2) how have you dealt with late royalty payments while you were building your network; and (3) how do you get franchisees to make additional investments in their stores, such as remodeling, new equipment, etc.? Using these answers we developed a profile of how the family principle is used at MBE and then compared MBE Israel's ML actions with that profile to determine whether a significant deviation had occurred.

Some ML actions correspond clearly to deviations from the standard way to manage the franchisor/franchisee relationship. Examples of such actions are frequent threats of termination, withholding support for minor reasons, and attempting to centralize activities that are normally considered to be responsibilities of the franchisees, such as marketing locally in their territory. Such actions conflict with the principle of treating franchisees like family instead of employees and working via persuasion rather than fiat.

Network performance.   Growth performance in early stage franchise organizations is best reflected by the number of franchises sold and stores opened (Bradach, 1998; Love, 1986). Same store sales growth is generally not used as a measure of growth until the network reaches a stable size and growth in the number of stores abates. The growth in the number of franchises is a key measure of performance because it provides a vital revenue stream of franchise fee payments from the sale of new franchise units. That revenue in turn funds the development of the central infrastructure that is necessary to support the growing network of stores until royalty payments from those centers are sufficiently substantial (Bradach, 1998). Network growth is not only used by academics to measure early franchise performance but is also one of the primary performance metrics both at MBE and in other franchising organizations (Bradach, 1998). Admittedly, using network growth as a performance metric may become problematic as a franchise organization matures[6] (Bradach, 1998), but in this study Israel was just being opened and network growth is considered to be the most suitable measure. Growth was measured as the number of new franchises sold by the end of each calendar quarter and was determined using archival data.

Inference

Establishing correlation

The data show that the decision concerning form of departure follows a clear pattern. The first decision was to significantly adapt the 52 week plan. Of the 330 actions to be taken in the first year only 68 were followed (20.6 percent), and the majority of these were delayed by up to six months. Even if one aggregates the minor steps into major milestones only one of seven major milestones (that of infrastructure development) was accomplished, and that only partially, in the first two years of operation with the rest being intentionally neglected. Even using the most conservative estimates this can clearly be considered a significant deviation.

Not only was this deviation significant in comparison with headquarters' standards, which is to fulfill all 330 actions in their proper sequence within the first year of operation, but also in comparison with many of the other international networks, particularly those which were well established and growing quickly at the time MBE entered Israel. Table 9.2 shows the number of steps followed by each of the 13 different international networks in existence prior to Israel (names are withheld for confidentiality reasons). While the number of steps Israel took can be pinpointed with accuracy due to the richness of the data, only a range can be determined for the other countries.

Table 9.2   Comparative patterns of MBE network growth

Country	Min. no. of steps in 52-week plan followed	Max. no. of steps in 52-week plan followed[a]	Cumulative no. of franchises sold after 2 years	Cumulative no. of franchises sold after 4 years	Cumulative no. of franchises sold after 6 years[b]	Cumulative no. of franchises sold after 8 years[b]
1	259	335	19	23	96	168
2	259	335	14	62	53	53
3	238	316	22	31	28	20
4	196	244	11	93	169	325
5	131	210	3	8	16	25
6	131	210	6	29	27	13
7	68	103	5	20	34	43
8	68	103	3	10	15	13
9	68	103	2	11	11	5
10	68	103	4	13	25	37
11	68	103	3	7	5	5
12	68	103	1	5	11	14
13	68	103	2	6	5	9
Israel	68	68	0	6	12	12

[a] Out of 330/335 possible steps (5 of the steps are only for those with an area franchisee structure).
[b] Cumulative number also includes stores closed.

This significant adaptation of the 52 week plan was followed approximately two years later, in 1998, with a decision to backtrack and re-approach the growth of the network by implementing the MBE system in the recommended way, following the steps outlined in the 52 week plan. Within the first year of this phase the remaining 262 steps were followed.

Two years later, in 2000, another decision was made to seriously depart from the system, this time involving adaptation of the knowledge concerning the "Family Principle," with MBE headquarters adopting a confrontational style of interaction with its franchisees and centralizing some franchise operations at headquarters. This is explicitly counter to headquarters' recommendations on managing the franchisor/franchisee relationship. Moreover, 93 percent of all MLs prior to Israel (and 84 percent including Israel and those that came after) followed the family principle extremely closely as recommended by MBE headquarters.

With only one exception prior to Israel all the MLs used a very accommodating, persuasive interaction style coupled with extended patience and forbearance for late royalty, or even non-payment, problems, and a clear respect for the franchisee as the primary interface with the customer. For instance, nearly all of the MLs, with the exception of Israel, approached the issue of late royalty payments with a lengthy process spanning six months or more that begins with personal phone calls and friendly letters of reminder. For franchisees that cannot pay due to financial difficulties (which is often interpreted broadly to include difficulties reaching break even) forbearance can be indefinite and involves substantial support in helping the franchisees become profitable. The need to approach franchisees with patience concerning late royalty payments is especially true for small networks where failure rates and negative referrals can be especially damaging. The following comment from the Austrian ML concerning a franchisee that had not paid royalties in over a year illustrates this approach and its importance for small networks:

> At the stage we are in of our development it is very difficult to take such a decision [terminating a franchisee]. There is the hope that gradually you will receive some part of it if not all. You tend to take the somewhat softer approach which we are doing.

Finally, the data also show that the growth of the network follows a clear pattern. While two pilot stores were operated by the ML between 1995 and 1997, no franchise units were sold in that period. This was followed by fast growth as franchise units were sold between 1998 and 1999. In 2000, however, the growth stalled again, with no new stores sold between 2000 and the end of the period of observation in July 2001. It is this stark empirical observation that we attempt to explain in the next section.

Overlaying the two patterns discussed above produces Table 9.3.

An analysis of the qualitative data also shows a clear correlation between the decision concerning form of departure and network growth. This correlation can be seen in the following rich description that details the MBE Israel experience from the beginning of the network until July, 2001.

First phase: presumptive adaptation and no growth.   Albert Alhadef bought the rights to develop the MBE franchise network in Israel in August 1995. MBE, as they do with all MLs, began the process of replicating their successful network in Israel with a series of intensive training sessions spanning multiple weeks. During these training sessions Albert was instructed in both building and operating a network and in establishing and operating a successful MBE store. The training included in-depth field experience. MBE also aided Albert in the transfer of franchising knowledge by providing him with extensive manuals detailing the codified knowledge of both how to build and run a franchise network as well as an MBE store. Finally, to aid in the replication of various successful MBE networks, MBE Headquarters ensured that Albert was introduced to the global MBE network and given access to MLs in other countries to serve as examples and references in establishing the network in Israel. The attempt in the training, the written materials, and access to the network was to transfer a success-proven system that would work in many environments worldwide.

With this wealth of available knowledge Albert opened the pilot store[7] in July 1996 and began focusing on building it and perfecting the sale of MBE services in Israel. From the beginning, Albert and the staff members that he hired believed that the basic MBE approach to both the business format and network growth had to be substantially adapted if it were to be successful in Israel. Many of the business services being offered in the United States were not even defined or established in their small country. The word "mailbox" itself, for example, had no meaning and having the mailbox logo in the front of stores meant little for attracting customers. Albert was concerned that the fit of the MBE concept in Israel was not tight enough to attract sufficient numbers of franchisees to build a network.

Table 9.3 Evolution of MBE Israel

	1995–1997	1998–1999	2000–2001
System adapted?	System adapted	System copied exactly	System adapted
No. of new franchises sold	0 (2 stores in operation, both owned by ML)	15	0 (in addition 3 existing stores are closed)

What initially attracted him to MBE, however, was the potential flexibility in the basic concept. He saw the flexibility in the business format as a tool to get MBE into the Israeli market.

> The MBE concept is so flexible that I don't think MBE home office has all the solutions. There's no way they can see all the needs of all the world and what is needed because the mission of MBE is that we will personalize a convenient business solution. There is no way you can think about all the system, what [services we] should give where (Albert).

By picking and choosing among the various components of the MBE business format Albert and his associates believed they could establish a profitable opportunity in Israel that would be easy for potential franchisees to detect. However, such an approach required a period of trial and error in the pilot store to determine what the right combination of services was for a general Israeli market.

Albert's strategy was to perfect the pilot store before selling franchises thereby proving the viability of MBE in the Israeli market and enticing an otherwise skeptical population to more easily buy into the MBE network. He believed that such a strategy would allow for even greater growth than the fastest growing MBE networks. Rather than expending significant amounts of time and money recruiting franchisees, as the plan calls for, Albert instead spent the majority of his effort the first two years perfecting the pilot store.

> We [were] doing in-store selling. We [were] staying behind the counter and selling stamps and making photocopies (Eitan – has not been introduced yet).

However, such an approach consciously violated the premises of the 52 week plan, as it purposely omitted steps outlined in the blueprint in order to focus on the pilot store. Out of a potential 330 actions in the plan he omitted 262, or 79.4% of them, in the first year and all but three or four of the ones he did implement were concerned solely with basic ML operations and the establishment of the pilot store. The 52 week plan called for numerous specific actions to recruit franchisees to be taken within the first six months with most of them beginning in the first month. These steps were neglected.

In an attempt to adapt to the perceived characteristics of the local environment, marked by skepticism and suspicion of new franchising schemes, Albert abandoned the underlying logic of the blueprint and adapted the corporate know-how on managing network growth to fit his own conception of key success factors. According to MBE instructions and the experience of other international MLs, by the end of the first period, December 1997, Albert should have sold nearly 14 franchises and have over half as many stores already in operation. Instead, he had not sold a single franchise yet and was still struggling to make the pilot store profitable.

The result was not as he had intended. Instead of a perfectly functioning, highly profitable pilot store that could attract potential franchisees the pilot center was not even profitable and he had zero network growth. In fact, the pilot center did not become profitable until nearly half the final number of franchise units had been added to the network. Nor was the pilot center even verging on breakeven at the end of 1997. Sales revenue growth had stalled and did not increase until critical mass in the network as a whole had been achieved. The growth following 1997 was not due to a perfected, Israeli version of the business concept (one well adapted to fit the Israeli market). First, the adapted model used in the pilot center had not achieved profitability. Second, the centers did not copy the pilot center model but each adapted the US model to match its own idiosyncratic local requirements. Clearly, presumptive adaptation of the know-how on managing network growth does not seem to be associated with the kind of results that Albert had intended.

Second phase: system for network growth copied closely and substantial growth.   In December 1997 Albert decided to send his Chief Operations Officer (COO), Eitan, to an MBE International conference in Milan, Italy. Italy was one of the more successful MBE international networks with nearly 200 stores established in a period of six years. At that conference Eitan had an opportunity to see a successful network first hand. He returned to Israel with a clearer picture of how the network was supposed to grow and the benefits of close adherence to the blueprint.

> The trip to Italy was a milestone for me, I think for all of us. I think Albert will agree with this milestone … December '97. It seems like every franchisor must … get to the point where you say, "Okay, let's start listening to others and what they are doing." (Eitan).

From December 1997 until the end of the period of observation Albert and his top managers shifted their policy from focusing on pilot store profitability to following the detailed blueprint that MBE had provided. During the initial period, when they had significantly adapted the system, they rarely asked for help with implementation problems. Having significantly adapted the system others could not help them much.

> We don't go back to the US. We have our own knowledge here. (Ari)

> Ask US for help? It might be the proper way, but we have created our own experience. (Albert)

In the second period, when they were trying to implement the system as closely as possible, they were in contact with successful MLs, such as those in Italy, Canada, the UK, and Portugal. Moreover, they began using IPEP, a diagnostic tool developed in the US geared to assess the degree of uniformity of their stores, a tool that allowed them to compare stores to the US standard along a number of dimensions. Personal contacts were used to compare their implementation with that in other countries. The following statement concerning one particular interaction with the Portuguese ML is indicative of the help in diagnosing implementation problems:

> He took things that may look like they are very big and complex and put them down to us and said, "This is nice and simple. Keep it like this. Keep it simple. Don't try to make this [more] difficult than it is." (Eitan)

With a new focus and compliance with the MBE recommended approach for managing network growth, the Israeli network grew from only one pilot store to two pilot stores plus 15 franchise outlets in two years. Israel was now among the fastest growing, young MBE networks at the time (growth often accelerates with age, but compared with other fairly new franchise networks they were now the second fastest growing ML in MBE history).

At first glance it might seem obvious that focusing on selling franchises would increase the size of the network. While this was the direct result of Albert's shift in thinking from adaptation to closer adherence to the knowledge assets it was not a shift in Albert's original intention. His intention from the beginning was to build a fast growing network. The shift, then, wasn't from a focus on growing the network, but from attempting to adapt the technique for growing the network to local conditions in order to achieve better than typical MBE growth. As he began to follow the pattern recommended by MBE Albert was finally meeting the original growth predictions of MBE when he bought the rights to build the MBE network in Israel.

Third phase: presumptive adaptation of the family principle, growth stalls. In December 1999, however, MBE Israel once again significantly departed from the system developed by MBE Headquarters, this time primarily in terms of the franchisor/franchisee relationship. In late 1999 Albert decided to shift his focus to a new business and promoted Eitan to be the new CEO of MBE Israel. Eitan had initiated the shift toward following the pattern for network growth outlined in the 52 week plan and was instrumental in implementing that plan. Furthermore, Albert had been phasing himself out for over a year before he promoted Eitan, with Eitan in charge of most of the phases of the business before he became CEO. While Albert was shifting his focus he still was frequently present. The only difference with Albert stepping away from the executive role was that Eitan became the primary interface with the franchisees instead of Albert. Other than the change described below the approach to building the network remained essentially the same.

Typically in a franchise organization the franchisor spends a large proportion of his/her time managing the relationship with the franchisees (Bradach, 1998; Kaufmann and Eroglu, 1998). The relationship between the network headquarters and the franchisees is important because, barring gross negligence, the franchisor has little ultimate authority over the franchisees and has to rely on relationships in order to ensure their cooperation in aspects of the business requiring coordination between franchisor and franchisee. Beyond that, managing the relationship appropriately is vital to the growth of the network because good relationships reflect in positive referrals to prospective franchisees. Albert had always been very accommodating in his approach to his franchisees even when there were difficulties in the relationship. That approach changed when Eitan became CEO.

As the network grew Albert and his top management team began to have problems with late royalty payments. The Israeli society is one characterized by a fear of ambiguous situations (such as the potential success of an untried franchise format),[8] a strong sense of the cost of time and money, a moderately strong sense of individuality,[9] coupled with a noted reluctance to accept and comply with developing social norms or the expectations of others (Mann, 1977). This environmental characteristic is most easily seen in the characterization of Israeli markets as requiring quick validation in what is a fast-paced, do-or-die atmosphere. As a consequence, new franchisees are under tremendous pressure to become successful quickly. The result of this cultural tendency in the MBE franchise network was for the franchisees to withhold royalty payments in order to use those funds as an interest-free short-term loan to expand their stores as quickly as possible. The norm of on-time royalty payments, typical in US MBE networks, was disregarded by franchisees that were frantically trying to swiftly recoup their investment, by capitalizing quickly on individual growth prospects.

The problem, however, was causing cash flow difficulties for the MBE Israel headquarters. Albert's approach was in line with the Family Principle and entailed persuasion, cajoling, negotiation, and individualized attention to the needs of each franchisee. Eitan's approach to dealing with these specific environmental characteristics, however, was a clear departure from the system advocated by MBE headquarters in San Diego. Instead of putting emphasis on maintaining the franchisor/franchisee relationship and finding individualized solutions to the problem, Eitan immediately confronted the franchisees and threatened to withdraw all ongoing support if royalty payments were not on time. Then, in an effort to control cash flow even more tightly he attempted to initiate policies aimed at centralizing operations with a majority of business being generated by headquarters through a centralized Internet interface and then implemented by the franchisees. This action was a clear departure from the Family Principle in that it turned the franchisor/franchisee relationship into a strained employer/employee relationship. The policy was also a clear departure from franchising principles in general where the franchisee acts as a semi-autonomous agent controlling the primary interface with the customer.

Eitan's policy changes put a strain on the all important franchisor/franchisee relationship. While the franchisees had been and continued to be profitable during this period, the policy changes altering the Family Principle resulted in open disputes between MBE Israel top management and the franchisees. Many of the franchisees were sufficiently unhappy that they decided to sabotage network growth by advising prospective franchisees against joining the MBE network. As this problem developed, the growth of the network faltered and then stalled with no new stores added following Eitan's promotion in December 1999. At the end of 2000 the situation deteriorated enough that Eitan was forced to leave the company and Albert brought in another CEO.

Figure 9.1 shows the growth pattern of the MBE Israel network along with the points demarcating the different phases where adaptation decisions were made.

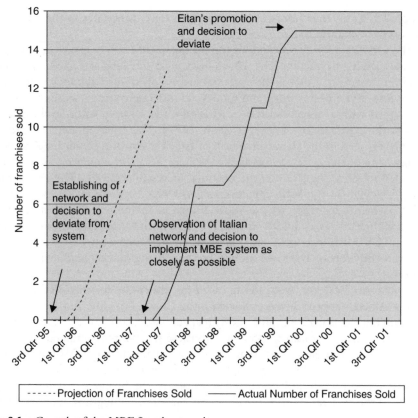

Figure 9.1   Growth of the MBE Israel network

Establishing causality

In retrospect, the MBE Israel saga could be analyzed as a naturally occurring, repeated-treatment quasi-experiment. Such a vantage point suggests a causal relationship between the form of departure and network growth. A quasi-experimental perspective is aptly suited to analyze situations where the researcher cannot control the incidence of the treatment but has rich access to data and exact knowledge of when the treatment occurs (Cook, 1991). The repeated-treatment design, in particular, is justified when the program is introduced to the entire population and the investigator has access to only one population (Cook et al., 1990).

The design is depicted below, and its most interpretable outcome occurs when the first observation (O_1) differs from the second (O_2), the third (O_3) differs from the fourth (O_4), and the O_3–O_4 difference is in the same direction as the O_1–O_2 difference.

$$O_1 \times O_2 \,/\, \times O_3 \times O_4$$

The treatment ($\times$) in our study occurs when the ML in Israel decides to presumptively adapt the MBE system for network growth. If the treatment has an effect on network growth we will expect that growth will be stagnant after each decision to adapt the system and that growth will accelerate following a decision to implement the standardized system. That is, O_1 (initial growth forecast developed by Albert and MBE headquarters in San Diego) will be higher than O_2 (observation after decision to adapt), O_3 (following decision to implement standardized system) will be higher than O_2 and the growth rate of O_4(following decision to adapt again) will be lower than O_3. This is exactly what we find and what Figure 9.1 illustrates.

Threats to validity

In this section we critically examine alternative explanations to our findings. Because the treatment is not applied randomly, inferring causality in a quasi-experimental setting necessitates a special effort to carefully weigh alternative explanations of the observed results. This task is particularly important in our setting because the treatment is endogenous, meaning that additional, possibly neglected, confounding factors may be correlated with the treatment.

However, while not completely resolving the issue, one of the strengths of a repeated-treatment, quasi-experimental design is that potential threats to validity have to follow the same on-off-on pattern as the treatment (the decision to presumptively adapt) (Cook and Campbell, 1979; Eisenhardt, 1989; Yin, 1989). While we cannot completely rule out the possibility that such events occurred, we are not aware of any event other than the treatment that followed this pattern fully. There were other factors, such as changes in the business climate that could have conceivably affected network growth. Upon scrutiny, however, we find that these factors remained constant across all three time periods or at least two of the three time periods.

Concerning the economic climate of Israel, we measured both quarterly economic indicators and average store revenue in the MBE Israel network from the middle until the end of the study to determine if a slowdown in economic growth was responsible for the decline in sales of new franchises during the last part of the period of observation. GDP increased during the entire period of the study but at a slightly decreasing rate during the last two years of the study. We constructed a measure of elasticity between the economic indicators and store revenue. The elasticity during the entire period is very small, ranging from -0.025 to 0.317 and is random with no clear pattern emerging. For the economic climate to have been the cause of the growth it should coincide, to some degree (although there may be a lag) with the pattern of network growth results. At the very least elasticity should be high or become significantly higher during the third period but we find that it does not.

Despite the overall economic climate, it is possible that lack of franchisee profitability (a possible motive for giving negative referrals to potential franchisees), rather than Eitan's policy changes, led to the decline in performance in the third period. However, for this factor to be the case one would expect either a precipitous decline in store revenues (data on store profitability is not available) at the time of Eitan's promotion (December 1999) or possibly a perennial lack of profitability with little hope for future prospects. Neither occurred in the MBE Israel network. Accounting for month to month variation in same store sales every single MBE Israel franchise saw steady increases in store revenue from inception through the end of 1999 with 86 percent seeing a steady increase through the end of 2000.

The average six-month revenue for all stores in operation for at least two months (to allow for minimal learning curve effects) in the first half of 1999 was 14.5 percent higher than the last half of 1998. The average from July to December 1999 was another 8.0 percent higher than the first six months of 1999 resulting in a year on year increase of 23.7 percent. Driven by two poor performing stores, the first six months of 2000 registered a 12 percent revenue decline; yet, by the end of 2000, revenues had rebounded to only a 1 percent decrease over year end 1999 figures. Even when decreasing the sample by increasing the required number of months in operation to three to allow for a longer learning curve, the year on year increase, between 1998 to 1999, is 21.6 percent.[10] Despite the mixed same store sales growth in 2000, lack of revenue does not seem to be the cause of the negative performance observed in the third period. For lack of revenue to be the cause of the observed pattern one would expect chronic low revenue or decreasing revenue for the period prior to Eitan's promotion. Otherwise one would expect to see franchise sales in the first six months of Eitan's tenure as CEO. While it is possible that no new stores were scheduled to be added at that point and declining revenue during the first six months of 2000 (even though only a few stores were declining) inhibited new franchisees from joining the network, one would expect to see the situation eased as revenues rebounded in the second half of 2000. Such was not the case.

Another possible threat is that the individuals at MBE Israel learned from the application of the treatment the first time and specifically avoided those problems the second time around. While top management did realize that a lack of growth at the beginning was directly due to not "listening to others" and subsequently copied the MBE system for network growth as closely as possible, they did not connect network growth with the concept of following the system as a whole. Instead they saw it as adherence to a particular part of that system, specifically the timing of selling franchises vis-à-vis the operation of the pilot store. The failure to learn from the first treatment is clearly seen by the departure from that same system during the last two years of the period of observation. At the time no one, including the observers, realized that departure from the system as a whole was the treatment being applied. The fact that the essence of the treatment was recognized retrospectively only enhances the validity.[11]

A third alternative explanation for the positive growth in the middle of the period of observation is that Albert was correct; perfecting the pilot store before selling franchises results in excellent growth. Yet, the pilot stores were never able to consistently break even until after there were sufficient numbers in the network to bring up the average revenue of all the stores in the network. Moreover, such a scenario would not explain the zero growth observed at the end of the period.

Another potential explanation for the positive growth could be the existence of a two-year lag between demonstration of the MBE business and actual franchisee recruitment. However, this is not the case in MBE Israel with the average time from demonstration to franchise sale of less than four months during the period in question. A time lag of nearly two years between demonstration of the concept and sale of the franchise would be required if such a lag were the cause of the pattern found in the data.

A sixth potential threat is that factors correlated with Eitan's promotion to CEO were responsible for the zero growth following that action. Such factors could be an increase in pressure for financial performance due to Albert's shift to a passive investor or possibly changes in Eitan's compensation package. Such factors, however, while being an alternative or complementary explanation for the decision to confront the franchisees concerning late royalty payments and for the decision to institute centralized operations do not alter the conclusion that Eitan's policy changes did in fact conflict with the Family Principle. Nor do such factors address the negative reaction of the franchisees which, according to all accounts, was in direct response to changes initiated by Eitan.

A final threat to validity is that employee turnover in the MBE network caused either the pattern of growth or the pattern of decline in the third period. Employee turnover could occur either through widespread turnover in headquarters or through a large-scale change in the way the business was operated outside of that detailed in the case. Through the period of observation, however, there were only incidental personnel changes at headquarters and, outside of the adherence to the 52 week plan, intentional changes in the franchisor/franchisee relationship, and Eitan's attempt at centralization, there were no major changes in the way the business was operated. Eitan's promotion to CEO was a major determinant in the second decision to deviate from the system for network growth. His promotion, however, did not result in a major change in other operating policies. Albert had been slowly removing himself from daily operations for some time before the promotion, leaving Eitan in charge of the day to day decisions and the actual operation of the network. The key change in Eitan's promotion was that Eitan, rather than Albert, became the primary ML interface with the franchisee. The centralization of operations was a major operating change. However, both pilot center and franchisee revenues grew during this period. Moreover, while it was a radical change for the operation of the stores this chapter is about adaptation of the system for network growth and the primary change in this policy in that regard was subordination of the franchisees to the level of employee.

Finally, we recognize that there may be instability in the measures or other unmeasured factors that might account for the results. While missing factors is a difficulty for most studies, this threat is typically heightened in a naturally occurring quasi-experiment due to the often endogenous nature of policy changes. However, while the possibility of significant, omitted variables may be higher, the repeated-treatment design substantially mitigates this threat. Moreover, data were gathered in real-time, as the events unfolded, over an eight-year period of time. During that entire period and beyond we had full access to the major parties, allowing us to follow closely the development of the MBE Israel network. During the period of observation and during interviews with all the principal players, no other factors emerged as either major policy changes or external factors that may have caused the observed pattern other than those discussed here. Other than the treatment, we know of no factors which were applied, removed, and re-applied and are unaware of any omitted variables which might possibly account for shifts in performance in any given time period.

Discussion and Conclusion

In mathematics and in the "exact" sciences the counterexample provides a constructive proof that a theorem or theory is not universally true and should therefore be abandoned or at least reformulated to exclude the offending example. Developing counterexamples is a standard part of creative research to determine the limitations of a proposed theorem.

Analogously, in the social sciences, an example of an approach that does not work as desired may point to serious shortcomings in the current system of beliefs, unless it is a bizarre case that is relatively rare and can safely be ignored. However, if the example points to a failure that can affect an important segment of the relevant population, a change in existing policy may be required. This is why the routine reporting of unwanted outcomes is a common method for identifying deficiencies in a system. Presumably these investigations will lead to changes in policy or procedures to reduce the chances of recurrence (Hoaglin et al., 1982).

We believe that MBE Israel, while being a conservative counterexample to the conventional wisdom of presumptive adaptation, is not an outlier. The example is representative to the extent that the setting is similar to that faced by other franchisees and the extent to which franchisees and others engaged in transfers of complex knowledge ascribe the same meaning to the form of departure decision as Albert did (Ilgen, 1986). In other words, generalizability of the MBE Israel example hinges on whether the setting of Israel is an outlier and whether other franchisees (or individuals and units engaged in the transfer of organizational practices) both within and outside MBE are faced with pressure to adapt to the local environment and the need to choose a starting form for that adaptation (i.e., the choice between presumptive adaptation or copying the franchise format or organizational practice as closely as possible).

Evidence from within the international MBE community, other franchising contexts, and the transfer of organizational practices outside of franchising indicates that both the choice of form of departure and the results obtained by Albert are not atypical. The correlation between the number of steps in the 52 week plan followed and the number of franchisees added each year for the entire MBE international network begins at 0.86 (statistically significant at the 0.05 level) in the second year of ML operation and decreases slowly to 0.51 by the eighth year and remaining statistically significant through the fifth year of operation. This result suggests that our findings are consistent with the experience of the larger MBE international network.

Moreover, through interviews conducted as part of a larger study involving knowledge transfer within the international MBE network, we find that nearly all of the MBE MLs have faced the issue of the form of departure for adaptation with varying decisions and varying results. Some MLs[12] utilized an approach similar to Albert's and presumptively adapted the MBE system for network growth, with the same tendency towards low growth results.

Other MLs adapted presumptively but to a lesser degree (neglected some, albeit fewer, steps in the 52 week plan) and found that adaptation created difficulties that slowed and even reversed growth. For example, one particular ML devoted significant up-front time altering lead generation materials to "ensure" a greater fit with local culture with the intent to thereby increase the rate of network growth. While such a move may have been warranted, the focus on changing the materials required significant time and money that needed to be spent on other aspects of network growth impairing its ability to support existing franchisees and resulting eventually in a revenue shortfall. The revenue shortfall led to a vicious cycle where lack of resources to spend on lead generation slowed down network growth which in turn curtailed support and revenue growth. Ultimately the ML ended the affiliation with MBE due to financial duress. Even relatively moderate and seemingly sensible presumptive adaptation created dynamics that led to poor network growth.

Other MLs, however, chose to follow the MBE system as closely as possible, with results opposite to Albert's. One example is the Italian ML.

> Our system is very close to the US . . . There was no point in buying a concept and then doing something else . . . We do it exactly like the US, not only in image but in business. (Italian ML)

Yet other MLs realized the need to adapt but chose to begin that adaptation from a faithful replica of the original practices, and then incrementally adapting only after the practices were sufficiently understood in the local context (not until significant time had passed). The Canadian ML, for instance, faithfully followed the US model for both network growth and the business format for the first 3–4 years of operation. At that point he began to adapt the business format by incrementally emphasizing the sale of document services over shipping. To support this shift in the business format he gradually shifted the lead generation process (a focus on document services requires a more technologically sophisticated franchisee) as well as the substance of the training franchisees received.

> I said "hey, this [the original MBE model] is a pretty successful concept," and I still believe it is probably one of the most successful, if not the most successful, service concepts in the world. . . . So, [concerning modifications] I went kind of slow to start with. (Canadian ML)

As reported in Table 9.2 previously, the results of these MLs are in stark contrast to those of Albert and others who engaged in significant presumptive adaptation.

Our conclusions could be generalized beyond MBE to the extent to which the lessons are transferable to other settings (Denzin and Lincoln, 1998). In the domain of franchising, such lessons seem especially applicable to organizations relying on a ML system. More generally, however, the MBE Israel example speaks to the broader phenomenon of choosing the form of departure in the transfer of franchising knowledge to franchisees at all levels. For instance, the proclivity for presumptive adaptation seems to be characteristic of franchising in general, not just MBE, and not just of the method for franchising growth. Franchisees often attempt to "improve" on the franchise system that they join by immediately introducing major modifications because they believe that they can quickly improve its profitability in their unique situation (Kaufmann and Eroglu, 1998; Seid and Thomas, 2000). Not only does the form of departure seem to be a decision commonly approached but the pattern of results obtained at MBE Israel also seems to be characteristic. Franchisees in general are warned explicitly to refrain from significant adaptation by franchisors as well as by franchising experts and many franchisees have learned the same lesson that Albert did (Bradach, 1998; Seid and Thomas, 2000). Some franchisors, recognizing this pattern, have enacted policies to overcome it. For example, Great Harvest Bread Co.

requires that its franchisees adhere closely to the original practice, allowing incremental modifications only after at least a year has passed (Great Harvest Bread, 1999).

While to some extent franchising may be a specialized setting because the locus of adaptation often lies with the recipient rather than headquarters, policies acknowledging the potential difficulties in choosing a form of departure too remote from the original practice occur in contexts other than franchising. Knowledge transfer policies at Xerox Europe and Intel are illustrative of the potential generalizability outside of the franchising domain. Xerox Europe, which has a long and distinguished history transferring best practices, demands that receiving units copy the practice exactly as it is performed at the source until it is able to achieve similar results (*Financial Times*, 1997). Intel also utilizes the copy exact policy when establishing new semi-conductor fabs, requiring engineers to replicate fab designs and work practices with exactitude (McDonald, 1998). In other words, both organizations strongly discourage presumptive adaptation.

The MBE Israel case thus suggests that the seemingly sensible idea of presumptively adapting a practice to fit a particular environment, to be responsive to local institutions, to attempt to anticipate local isomorphic pressures may be counterproductive when transferring an insufficiently well-understood practice across borders. This finding at the very least suggests that the form of departure for adaptation is an important managerial choice that has thus far received little consideration. Such a decision is different from the decision to initiate the transfer and deserves consideration in its own right. This finding is also a note of caution against engaging in extensive presumptive adaptation.

As the Great Harvest Bread Co. (Great Harvest Bread, 1999), Intel (McDonald, 1998), and Xerox Europe (*Financial Times*, 1997) examples illustrate, presumptive adaptation is not a necessary condition for successful transfer. Rather than beginning the transfer by actively engaging in presumptive adaptation, the transfer process can begin instead by creating, in the new environment, a replica of an existing working practice and then systematically fine tuning it, by introducing modifications in a controlled way, until satisfactory results are achieved. Such a conservative approach to presumptive adaptation may be more appropriate when either the practice being transferred or the relevant environment is complex or ambiguous. In such a context this approach may allow the recipient unit to better approximate the appropriate final form by maximizing the information contained in the original example when the other relevant criteria cannot be fully specified ex-ante.

The question then becomes how different from the original practice could the form of departure be in the new setting before the diagnostic value of the original template is effectively lost, i.e., before it becomes comparatively more efficient to resort to trial and error than to continue to use the original for diagnosis. Indeed, for even moderately complex practices, a small departure from the original may create major problems. The sensitivity to the form of departure is compounded by the fact that the host environment is often not well understood, even by the receiving unit. Nor, given the fact that the practice is new to the receiving unit, is the interaction between the adapted practice and systemic effects likely to be completely understood (Ghoshal and Westney, 1993). Thus, presuming that adaptation can be planned and implemented in advance entails presuming extraordinary understanding and foresight not just for the recipient (the usual subject) but the source as well. Yet, a form of departure identical to the original practice may turn out to be unrealistic. Some obvious features may have to be modified from the start.

It would seem that the lesson from MBE Israel's experience is thus manifold. First, it confirms the form of departure for adaptation to be a major managerial consideration. Second, it would seem that the choice of a form of departure that is closest to the one of the original example maximizes the possibilities of drawing on the experience embedded in that example to grow a network of stores in the new environment. This form of departure is qualitatively different from one where substantial modifications are introduced ahead of the implementation. Minimizing presumptive adaptation, i.e., choosing a starting form that is as close to the original example as possible, seems to have been the most efficient and effective way to proceed.

Thus, MBE Israel's experience suggests that the fact that a practice will eventually be adapted to fit a new environment better does not necessarily entail that presumptive adaptation is necessary, i.e., that the form of departure for the process of adaptation must be a significantly modified practice. In this sense, the MBE case serves as a striking counterexample to such an assumption. It suggests that the form of departure for the adaptation process has to be carefully chosen. Beginning the transfer process by introducing modifications to a working practice before implementing it in another location, or beginning the adaptation process with a large change from the original, could have deleterious consequences. A seemingly obvious form of departure for adaptation may in fact prove incorrect. Adaptation to a new environment may be greatly facilitated by beginning from a different starting form, one that helps preserve to the extent possible the diagnostic value of the working example.

These conclusions suggest a number of directions for future research. Of primary importance is specifying the set of possible starting forms from which to begin the process of adaptation and identifying the primary contingencies that would determine the choice of the most appropriate one. Of importance also is specifying the factors that account for varying levels of presumptive adaptation.

Perhaps an even more fundamental question raised by our study is whether and to what extent presumptive adaptation of any kind could be beneficial. Our findings suggest the troubling hypothesis that any form of presumptive adaptation, i.e., of adaptation that relies on presumed characteristics of a host environment, may in the end prove counterproductive. When the intent is to leverage existing knowledge, a strong contender for the correct form of departure seems to be the original practice.

Acknowledgments

The authors acknowledge helpful comments from Sid Winter, Therese Flaherty, Nicolaj Siggelkow, Lori Rosenkopf, Participants at the Strategic Management Society 2002 conference and Seminars at INSEAD.

Notes

1. Knowledge assets, in general, are considered by many to be central to competitive advantage in a wide variety of settings including MNCs (Argote and Ingram, 2000; Eisenhardt

and Martin, 2000; Gupta and Govindarajan, 2000; Nelson and Winter, 1982; Teece et al., 1997; Zander and Kogut, 1995).

2. We chose to study network growth rather than the operation of individual stores for a number of reasons. First, it enables us to use a repeated-treatment, quasi-experimental research design rather than the non-equivalent groups post-test only design the study of individual stores would require. The latter design is substantially weaker in terms of internal validity. Second, while one could potentially overcome the inherent weaknesses of the latter design it would require a deep level of access. We had virtually unfettered access to MBE Israel headquarters but had limited access to the individual franchisees, making it impossible to adequately address the threats to validity that arise from the use of a non-equivalent groups post-test only research design.

3. Confidentiality reasons prevent us from revealing exact details from the 52 week plan.

4. The limitations of the contract as a governance tool and the fundamental importance of persuasion have been recognized as critical to franchise systems in general (Bradach, 1998; Seid and Thomas, 2000).

5. The MLs interviewed in this regard include those from Poland, Mexico, Malaysia, Austria-Hungary, the Caribbean, the UK, Portugal, Singapore, Philippines, Central America, Andean region, France, Canada, Japan, Italy, and Turkey.

6. When markets become saturated franchise organizations often turn to maximizing the units they already have.

7. A pilot store is a model store, the first to be opened in a particular geographic area, which is run by the ML as a tangible exemplar of how to operate a franchise unit.

8. Israel ranks nineteenth on Hofstede's (1997) cultural indices for uncertainty avoidance with a score of 82 as compared to a US score of 46 and an average across all 53 countries in his sample of 65.

9. Israel ranks nineteenth on Hofstede's (1997) cultural indices for individualism with a score of 54 as compared to a US score of 91 and an average across all 53 countries in his sample of 43.

10. Because the same store revenue was generally increasing for all stores during this period, extending the cutoff date for including stores in the sample will naturally decrease the year-to-year percentage increase. However, even increasing the cutoff to 6 months to allow for a longer learning curve yields a 12.5 percent year-to-year increase in sales at the time Eitan became CEO.

11. Campbell and Overman (1988) reach a similar conclusion about the likelihood of social threats to validity in their study of the Connecticut crackdown on speeding.

12. Names withheld for confidentiality reasons.

References

Anand, J. and Kogut, B. 1997: Technological capabilities of countries, firm rivalry and foreign direct investment. *Journal of International Business Studies*, 28, 445–465.

Argote, L. and Ingram, P. 2000: Knowledge transfer: A basis for the competitive advantage of firms. *Organizational Behavior and Human Decision Processes*, 82, 1–8.

Baron, J.N., Hannan, M.T., and Burton, M.D. 1999: Building the iron cage: Determinants of managerial intensity in the early years of organizations. *American Sociological Review*, 64, 527–547.

Bartlett, C.A. and Ghoshal, S. 1989: *Managing across Borders: The Transnational Solution*. Boston, MA: Harvard Business School Press.

Bradach, J.L. 1998: *Franchise Organizations*. Boston, MA: Harvard Business School Press.

Brannen, Y. and Wilson, J.M. 1996: What does Mickey Mouse mean to you? *Financial Times*, April 26, 14–16.

Burgelman, R.A. 1983: A process model of internal corporate venturing in the diversified major firm. *Administrative Science Quarterly*, 28, 223–244.

Buzzell, R.D. 1968: Can you standardize multinational marketing? *Harvard Business Review*, (November/December), 102–113.

Campbell, D.T. and Overman, E.S. 1988: *Methodology and Epistemology for Social Science: Selected Papers*. Chicago, IL: University of Chicago Press.

Cantwell, J. 1989: *Technological Innovation and the Multinational Corporation*. Oxford, UK: Basil Blackwell.

Caves, R.E. 1996: *Multinational Enterprise and Economic Analysis* (2nd edn). Cambridge, UK: Cambridge University Press.

Cook, T.D. 1991: Clarifying the warrant for generalized causal inferences in quasi-experimentation. In M.W. McLaughlin and D.C. Phillips (eds.), *Evaluation and Education: At Quarter Century: Ninetieth Yearbook of the National Society for the Study of Education*. Chicago, IL: University of Chicago Press, 115–145.

Cook, T.D. and Campbell, D.T. 1979: *Quasi-experimentation: Design and Analysis Issues for Field Settings*. Boston, MA: Houghton Mifflin Company.

Cook, T.D., Campbell, D.T., and Peracchio, L. 1990: Quasi experimentation. In M.D. Dunnette and L.M. Hough (eds.), *Handbook of Industrial and Organizational Psychology*, 2nd edn, vol. 1. Palo Alto, CA: Consulting Psychologists Press, 491–576.

Cui, G. and Liu, Q. 2001: Executive insights: Emerging market segments in a transitional economy: A study of urban consumers in China. *Journal of International Marketing*, 9, 84–106.

Denzin, N. and Lincoln, Y. 1998: *Handbook of Qualitative Research*. Thousand Oaks, CA: Sage.

Douglas, S.P. and Wind, Y. 1987: The myth of globalization. *Columbia Journal of World Business*, 22, 19–29.

Dunning, J.H. 1977: Trade, location of economic activity and the MNE: A search for an eclectic approach. In B. Ohlin, P.O. Hesselborn, and P.M. Wijkman (eds.), *The International Allocation of Economic Activity*. New York: Holmes & Meier, 395–418.

Eisenhardt, K. 1989. Building theory from case study research. *Academy of Management Review*, 14, 532–550.

Eisenhardt, K.M. and Martin, J.A. 2000: Dynamic capabilities: What are they? *Strategic Management Journal*, 21, 1105–1121.

Financial Times 1997: Xerox makes copies. *Financial Times*, July 14.

Ghoshal, S. and Westney, D.E. 1993: *Organizational Theory and the Multinational Corporation*. New York: St Martin's Press.

Gielens, K. and Dekimpe, M.G. 2001: Do international entry decisions of retail chains matter in the long run? *International Journal of Research in Marketing*, 18, 235–259.

Great Harvest Bread 1999: *Apprenticeship Agreement, 2*. Great Harvest Bread Co., Dillon, MT.

Griffith, D.A., Hu, M.Y., and Ryans, J.K., Jr. 2000: Process standardization across intra and inter-cultural relationships. *Journal of International Business Studies*, 31, 303–324.

Gupta, A.K. and Govindarajan, V. 2000: Knowledge flows within multinational corporations. *Strategic Management Journal*, 21, 473–496.

Hannan, M.T., Burton, M.D., and Baron, J.N. 1996: Inertia and change in the early years: Employment relations in young, high-technology firms. *Industrial and Corporate Change*, 5, 503–536.

Hannon, J.M., Huang, I.C., and Jaw, B.S. 1995: International human resource strategy and its determinants: The case of subsidiaries in Taiwan. *Journal of International Business Studies*, 26, 531–554.

Hoaglin, D.C., Light, R.J., McPeek, B., Mosteller, F., and Stoto, M.A. 1982: *Data for Decisions: Information Strategies for Policymakers*. Cambridge, MA: Abt Books.

Hofstede, G. 1997: *Culture and Organizations: Software of the Mind*. New York: McGraw-Hill.

Hymer, S.H. 1976: *The International Operations of National Firms: A Study of Direct Investment*. Cambridge, MA: MIT Press.

Ilgen, D.R. 1986: Laboratory research: A question of when, not if. In E.A. Locke (ed.), *Generalizing from Laboratory to Field Settings: Research Findings from Industrial-Organizational Psychology, Organizational Behavior, and Human Resource Management*. Lexington, MA: Lexington Books, 257–266.

Kashani, K. 1989: Beware the pitfalls of global marketing. *Harvard Business Review*, 67, 91–98.

Kaufmann, P.J. and Eroglu, S. 1998: Standardization and adaptation in business format franchising. *Journal of Business Venturing*, 14, 69–85.

Kirkman, B.L., Gibson, C.B., and Shapiro, D.L. 2001: "Exporting" teams: Enhancing the implementation and effectiveness of work teams in global affiliates. *Organizational Dynamics*, 30, 12–29.

Kogut, B. and Zander, U. 1993: Knowledge of the firm and the evolutionary theory of the multinational enterprise. *Journal of International Business Studies*, 24, 625–646.

Kostova, T. 1999: Transnational transfer of strategic organizational practices: A contextual perspective. *Academy of Management Review*, 24, 308–324.

Kostova, T. and Roth, K. 2002: Adoption of an organizational practice by subsidiaries of multinational corporations: Institutional and relational effects. *Academy of Management Journal*, 45, 215–233.

Kostova, T. and Zaheer, S. 1999: Organizational legitimacy under conditions of complexity: The case of the multinational enterprise. *Academy of Management Review*, 24, 64–81.

Lawrence, P. and Lorsch, J. 1967: *Organization and Environment*. Boston, MA: Harvard University, Graduate School of Business Administration, Division of Research.

Lemak, D.J. and Arunthanes, W. 1997: Global business strategy: A contingency approach. *Multinational Business Review*, 5, 26–37.

Leonard-Barton, D. 1988: Implementation as mutual adaptation of technology and organization. *Research Policy*, 17, 251–267.

Lippman, S.A. and Rumelt, R.P. 1982: Uncertain imitability: An analysis of interfirm differences in efficiency under competition. *Bell Journal of Economics*, 13, 418–438.

Love, J.F. 1986: *McDonald's: Behind the Arches*. New York: Bantam Books.

Luo, Y. 2000: Determinants of local responsiveness: Perspectives from foreign subsidiaries in an emerging market. *Journal of Management*, 27, 451–477.

Mann, L. 1977. The effect of stimulus queues on queue-joining behavior. *Journal of Personality and Social Psychology*, 35, 437–442.

McDonald, C.J. 1998: The evolution of Intel's Copy Exactly! technology transfer method. *Intel Technology Journal*: http://www.intel.com/technology/itj/q41998/articles/art_41992.htm.

Miles, M.B. and Huberman, A.M. 1984: *Qualitative Data Analysis: A Sourcebook of New Methods*, Newbury Park, CA: Sage.

Morosini, P., Shane, S., and Singh, H. 1998: National cultural distance and cross-border acquisition performance. *Journal of International Business Studies*, 29, 137–158.

Nelson, R. and Winter, S. 1982: *An Evolutionary Theory of Economic Change*. Cambridge: MA, Belknap Press.

Nohria, N. and Ghoshal, S. 1997: *The Differentiated Network*. San Francisco, CA: Jossey-Bass Publishers.

Onkvisit, S. and Shaw, J.J. 1987: Standardized international advertising: A review and critical evaluation of the theoretical and empirical evidence. *Columbia Journal of World Business*, 22, 43–55.

Penrose, E.T. 1959: *The Theory of Growth of the Firm*. Oxford: Basil Blackwell.

Prahalad, C.K. and Doz, Y.L. 1987: *The Multinational Mission: Balancing Local Demands and Global Vision*. New York: Free Press.

Prahalad, C.K. and Lieberthal, K. 1998: The end of corporate imperialism. *Harvard Business Review*, 76, 68–79.

Rivkin, J.W. 2000: Imitation of complex strategies. *Management Science*, 46, 824–844.

Robert, C., Probst, T.M., Martocchio, J.J., and Drasgow, F. 2000: Empowerment and continuous improvement in the United States, Mexico, Poland, and India: Predicting fit on the basis of the dimensions of power distance and individualism. *Journal of Applied Psychology*, 85, 643–658.

Rosenzweig, P.M. and Nohria, N. 1994. Influences on human resource management practices in multinational corporations. *Journal of International Business Studies*, 25, 229–251.

Scott, W. R. 2001: *Institutions and Organizations* (2nd edn). Thousand Oaks, CA: Sage.

Seid, M. and Thomas, D. 2000: *Franchising for Dummies*. Foster City, CA: IDG Books Worldwide.

Siggelkow, N. 2002: Evolution toward fit. *Administrative Science Quarterly*, 47, 125–159.

Sorge, A. 1991: Strategic fit and the societal effect: Interpreting cross-national comparisons of technology, organization and human resources. *Organization Studies*, 12, 161–190.

Szulanski, G. 1996: Exploring internal stickiness: Impediments to the transfer of best practice within the firm. *Strategic Management Journal*, 17, 27–43.

Teece, D.J. 1986: Profiting from technological innovation: Implications for integration, collaboration, licensing and public policy. *Research Policy*, 15, 285–305.

Teece, D., Pisano, G., and Shuen, A. 1997: Dynamic capabilities and strategic management. *Strategic Management Journal*, 18, 509–533.

Tolbert, P.S. and Zucker, L.G. 1983: Institutional sources of change in the formal structure of organizations: The diffusion of civil service reforms, 1880–1935. *Administrative Science Quarterly*, 23, 22–39.

von Hippel, E. 1994: "Sticky information" and the locus of problem solving: Implications for innovation. *Management Science*, 40, 429–439.

Westney, D.E. 1987: *Imitation and Innovation: The Transfer of Western Organizational Patterns to Meiji Japan* (first edn). Cambridge, MA: Harvard University Press.

Westphal, J., Gulati, R., and Shortell, S. 1997: An institutional and network perspective on the content and consequences of TQM adoption. *Administrative Science Quarterly*, 42, 366–394.

Williamson, O.E. 1975: *Markets and Hierarchies: Analysis and Antitrust Implications*. New York: The Free Press.

Winter, S.G. and Szulanski, G. 2001: Replication as strategy. *Organization Science*, 12, 730–743.

Yan, R. 1994: To reach China's consumers, adapt to guo qing. *Harvard Business Review*, 72, 66–74.

Yin, R.K. 1989: *Case Study Research* (revised edn). Newbury Park, CA: Sage.

Yip, G.S. 1989: Global strategy: In a world of nations? *Sloan Management Review*, 31, 29–41.

Zander, U. and Kogut, B. 1995: Knowledge and the speed of the transfer and imitation of organizational capabilities: An empirical test. *Organization Science*, 5, 76–92.

Appendix 9.1

The MBE statement of culture and core values reproduced below (italics added for emphasis) can be found at the following web address: http://www.mbe.com/ambe/cacu.html.

MBE Culture

At MBE, we pride ourselves on maintaining an atmosphere of teamwork and camaraderie, a spirit that permeates our entire corporate culture. For this reason, we refer to the collective network of MBE corporate employees and franchisees as the *MBE Family*.

We understand the importance of a comfortable work environment that fosters growth, both personally and professionally. Our primary goal is to focus on customer intimacy while adhering to our core values of caring, honesty, fairness, integrity, trust, respect, commitment and accountability. A shared mission and core values are the heart and soul of the Mail Boxes Etc. culture. The MBE mission statement and core values have permanence because they grew out of a collaborative process that included every member of the MBE corporate office team.

Our Mission Statement

Making business easier worldwide through our service and distribution network, delivering personalized and convenient business solutions with world-class customer service.

Our Core Values

Respect, Accountability, Fairness, Trust, Caring, Commitment, Honesty, and Integrity

... Likewise, the officers who comprise the MBE Leadership Council wholeheartedly embrace the concept of "servant leadership" in their dealings with members of the MBE family. They, too, recognize that when we treat one another as "customers" we create an environment in which mutually beneficial relationships are developed and nurtured.

PART III

Superior Management and Governance Practices

A Bayesian Application of the Resource-based View: Narrowing the Gap between Theory and Practice

Mark H. Hansen, Lee T. Perry, and C. Shane Reese

Introduction

The resource-based view of the firm (RBV) offers a theoretical explanation of competitive advantage which is based on differences in firm resources (Barney, 1991; Peteraf, 1993; Rumelt, 1984; Wernerfelt, 1984). RBV logic is nearly ubiquitous as a *practical* tool as evidenced by its coverage in strategy classes, textbooks, and journals with largely managerial audiences (e.g., Collis and Montgomery, 1995; Hitt et al., 2001). Scholars have also relied upon the RBV in examining the relationship between firm resources and economic performance (Bergh, 1998; Deephouse, 2000; Hult and Ketchen, 2001). And yet, challenges continue to be registered by some academicians about the *theoretical* validity of RBV explanations of competitive advantage (Priem and Butler, 2001a). The apparent gap between the utility of the RBV as a practical tool and its utility as a theoretically sound explanation of competitive advantage deserves attention.

An observation from production agriculture is illustrative of this gap. In southeastern Idaho, farmers who grow potatoes have access to essentially the same resources. Sources of seed potatoes, fertilizers, equipment, and labor are common to all farmers in the region. Weather, air quality, and water quality are likewise common to all these farmers. Soil quality varies only slightly depending on the amount of sand in the soil. These farmers have access to the same markets. Given this set of circumstances, the RBV as a practical tool would predict that no farmer is likely to realize a competitive advantage vis-à-vis other farmers in the region. However, some farmers clearly enjoy a competitive advantage as evidenced by their survival, expansion, and wealth relative

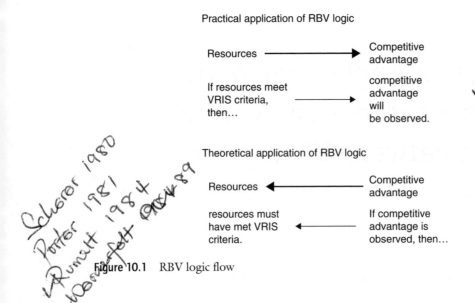

Practical application of RBV logic

Resources ⟶ Competitive advantage

If resources meet VRIS criteria, then... ⟶ competitive advantage will be observed.

Theoretical application of RBV logic

Resources ⟵ Competitive advantage

resources must have met VRIS criteria. ⟵ If competitive advantage is observed, then...

Figure 10.1   RBV logic flow

to their neighbors, some of whom are forced into bankruptcy. Thus practical prediction of no competitive advantage and the need to offer a theoretical explanation of observed competitive advantage seem to arise from homogeneously distributed resources. The incongruency in this example between practical prediction and theoretical explanation of observation is indicative of the RBV's gap between theory and practice.

One way to conceptualize the gap between the RBV's practical and theoretical utility is to consider the point at which competitive advantage becomes operative. Typically, competitive advantage is the endpoint in practical applications of the RBV and the beginning point in theoretical applications (see Figure 10.1). Perhaps the most common use of the RBV as a practical tool is the *ex ante* analysis of strategic actions, with a focus on predicting whether or not a resource is likely to lead to competitive advantage (e.g., Barney, 2002 – VRIO framework). If evidence suggests that a resource is valuable, rare, costly to imitate, and without close substitutes (VRIS) RBV logic holds that a competitive advantage will accrue to the owner of that resource. This logic is based upon several well-accepted economic principles such as scarcity and price theory (Peteraf, 1993; Rumelt, 1984; Stigler, 1966). Resource-based logic, thus applied, is difficult to refute.

On the other hand, the more theoretical application of the RBV involving the explanation of competitive advantage when it is observed, or the explanation of why competitive advantage is not observed, has been criticized by theorists (Priem and Butler, 2001b). These explanations of observed competitive advantage (or lack of it) would naturally seem to rest on the argument that the resources involved must (not) have been valuable, rare, costly to imitate, and without close substitutes. However, critics of the RBV point out that such reasoning is problematic in the absence of careful measurement of these four characteristics because such reasoning is not falsifiable (Priem and Butler, 2001b). Specifically, measurement of the *value* of a resource is problematic because the measurement of economic performance and resource *value* is confounded (Powell, 2001). This criticism is then generalized to the theory as a whole, calling into question the validity of the theory in a practical as well as theoretical sense.

Thus, a fundamental gap is observed between the accepted practical utility and the accepted theoretical utility of the RBV. This gap is especially interesting in light of the observation that the argument from competitive advantage back to resource characteristics rests on the same well-accepted economic principles as the argument from resource characteristics to competitive advantage. Although some research suggests that this gap stems from an inherent tautology in the RBV, we suggest that the gap is more appropriately attributed to a subtle form of a logical fallacy known as *post hoc ergo propter hoc*, meaning that because *B* follows *A*, *B* must have been caused by *A*. In other words, the tautology is not inherent in the economic logic underlying the RBV, rather the tautology results from the fallacious application of the economic logic. Therefore, we argue that narrowing the gap between the practical and theoretical utility of the RBV is largely a matter of recognizing and avoiding a *post hoc ergo propter hoc* logical fallacy.

This chapter offers two main suggestions for avoiding *post hoc ergo propter hoc* reasoning and thereby narrowing the gap between theory and practice. First, a modification of the RBV framework is proposed that argues for an explicit recognition of the distinction between resources and services made by Penrose (1995 [1959]). This distinction enhances the firm-level focus of the RBV. Second, an argument is made for more careful alignment of theory and methodology when applying the RBV. A Bayesian hierarchical modeling methodology is proposed because of the congruency between this methodology and the firm-level nature of the RBV. Then, the modified RBV is applied empirically using the proposed Bayesian hierarchical model to demonstrate how such an approach may be used to address a variety of issues. Finally, a discussion section explores the implications of the proposed RBV modifications and the Bayesian modeling approach.

Towards Informative Specificity

The subtle form of a *post hoc ergo propter hoc* logical fallacy to which some RBV explanations of competitive advantage may be subject stems from an overly general definition of resources and a vague pathway from resources to competitive advantage. Over-generalization and definitional vagueness create a context in which theories are difficult to falsify. The challenge is that the refutation of a proposition seems to be impossible when that proposition lacks what we refer to as informative specificity.[1] A statement (argument, proposition, hypothesis, etc.) has the quality of informative specificity if that statement conveys sufficient information to render the statement both useful and contestable. For example, the statement that the boiling point of water is 212.0 °F at sea level and 208.4 °F at an elevation of 2,000 ft is packed with informative specificity. This statement is useful and it can be contested in an experimental setting.

On the other hand, the statement '*A* causes *B*' lacks informative specificity when *how A* causes *B* is not satisfactorily explained. The statement is difficult to refute because one is hard pressed to know exactly *what* is to be refuted. Whenever *B* is observed one can easily slip into the logical fallacy of accepting the proposition since *B* followed *A* as predicted. This reasoning is especially seductive if the original proposition that *A* causes *B* is intuitively appealing. Ultimately, the logical fallacy is exposed by returning to the original statement and asking *how A* causes *B* – a question meant to reveal whether sufficient informative specificity exists.

Explanations of differing levels of heat produced in a forge offer an interesting parallel to RBV explanations of firm performance. The theoretical argument that superior levels of heat in a forge are produced through superior combinations of air and fuel would appear to be similarly tautological to RBV explanations of firm performance. It is difficult to argue with the statement that superior air and fuel produce superior forge heat. Moreover, who would dispute the argument that observed superior forge heat was produced by superior combination of air and fuel? However, both explanations lack informative specificity. If the theoretical argument is refined to include a specific assertion about *how* the air and fuel are mixed to produce superior heat in a forge, the tautology disappears since different mixtures and mixing methods of air and fuel can be tested.

The above example suggests that the danger of committing a *post hoc ergo propter hoc* logical fallacy is especially high when the causal pathway is so vaguely and generally defined that falsification is not possible. The inability to falsify a statement that lacks informative specificity gives rise to the criticisms of tautology like those leveled at the RBV (Priem and Butler, 2001b). Logical fallacy and tautology can both be avoided by applying sufficient informative specificity in defining causal pathways from resources to competitive advantage.

An important point to recognize about RBV logic is that it may well be correct even if its applications are subject to logical fallacy and tautology. The enduring practical utility of the RBV is a testimonial to the fact that most people assume that competitive advantage is largely determined by firm resources (Barney, 2001). Nevertheless, greater informative specificity may pre-empt criticisms of logical fallacy and tautology and thereby narrow the gap between the practical and theoretical utility of the RBV.

Resources and Services

Edith Penrose's book, *The Theory of the Growth of the Firm* (1995 [1959]), is widely considered to be the RBV's seminal work. If her book is the primary seminal work, then the works of Wernerfelt (1984), Rumelt (1984), Barney (1986; 1991), Conner (1991), Mahoney and Pandian (1992), Amit and Shoemaker (1993) and Peteraf (1993), may properly be called secondary seminal works that followed decades later. As is often the case (e.g., transaction cost theory with Coase, 1937, followed by Alchian and Demsetz, 1972 and Williamson, 1975), these secondary seminal works expand and build upon a few of the "big ideas" of the primary seminal work. Most secondary seminal works in the RBV appear, however, to have ignored one of Penrose's most important "big ideas" – the distinction between *resources* and the *services*[2] those resources can render. Mahoney and Pandian (1992) is a notable exception – they clearly recognize the significance of Penrose's distinction. Also, in the opening paragraph of Wernerfelt's 1984 article he recognizes that "Most products require the services of several resources and most resources can be used in several products" (p. 171). Beyond these recognitions, the distinction between resources and services is largely forgotten in the RBV literature.

About the distinction between resources and services, Penrose (1995: 25) wrote:

> The important distinction between resources and services is not their relative durability; rather it lies in the fact that resources consist of a bundle of potential services and can, for the most part, be defined independently of their use, while services cannot be so defined, the very word "service" implying a function, an activity. As we shall see, it is largely in this distinction that we find the source of the uniqueness of each individual firm.

Penrose's assertion that the source of firm uniqueness is to be found in the distinction between resources and services is very different from the current prevailing view that resources *per se* are the source of firm uniqueness. We argue that this distinction has important implications for the RBV – it provides informative specificity about how resources create superior economic value.

Why the distinction matters

According to Barney, the RBV rests on two important assumptions: (1) that firms may be heterogeneous with respect to the strategic resources they control, and (2) that these resources may not be perfectly mobile across firms (1991: 101). Heterogeneity and imperfect mobility may well be necessary conditions for competitive advantage (Peteraf, 1993). However, heterogeneity and imperfect mobility with respect to a firm's resources may not be a necessary condition for competitive advantage. A firm's heterogeneous and imperfectly mobile *services* may yield a competitive advantage.

The distinction between resources and services is important because it allows for the possibility that relatively homogeneous resources may be transformed into relatively heterogeneous services, and that such heterogeneous services are, in fact, the more proximal source of competitive advantage. Explanations of firms that achieve extraordinary returns with only ordinary resources become more theoretically satisfying when viewed through this modified RBV lens. This argument builds on Penrose's notion of a firm's "subjective productive opportunity" which refers to what the firm "thinks it can accomplish" given its resources (1995: 41). It is also consistent with Barney's (1986) reasoning that some firms are better than other firms in recognizing sources of potential value in factor markets. What a firm does with its resources would appear to be at least as important as which resources it possesses. The subtle, yet profound, implication is that firms with homogeneously distributed resources may nevertheless realize competitive advantage.

While the distinction between resources and services may not open Priem and Butler's (2001a) "exogenous black box"[3] it does improve understanding about their "process black box." Coming at it from a slightly different angle, but making substantially the same point, Alchian and Demsetz (1972: 793) observed that "efficient production with heterogeneous resources is a result not of having better resources but in knowing more accurately the relative productive performances of those resources." One might argue within the current RBV framework that a pristine spring which produces pleasant tasting water is a potential source of competitive advantage for the owner of the spring (while conceding that the value of that resource was determined in ways that are exogenous to the RBV theory developed in Barney's 1991 article (Barney, 2001; Priem and Butler, 2001b). The interesting question to the strategist is: How does the owner of the spring actually realize that competitive advantage? Two possibilities would appear to be either selling the spring itself (a factor market) or bottling the water and selling bottled water (a product market). Barney's (1986) "factor markets" paper describes the conditions under which value might be realized in the selling of the spring itself. One could also call on several other works in the RBV to argue that the owner of the spring will enjoy a sustainable competitive advantage only if the bottling, selling, and distribution of the water results in bottled water that is valuable, rare, costly to imitate, and non-substitutable (Barney, 1991; Peteraf, 1993; Wernerfelt, 1984). And therein lies the "process black box," especially in regard to endogenous value creation. When, where, and, especially, how will the resources of the firm be useful in producing bottled water that results in superior economic performance for the firm?

In the product market scenario it is implicitly understood that the value of the spring is ultimately dependent upon the resources that the firm is able to bring to bear on the process of bottling, selling, and distributing the water. However, in order to move beyond this well-accepted, implicit understanding, the difference between the resources and the services provided by those resources must be considered. By recognizing the distinction between resources and the services those resources can generate, the possibility exists that identical sets of productive resources may provide different services that result in different levels of economic performance. The resources–services distinction allows an examination of the pathway from resources to services to economic performance, rather than simply imputing value directly to the spring when superior economic performance is observed.

Two classes of resources

The explicit distinction that Penrose (1995) makes between resources and services is consistent with the distinction she makes between resources and the administration of those resources. Administration, of course, refers to the role of the managers (or entrepreneurs) of the firm in determining how the resources of the firm are to be used. Early on in the development of her theory, Penrose is careful to distinguish between productive resources and the "administrative decisions" that govern the use of resources. Later in her theoretical development she clearly includes managerial talent as a resource. Thus, in Penrose's framework two classes of resources are implied: "productive resources" and resources that exercise discretion over the use of "productive resources."

We simply adopt Penrose's (1995) term to refer to "productive resources." Productive resources include the physical resources of a firm, the knowledge embedded in the human capital of the firm (including non-strategy making managers), and other intangible resources such as reputation, brand equity, etc. In an attempt to bring further informative specificity and clarity to these two classes of resources we refer to the second class of resources as *catalytic resources*. Catalytic resources refer to the knowledge and skill of those managers and non-managers who exercise discretion over the use of a firm's productive resources. The role of management and boards of directors in determining the strategic direction of firms is well established in the literature (Barney, 1995; Castanias and Helfat, 1991; Sundaramurthy and Lewis, 2003). A firm's catalytic resources may be viewed as the ability of the firm's leaders to conceive of combinations or bundles of productive resources that will produce unique and valuable services.

The distinction between productive and catalytic resources may be better understood by considering how it relates to the capabilities, routines, and dynamic capabilities frameworks. Capabilities and routines would generally be considered among the productive resources of firms (Andrews, 1980; Dosi et al., 2000; Winter, 1995). Like other productive resources, capabilities and routines can be bundled in various ways to produce services. For example, a firm may have a capability or routine of working sheet metal that could be utilized to produce toasters or refrigerators depending on the administrative decisions of managers.

The term "dynamic capabilities" is broader in that it spans catalytic resources and productive resources. Dynamic capabilities refer to a firm's ability to "integrate" and "reconfigure" the resource base of a firm, as well as the ability to "deploy" or "release" resources (Eisenhardt and Martin, 2000; Teece et al., 1997). The integration and reconfiguring of a firm's resource base involves the catalytic resources of the firm and the releasing or deploying of resources involves the productive resources of the firm. A firm may have some dynamic capabilities that are catalytic resources and other dynamic capabilities that are productive resources.

Alternatively, catalytic resources would include what Makadok (2001) refers to as resource-picking and capability building mechanisms because catalytic resources are used in picking resources as well as in deciding which capabilities would be developed and used in transforming productive resources into services.

Similar overlap exists between catalytic resources and higher order routines (Dosi et al., 2000). While most routines would be considered as part of a firm's productive resources, some higher order routines involving the bundling of resources may properly be considered catalytic resources. Thus, in this modified RBV framework catalytic resources (one form of dynamic capabilities) are employed in exercising discretion over productive resources, including the capabilities, some dynamic capabilities, routines, and competencies as well as the tangible and other intangible resources of firms.

A model for converting resources into services

A rather simple modification of the RBV framework can yield significantly enhanced insights into the generation of competitive advantage. We argue that the catalytic resources of a firm act on that firm's productive resources to generate services, which, in turn, may lead to competitive advantage and superior economic performance. The model focuses attention on the administrative decisions that convert resources into services (see Figure 10.2). These administrative decisions may consist of rebundling

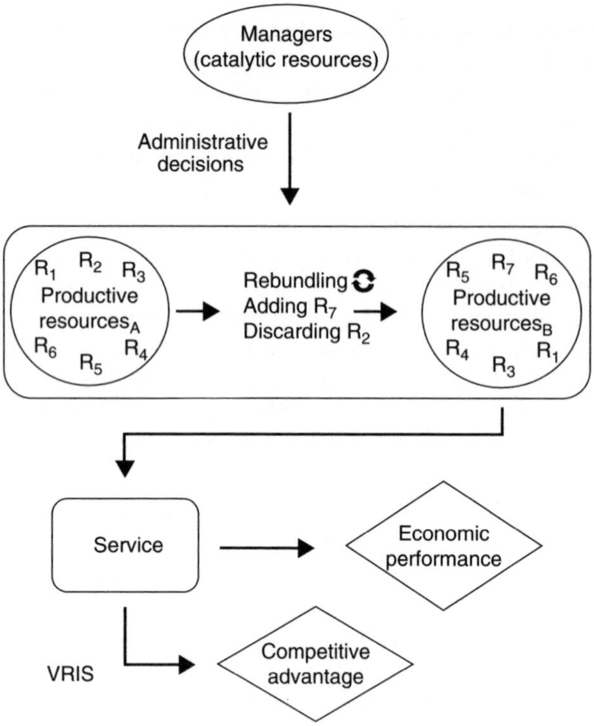

Figure 10.2   Modified RBV logic flow

the existing resources of the firm, adding new resources, discarding resources, or more likely, some combination of the three. Services are generated as a result of the administrative decisions that configure the firm's resources in a particular way. The services thus generated may result in competitive advantage and possibly superior economic performance if the services meet the VRIS criteria.

This modified RBV framework is substantially different from what has emerged in the secondary seminal works in the RBV. Secondary seminal works adopt a very general, all-inclusive definition of resources and link those resources directly to competitive advantage. Wernerfelt defines resources as "anything which could be thought of as a strength or weakness of a firm" (1984: 172). Barney (1991) also adopts a definition of resources that includes "all assets, capabilities, organizational processes, firm attributes, information, knowledge, etc. controlled by a firm that enable the firm to conceive of and implement strategies that improve its efficiency and effectiveness (Daft, 1983)." The modified RBV framework recognizes two types of resources: one which acts upon the other. Also, this model recognizes the *services* step between resources and competitive advantage. These simple recognitions allow meaningful explanations of competitive advantage – especially if that competitive advantage appears to spring from homogeneously distributed resources.

Most RBV scholars would agree that there is an implicit understanding that services provided by resources are what actually generate value, but explanations of competitive advantage typically link observed superior economic performance directly to resources without considering the services that are immediately proximal to the competitive advantage. Such explanations do not account for the extraordinary success of a few Idaho potato farmers or the superior economic returns earned by firms that possess relatively homogeneous resources. Recall that Penrose (1995) argued that firm heterogeneity resulted largely from differences in the *services* different firms were able to offer. Differences in services stem primarily from differences in the administrative decisions made concerning productive resources that, for the most part, are widely available to competing firms.

Recognizing the distinction between catalytic and productive resources and the distinction between resources and services makes the role of strategy-making managers and non-managers an explicit part of the RBV, and it further fills the "process black box" between resources and superior economic performance (Priem and Butler, 2001a). As indicated in Figure 10.2, administrative decisions include: (1) re-bundling existing productive resources of the firm, and/or (2) altering the productive resource endowment of the firm through acquisition and/or divestiture (Makadok, 2001). In this context, the capabilities and routines of the firm comprise a critical component of a firm's productive resources (Eisenhardt and Martin, 2000; Nelson and Winter, 1982) because the services produced will be a function of the combination of productive resources. However, some administrative decisions will be superior in creating combinations of productive resources.

The superiority of administrative decisions is based on the resource bundles they create and the market appropriateness of services created from bundled resources. For example, people at Nucor Steel, most notably Kenneth Iverson, acquired new productive resources – a Whiting electric arc furnace, a Concast continuous-casting machine, and a Swedish rolling mill – to pioneer minimill steel-making in the US. USX, on the other hand, continued to deploy conventional steel-making technologies while taking aggressive steps to increase mill efficiency (e.g., labor efficiency improved from more than nine labor hours per ton of steel produced in 1980 to just under three hours per ton in 1991). The limitation for USX was not a resource limitation *per se*; its resources far surpassed those of Nucor. Rather it was a limitation in the administrative discretion exercised over those resources. The managers of Nucor Steel appeared to realize that the productive resources associated with new minimill technology had the potential of reshaping the market demand characteristics of the steel industry, while the leaders of USX appeared to make decisions that assumed no such industry change (see Christensen, 1997 about "disruptive technologies"). Therefore, the actual value created by Nucor Steel has far surpassed that of USX (now United States Steel) over the last two decades.

Thus, in the modified RBV framework administrative decisions about how productive resources are to be bundled and converted into services are of primary concern. This model facilitates the explanation of extraordinary performance by firms whose resources may not meet VRIS criteria. Increasing informative specificity about the pathway from resources to competitive advantage helps to avoid *post hoc ergo propter hoc* logical fallacies and helps to move the RBV further toward "theory status" (Priem and Butler, 2001a).

Empirical Application of the "Modified" RBV

Theoretical considerations

The apparent gap between the theoretical utility of the RBV as a theory and the practical utility of RBV logic can be further bridged by adopting a more appropriate methodology for empirically applying the RBV with the resources-services modifications proposed above. The first step in understanding what a more appropriate methodology might be is to recognize the nature of the theory itself. Indeed the theory is intended to explain why some firms do better economically than other firms (Barney, 1991; Collis and Montgomery, 1995). Clearly the RBV is a theory of outliers – firms that are different enough from other firms that competitive advantage accrues to these outlier firms. Thus, an appropriate methodology would be one that allows for a focus on truly firm-specific phenomena.

Although considerable empirical research has been done using RBV reasoning, the congruency between the theory and the methods used deserves a closer look. Several studies examine the relationship between resources and/or capabilities possessed by a firm and the economic performance of the firm (Bergh, 1998; Hult and Ketchen, 2001; Maijoor and van Witteloostuijn, 1996; Miller and Shamsie, 1996; Perry-Smith and Blum, 2000). Most of the empirical studies done in this area are based on traditional (classical) statistical approaches, generally a form of regression analysis. These studies typically focus on whether there is a statistically significant association between a resource and/or capability and economic performance.

A statistically significant, positive association between a resource and performance in a study using regression analysis indicates that, on average, the more of that resource a firm possesses, the more positive the economic performance of that firm. Such a result provides evidence that a relationship exists between a resource and performance, and it informs us about the confidence we can have in the relationship existing across repeated samples (Cohen and Cohen, 1983). However, no comment can be made as to a specific probability that such a relationship exists in a given firm.

There are other important issues to be considered in terms of the congruency between such results and RBV theory. First, the results are based on averages across the sample. A regression approach is not intended to focus on the effects of specific firms. In fact, if an observation (firm) is found to be influential and it can be demonstrated that the observation is an outlier, then the observation could justifiably be removed from the analysis. Furthermore, random and fixed effects models are used to control for the "firm effect" in panel data (Johnson and DiNardo, 1997) to ensure that the lack of independence among variables and observations due to a firm being in the sample repeatedly does not bias results. This seems to be incongruent with RBV logic. Although these random and fixed effects could conceivably be used to examine individual firms, the interpretation of results would be subject to the same limitations of regression analysis. Additional analysis, including graphing, could be done to identify influential observations in order to determine how widely held the resource is among firms in the sample (Cohen and Cohen, 1983). Without such additional analysis there is no way of knowing if an association is the result of a widely held resource or if the resource is held by only a very few firms that are able to achieve extraordinary economic performance because of the resource. We, however, know of no study in which this type of additional analysis has been done.

In addition, a positive association between a resource and performance says nothing about superior economic performance or competitive advantage. Such a finding does suggest that firms without that resource may be at a disadvantage, but one cannot conclude that possessing that resource confers a competitive advantage. The limitations of traditional statistical approaches lead to the conclusion that there is an important lack of congruency between RBV theory and regression-type analysis.

As Rumelt suggests: "strategy analysis must be situational. Just as there is no algorithm for creating wealth, strategic prescriptions that apply to broad classes of firms can only aid in avoiding mistakes, not in attaining advantage" (1984: 569). Congruency between RBV theory and an empirical methodology requires a methodology that can isolate the effects of individual firms and allow for meaningful interpretation of firm-level results. We propose a Bayesian approach because it allows such an examination of firm-specific phenomena.

The Bayesian approach

Bayesian methods are ideal for examining the types of issues inherent in the RBV, and more specifically for those raised in this chapter. A helpful overview of basic concepts in Bayesian methods is provided by Berry (1996). The Bayesian class of methods is characterized by the use of sources of data external to the data of immediate interest. This external information is often called *prior* information, and it is usually captured in terms of a probability distribution based on such things as previous studies, expert opinion, and historical information. Bayesian methods get their name from Bayes' Theorem, which asserts

$$\Pr(A \mid B) = \frac{\Pr(B \mid A)\Pr(A)}{\Pr(B)},$$

where A represents the unknown parameter (vector), and B represents the data. The formula asserts that the probability of observing unknown parameters conditional on the observed data is proportional to the probability of the data conditional on the unknown parameters, $\Pr(B \mid A)$, (more commonly known as the likelihood function) multiplied by the prior probability of the unknown parameters, $\Pr(A)$, which represents the prior information referred to earlier.

Bayesian hierarchical models (Draper et al., 1992) are general and powerful modeling tools that extend basic Bayesian methods to allow a rich class of models. The central idea behind hierarchical modeling is that each observation (or group of observations) is allowed to have a separate parameter or distribution. In the present case, the parameter of each firm is assumed to come from a population of such parameters. The primary distinction between Bayesian hierarchical models and classical alternatives (such as regression models, including random and fixed effects models (Cohen and Cohen, 1983; Haveman, 1993; Johnson and DiNardo, 1997)) are that (1) Bayesian hierarchical models provide complete distributional estimation (instead of point and/or interval estimates), (2) Bayesian hierarchical models allow for predictive inference while classical procedures allow only estimation and inference to observed firms (i.e., they are not predictive), and (3) Bayesian hierarchical models allow decision makers to make probability statements about decisions on a firm basis with the inclusion of uncertainty while classical procedures do not allow such statements (Berry, 1996). In a classical statistical framework the models posed in this work would typically produce identifiability problems.

A key element of this Bayesian methodology is the notion of a "borrowing of strength" across observations made possible by the fact that the parameters come from the same distribution (Carlin and Louis, 1996). Besides better estimation of individual (or firm) specific parameters, the distribution of parameters provides a predictive capability that is often desirable in management problems. For example, this method allows for specific probability statements as to the effects of one or more constructs (variables) on other constructs. In other words, the probability that a particular action will affect an outcome can be known. Such interpretation is not possible with a classical approach.

Applying the RBV

The aim of the Bayesian approach presented in this chapter is to demonstrate that questions naturally arising from the application of the RBV to organizational phenomena may be addressed and answered using a methodology that is consistent with RBV theory. This approach is not a "test" of RBV theory. It is not intended to somehow "solve" the tautology for which the RBV is sometimes criticized (Priem and Butler, 2001a, b). There are no universal hypotheses developed that link resources to competitive advantage across all firms. Rather, a statistical model is posed, based on the modified RBV framework that can be used to answer a variety of questions about individual firms, specific industries, and the sample as a whole.

Conceivably, all the elements of the framework depicted in Figure 10.2 could be measured either directly or through some proxy. However, such measurement would be fraught with confounding effects (Powell, 2001). More importantly, such measurement of each element of the model would be unnecessary. The pivotal point in the modified RBV framework is the administrative decision(s) that leads to services, and ultimately to economic performance. The general firm-level question suggested by the modified RBV framework is: What are the effects of administrative decisions on the economic performance of firms? This question can be addressed using measures of administrative decisions and economic performance. This approach makes sense in a framework where the focus is on *how* a firm bundles its resources as opposed to *which* resources a firm possesses.

Tautology is thus avoided – not solved – by focusing on directly measurable phenomena that are not subject to confounding effects nor to any *post hoc ergo propter hoc* logical fallacy through the imputation of unmeasurable VRIS characteristics to resources or services. There is no claim made in the modified RBV framework that administrative decisions meet VRIS criteria.

Resources and services are noticeably absent from the empirical application of the RBV presented here. Although this observation may seem illogical given the arguments for recognizing the distinction between resources and services presented above, it is precisely this distinction that makes the focus on administrative decisions sensible. The distinction between resources and services is a recognition that a transformation of a firm's productive resources must take place in order for services to be generated. Administrative decisions are critical to this transformation. By examining administrative decisions and economic performance we can learn about a firm's ability to transform productive resources into services even if we do not measure resources and services. Furthermore, some of the most important resources and services of a firm may well be intangible and/or unobservable (Barney, 1991). These unobservable phenomena are nevertheless accounted for in the modified RBV framework because we know they exist, even if we are unable to observe them (Godfrey and Hill, 1995). The use of evidence in court proceedings and the study of quantum mechanics are examples of observable phenomena being used to link together the elements of a model, some of which are unobservable phenomena. Examining administrative decisions and economic performance can likewise inform us about a firm's ability to convert resources into services.

Competitive advantage is another important element of the modified RBV framework (see Figure 10.2). The modified RBV framework suggests that competitive advantage will be generated by the services flowing from productive resources as a result of administrative decisions. Any competitive advantage a firm may have will be latently present in the administrative decisions and the economic performance achieved by that firm, assuming that competitive advantage has not been bid away by stakeholders (Coff, 1999). In the Bayesian model proposed here, we are able to isolate the firm effect on economic performance through the "borrowing of strength" from the data contained in the entire sample (Carlin and Louis, 1996).

We propose that this firm effect may be viewed as an indicator of any competitive advantage that a specific firm may possess. In short, the firm effect is the probability that the focal firm will achieve economic performance that is either less than or greater than what would be expected of a firm that took exactly the same administrative decisions or actions as those taken by the focal firm. A positive firm effect thus indicates the probability that the focal firm possesses some competitive advantage that will allow that firm to achieve economic performance greater than what would be predicted by the actions taken by that firm. The firm effect calculated from the data in this study indicates that a competitive advantage exists, but it cannot specifically identify what resource or service generates that advantage. However, with additional, more fine-grained data such resources and services could be identified.

The ability to estimate a directly unobservable competitive advantage without relying on a pairwise, direct comparison of that firm's economic performance with the performance of other firms is an important contribution of this Bayesian approach. Although the economic performance of each firm in the sample enters into the calculation of the firm effect, competitive advantage is estimated in light of other factors influencing economic performance. Concerns of tautology diminish when competitive advantage and economic performance can be considered separately.

Perhaps the most powerful implication of the firm effect is that it can be combined with a set of hypothetical actions to answer "What if?" questions. For example, a probability distribution can be calculated for the economic effect of a firm taking a set of specific actions. Such a probability is based on the actions of the firm in the past, the economic performance of the firm in the past, the actions of all other firms in the sample, and the economic performance of all other firms in the sample. This ability to make a prediction about a specific firm is the very essence of the RBV, both theoretically and practically.

The Bayesian model developed here also allows for the calculation of an industry effect. This measure is the probability that the industry in which a firm operates affects the economic performance of that firm. The firm effect and the industry effect calculated in this model are not merely a matter of controlling for firm and industry effects as would be done in a classical statistical approach. Here, these effects are calculated for each individual firm and for each industry in the sample. Again, this modeling is congruent with the firm level nature of RBV theory.

Data collection

The phenomena of interest in this chapter are administrative decisions and the resulting economic performance of firms. We chose to study firms that had recently appointed new CEOs. This context was chosen because it is a setting in which a new leader (catalytic resource) inherits a set of productive resources. Newly appointed CEOs have the opportunity and challenge to: (1) do nothing, or very little, to the resource base of the firm, (2) re-bundle the existing resource base of the firm, or (3) change the resource base of the firm through acquisition, divestiture, etc. Although all CEOs have these same opportunities and challenges to varying degrees throughout their tenure, we selected our sample based on new CEOs in an effort to capture the administrative decisions of those who have recently been given authority, perhaps even a mandate, to adjust the bundling of the firm's productive resources.

Data were collected on 195 Fortune 500 firms that changed CEOs during the period 1980–96. Using the *Wall Street Journal Index* data were gathered concerning major administrative decisions, including buying business units, selling business units, financial restructuring, organizational restructuring (shuttering divisions, consolidating divisions, etc.), layoffs, hiring, key personnel changes, and alliance formation. These data were gathered and cross-checked by two graduate students to ensure that announcements were accurately and consistently categorized. These categorizations were then reviewed by one of the co-authors. Financial performance data were gathered from Compustat for each firm. These data were gathered for the year preceding the new CEO's appointment and for the first three years of each new CEO's tenure.

Bayesian Hierarchical Model

In our case we have employed a somewhat complex Bayesian hierarchical model to address the question posed above. We employ a Bayesian hierarchical linear model (Broemeling, 1985) for examining the effects of administrative decisions, firms, and industries on economic performance. We model two types of performance – an accounting measure (net income/sales) and a market measure (stock market return, including dividends). Here, both response variables are continuous and a normal hierarchical model is reasonable. The performance parameter is expressed as a function of the firm (where each firm has its own effect) as well as the industry and the administrative decisions made, such as selling units, buying units, personnel actions, etc. The model we pose is:

$$performance = firm(industry) + industry + year + \sum_{j=1}^{10} \beta_j action_j$$

where we allow each industry and each firm to have its own effects (making the model a Bayesian hierarchical model). A more general form of this model has been explored in Berry et al. (1999), and a more detailed explanation of the model is presented in Appendix 10.1. This model allows for individual firm contribution as well as industry average contribution (four digit SICs) in addition to the action-based contributions to the economic performance of the firm.

All computation was done using Markov Chain Monte Carlo methods as reviewed in Gilks et al. (1996). The priors used in these calculations have little, if any, effect on the results for two reasons. First, prior distributions were assumed to be relatively "flat", which has the effect of ensuring that the influence of the prior distributions on the posterior distributions will be minimal (Berry, 1996). Second, due to the reasonably large sample size the effect of prior distributions was minimal. Several choices for prior distributions were also analyzed and found to have little effect on the resulting posterior distributions. Thus, although priors are necessary to perform the calculations, the priors that were chosen minimally influence the results of the analysis. Posterior predictive checks of the model (analogous to residual analysis) presented in Gelman et al. (1995) indicated a good fit.

Results and Discussion

Although the focus of interest is at the firm level, the Bayesian hierarchical model used here can also provide information about average effects across the sample. We present several sample-level results and compare these results to those one would obtain from a classical statistical approach. We then present firm- and industry-level results.

One of the advantages of the Bayesian approach is that much of the information generated by the analysis can be graphically represented as posterior distributions. These graphical representations contain much more information than a single metric. However, probability statements can also be represented in a single metric. Table 10.1 indicates the probability that each of the administrative decisions (actions) measured will have an effect on accounting measures of economic performance and market measures of economic performance. The probabilities in Table 10.1 give no indication of the size of effect.

These same results can also be shown graphically. Notice in Table 10.1 that the probability is 0.8111 that buying business units will have a positive effect on accounting measures of performance. The graph in Figure 10.3 shows how that probability is distributed.

The peak of the curve appears to be centered over approximately 0.005, indicating that the most likely effect on accounting returns of buying a business unit is an increase in performance of about 0.5 percent. There is a small area under the curve

Table 10.1   Probabilities of effects of actions on performance

Actions	Accounting returns	Market returns
Buying units	0.8111	0.9671
Selling units	0.5584	0.0791
Organization restructuring	0.9274	0.4781
Alliances	0.4571	0.0519
Hiring	0.5867	0.8848
New markets	0.4646	0.5983
Financial restructuring	0.0516[a]	0.9828
Personnel changes	0.1169	0.0032
Layoffs	0.3082	0.4341
New products	0.7434	0.9687

[a] values below 0.5 indicate a probability of a negative effect, thus 0.0516 indicates a strong probability $(1 - 0.0516 = 0.9484)$ of a negative effect.

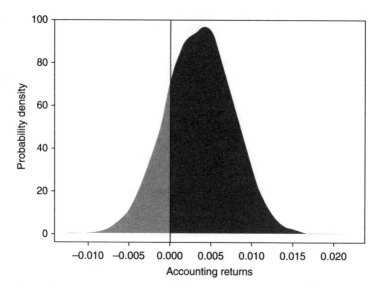

Figure 10.3   Effect of buying units on accounting returns

that lies to the left of zero, representing the 0.1889 probability that the effect of buying a business unit is negative. It is important to note that these results do not represent a confidence interval nor are they "significant" because they have passed a "p-value" threshold. These results are the actual probabilities based on the data in this sample.

The probabilities reported in Table 10.1 may be used to answer a variety of questions about which actions, on *average*, are likely to lead to which outcomes. Such results may serve as a useful point of departure in theory building focused on the pathway from resources to economic performance. These results may also give pause to our previously held convictions concerning the effects of certain actions on economic performance. For example, recent studies examining the cumulative abnormal returns (CAR) of acquirers indicate that acquiring firms usually experience a negative effect on market returns (Anand and Singh, 1997; Capron and Pistre, 2002; Hayward, 2002; Wright et al., 2002). Table 10.1 indicates that buying business units has a probability of 0.8111 of a positive effect on accounting returns and a probability of 0.9671 of a positive effect on market returns. These results appear to be directly opposed to recent CAR studies. However, the data in our sample are fundamentally different from the data used in CAR studies. The present study examines year-end returns over several years as opposed to stock market reaction during a brief window surrounding the announcement of the acquisition. This study is also based on data from the first three years of a new CEO's tenure. Whereas CAR studies attempt to meticulously avoid confounding effects by using a brief window, this model offers a probability distribution of the effect of buying units, in the presence of other significant actions, over a several-year period. In the present sample of firms, after accounting for the effects of all the other actions measured – the firm effect, industry effect, and year effect – there is a high probability that a firm that buys a business unit will experience, over a several-year period, a positive economic performance effect, albeit a very small one.

Figures 10.4 and 10.5 show the probability distributions for the effects of each action on accounting returns and market returns, respectively. The dark-shaded area (to the right of zero) under the curve represents the probability that the effect on performance is positive and the light-shaded area (to the left of zero) indicates the probability of a negative effect. Graphs in which the dark- and light-shaded areas are roughly equal indicate that the probability of a positive versus a negative effect is roughly equal. Note that this is different from saying that there is no effect. For example, in Figure 10.4, the probability distributions for both selling units and hiring indicate that the probability of a positive versus negative effect is roughly equal. However, the shape of the distribution for selling units indicates that the effect is almost certain to lie between −1 percent and 1 percent, while the shape of the distribution for hiring indicates that the effect is spread from −3 percent to 3 percent. These graphs convey a tremendous amount of information in a simple, straightforward manner.

The results reported in Table 10.1, Figures 10.3, 10.4, and 10.5 are similar in nature to other empirical RBV work in that they reflect the *average* effect of the various administrative decisions. However, these results are fundamentally different in terms of their interpretation. Results from a classical approach would correctly be interpreted to mean that if the sample were repeated infinitely the results obtained would include the correct parameters 99 percent of the time assuming a p-value of 0.01. A problem with classical approaches is that there is no way to know, with a specific sample, if the results are part of the 99 percent that is correct or the 1 percent that is incorrect. Thus, classical approaches allow us to say nothing about probabilities. On the other hand, the Bayesian results reported here are, in fact, probability statements.

The unique value of this Bayesian approach is *not* the ability to predict average effects across firms; it is the ability to generate probabilities for individual firms and

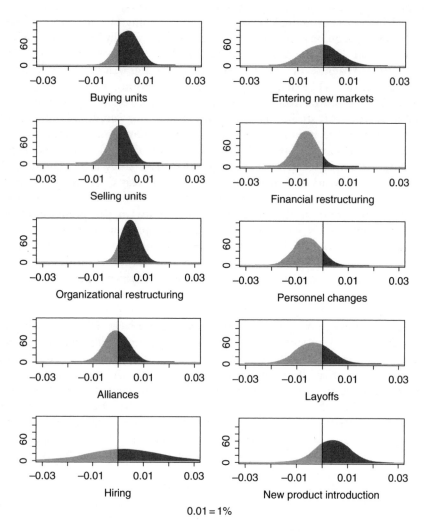

Figure 10.4   Probability distribution of effect on accounting returns

specific industries. Figure 10.6 shows the probability distribution of the firm effect of Micron and the industry effect of the primary industry in which Micron operates (SIC 3674) on market measures of economic performance. Micron had a larger firm effect on market returns than any other firm in the sample. The firm effect distribution in Figure 10.6 peaks around 63 percent, indicating the most likely effect on economic performance. Also, the distribution lies almost completely to the right of zero, suggesting that the probability of a positive effect on market returns is nearly 1.0 (above 0.9999). Specifically, the distribution shown in Figure 10.6 indicates that Micron is virtually certain to achieve higher market returns than would be expected

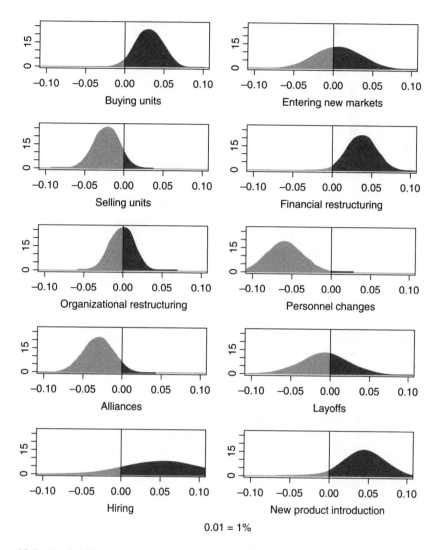

Figure 10.5   Probability distribution of effect on market returns

for an "average" firm in the sample taking the same actions that Micron actually took. We interpret this as strong evidence of a competitive advantage for Micron at the time (1993–96).[4]

The firm effect of Micron and its industry effect are both stronger than any of the administrative decisions studied. There is a difference between the firm effect and industry effect for Micron of nearly 30 percent (63 percent firm effect versus 33 percent industry effect). The differences in these two distributions have potentially interesting implications for the debate of industry versus firm effects (McGahan and Porter, 1997; Rumelt, 1991; Schmalansee, 1985) because there are many firms in the sample whose firm effect was less than the industry effect. This Bayesian approach

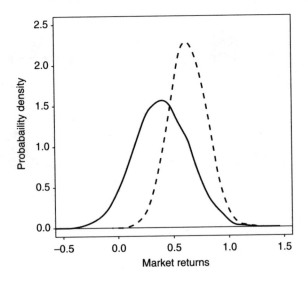

Figure 10.6 Industry and firm effect

facilitates a comparison of individual firm effects to industry effects. It is also possible to compare industry effects across industries. Such a comparison may also be useful in industrial organization research (e.g., tests of Porter's Five Forces Model (Porter, 1990)).

We are able to calculate the probabilities of firm effects and industry effects for each firm and industry in the sample. However, we are unable to calculate the probabilities for the effects of specific administrative decisions for specific firms because our data is currently limited to four years. With data from several more years, we will be able to calculate the probabilities of the effects of specific actions on specific firms.

Another interesting analysis that can be performed with our current dataset and this Bayesian approach is to ask "What if?" questions about a set of actions a firm may be considering. We constructed two strategy scenarios: a refocusing scenario and a diversification scenario. The refocusing scenario consisted of selling two business units, one organizational restructuring, one key personnel change, and one layoff. The diversification scenario included buying two business units, one financial restructuring, one key personnel change, one hiring, and one alliance. The probability distributions for the effects of these scenarios on the market performance of individual firms can be calculated, taking into account the relevant firm effect and industry effect. Figure 10.7 shows the effects of the two scenarios on Micron. The distribution of the firm effect for Micron was centered over 63 percent before being combined with the scenarios, indicating a considerable competitive advantage. The diversification scenario moved the distribution to the right, indicating an improvement in the effect for Micron of about 9 percent. The refocus scenario moved the distribution to the left by about 8 percent. Thus, for Micron there is a difference in effect of about 17 percent between the two scenarios. Again, the point is not to demonstrate that one strategy is better than another. Rather, the point of the analysis is to show that

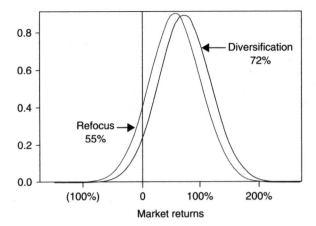

Figure 10.7   Market performance effect of scenarios on Micron

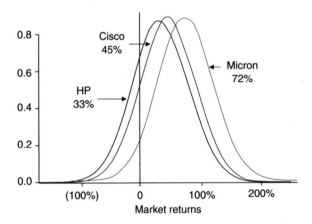

Figure 10.8   Effect of diversification scenario

this Bayesian methodology can be used to see which strategy is likely to produce the most favorable results for a specific firm.

Figure 10.8 shows the effects of the diversification strategy on three different firms: Micron, Cisco, and Hewlett-Packard (HP). Each of these three firms had unique firm effects before being combined with the effects of the diversification scenario. Combining the firm effects with the diversification scenario resulted in the three distributions. Many different analyses may be performed by combining firm effects and actions taken.

Limitations

Perhaps the greatest limitation of this study is the liability of newness. This study is an effort to demonstrate that there is a reasonable alternative to the way scholars have thought about and applied the RBV. We suspect that some scholars may resist the notion that a picture – a posterior distribution – can actually convey enough information to be meaningful in a research or practical setting. We suspect that some will resist the notion of using prior information to establish prior distributions. Our hope is that more work can be done that will, in time, prove convincing to skeptics.

Measures of discretion used in this study are admittedly coarse-grained given that administrative decisions and the impact of those decisions may vary greatly across firms. However, the Bayesian approach used here assumes that each firm has its own distribution of parameters; therefore, the effect of an action is treated with specific regard to the firm that took the action. The fact that buying a business unit is of different significance to different firms is thus captured and accounted for in this methodology. Of course more fine-grained measures would allow researchers to study more specific details of administrative decisions.

The generalizability of this study is limited by our choice to study firms with newly appointed CEOs. It would be inappropriate to generalize the relationship between an administrative decision and economic performance in this study to a population of firms whose CEOs were not newly appointed. However, on an individual basis the results obtained for a given firm are generalizable to other firms if the other firms are "exchangeable" (Berry, 1996), meaning that the other firms are substantially similar to the firm in this sample. Of course, this begs the question, "How similar is substantially similar?" There is no test for this, and it remains a question of judgment. Having stated the limitation, it is important to note the congruency between appropriate generalization and the RBV. If a relationship could be appropriately generalized to a larger population, such a generalization would seem to violate the rareness notion inherent in the RBV.

Conclusion

This study is a first step in a research stream that will hopefully increase the usefulness of the RBV and bring greater clarity to important organizational phenomena. The explicit recognition of the resources–services distinction allows researchers to develop arguments about the pathway from resources to superior economic performance with sufficient informative specificity that the *post hoc ergo propter hoc* logical fallacy is not problematic. Although this study is exploratory and coarse-grained, it will hopefully encourage others to develop more fine-grained analysis of the relationships among resources, services, competitive advantage, and economic performance.

We urge scholars to consider the implications of the modified RBV framework proposed here with regard to the generation of competitive advantage from productive resources that are homogeneously distributed among firms. Skeptics will argue that catalytic resources are simply another class of resource and, therefore, current conceptualizations of the RBV adequately explain all instances of competitive advantage. However, such arguments require a direct link between managers (catalytic resources) and competitive advantage, thereby failing to account for the process of converting productive resources to services. We hope that scholars will be motivated to develop increasingly satisfying explanations of competitive advantage, which account for the resources-to-services process.

The Bayesian methodology introduced in this chapter is much more consistent with the RBV as a theory of outliers than traditional classical statistical approaches. The ability to focus on individual firms is one of the greatest strengths of the Bayesian approach. It is our hope that researchers and managers alike will recognize the power of being able to make probability statements at the actual firm level. As suggested by the pattern of results reported in Table 10.1, this approach may also call into question some long-held assumptions about the effects of particular administrative decisions on firm performance. We encourage research efforts aimed at examining these long-held assumptions using emerging tools such as the Bayesian hierarchical modeling used in this chapter.

The history of Micron juxtaposed against the results obtained in this study suggests some interesting avenues for research. As Micron grew from a four-person start up, the firm began to amass resources. We suspect that early on in the history of the firm most of these resources were widely available in the market. Over time, Micron developed proprietary technologies for manufacturing and testing chips. Do we have adequate theoretical explanations for the development of heterogeneous productive resources from homogeneous productive resources? Another interesting pattern in Micron's history is that it has had substantial losses in five of the last six years, even though the company appeared to have a competitive advantage in the mid-1990s. Does Micron still have a competitive advantage? Can a firm with a history of financial losses have a competitive advantage? The firm continues to enjoy high market share and to win quality and innovation awards (www.micron.com/ir/profile.html). Are there better measures of competitive advantage that could capture organizational successes that may not immediately fall to the bottom line? These issues represent significant research opportunity.

Hopefully this chapter will help to bridge the gap between the RBV as a theory and the practical application of the RBV as a management tool. This work should be viewed as an extension of the RBV and the beginning of an exciting methodological path for researchers and practitioners. Finally, the potential for de-constructing and re-examining decades-old management research using the Bayesian approach should be recognized as a means of improving theoretical understanding and modern management practice.

Notes

1. Informative specificity is a foundation of the experimental method – when reporting research methods a researcher is expected to provide sufficient informative specificity to recreate the original research.
2. Service(s) is used throughout the chapter in the Penrosean sense of the word. Thus, services refer to outputs of the resources of the firm such as products, services (in the traditional sense), benefits, etc.
3. While we agree with Priem and Butler (2001a) and Barney (2001) that resource value is determined from a source exogenous to the RBV, this is not a particularly interesting issue to strategists when compared to how superior economic value is created through the transformation of resources into services. Analogously, knowing something about how specific cards end up in the hands of specific poker players may ultimately enhance our understanding of the game of poker, but it would require much more effort and is likely

to lead to much less understanding than efforts to learn about how poker players win by playing the cards they are dealt. In many ways, strategists are like poker players – on a given night they are either lucky or unlucky in terms of the cards they are dealt, but those with superior knowledge of the game of poker will often find ways to win even when they are unlucky. RBV theorists argue that competitive advantage results from superior knowledge, or luck, or some combination of the two (Barney, 1986; Dierickx and Cool, 1989; Rumelt, 1984), but their attention naturally ebbs toward superior knowledge, because they recognize that strategists can do something with insights about superior knowledge (i.e., Thomas and Tymon, 1982, would assert they have the potential for "operational validity"), while there is little strategists can do with insights about luck.

4. Micron reported losses of over $1 billion for fiscal year 2003 even though the company is second in DRAM market share worldwide (www.micron.com/ir/profile.html).

References

Alchian, A. and Demsetz, H. 1972: Production, information costs and economic organization. *American Economic Review*, 62, 777–795.

Amit, R. and Shoemaker, P. 1993: Strategic assets and organizational rents. *Strategic Management Journal*, 14, 33–46.

Anand, J. and Singh, H. 1997: Asset redeployment, acquisitions and corporate strategy in declining industries. *Strategic Management Journal*, 18 (Summer Special Issue), 99–118.

Andrews, K. 1980: *The Concept of Corporate Strategy* (rev. edn). Chicago, IL: Richard D. Irwin.

Barney, J. 1986: Strategic factor markets: expectations, luck and business strategy. *Management Science*, 32, 1231–1241.

Barney, J. 1991: Firm resources and sustained competitive advantage. *Journal of Management*, 17, 99–120.

Barney, J. 1995: Looking inside for competitive advantage. *Academy of Management Executive*, 9, 49–61.

Barney, J. 2001: Is the resource-based "view" a useful perspective for strategic management research? Yes. *Academy of Management Review*, 26, 41–57.

Barney, J. 2002: *Gaining and Sustaining Competitive Advantage* (2nd edn). Upper Saddle River, NJ: Prentice Hall.

Bergh, D. 1998: Product-market uncertainty, portfolio restructuring, and performance: An information-processing and resource-based view. *Journal of Management*, 24, 135–155.

Berry, D. 1996: *Statistics: A Bayesian Perspective*. New York: Duxbury Press.

Berry, S., Reese, C.S., and Larkey, P. 1999: Bridging different eras in sports. *Journal of the American Statistical Association*, 58, 827–843.

Broemeling, L. 1985: *Bayesian Analysis of Linear Models*. New York: Marcel Dekker.

Capron, L. and Pistre, N. 2002: When do acquirers earn abnormal returns? *Strategic Management Journal*, 23, 781–794.

Carlin, B. and Louis, T. 1996: *Bayes and Empirical Bayes Methods for Data Analysis*. London: Chapman and Hall.

Castanias, R. and Helfat, C. 1991: Managerial resources and rents. *Journal of Management*, 17, 155–171.

Christensen, C. 1997: *The Innovator's Dilemma: When New Technologies Cause Great Firms to Fail*. Boston, MA: Harvard Business School Press.

Coase, R. 1937: The nature of the firm. *Economica*, 4, 386–405. Reprinted in J.B. Barney and W.G. Ouchi (eds.), *Organizational Economics*. San Francisco, CA: Josey-Bass, 1986, 80–98.

Coff, W.C. 1999: When competitive advantage doesn't lead to performance: The resource-based view and stakeholder bargaining power. *Organization Science*, 10, 119–213.

Cohen, J. and Cohen, P. 1983: *Applied Multiple Regression/Correlation Analysis for the Behavioral Sciences*. Hillsdale, NJ: Lawrence Erlbaum.

Collis, D. and Montgomery, C. 1995: Competing on resources: Strategy in the 1990s. *Harvard Business Review*, 73, 118–128.

Conner, K. 1991: A historical comparison of resource-based theory and five schools of thought within industrial organization economics: Do we have a new theory of the firm here? *Journal of Management*, 17, 121–154.

Daft, R. 1983: *Organization Theory and Design*. New York: West.

Deephouse, D. 2000: Media reputation as a strategic resource: An integration of mass communication and resource-based theories. *Journal of Management*, 26, 1091–1112.

Dierickx, I. and Cool, K. 1989: Asset stock accumulation and sustainability of competitive advantage. *Management Science*, 35, 1504–1511.

Dosi, G., Nelson, R., and Winter, S. 2000: The nature and dynamics of organizational capabilities. In G. Dosi, R.R. Nelson, and S.G. Winter (eds.), *The Nature and Dynamics of Organizational Capabilities*. New York: Oxford University Press.

Draper, D., Gaver, D., Goel, P., et al. 1992: Selected statistical methodology of combining information. In D. Cochran and J. Farrally (eds.), *Combining Information: Statistical Issues and Opportunities for Research*. Washington, DC: National Academy Press, 197–217.

Eisenhardt, K. and Martin, J. 2000: Dynamic capabilities: What are they? *Strategic Management Journal*, 21, 1105–1121.

Gelfand, A. and Smith, A. 1990: Sampling-based approaches to calculating marginal densities. *Journal of the American Statistical Association*, 85, 398–409.

Gelman, A., Carlin, J., Stern, S., and Rubin, D. 1995: *Bayesian Data Analysis*. London: Chapman and Hall.

Gilks, W., Richardson, S., and Spiegelhalter, D. 1996: *Markov Chain Monte Carlo in Practice*. London: Chapman and Hall.

Godfrey, P. and Hill, C. 1995: The problem of unobservables in strategic management research. *Strategic Management Journal*, 16, 519–533.

Haveman, H. 1993: Organizational size and change: Diversification in the savings and loan industry after deregulation. *Administrative Science Quarterly*, 38, 20–50.

Hayward, M. 2002: When do firms learn from their acquisition experience? Evidence from 1990–1995. *Strategic Management Journal*, 23, 21–39.

Hitt, M., Ireland, R., and Hoskisson, R. 2001: *Strategic Management: Competitiveness and Globalization* (4th edn). Cincinnati, OH: South-Western.

Hult, G. and Ketchen, D. 2001: Does market orientation matter? A test of the relationship between positional advantage and performance. *Strategic Management Journal*, 22, 899–906.

Johnson, J. and DiNardo, J. 1997: *Econometric Methods* (4th edn). New York: McGraw-Hill.

Mahoney, J. and Pandian, J. 1992: The resource-based view within the conversation of strategic management. *Strategic Management Journal*, 13, 363–381.

Maijoor, S. and van Witteloostuijn, A. 1996: An empirical test of the resource-based theory: Strategic regulation in the Dutch audit industry. *Strategic Management Journal*, 17, 549–569.

Makadok, R. 2001: Toward a synthesis of the resource-based and dynamic-capability views of rent creation. *Strategic Management Journal*, 22, 387–401.

McGahan, A. and Porter, M. 1997: How much does industry matter, really? *Strategic Management Journal*, 18, 15–30.

Micron Technology, Inc. 2003: Company website: www.micron.com/ir/profile.html. Accessed October 26, 2003.

Miller, D. and Shamsie, J. 1996: The resource-based view of the firm in two environments: The Hollywood film studios from 1936 to 1965. *Academy of Management Journal*, 39, 519–543.

Nelson, R. and Winter, S. 1982: *An Evolutionary Theory of Economic Change*. Cambridge, MA: Harvard University Press.

Penrose, E. 1995 [1959]: *The Theory of the Growth of the Firm* (3rd edn). New York: Oxford University Press.

Perry-Smith, J. and Blum, T. 2000: Work-family human resource bundles and perceived organizational performance. *Academy of Management Journal*, 43, 1107–1117.

Peteraf, M. 1993: The cornerstones of competitive advantage: A resource-based view. *Strategic Management Journal*, 14, 179–191.

Porter, M. 1990: *Competitive Strategy*. New York: Free Press.

Powell, T. 2001: Competitive advantage: Logical and philosophical considerations. *Strategic Management Journal*, 22, 875–888.

Priem, R. and Butler, J. 2001a: Is the resource-based "view" a useful perspective for strategic management research? *Academy of Management Review*, 26, 22–40.

Priem, R. and Butler, J. 2001b: Tautology in the resource-based view and the implications of externally determined resource value: Further comments. *Academy of Management Review*, 26, 57–66.

Reese, S., Calvin, J., George, J., and Tarpley, R. 2001: Estimation of fetal growth and gestation in bowhead whales. *Journal of the American Statistical Association*, 96, 915–938.

Rumelt, R. 1984: Towards a strategic theory of the firm. In R. Lamb (ed.), *Competitive Strategic Management*. Englewood Cliffs, NJ: Prentice-Hall, 556–570.

Rumelt, R. 1991: How much does industry matter? *Strategic Management Journal*, 12, 167–185.

Schmalansee, R. 1985: Do markets differ much? *American Economic Review*, 75, 341–351.

Stigler, G. 1966: *The Theory of Price*. New York: Macmillan.

Sundaramurthy, C. and Lewis, M. 2003: Control and collaboration: Paradoxes of governance. *Academy of Management Review*, 28, 397–415.

Teece, D., Pisano, G., and Shuen, A. 1997: Dynamic capabilities and strategic management. *Strategic Management Journal*, 18, 509–533.

Thomas, K. and Tymon, W. 1982: Necessary properties of relevant research: Lessons from recent criticisms of the organizational sciences. *Academy of Management Review*, 7, 345–352.

Wernerfelt, B. 1984: A resource-based view of the firm. *Strategic Management Journal*, 5, 171–180.

Williamson, O. 1975: *Markets and Hierarchies: Analysis and Antitrust Implications*. New York: Free Press.

Winter, S. 1995: Four Rs of profitability: Rents, resources, routines, and replication. In C. Montgomery (ed.), *Resource-based and Evolutionary Theories of the Firm: Toward a Synthesis*. Hingham, MA: Kluwer Academic Publishers.

Wright, P., Kroll, M., Lado, A., and Van Ness, B. 2002: The structure of ownership and corporate acquisition strategies. *Strategic Management Journal*, 23, 41–53.

Appendix 10.1

Bayesian approaches are characterized by a probabilistic specification of the problem. The fundamental notion behind any Bayesian analysis is Bayes' Theorem which states:

$$\pi(\theta \mid y) = \frac{f(y \mid \theta)\pi(\theta)}{\int f(y \mid \theta)\pi(\theta)\partial\theta}$$

where θ represents the unknown parameters we wish to estimate and y represents the response or dependent variable. The left-hand side of Bayes' Theorem $\pi(\theta \mid y)$ is called the posterior distribution and represents the state of knowledge about θ after observing the data. The right-hand side of Bayes' Theorem consists of three pieces of information:

- a likelihood function, $f(y \mid \theta)$
- a prior distribution, $\pi(\theta)$
- and a normalizing constant, $\int f(y|\theta)\pi(\theta)\partial\theta$.

The likelihood function is commonly used in classical statistical analyses and represents the information contained in the data. The prior distribution represents the state of knowledge about the unknown parameters before any data has been collected. The normalizing constant ensures that the posterior distribution is, in fact, a probability distribution. The normalizing constant is also the piece that made application of Bayesian methods difficult until the early 1990s. Gelfand and Smith (1990) present a computational tool called Markov Chain Monte Carlo, which allows a very general purpose technique for simulating values from the posterior distribution. These simulated values can then be used to make inference based on the posterior distribution. That is, the simulated observations essentially act as a surrogate for calculation of the normalizing constant (and can, in fact, be used to estimate the normalizing constant). This realization was made possible by advancements in computational speed and accuracy.

In the case of RBV theory, we call economic performance (market returns and accounting returns) for company i ($i = 1, \ldots, 175$) in year j ($j = 1, \ldots, 4$), Y_{ij}, and use as our model

$$Y_{ij} \sim N(\mu_{ij}, \sigma_j^2)$$

where the notation above indicates a normal distribution with mean μ_{ij} and variance. σ_j^2. Our model seeks to estimate not only aggregate measures of the effect of specific actions, X_{ijk} ($k = 1, \ldots, 10$), but also a firm specific effect. The model we propose then is:

$$\mu_{ij} = \eta_{ij} + \sum_{i=1}^{k} \beta_{jk} X_{ijk}$$

where the important point in the model is that each firm is given its own effect. While this type of modeling can be couched in so-called fixed-effects models (Johnson and DiNardo, 1997) (these are commonly called random effects models in the statistics literature), a compelling argument can be made that what is really desired is a probability distribution for each of the firm specific effects. This probability distribution can be obtained through the use of Bayes' Theorem presented above. In the case of economic performance, the likelihood function is:

$$f(y \mid \theta) = (2\pi\sigma_j^2)^{-175/2} \exp\left(-\sum_{i=1}^{175}\sum_{j=1}^{4}\left(y_{ij} - \left(\eta_{ij} + \sum_{k=1}^{10}\beta_{jk}X_{ijk}\right)^2 / 2\sigma_j^2 \right) \right)$$

where $\theta = (\eta_{1,1} \ldots, \eta_{4,175}, \beta_1 \ldots, \beta_{10}, \sigma_1, \ldots, \sigma_4)$ is the entire set of parameters for which inference will be made.

The prior distribution must be specified for the entire set of parameters. It is this next step that distinguishes our hierarchical Bayesian approach from a standard Bayesian approach. Our prior distributions for market returns are as follows:

$$\eta_{ij} \sim N(\lambda_j, \tau_j^2)$$

$$\lambda_j \sim N(0,10)$$

$$\tau_j^2 \sim IG(3,1000)$$

$$\beta_{jk} \sim N(0,10)$$

$$\sigma_j^2 \sim IG(3,1000)$$

The interpretation of this formulation is that the firm specific effects are modeled by a conditionally independent hierarchical model. It suggests that the firm specific effects vary according to a normal distribution and that the mean of that distribution has a normal distribution with mean 0 and variance 10. In other words, this prior distribution suggests that the effect of any one firm on market returns, with only a very small probability, result in more than a 300 percent change (increase or decrease). This is a very diffuse prior given that no observed market return was greater than 160 percent. Furthermore, our prior distribution assumes that each action taken will have an effect of no more than a 300 percent change in market returns (again, a fairly liberal assumption). The variance prior distributions (σ_j^2, τ_j^2) are both inverse gamma distributed (abbreviated above as IG). They each assume that the standard deviation of both the firm effects (τ) and the error standard deviation (σ) are, with only very small probability, larger than 50 percent. Again, this prior distribution is very diffuse. We used more diffuse distributions and found little to no difference in the results and were satisfied that this choice was not critical given the appreciable sample size. For more discussion on sensitivity to these choices, Reese et al. (2001) has a good discussion for how one would address this issue in a more rigorous manner.

The choices above give rise to the following formula for the prior distribution, $\pi(\theta)$,

$$\pi(\theta) = \prod_{i=1}^{175}\prod_{j=1}^{4}(2\pi\tau_j^2)^{-1/2}\exp(-(\eta_{ij} - \lambda_j)^2/2\tau_j^2)$$

$$\times (2\pi 10^2)^{-1/2}\exp(-(\lambda_j)^2/2(10^2))$$

$$\times \frac{1}{1000^3\Gamma(3)}(\tau_j^2)^{-(3+1)}\exp(-1/1000\tau_j^2)$$

$$\times \prod_{j=1}^{4}\prod_{k=1}^{10}(2\pi 10^2)^{-1/2}\exp(-(\beta_{jk})^2/2(10^2))$$

$$\times \prod_{j=1}^{4}\frac{1}{1000^3\Gamma(3)}(\sigma_j^2)^{-(3+1)}\exp(-1/1000\sigma_j^2)$$

The last piece of information that is necessary to find is the normalizing constant. As mentioned earlier, there are many problems where this is difficult, if not impossible, to compute. Given the formula for the likelihood function and the prior distributions above, this calculation is infeasible for our model. Thus, we employ a Markov Chain Monte Carlo (MCMC) procedure to estimate the joint posterior distribution. The details of this computational procedure can be found in the article by Gelfand and Smith (1990). It is worth noting that the computations used in this chapter (after debugging and original coding) took about 10 hours of computational time on a fast desktop computer. This time includes the model comparison made using Bayes' Factors.

The result of applying such a procedure is a sample of observations from the joint posterior distribution of the CEO action effects, the variance parameters, and most important to our particular model, the firm specific effects. These posterior distributions provide a fully probabilistic assessment of the contribution of each firm to the return on investment. This effect is estimated in the presence of the actions that could be taken, and represents all of the actions/features of each firm that add (or subtract) value above and beyond that which the actions taken reveal. An important difference between this posterior distribution of firm effects and traditional statistical inference is that traditional statistical inference makes statements about these effects over a long run average and in repeated sampling. Bayesian inference allows a more direct interpretation based on probability which is a highly effective tool for decision makers.

CHAPTER ELEVEN

How Much Do Middle Managers Matter, Really? An Empirical Study on their Impact on Sustained Superior Performance

Johanna Mair

Introduction

Strategic management research is concerned with identifying the sources of sustained superior performance (Rumelt et al., 1994). Based on different theories and methodologies scholars have suggested market positions (Porter, 1980), idiosyncratic and inimitable firm specific resources (Lippman and Rumelt, 1982; Wernerfelt, 1984) or dynamic capabilities (Teece et al., 1997) as its primary sources. Although important, these empirical studies have predominantly focused on how important top management strategic *decisions* affect competitive advantage or above average returns. In contrast, the impact of middle managers' entrepreneurial *actions* on superior performance has received only limited attention. Furthermore, previous empirical studies have concentrated on performance measured primarily at the organizational level and investigated performance differences *between* firms or clusters of firms. Only a few have recognized the performance potential at the sub-unit level and examined variance *within* one company or division.

The objective of this chapter, therefore, is to steer research attention to this important topic by showing how middle manager entrepreneurial actions may affect sub-unit performance and, hence, be an effective tool for counteracting the low-growth syndrome of large established organizations. I, thus, complement existing empirical research by emphasizing actual behavior instead of decision making, by focusing on middle instead of top managers, and by stressing the importance of examining superior performance over time at the sub-unit rather than just the corporate level. In more detail, I develop a fine-grained, context specific measurement instrument to capture middle managers' entrepreneurial behavior defined as pursuing opportunities through the innovative use of resource combinations as this notion has been assumed to affect various dimensions of superior performance such as competitive advantage and above-normal returns (Covin and Miles, 1999), growth (Penrose, 1995), and renewal (Ghoshal and Bartlett, 1995). I collected survey data on this entrepreneurial behavior measure from 118 middle managers of a large European financial and tested its effect on objective sub-unit performance data collected over three consecutive years (1997–1999).

In the next section, I elaborate on middle management entrepreneurial behavior as an effective means to renew established organizations and lay out the theoretical arguments for linking it to sustained superior performance, namely to profitable growth. In the following section, I summarize the research design, data analysis, and present the empirical results. To conclude, I discuss the main findings, contribution to the literature, and managerial implications.

Theoretical Arguments

Defining entrepreneurship in organizations

While business press and scholars alike typically conceive entrepreneurial behavior as an efficacious means to stimulate continual innovation, growth, and value creation (Hamel, 1999), rigorous empirical research linking entrepreneurial activities and superior performance remains scarce (Covin and Slevin, 1991; Zahra and Covin, 1993). Furthermore, previous empirical studies have mainly looked at *grand entrepreneurship*, i.e., discrete entrepreneurial events such as the creation of new organizations (Gartner, 1988), new ventures (Vesper, 1985), new entry (Lumpkin and Dess, 1996), or new product development (von Hippel, 1977). While important for traditional entrepreneurship research, such narrow definitions remain inapplicable to various entrepreneurial phenomena occurring in large established companies. In this study, I adopt a less heroic view and emphasize *day-to-day entrepreneurship* aiming at "getting things done in an entrepreneurial – innovative and unusual – way."

Following a behavioral research tradition (Stevenson and Jarillo, 1990), I view entrepreneurship within established organizations as a set of interlocking opportunity-based activities by competent and purposeful individuals, who – through their actions – can make a difference. For the purpose of this chapter, I, thus, define entrepreneurial behavior as

> a set of activities and practices by which individuals at multiple levels autonomously generate and use innovative resource combinations to identify and pursue opportunities.

While innovation, autonomy and opportunities are defining elements of entrepreneurship in general (Lumpkin and Dess, 1996; Miller, 1983; Stevenson and Jarillo, 1990), entrepreneurial behavior within large organizations is distinct. It includes a spectrum of activities ranging from independent/autonomous to integrative/cooperative behavior (Ghoshal and Bartlett, 1994; Kanter, 1982). Within large organizations entrepreneurial managers build on the uniqueness of their units and at the same time profit from similarities with other units. They continuously balance "exploration" of new resource combinations with "exploitation" of existing organizational capabilities (Normann, 1977). Moreover, entrepreneurial behavior within such companies is not constrained by organizational boundaries but rather implies heedful stretching of such boundaries.

Middle managers and entrepreneurship

Previous – mainly process oriented – research has shown that middle managers assume an active role in both strategy implementation and strategy formulation. They translate organizational goals and strategy into concrete actions (Uyterhoeven, 1972); they convert autonomous managerial action into strategic intent (Burgelman, 1983a); and they ensure efficient allocation, transfer, and sharing of resources and capabilities (Bower, 1970; Ghoshal and Bartlett, 1998; Nonaka, 1988) by exerting upward, downward, and sideways influence.

More recently, however, researchers have emphasized the importance of the middle managers' role in fostering entrepreneurial initiatives in established organizations (see Hornsby et al., 2002 for a review). While all organizational actors can be entrepreneurial by definition, middle managers are seen as vital to translate initiatives developed at the front into organizational outcomes (Burgelman, 1983b). "Entrepreneurial" middle managers not only seek and pursue opportunities; they also bring them to life (Kanter, 1982). They actively promote ideas, build support, overcome resistance, and ensure that the innovative ideas are implemented and followed up (Howell and Higgins, 1990).

While we have gained a comprehensive understanding about the nature of middle managers' activities, we still know relatively little about their consequences on tangible performance. The few existing empirical studies are typically based on abstract categories of activities and they assess performance implications at the organizational level. Woolridge and Floyd (1990), for example, relate middle managers' involvement in strategy making to performance measured at the organizational level. Little empirical research has looked at the effect of specific managerial activities, especially entrepreneurial behavior, on sustained performance at the sub-unit level, likely the most appropriate level to assess middle managers' impact.

Middle manager entrepreneurial behavior and sustained superior performance

This chapter suggests that entrepreneurial behavior of middle managers stimulates sustainable superior performance. I first define sustainable superior performance as profitable growth and then make the arguments on how middle manager entrepreneurial behavior affects it.

Growth hardly represents an organizational goal in itself, and neither is it a guarantee for value creation (Canals, 2001). *Profitable* growth, on the other hand, integrates growth and profitability, two of the main aspects of economic performance, and provides a more adequate point of reference for superior performance. It reflects a company's ability to innovate, to stay in close touch with customers and markets, to enhance employee commitment, and attract investors (Canals, 2001), and is viewed as a viable indicator for organizational effectiveness, value creation, and sustained competitiveness (Stonham, 1995). Despite its relevance, profitable growth has received only limited attention in empirical studies and, therefore, still remains a highly elusive phenomenon.

The main theoretical argument of this chapter, i.e., the positive link between middle managers' entrepreneurial behavior and profitable growth, comes from early works in the strategic management field. Edith Penrose's "theory of the firm" (1995 [1959]) asserts that growth critically depends on *individual managers carrying out new ideas.* "Entrepreneurial services," defined as innovative use of resources, are central to purposive effective (growth-oriented) behavior, and are required in all organizations (Penrose, 1995). A number of authors broadened this argument to discuss the role of managerial competence. Ghoshal et al. (1999), for example, stress the importance of quality of managerial actions in eliciting growth, and Normann (1977) points to the reciprocal relations between vision and concrete managerial action as a basic condition for growth.

The positive link between middle managers' entrepreneurial behavior and profitable growth can be seen through the defining elements of entrepreneurial behavior, innovation and opportunities. Opportunities, conceived as future states that are both desirable and feasible (Stevenson and Jarillo, 1990), make growth possible, while *innovative approaches* to pursue these opportunities ensure profits. Innovation as viewed in this chapter is not limited to technological development but can be understood as a process through which resources are developed and utilized to generate higher quality or lower cost processes, products, and services.

It is important to note that opportunities arise inside and outside the organization. Innovative approaches to capture opportunities outside the sub-unit or organization, for example, include proactive ways to search and pursue business and market opportunities as well as to approach customers. Such activities elicit first-mover advantages, which in turn may create sustainable competitive advantage and result in profitable growth. Inside the business unit, resources can be employed innovatively to develop or adapt products and processes, to lead people, and to organize and structure the unit. Approaching processes and procedures in innovative ways may result in the building of dynamic organizational capabilities, which could in turn stimulate profitable growth and overall organizational effectiveness and competitiveness (Teece et al., 1997).

In summary, three innovative and opportunity based activities define middle managers' entrepreneurial behavior: first, in the way they lead and guide their subordinates; second, in the way they build and organize their unit, and third, in the way they meet customer and market challenges. It is the set of these activities that are vital to induce profitable growth at the sub-unit level.

Based on these arguments I propose:

Proposition: Middle managers' entrepreneurial behavior has a positive effect on profitable growth in the unit they are responsible for.

Methods

I chose a one-company research design to capture the phenomenon, and to develop context-specific measurement instruments. This design also allowed me to reduce "noise" by holding constant several important determinants of entrepreneurial behavior at the firm level, such as incentives systems, corporate culture, and official information flow.

Setting

The company chosen, ABN-Amro, belongs to the highly concentrated Dutch retail financial services industry. After a wave of consolidation and restructuring in the 1990s, the big three Dutch financial institutions, ABN-Amro, Rabobank and ING Bank owned approximately 85 percent of the 6,650 retail branches in the Netherlands. Given this restructuring and gradual reduction of retail branches, the number of inhabitants serviced by each branch doubled. Furthermore, the demand growth in short and medium-term loans was hovering around 15 percent per annum, and mortgages at approximately 20 percent per annum, both very much correlated to economic growth. In summary, the Dutch retail financial services industry appeared to be highly attractive.

Yet these incumbent banks still found it increasingly difficult to achieve profitable growth despite their high concentration and favorable demand growth prospects. Increasingly demanding customers, intensified competition from abroad and non-financial institutions together with new and cheaper methods of distribution posed significant threats to the incumbents. For example, Spaarbeleg Bank (AGEON), a small niche player, entered the market providing products via non/traditional distribution channels and captured 6.5 percent of the Dutch population within 5 years. Profitability in the strong mortgage market was challenged by fierce competition on the asset side of the balance sheet as new players with more favorable cost structures entered and exerted pressure on the margins. And non-financial institutions such as retail chains gained momentum. As a result of these threats, the large retail banks had to think of innovative ways to increase efficiency. Fostering cross-selling of financial products and services, re-thinking distribution platforms, redesigning branches, modifying sales incentive policies, and focusing on cost efficiency were seen as essential to ensure profitable growth. While the large banks established broad efficiency targets at the corporate level, they became increasingly aware that implementation of these targets required the entrepreneurial effort of all employees.

In 1997, ABN-Amro launched a project to promote entrepreneurial behavior, and accordingly reshuffled its Dutch retail banking operations. The company divided the Netherlands into approximately 200 micro markets each run by an area manager. Each of these independent sub-units belonged to one of 11 regional units. Area managers, who formally reported to a general regional manager, were now expected to manage their unit in an entrepreneurial way and diffuse an entrepreneurial spirit throughout. In other words, area managers were given considerable autonomy in leading and guiding their subordinates, building and organizing their units, and approaching customer and market challenges. In return, they became increasingly accountable for the financial results of their units. It is thus these activities of these area managers – middle managers – and their impact on profitable growth in their areas (sub-unit) that is at the center of this study.

Sample and procedures

Following March and Sutton (1997), who predicted retrospective biases in self-reported performance variables but not in assessing independent variables, I used objective sources (company archives) to collect performance data for the period 1997–99, and relied on self-reported data to assess entrepreneurial behavior.

Procedure.   The data collection process included: (1) forty semi-structured interviews (with middle managers, their bosses and subordinates) to operationalize entrepreneurial behavior and develop an adequate measurement instrument; (2) a comprehensive questionnaire completed by middle managers to assess entrepreneurial behavior; and (3) the collection of objective performance data over time.

Sample.   Out of a total population of 207 area managers, 150 managers answered the questionnaire (response rate of 72 percent). To follow performance over time (1997 until the end of 1999) and to ensure comparability, I delimited the analysis to the 121 middle managers that assumed their job with the launch of the entrepreneurial project at ABN-Amro at the beginning of 1997. Three additional areas (units) had to be excluded from the analysis: the national airport because of its particularities with respect to both business and inhabitants, and two areas where no performance data was available. Thus the final sample (N) consisted of 118 areas (units).

   I evaluated non-response biases by comparing regional distribution, size, and performance of the units in the "returned" sample with the ones in the "not-returned" sample. No significant differences were found. As suggested by the relevant literature, I eliminated social desirability effects as much as possible by clarifying introductions and accurate phrasing of questions (Rossi et al., 1983).

Respondents.   The sample of managers who returned the questionnaire and started their job in 1997 exhibited the following characteristics. Four percent of all middle managers in the return sample were female, and 71 percent of all respondents were less than 50 years old. The educational level was quite elevated: 77.3 percent have enjoyed higher education (39 percent held university degrees). These results were consistent with the distribution in the overall population of middle managers working for ABN-Amro in the Netherlands. On average, managers in the sample had been with the company for 22 years and were responsible for 59 employees. Depending on the size of unit, the latter number ranged between 14 and 217 employees.

Measures

Dependent variable.   Profitable growth was assessed over a period of three years. I created a profitable growth index that compared 1997 net income with those of 1999

(1997 = 100). This information was based on objective data that was collected directly from the company.

Independent variable.   I conducted a series of interviews with middle (area) managers, subordinates, bosses and internal/external experts to create a context-specific instrument to measure middle manager entrepreneurial behavior. Following the distinct steps suggested by the literature on scale development (Rossi et al., 1983), I generated different items and pre-tested the scale with a sample of middle managers. The final scale included questions about the extent to which middle managers engaged in particular entrepreneurial activities (1 "no extent", to 7 "to a great extent"). The five items constituting the final scale (see Appendix 11.1) capture the main defining elements of entrepreneurial activity in large traditional organizations, i.e., innovation, autonomy, and opportunity. They are targeted at activities related to the renewing of organizational processes and structure, to guiding employees, and to proactively approaching customers and markets. In other words, the items reflect the spectrum of activities associated with entrepreneurial management within an established organization. The final scale demonstrated highly satisfactory internal reliability (Cronbach alpha = 0.76).

Control variables.   To assess change in financial results (i.e. profitable growth) properly, I controlled for the initial financial results (Finkel, 1995). By controlling for these initial values, I take into account the likely negative correlation between initial scores on a variable and subsequent change, a phenomenon generally known as "regression to the mean."

While literature in organizational behavior has extensively argued that superior performance can to a large extent be attributed to the person, strategic management literature has traditionally emphasized situational characteristics such as size and/or the level of competitiveness as the critical variables. Attempting to reconcile both literatures, I controlled for personal characteristics of the managers as well as for the particular characteristics of their units. Personal characteristics reflect gender, age, level of education, and professional background. I used dummy variables for all of these characteristics: gender (male/female), age (above/below 50), education (high: university or higher vocational education/secondary or primary school), and professional background (similar position as middle managers in same geographical location/another position within the domestic division).

To control for unit-specific characteristics, I included variables reflecting the particular region where the unit is located, the size of the unit, the level of wealth in the area, the degree of micro market competition, and the economic development in the area as an indicator for demand growth. I used dummy variables to indicate the unit (in an 11-region total); the number of full-time employees as a proxy for the size of the unit; the average prices of houses as an indicator for the level of wealth in the unit; the number of inhabitants per branch as an estimate for the level of competition; and growth in the number of small and medium enterprises (SMEs) as a proxy for the economic development in the area.

Data Analysis and Results

I conducted multiple regression analysis (OLS) to test the proposition that middle managers instigate profitable growth by engaging in entrepreneurial behavior. Table 11.1 presents the descriptive statistics (means and standard deviations) and Pearson correlation matrix for all variables. To check for multicollinearity, I assessed Variance Inflation Factor (VIF) and tolerance statistics, which both indicate acceptable levels and did not compromise the theoretical and empirical validity of the study.

The data were analyzed in two steps. In the first step, I included entrepreneurial behavior and controlled for initial financial results (model 1). In the second model, I added personal and unit-specific characteristics as control variables. Table 11.2 illustrates the results of the multiple regression analysis. Both models were highly significant ($F = 4.89$ and $F = 3.72$, $p < 0.001$). Model 1 explained 8 percent of the variance in profitable growth. The main proposition of this chapter was supported: entrepreneurial behavior of middle managers exerted a significant and positive effect on profitable growth (0.18, $p < 0.05$) even after controlling for the initial level of profits.

In model 2, I consider the effect of personal characteristics and unit-specific characteristics. This comprehensive model explained 43 percent of variation in profitable growth and the change in variance explained was highly significant (F-test of difference $= 3.39$, $p < 0.01$). Besides the principal independent variable entrepreneurial behavior (0.14, $p < 0.1$), a number of variables reflecting personal characteristics significantly affected profitable growth. Gender had a significant negative effect on profitable growth (-0.16, $p < 0.05$), suggesting that units managed by female managers perform better than units managed by male managers. However, it is important to note that the number of female area managers is relatively small. Only 3.4 percent of the managers in the sample were female. The level of education had a significant negative effect on profitable growth (-0.19, $p < 0.05$) suggesting that units managed by managers with university degrees or higher vocational training economically perform worse than those run by managers that merely enjoyed primary or secondary education. Finally, the professional background of middle managers also significantly affected profitable growth. Managers who did not change position and location exhibited a significantly lower growth in profits (-0.23, $p < 0.01$) than their colleagues who changed both content and place.

In contrast to variables reflecting personal characteristics, only a few control variables regarding the specific business units showed significant effects on profitable growth. The region of Ostbrabant exhibited significantly higher levels of profitable growth (0.24, $p < 0.05$) than the region of Amsterdam, which is not surprising as most of the Dutch multinationals have their headquarters in this region.[1] The region of Overijssel, on the other hand, showed significantly lower profitable growth (-0.22, $p < 0.1$), which can be attributed to the relatively weaker economic situation in this area. Also the size of the unit had a highly significant and positive effect on profitable growth (0.59, $p < 0.01$), most likely driven by market share effects (the correlation of between size and profits, rather than profit growth is highly significant.) The coefficient for growth in the number of SMEs was significant though negative

Table11.1 Descriptive statistics and Pearson correlations ($N = 118$)

	Mean	Std. Dev.	(1)	(2)	(3)	(4)	(5)	(6)	(7)	(8)	(9)	(10)	(11)	(12)	(13)	(14)	(15)	(16)	(17)	(18)	(19)	(20)
1 Ln Profit Growth	4.88	0.17	—																			
2 Entrep. Behavior	4.71	0.93	0.19*	—																		
3 Ln Fin. Result	8.11	0.80	-0.22	-0.04	—																	
4 Size	60.37	44.17	-0.16	-0.02	0.84**	—																
5 Region Limburg	0.05	0.22	0.22*	0.07	-0.25**	-0.20*	—															
6 Region Den Haag	0.06	0.23	0.02	-0.15	0.07	0.02	-0.06	—														
7 Region Zuid West	0.11	0.31	-0.001	0.16	0.08	-0.01	-0.08	-0.09	—													
8 Region Utrecht	0.08	0.28	-0.80	0.06	0.25**	0.11	-0.07	0.08	-0.11	—												
9 Region Gelderland	0.11	0.31	-0.30	-0.03	-0.71	-0.01	-0.08	-0.09	-0.12	-0.11	—											
10 Region Overijssel	0.09	0.29	-0.15	-0.07	-0.16	-0.07	-0.07	-0.08	-0.11	-0.10	-0.11	—										
11 Region Noord	0.11	0.31	0.03	0.12	0.12	0.07	-0.08	-0.08	-0.12	-0.11	-0.12	-0.11	—									
12 Region Haarlem	0.09	0.29	-0.05	0.00	-0.08	-0.09	-0.07	-0.08	-0.11	-0.10	-0.11	-0.10	-0.11	—								
13 Region Rotterdam	0.15	0.36	0.13	-0.01	0.04	0.04	-0.10	-0.11	-0.15	-0.13	-0.15	-0.14	-0.15	-0.14	—							
14 Region Ostbrabant	0.07	0.25	-0.14	-0.16	0.12	0.05	-0.06	-0.07	-0.10	-0.08	-0.10	-0.09	-0.10	-0.09	-0.11	—						
15 Ln Competition	7.74	0.43	-0.14	-0.15	0.07	0.11	-0.13	0.14	-0.34**	-0.20*	-0.01	0.01	-0.31**	0.02	0.22*	0.08	—					
16 Wealth	122513.34	25384.29	-0.13	-0.08	0.10	-0.09	-0.07	0.10	-0.24**	0.44**	0.08	-0.14	-0.39**	0.23*	-0.12	0.13	0.27**	—				
17 Eco. Development	119.55	19.49	-0.15	-0.08	0.40	0.06	-0.05	-0.04	-0.09	-0.03	0.06	-0.06	0.02	-0.09	0.06	0.10	0.11	-0.13	—			
18 Education	0.76	0.43	-0.25**	-0.14	0.20*	0.14	0.04	0.06	-0.06	-0.12	0.01	-0.03	0.01	-0.10	0.02	0.07	0.13	0.10	-0.01	—		
19 Age	0.33	0.47	-0.06	0.01	0.11	0.12	0.08	0.06	0.27**	-0.02	0.04	0.09	0.04	0.02	-0.25**	-0.05	-0.15	-0.07	-0.12	-0.07	—	
20 Gender	0.97	0.18	-0.82	-0.05	-0.08	-0.01	0.04	0.05	0.07	-0.28	0.07	0.06	0.07	0.06	-0.18*	0.05	-0.17	-0.20*	0.02	0.01	0.13	—
21 Background	0.42	0.49	-0.22*	0.02	-0.20*	-0.29**	0.11	-0.14	0.03	0.05	-0.03	-0.04	0.08	-0.10	0.02	0.04	-0.40	0.06	0.14	-0.09	0.13	-0.03

*$p < 0.10$; **$p < 0.05$; ***$p < 0.001$.

Table 11.2   Results of multiple regression: effect of entrepreneurial behavior on profitable growth

Variables	Model 1 Profit growth[a]	t-statistic	Model 2 Profit growth[a]	t-statistic
Entrepreneurial behavior	0.18**	2.01	0.14*	1.74
Initial level of performance	(0.02)	−2.32	(0.02)	−4.28
Financial results in 1997[a]	−0.21**		−0.75***	
	(0.02)		(0.04)	
Personal characteristics				
Gender (1=male)			−0.17**	−1.99
			(0.08)	
Age (1=>50)			−0.02	−0.19
			(0.03)	
Education (1 = higher education)			−0.19**	−2.24
			(0.03)	
Background: similar position as area manager in the same geographical location			−0.23**	−2.61
			(0.03)	
Characteristics of unit				
Region Limburg			0.13	1.20
			(0.08)	
Region Den Haag			0.07	0.66
			(0.08)	
Region Zuid West			−0.04	−0.28
			(0.07)	
Region Utrecht			0.01	0.11
			(0.08)	
Region Gelderland			−0.07	−0.51
			(0.06)	
Region Overijssel			−0.22*	−1.85
			(0.07)	
Region Noord			−0.07	−0.52
			(0.07)	
Region Haarlem			−0.05	−0.42
			(0.07)	
Region Rotterdam			−0.06	−0.40
			(0.06)	
Region Oostbrabant			0.24**	2.26
			(0.07)	
Competition[a]			−0.13	−1.32
			(0.04)	
Wealth			−0.8	−0.64
			(0.00)	
Size			0.60***	3.55
			(0.001)	
Economic Development			−0.14*	−1.68
			(0.001)	
F	4.89**		3.72***	
F change			3.39***	
R^2	0.08		0.43	
Adjusted R^2	0.06		0.32	

$n = 118$.

Values are standardized estimates. Standard error terms appear in parentheses.

[a] Logarithm.

* $p < 0.10$; ** $p < 0.05$; *** $p < 0.001$.

(-0.14, $p < 0.1$). However, the coefficients for competitiveness and wealth were not significant. Finally, the initial level of financial results did exert a significant effect on sub-unit profitable growth in model 1 (-0.21, $p < 0.05$) and model 2 (-0.74, $p < 0.1$).

Discussion and Implications

In this study, I advanced and tested the idea that middle managers' entrepreneurial behavior, conceptualized as their innovative use of resource combinations to explore and exploit opportunities, triggers profitable growth within sub-units. While prior literature in strategic management has largely overlooked middle managers' potential to achieve sustained superior performance, my analysis reveals that their entrepreneurial behavior is significantly associated with profitable growth and therefore constitutes an important lever to create sustained superior performance in established organizations.

This finding corroborates earlier, mainly theoretical, claims about the importance of the quality of managerial actions in eliciting superior performance and growth (Ghoshal et al., 1999). Furthermore, it substantiates Penrose's idea that growth critically depends on individual managers carrying out new ideas and engaging in "entrepreneurial services" (Penrose, 1995). Indeed, this idea has been followed upon recently by scholars advocating a "new theory of economic growth" arguing that individuals (and companies) exploring and implementing new and better ways of doing things rather than capital or raw materials trigger economic growth (Romer, 1989).

In addition, the results suggest that personal characteristics of the entrepreneurial actors – largely ignored by previous strategic management research – do matter. According to my data, female middle managers – although representing only a small percentage of the overall population – do significantly better in achieving profitable growth in their units. The same holds for managers with a, relatively speaking, lower level of education. Managers holding degrees from primary or secondary school seem to be more successful in triggering profitable growth in middle management positions than their "highly" educated colleagues. One interpretation of this finding goes back to the "socially created" perception of the job of middle managers. Very often middle management positions are merely considered as "necessary" steps on the career ladder within large organizations. As for many career-oriented managers holding university or comparable degrees, they represent a temporary placement on the way to the top (management); therefore, the relative effort put into managing the unit is moderate. On the other hand, for managers with a low educational background, middle manager positions represent a superb opportunity to demonstrate their managerial competence. Furthermore, as these managers in general hold their positions for longer periods of time, they also tend to put in more effort and "care." The data also reveals a significant effect of the professional background of middle managers on profitable growth, suggesting that managers might be more successful in stimulating profitable growth if they are not stuck for too long with the same job in the same location.

Situation and unit-specific control variables partially exerted significant effects on profitable growth. The significant and positive effect of size suggests that larger units do better in triggering profitable growth. While overall results on the effect of sub-unit size on organizational performance are mixed (see Dalton et al., 1980 for a review), this finding corroborates claims that larger units have the necessary resources and involve a critical mass of activities to ensure superior performance (Bantel and Jackson, 1989). In the context of ABN-Amro, managers of small areas composed of 2 or 3 bank branches very often do not have the means to explore and exploit opportunities in an innovative way. Building on a larger base of customers and employees managers of larger areas might encounter more possibilities to act proactively and have more bargaining power with respect to autonomy in pricing, human resources issues, and the way they structure their area. Finally, the negative relationship between economic development and profitable growth could be related to the fact that growth of the number of SMEs in the area might be a valuable indicator for economic development; however, it does not necessarily have a direct effect on the bank's core business which relies on retail clients and only to a smaller percentage on SMEs.

Contribution, Limitations and Future Research

This chapter integrates literatures on middle managers, the sources of sustained superior performance, and entrepreneurship within established organizations. It complements and advances existing research as follows. First, in contrast to prior research on middle managers, it goes beyond describing roles and tasks of effective middle managers and offers insights on how specific actions aligned with the strategic vision of an organization translate into superior performance. Second, the chapter tackles the elusive phenomenon of sustained superior performance *within* large organizations. I complement and extend existing literature by elucidating how sustained superior performance – measured in terms of profitable growth – is generated through distinct managerial activities at the sub-unit level. Hence, the study corroborates earlier claims that growth is not merely based on capital and raw materials but significantly depends on human initiative and creativity (Canals, 2001; Ghoshal et al., 1999; Penrose, 1995). Third, I broaden existing literature on entrepreneurship within established organizations by adopting a less heroic view and emphasizing day-to-day entrepreneurship. Expanding the range of activities constituting entrepreneurial behavior, I offer a conceptualization that is applicable to a number of phenomena in large traditional organizations that would be excluded if merely looking at grand entrepreneurship, i.e., new venture creation or new product development. Finally, the chapter addresses and fills methodological gaps detected in previous research on middle managers and entrepreneurship within established firms. I adopted methods appropriate for an "infant field" lacking an advanced paradigm and concentrated on linking specific managerial activities to superior results at the sub-unit level rather than testing general theory (Bygrave, 1989; Goodman et al., 1983; Scott, 1977). Also, while traditional research mainly remained on the descriptive level, I developed fine-grained context-specific measurement instruments based on qualitative insights to assess effective (entrepreneurial) behavior. Adequate measurements are fundamental for further theory development as well as for deriving meaningful implications for managerial practice (Lumpkin and Dess, 1996).

Nonetheless, a few limitations of the study and suggestions for future research should be pointed out. First, while the explorative nature of the research project asked for a one-company research design, additional studies are needed to establish external validity of the measurement instrument and to allow for a generalization of the findings. Second, profitable growth was assessed by taking into consideration the 3 years succeeding the launch of the entrepreneurial project at ABN-Amro. It can be argued that to accurately estimate time lag effects, a larger time horizon needs to be considered (Zahra et al., 1999). Third, although capturing behavior over 3 years, for accessibility reasons, entrepreneurial activity was assessed at one point in time, future analysis would benefit from measuring entrepreneurial activity longitudinally, i.e., at various points over time. Finally, future research would also gain from controlling for past performance. In this study, as units and management positions were newly created in 1997, data on past performance and activities did not exist.

Implications for Managerial Practice

Contrary to popular press, which has repeatedly described middle managers as "corporate dinosaurs," this study suggests that middle managers do add value. Their entrepreneurial behavior is significantly associated with sustained superior performance. The findings of this chapter suggest that entrepreneurial behavior represents a viable means to manage large established organizations and sustain profitable growth. It is important to note that in these organizations acting entrepreneurial typically implies "freedom within boundaries." In the context of ABN-Amro, these boundaries consisted in explicit rules such as limited credit risk authorities or implicit rules such as not cannibalizing business of other areas. The implications for top management are straightforward. We know that top management assumes a critical role in fostering entrepreneurial behavior (Ghoshal and Bartlett, 1994). However, this role cannot be limited at delineating an appropriate strategic vision, shaping formal organizational structure and processes, incentive and information systems, or providing the necessary resources. To make entrepreneurial approaches sustainable and profitable, top management needs to mold the "behavioral" context; i.e., it needs to empower middle managers (Spreitzer, 1996) and build the appropriate levels of support, stretch, discipline, and trust, to nurture entrepreneurial initiative at the sub-unit level (Ghoshal and Bartlett, 1994).

Note

1. The particular regions are coded as dummy variables. Ten dummy variables (for 11 regions) were created with the region of Amsterdam used as the region of reference.

References

Bantel, K. and Jackson, S. 1989: Top management and innovations in banking: Does the composition of the top team make a difference? *Strategic Management Journal*, 10, 107–124.

Bower, J. 1970: *Managing the Resource Allocation Process: A Study of Corporate Planning and Investment*. Boston, MA: Harvard Business Press.

Burgelman, R. 1983a: A model of the interaction of strategic behavior, corporate context and the concept of strategy. *Academy of Management Review*, 8, 61–70.

Burgelman, R. 1983b: Corporate entrepreneurship and strategic management: Insights from a process study. *Management Science*, 29, 1349–1364.

Bygrave, W. 1989: The entrepreneurship paradigm (I): A philosophical look at its research methodologies. *Entrepreneurship Theory and Practice*, 14, 7–26.

Canals, J. 2001: How to think about corporate growth? *European Management Journal*, 19, 587–598.

Covin, J. and Miles, M. 1999: Corporate entrepreneurship and the pursuit of competitive advantage. *Entrepreneurship Theory and Practice*, 23, 47–63.

Covin, J. and Slevin, D. 1991: A conceptual model of entrepreneurship as firm behavior. *Entrepreneurship Theory and Practice*, 16, 7–25.

Dalton, D., Todor, W., Spendolini, M., Fielding, G., and Porter, L. 1980: Organization structure and performance: A critical review. *Academy of Management Review*, 5, 49–64.

Finkel, S. 1995: *Causal Analysis with Panel Data*. Thousand Oaks, CA: Sage.

Gartner, W. 1988: "Who is an entrepreneur?" is the wrong question. *American Journal of Small Business*, 12, 11–32.

Ghoshal, S. and Bartlett, C. 1994: Linking organizational context and managerial action: The dimensions of quality of management. *Strategic Management Journal*, 15, 91–112.

Ghoshal, S. and Bartlett, C. 1995: Building the entrepreneurial corporation: New organizational processes, new managerial tasks. *European Management Journal*, 13, 139–155.

Ghoshal, S. and Bartlett, C. 1998: *The Individualized Corporation: A Fundamentally New Approach to Management*. London, UK: Heinemann.

Ghoshal, S., Bartlett, C., and Moran, P. 1999: A new manifesto for management. *Sloan Management Review*, 40, 9–20.

Goodman, P., Atkin, R., and Schoorman, F. 1983: On the demise of organizational effectiveness studies. In K. Cameron and D. Whetten (eds.), *Organizational Effectiveness: A Comparison of Multiple Models*. San Diego, CA: Academic Press, Inc. 163–183.

Hamel, G. 1999: Bringing Silicon Valley inside. *Harvard Business Review*, 77, 70–84.

Hornsby, J., Kuratko, D., and Zahra, S. 2002: Middle managers' perception of the internal environment for corporate entrepreneurship: Assessing a measurement scale. *Journal of Business Venturing*, 17, 253–273.

Howell, J.M. and Higgins, C.A. 1990. Champions of technological innovation. *Administrative Science Quarterly*, 35, 317–330.

Kanter, R. 1982: The middle manager as innovator. *Harvard Business Review*, 60, 95–105.

Lippman, S. and Rumelt, R. 1982: Uncertain imitability: An analysis of interfirm differences in efficiency under competition. *Bell Journal of Economics*, 13, 418–438.

Lumpkin, G. and Dess, G. 1996: Clarifying the entrepreneurial orientation construct and linking it to performance. *Academy of Management Review*, 21, 135–172.

March, J. and Sutton, R. 1997: Organizational performance as a dependent variable. *Organization Science*, 8, 698–706.

Miller, D. 1983: The correlates of entrepreneurship in three types of firms. *Management Science*, 29, 770–791.

Nonaka, I. 1988: Toward middle-up-down management: Accelerating information creation. *Management Science*, 29, 9–18.

Normann, R. 1977: *Management for Growth*. Chichester, UK: John Wiley & Sons.

Penrose, E. 1995: *The Theory of the Growth of the Firm* (3rd edn [1959]). Oxford, UK: Oxford University Press.

Porter, M. 1980: *Competitive Strategy*. New York: Free Press.

Romer, P. 1989: Capital accumulation in the theory of long-run growth. In R.J. Barro (ed.), *Modern Business Cycle Theory*. Cambridge, MA: Harvard Univerity Press, 51–127.

Rossi, P., Wright, J., and Anderson, A. (eds.) 1983: *Handbook of Survey Research*. San Diego, CA: Academic Press.

Rumelt, R., Schendel, D., and Teece, D. 1994: *Fundamental Issues in Strategy*. Cambridge, MA: Harvard University Press.

Scott, W. 1977: Effectiveness of organizational effectiveness studies. In P. Goodman and J. Pennings (eds.), *New Perspectives on Organizational Effectiveness*. San Francisco, CA: Jossey-Bass, 63–95.

Spreitzer, G. 1996: Social structural characteristics of psychological empowerment. *Academy of Management Journal*, 39, 483–504.

Stevenson, H. and Jarillo, J. 1990: A paradigm of entrepreneurship: Entrepreneurial management. *Strategic Management Journal*, 11, 17–27.

Stonham, P. 1995: New view of strategy: An interview with C.K. Prahalad. *European Management Journal*, 13, 130–138.

Teece, D., Pisano, G., and Shuen, A. 1997: Dynamic capabilities and strategic management. *Strategic Management Journal*, 18, 509–533.

Uyterhoeven, H. 1972: General managers in the middle. *Harvard Business Review*, 67, 136–145.

Vesper, K. 1985: A new direction, or just a new label? In J. Kao and H. Stevenson (eds.), *Entrepreneurship: What It Is and How to Teach It*. Boston, MA: Harvard Business School, 62–76.

von Hippel, E. 1977: Successful and failing internal corporate ventures – an empirical analysis. *Industrial Marketing Management*, 6, 163.

Wernerfelt, B. 1984: A resource-based view of the firm. *Strategic Management Journal*, 5, 171–180.

Woolridge, B. and Floyd, S. 1990: The strategy process, middle management involvement, and organizational performance. *Strategic Management Journal*, 11, 231–241.

Zahra, S. and Covin, J. 1993: Business strategy, technology policy and firm performance. *Strategic Management Journal*, 14, 451–478.

Zahra, S., Jennings, D., and Kuratko, D. 1999: The antecedents and consequences of firm-level entrepreneurship: The state of the field. *Entrepreneurship Theory and Practice*, 24, 45–65.

Appendix 11.1: Scale to assess entrepreneurial behaviour

To what extent did you carry out the following activities in your job as rayon manager over the last years?	To no extent						To a great extent
1. Changing procedures to facilitate client contact within the rayon[a]	1	2	3	4	5	6	7
2. Promoting entrepreneurial behavior of employees with initiatives that went beyond the ones suggested by head-office	1	2	3	4	5	6	7
3. Proactively approach new customers	1	2	3	4	5	6	7
4. Actively investigating new market opportunities within the rayon	1	2	3	4	5	6	7
5. Encouraging your employees to develop new ideas on how to do business	1	2	3	4	5	6	7

[a] The term rayon refers to area (sub-unit).

CHAPTER TWELVE

Impacts of Justification Behavior: The Forgotten Costs of Corporate Governance?

Michael Nippa and Kerstin Petzold

Introduction

Strategic management concerns creating value, sustaining competitive advantage, and achieving company growth and survival (Grant, 1998). Yet these objectives are not ends in themselves, but means to satisfy the interests of different stakeholders of the firm. If managers were the owners of the firm, making strategic decisions would be relatively simple; conflicts would be avoided. But it is argued that if the management function is separated from the ownership of the firm, fundamental conflicts arise. If not prevented by external constraints, top managers may exploit shareholders by pursuing their personal objectives rather than maximizing shareholders' wealth (e.g. Williamson 1985). Indeed, Shleifer and Vishny (1997: 737) summarize this conflict, the basis of the corporate governance field, in three straightforward questions: "How do the suppliers of finance get managers to return some of the profits to them? How do they make sure that managers do not steal the capital they supply or invest it in bad projects? How do suppliers of finance control managers?"

Corporate governance research develops, analyzes, discusses, and proposes various measures to prevent shareholders from being fleeced by managers (Denis, 2001; Hart, 1995; Shleifer and Vishny, 1997; Tirole, 2001). Researchers have focused on two main topics: systems for monitoring (and punishing) top management behavior that prevent deviation from shareholders' interests; and incentives that reward top management for achieving objectives deemed important to owners (see e.g. Tosi et al., 2000).

Despite the substantial research in corporate governance, the empirical results have not been particularly satisfying. For example, under the first topic, if top management has not achieved the expected objectives, it still takes a long time before they are removed either internally or through a hostile takeover (Jensen and Murphy, 1990b; Porter, 1992). For example *Business Week* named John Akers, then CEO of IBM, in March 1992 to be one of 25 executives to watch (*Business Week*, 1992). He stepped down in January 1993. Conyon and Florou (2002) find that corporate performance must fall dramatically to force a senior executive job separation. However, there is also a downside in firing a CEO (Mahajan and Lummer, 1993; Wiersema, 2002).

Likewise, the second measure, i.e. linking top management compensation with firm performance, has not led to the expected management motivation and behavior (e.g. Abowd and Kaplan, 1999; Fehr and Falk, 2001). Indeed, many of the recent accounting scandals and obvious cases of corporate frauds such as Enron, Tyco, Vivendi, or Worldcom, provide high profile evidence that linking the compensation to the firm's share performance might create counterproductive side-effects. Furthermore, empirical support for "optimal incentive contracts" as proposed by principal–agent theory is still missing (Barkema and Gomez-Mejia, 1998; Coles et al., 2001; Tosi et al., 2000).

This lack of evidence of the proper management behavior from incentive contracts, and the delay in punishing management for poor behavior and/or outcomes may lead to two totally different conclusions. On the one hand, one can take this as a proof of the inadequacy of these measures and consequently the underlying theory. On the other hand, it can lead to an even more intensified monitoring to ensure managerial compliance. In practice we are witnessing the latter. New laws such as the Sarbannes–Oxley Act in the US and *KonTraG* in Germany have been enacted; reporting obligations have been increased; quasi-voluntary codes have been established, and new supervisory institutions have been implemented.

Without a doubt, these actions may indeed increase managerial compliance; however, they neglect interactive processes between actors within a dynamic environment. Implementing and imposing corporate governance measures in order to cause a desired behavior induces managerial reaction and ultimately justification behavior. Justifying decisions or behavior is a common social expression. Given the research on justification behavior within psychology and sociology (Lerner and Tetlock, 1999), the phenomenon is understudied in strategic decision making and corporate governance (exceptions are Bettman and Weitz, 1983; Staw et al., 1983; Tsang, 2002 for justifications of firm performance and Granlund et al., 1998 for justification of single decisions).

The primary objective of this chapter, therefore, is to explore justification behavior within the context of strategic decision making and corporate governance mechanisms. We will do so by answering the following research questions:

- What causes the justification of strategic decisions by top management?
- Which kind of organizational mechanisms emerge as a consequence of specific justification needs?
- How can major variables of justification processes be integrated in a basic corporate governance model?
- To what extent does justification behavior impact the efficiency of corporate governance monitoring measures?

In order to provide answers to the research questions, the chapter is structured as follows. First, we outline the concept of justification behavior in organizations. Second, we develop three propositions. Finally, we build and discuss a preliminary model of justification induced management behavior and derive implications for management and corporate governance.

Conceptualization of Justification Behavior

Principal–agent theory and justification

Corporate governance literature relies primarily on financial and organizational economics in general and principal–agent theory in more detail (see e.g. Hawley and Williams, 2000; Turnbull, 1997 for a review.). A "simple financial model" can be understood as the starting point and dominant way of thinking within the recent debate of corporate governance issues (Turnbull, 2000: 23). The theory concerns how one party, the principal or shareholder, who delegates work to another, the agent or top management, can achieve the most efficient compensation arrangement (Alchian and Demsetz, 1972; Eisenhardt, 1989; Jensen and Meckling, 1976). The two parties are assumed to be utility maximizers, i.e. to be acting in their own best interests (Jensen and Meckling, 1976). Both parties would prefer to cooperate for the maximization of their respective competitive positions (Fama, 1980); however, three fundamental assumptions make the fixing of these contracts difficult: environmental uncertainty, information asymmetry, and goal conflict.

First, when the environment is uncertain, the principal cannot verify the agent's intentions by only examining his performance outcomes. The outcomes may be due to environmental factors such as recessions, competitive reactions etc. that are beyond the agent's control. While they may attempt to incorporate many possible environmental contingencies, it is unlikely that they can anticipate all of them.

Second, even if the environment were certain, the principal may still not fully know the agent's abilities or what he has actually done. In such cases, agent opportunism may arise. Moral hazard refers to the problem of shirking or the agent's lack of effort (Holmström, 1979). The second problem concerns adverse selection, or the misrepresentation of the agent's ability (Akerlof, 1970).

Finally, the agent may not always act in the best interest of the principal since the two parties' goals are not likely to be identical or compatible (Holmström, 1979). For example, the agent may be risk averse, preferring to maximize his compensation with the minimum of effort (Coughlan and Sen, 1989). Indeed, top management may have incentives to increase the size of the firm, regardless if it increases shareholder wealth, because executive compensation has been typically related to firm size (Donaldson, 1984; Jensen and Murphy, 1990a; Murphy, 1985). The principal, on the other hand, is assumed to be risk neutral striving for maximum profits, with the agent's utility acting as one of his constraints.

Because of these three fundamental assumptions, the principal encounters costs in monitoring and enforcing the agent's behavior, costs in measuring or sorting out the factors other than the agent's efforts that might have led to specific outcomes and a residual loss due to divergence between the expected and actual outcomes (Jensen and Meckling, 1976). Thus, the challenge for the principal is to write the most efficient contract that compensates the agent for work performed but protects the principal as much as possible (Jensen and Meckling, 1976).

If the principal can, with limited monitoring costs, reduce information asymmetry and sanction the agent for deviant behavior, then the principal can rely on a behavior-based contract, such as a salary. However, due to adverse selection and moral hazard, agent behavior may be very costly to monitor and verify. Furthermore, diverse shareholders have few incentives to actively pressure management because they would privately bear the monitoring and influence costs for public benefit. While in theory shareholders elect a board of directors to represent their interests, they are more often captured by management (Jensen, 1993). This leaves agents with substantial strategic decision-making discretion. While the board of directors may ultimately remove management, or the company may be subject to a hostile takeover or proxy contest, their effects are considered too slow (Porter, 1992).

Principals may implement an outcome-based contract such as pay-for-performance and stock options stipulating performance targets for top management. Yet, in these systems there may be the difficulty of measuring the link between the agent's actions and the observed outcomes. Indeed, linking top management compensation with firm performance has not led to the expected management motivation and behavior (e.g. Abowd and Kaplan, 1999; Fehr and Falk, 2001). Rather, it has led to 'game playing' to increase the share price as witnessed by such high profile examples as Enron and Tyco.

In summary, efficient corporate governance consists of identifying and implementing institutions; i.e. rules and incentives that align management decisions and behavior with the owners of the firm. Efficiency directly results from the comparison of costs and benefits as ascribed to the principal. Furthermore, the lack of evidence of the proper management behavior from incentive contracts, and the delay in punishing management for poor behavior and/or outcomes has led to further adherence to the theory. Intensified monitoring has indeed increased. New laws such as the Sarbannes–Oxley Act in the US and *KonTraG* in Germany have been enacted; reporting obligations have been increased; quasi-voluntary codes have been established, and new supervisory institutions have been implemented – all in an effort to limit aberrant behavior.

However, further adhering to the theory neglects the interactive character of the manager–investor relationship. It fails to take into account additional costs of justification behavior. We suggest that managers react to additional monitoring and controlling measures by implementing specific organizational mechanisms to cope with increased information needs and justification necessities. Taking these costs into account, traditional corporate governance measures, especially increased monitoring, may turn out to be inefficient or even counterproductive. Given the dearth of research in justification behavior in strategic management, strategic decision making and corporate governance, we proceed to further develop the construct before developing the propositions.

Justification triggers

There are neither comprehensive contributions with regard to justification behavior within organizations nor research insights on the impacts of justification for corporate governance. Thus a general definition and characterization of organizational justification is missing, too. As justification behavior is mainly studied within disciplines such as sociology and philosophy we draw upon concepts and arguments found there.

We define justification as an activity in which individuals try to legitimate their intended or actual behavior and decision to a norm-setting or norm-auditing person or institution they depend on. The essential importance of demonstrating and communicating compliance with explicit and implicit values and norms of the evaluator is emphasized in the following definition: "an act, a strategy, a practice, an arrangement, or an institution, that typically involves showing to be prudentially rational, morally acceptable or both" (Simmons, 1999: 740). Referring to and applying philosophical definitions and socio-psychological concepts, three conditions have to be in place in order to trigger justification: *decision ambiguity* (Krogh and Grand, 2000), *dependence* (Tetlock, 1985, 1999), and *demand* based on specific expectations (Caldwell and O'Reilly, 1982).

Decision ambiguity.   One fundamental precondition for the emergence of justification processes is decision ambiguity. Compared with tactical and operational decisions, strategic decisions can be characterized as novel, complex and highly uncertain (e.g., Schwenk, 1995; Schwenk and Thomas, 1988). By definition, strategic decision making requires analyses of aggregated and abstract qualitative and quantitative information and data to position the company over the long term. But this information and data do not represent a "single independent reality," rather they are "continually (re)constituted [as well as (re)constructed] by human beings though linguistic and symbolic means" (Tsoukas, 1993: 324, original references omitted). Indeed, the decision and the process of decision making become subjects of interpersonal evaluation based on individual preference systems. Cause-effect and means-end relationships can be supposed, but hardly identified explicitly. As a result, managers may rely more on intuition than pure analysis (Hammond et al. 1987; Simon 1987). Yet, under increasing decision ambiguity, interpretation and evaluation still has to be meaningful (Smircich and Morgan, 1982) such that the decisions can be explained, rationalized, and legitimized (see Pfeffer, 1981: 4).

Dependence.   While strategic decisions are ambiguous and, therefore, trigger perceived justification, its justification will increase as the decision maker depends more on third parties (Tetlock, 1985). Whether and to what extent does corporate management depend on shareholders? Put differently, to what extent are shareholders becoming more powerful? (see, e.g., Emerson, 1962).

The traditional answer to this question has been straightforward. Diverse shareholders do not have the power to enforce management to comply with their interests. Management has an information advantage; shareholders do not want to bear the monitoring costs for public benefit (Berle and Means, 1932); and the board of directors, while supposedly representing the interests of shareholders, are more often captured by management (Jensen, 1993). Therefore management could act independently and could exploit shareholder rents opportunistically. Consequently, proposed and implemented mechanisms of corporate governance strive for providing shareholders with increased power (Shleifer and Vishny, 1997: 739).

Certainly the trends in corporate governance are moving in this direction and can be related to a taxonomy of three types of power: coercive, legitimate, and reward (see e.g., Yukl, 1981). First, the more recent enacted laws and precedents increase the coercive power of shareholders and investors as their claims are grounded in codified law and can be asserted. The threat of being called to account enforces legal conformity of managers. Additionally they will produce corresponding signals of compliance.

Secondly, larger investors may claim legitimate power as they subscribe significant amounts of capital. Indeed, statistics prove a dramatic shift in the concentration of shareholders. The percentage held by institutional investors in US publicly traded companies increased from 16 percent in 1960 to 57 percent (Ryan and Schneider, 2003).

Finally, newly introduced or extended performance-related incentive schemes give shareholders reward power. Stock-based compensation schemes attach, for instance, large portions of monetary management rewards to the firm's performance as assessed by the market. As the shareholders' assessment of management decisions is reflected in the share price, and pay-for-performance compensation schemes are based on the share price, the income of top management depends on the shareholders' assessment of their decisions and behavior. Thus shareholders should have the power to punish "wrong" decisions and to award "right" ones. To avoid punishment or to obtain additional rewards the dependent manager has to comply.

Demand.   Finally, justification will not occur, if potential or actual "claimants" do not demand it from the dependent person (Ashforth and Gibbs, 1990; Caldwell and O'Reilly, 1982). For example, one would abstain from justifying norm-conflicting behavior, e.g. showing up late at work, even in front of a powerful supervisor, if she or he does not expect or demand such a justification behavior. Thus, expressing demand for justification, especially from more powerful parties, will lead to increased justification. This relationship assumes (a) the existence of explicit or implicit norms and preferences, (b) means to value compliance with these norms and preferences, and (c) the expectation that the decision or behavior will hurt these norms or preferences.

These assumptions are certainly addressed in corporate governance. For example, new laws such as the Sarbannes–Oxley Act in the US and *KonTraG* in Germany have been enacted. Reporting obligations have been increased; quasi-voluntary codes have been established; new supervisory institutions have been implemented; and institutional investors are demanding more comprehensive information about strategic decisions through investor conferences. Clearly, these actions are not only to limit aberrant behavior but also to increase justification demand. Indeed, the more it is presumed, communicated, or proved with respect to individual cases that managers behave opportunistically, hurt shareholder interests, and "steal" from them, the greater the expressed demand for justification, as recently shown by these new changes in corporate governance.

In summary, the three conditions to trigger increased justification behavior, dependence, decision ambiguity, and demand, are certainly in place in corporate governance mechanisms. As these conditions increase, which apparently is the trend, top management may implement specific organizational mechanisms to cope with increased information needs and justification triggers. They may not only invest in further justification tactics but may also change their strategies to "please" the investors; yet, compliance to these standard strategies, i.e. strategies investors would like to see, may, in fact, reduce the company's chance to gain any competitive advantage. In the following section, we develop propositions and a basic framework on how the justification process impacts the relationship between shareholders and management and how it might add to corporate governance costs.

Model and Development of Propositions

We build our model on basic assumptions used by standard economic theory. We propose to broaden the agency theory perspective, namely by considering interactive behavior of both actors: the principal and agent. If interactive processes are taken into account, a more complete view of corporate governance systems will evolve. Hence, economic evaluation of specific corporate governance measures is improved, too. Additionally the model will help to understand elements and processes underlying justification behavior. Thus interaction and communication between managers and important stakeholder can be improved as well.

Behavioral modifications induced by justification triggers

As a consequence of perceived justification triggers, individuals and groups change their behavior and decision making (e.g. Huber and Seiser, 2001; McMackin and Slovic, 2000). These behavioral modifications can be differentiated in three ways before and after the decision is made, as shown in Figure 12.1. First, persons under justification pressure may change his or her decision according to what they think the shareholders want. Secondly, individuals perceiving or facing the need for justification may modify their decision making process, for example, by searching for additional information. Whereas these behavior modifications occur mainly prior to making the decision, justification pressure may also result in behavior modifications during the interaction between the decision maker and the claimant.

Decision modification.   Apart from reversible decisions, which might be changed under justification pressure even after being made, modifications of decisions are likely to occur, if top management knows about the need for justification in advance, before committing to a decision (Lerner and Tetlock, 1999). Top management may deviate from their independent decision, if the perceived or assumed preference system of the claimant differs from their own, irrespective of the clarity of expectations and evaluation criteria. For example, clarity about preference systems has been shown to enhance decision-maker conformity (Brown, 1999; Payne et al., 1993). Yet, other studies have also shown that under the condition of fuzzy expectations, preferences, and evaluation criteria, decision makers will choose alternatives, which are less risky (Curley et al., 1986; Taylor, 1995), most probably minimize potential losses (Tetlock and Boettger, 1994), or represent a middle option in a choice set (Simonson, 1989).

With regard to these behavioral consequences, the question arises whether this deviation from an originally intended decision is economically favorable or not. While it

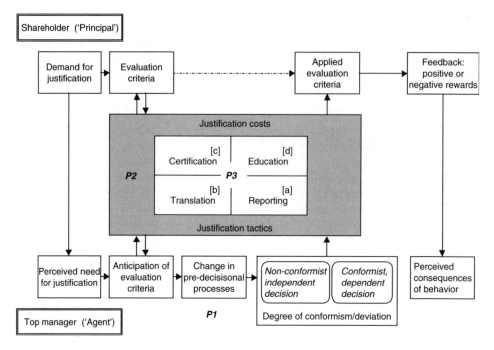

Figure 12.1   An interaction based model of justification behavior in corporate governance

has been argued that due to accountability inefficient decisions may arise (Adelberg and Batson, 1978; Lerner and Tetlock, 1999; Tetlock, 1998), the crucial criterion is the measure of efficiency. Within decision experiments often very restrictive assumptions underlie the definition of an error (Hertwig and Gigerenzer, 1999; Mellers et al., 1998). However, from our point of view these results need more and deeper investigation, before they might be used as propositions in a corporate context.

Modifications of the strategic decision making process.   Justification pressure or needs may not only impact the decision made, but also the processes that lead to the decision (Hagafors and Brehmer, 1983). If management expects justification pressure, they most probably will take it into account. Indeed, studies have shown that justification pressure may lead to postponement of decisions (Hastie and Pennington, 2000; Tetlock and Boettger, 1994), more attention to evaluation and selection issues (Lerner and Tetlock, 1999), and intensified information gathering (Huber and Seiser, 2001; Lerner and Tetlock, 1999). Thus, independently from its impact on the decision itself, such modifications of the decision-making process will result in extra time, effort, and costs. Therefore, we can make the following proposition:

> *Proposition 1*:   An increase of justification pressure leads to additional costs on the part of the management, as they will allocate more organizational resources on pre-strategic decision-making processes.

Modifications of the interaction between management and shareholders.   Management may also modify behavior and institute measures to influence the shareholders' expectations, preferences, and evaluation criteria. We will use the term "justification tactics" to indicate activities managers may use to change the shareholders' understanding or to at least "prove" conformity to their existing expectations and evaluation criteria. Based on previous experimental research, we can distinguish four justification tactics. Each will be validated by examples at the organizational level.

First, individuals, under justification pressure, communicate their decisions more intensively and in more detail to evaluators (Huber and Seiser, 2001). We will call this kind of justification tactic "reporting" (refer to [a] in Figure 12.1). Investor relations departments can be seen as an example of how managers report their decisions to shareholders. These organizational sub-units typically answer shareholder questions, offer information, compile reports, and arrange investor conferences. Indeed, a direct link can be seen between increased justification pressure and intensified reporting and communication. For example, the number of investor relations departments (Rao and Sivakumar, 1999) and the expenditures to investor communication (IRES, 2000) has been steadily increasing.

Secondly, it has been observed that decision makers reformulate their reasons to demonstrate conformity with evaluators' measurement scales (Koonce et al., 1995; Lerner and Tetlock, 1999; Lord, 1992). For example, they may translate relevant parts of their decision-making process and the final decision into the "language" of the evaluators. We will call this justification tactic "translation" (refer to [b] in Figure 12.1). In practice, management may use more formal analytic tools to justify their strategic decisions to shareholders. For example, rather than justifying negative net present value projects as "strategic" or through personal favors, management may be pressured into using more formal accepted methods such as real options (Amram and Kulatilaka, 1999; Trigeorgis, 1996) or value-based management approaches (e.g., Stern et al., 1996).

Thirdly, decision makers may decide to use the power of references in order to convince evaluators that their decisions are aligned to expectations or norms (Huber and Seiser, 2001; Wood and Kallgren, 1988). In many cases, well-reputed and accepted experts are chosen to prove conformity. This justification tactic can be subsumed under the term "certification" (refer to [c] in Figure 12.1). Indeed, management consultants have become the means to legitimize managerially favored alternatives by providing an accepted, valid, sometimes unquestionable reference promoting the decision (Nippa and Petzold, 2002). The reference power of consultants is first of all based on their independence, which signals objectivity. Secondly, it is based on their reputation of employing superior or, at least, excellently trained human capital for solving certain management problems. Finally, well-defined and widely accepted management consulting concepts or fashions (Abrahamson, 1996), such as re-engineering, benchmarking, value based management, portfolio planning etc., provide a decision logic (Krogh and Grand, 2000) albeit temporarily (Abrahamson and Fairchild, 1999) that helps justify decisions. Put together, these three factors offer a strong qualitative rationale for managers who might face justification pressure regarding a strategic decision.

The fourth justification tactic, "education" (refer to [d] in Figure 12.1) goes beyond mere one-directional signaling and information flow, i.e. from the decision maker to the evaluator. In order to initiate a learning process with the evaluator, the decision maker invests in mutual interaction as she depends on feedback about learning success. As emphasized by some researchers, external constituencies do not necessarily possess appropriate knowledge for decision evaluation (Nonaka and Takeuchi, 1996). Due to their novel, complex, and uncertain nature, strategic decisions may often incorporate tacit knowledge (Brockmann and Anthony, 2002; Brockmann and Simmonds, 1997). In these situations, reporting, transforming, and certification may not be sufficient; the shareholder may not be able to understand the information. Thus top management may not only provide the shareholders with information, but also with interpretative knowledge through education. Educating is a time-consuming effort and requires an intensive involvement on both sides. For example, Useem (1993) found that management's widespread concern for short-term shareholder impatience was met by significant educational efforts.

While all justification tactics aim to influence the reasoning of the evaluator through intensified communication and interaction, they come at a potentially significant cost. Therefore we make the following proposition:

> *Proposition 2*:   An increase of justification pressure leads to additional costs on the part of the decision makers, as they will allocate more organizational resources on the interaction with evaluators, i.e., justification tactics such as reporting, translation, certification, or education.

Furthermore, we suggest that the decision maker will choose a specific justification tactic or a certain combination of tactics as a reaction to specific internal and external contingencies. For example, these contingencies may come from the characteristics of the claimants or the competitive environment or from the personality of the decision maker or the strategic task.

Contingent choices of justification tactics

Each justification tactic shows special characteristics and results in a different form of interaction and communication between the decision maker and the evaluator. It can be assumed each can be used more efficiently in different situations. As mentioned above, justification tactics are widely acknowledged and simultaneously used within the corporate world. This leads to the question: What justification tactic is most efficient depending on what kind of contingencies? Referring to practice we assume that managers who face justification pressure choose justification tactics rather arbitrarily or intuitively at best and apply all of them without reflecting actual needs. As a consequence they may end up with inefficient solutions to justification problems.

We propose using basic characteristics of knowledge exchange, namely dissemination and explicability of information and knowledge (e.g., Zack, 1999) as the basis for choosing justification tactics. Justification behavior in general and the choice of preferred justification tactics may vary as a consequence of the level of evaluator's appropriate interpretative knowledge of the strategic decision. If there is a generally accepted knowledge base then decisions can be explained by relying on that knowledge. If not, top management has to manage it. Furthermore, decision makers may

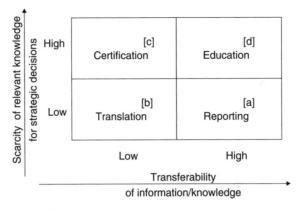

Figure 12.2   Knowledge characteristics as contingencies of justification tactics

apply appropriate justification tactics as a reflection of the perceived transferability of information and knowledge. Depending on whether decision relevant information can be transferred and the necessary knowledge can be explained – as a precondition for transferring – one will simply transfer the information or have to rely on some kind of coding. By combining these two dimensions one obtains a basic framework – see Figure 12.2 – that supports the rational choice of appropriate justification tactics with regard to the actual requirements.

To explain this framework in more detail, we will exemplarily describe the two quadrants [b] and [c]. If there are, for instance, accepted forms of expressing strategic decision problems and corresponding solutions on both sides – i.e. high levels of relevant knowledge – but top management uses different – probably even more efficient – conceptualizations and explanations within the decision-making process, then there will be a need to translate them into an appropriate form. If the translation format is well understood it may be the appropriate way to demonstrate conformity to shareholders, even if the original idea cannot be easily explained in the first place [b].

In the case of low level of relevant knowledge to evaluate strategic decisions on the part of non-expert evaluators and low transferability, certification becomes an option. Since certificates transmit expressive meaning, reason is provided by the certificate itself. Such kind of justification confirms the correctness of the decision with respect to the relevant norms without relying on any direct decision relevant knowledge or information [c].

Based on these arguments, we make the following proposition:

> *Proposition 3*:   The effectiveness of justification tactics such as reporting, translation, certification, and education depends on the dissemination and transferability of specific interpretative knowledge.

In summary, any justification process is initiated by a subjectively perceived need and necessity for justification on the part of the manager (i.e., the ambiguity of strategic decisions). We have demonstrated that the power of shareholders and their demand for justification has been increasing.

As shown in Figure 12.1, an initial reaction to justification needs, top management will analyze existing or gather additional information about the evaluation criteria most probably applied by shareholders. The main consequences arising from justification needs are threefold. Management may spend more organizational resources on pre-decision-making processes (Proposition 1). Depending on various factors such as personality of the decision maker, power balance, and characteristics of the decision itself, the decision maker may deviate from the decision taken without justification needs in order to show conformity to external expectations. Furthermore, management may intensify shareholder interaction and communication and will use scarce resources to implement appropriate justification tactics (Proposition 2). Finally, taking a normative perspective we propose to use dissemination and explicability of information and knowledge in order to select the most efficient justification tactic with regard to specific contingencies (Proposition 3).

Finally, the strategic decision will be evaluated by the shareholder. As a rule shareholders will communicate the result of their evaluation directly through positive or negative rewards (e.g., praise, complaints) but even more do so indirectly by selling their stake or buying one. Based on this evaluation managers will keep up, modify, or refrain from using their justification tactics. Without a doubt, additional elements and interdependencies exist and will be integrated into the basic model in the future. The shareholders' perception of applied justification tactics by managers will determine, for instance, their future justification demands. Similarly, the reaction to justification tactics by the shareholder will have an impact on the future justification behavior of the manager.

Discussion and Conclusions

First, we believe that our model has implications for agency theory in general and corporate governance in particular. Our model suggests that expected increases in shareholder rents ascribed to specific means of corporate governance may be illusory. Intensified dependency will cause reactive justification efforts on the part of the manager. These justification costs have to be regarded as additional agency costs on the part of the agent, which indirectly affect the principal as organizational resources are used for justification purposes. Thus resources available for investment suffer. Indeed, including these previously forgotten costs of corporate governance may lead to different decisions regarding corporate governance measures.

Secondly, it has been argued that management can improve its competence based trustworthiness by choosing appropriate language and labeling of decision explanations (Elsbach and Elofson, 2000). We argue that these decision explanations through the four justification tactics – reporting, translation, certification, and education – should be guided by the dissemination and transferability of specific information and knowledge necessary for an appropriate evaluation of the strategic decision.

Thirdly, our model also has implications for the knowledge-based theory of the firm (e.g. Fransman, 1994; Spender, 1996). Until recently this theory adheres to an internal perspective of the firm. External constituencies and their possible impact on the firm remain disregarded (Cohendet et al., 1998). The preliminary model we developed in our chapter, however, indicates how knowledge creation within firms may be influenced by external constituencies. Indeed, any external claim on the provision of decision rationales controls the type of knowledge produced.

Several limitations of the study need to be noted, which could lead to future research. First, the basic propositions we have outlined need both operationalization and empirical testing. Additionally new propositions should be derived. It has been mentioned, for instance, that justification pressure and justification induced behavior will lead under certain circumstances to modifications of strategic decisions. It has been shown that firms which are owned to a decisive degree by short-term orientated institutional investors decrease their innovative activity (Bushee, 1998; Petzold, 2002). Furthermore, management approaches which are approved by external constituencies may lead to inefficient resource allocations (Palliam and Shalhoub, 2002; Shleifer and Vishny, 1994). We believe that these findings could indeed profit from considering justification behavior.

The dissemination and transferability of specific information and knowledge has been proposed to be a determinant of the appropriateness of a specific justification tactic. This determinant should be related to a more precise cost argument within future research. It would permit us to see how traditional corporate governance mechanisms (outsiders, ownership, CEO and chairman of the board separation, pay for performance, etc.) and their efficiency may be impacted due to justification needs. Furthermore, the characterization of specific information and knowledge needs related to appropriate evaluation of strategic decisions could be used as an explanatory variable for differences in corporate governance structures found in practice. For instance, industry-related factors explain to a major degree variances found in governance variables (Coles et al., 2001). As each industry (e.g., mature or growing) relies on different kinds of knowledge, this may cause differences in monitoring and, hence, strategic decision justification.

Finally, management's choice to apply one over another may be moderated by, for example, the characteristics of the decision, the decision maker, or the perception of external constituencies. Research regarding these moderating factors may unearth the efficiency of different justification tactics in more detail. Furthermore, it may be suggested that justification can be circumvented, for instance by co-optation (Bacharach and Lawler, 1998) or by the communicator's credibility, as well (Ashforth and Gibbs, 1990). These examples show clearly a number of options for extending the proposed model. We hope that in spite of these limitations, new light has been shed on the topic of justification, corporate governance, and strategic decisions.

Acknowledgments

The authors are grateful to the SMS book series editors for valuable comments and suggestions. Special thanks are owed to James Henderson, who was extremely helpful in improving the arguments put forth in the paper. We also would like to thank Joan van Aken and the participants at the EIASM workshop on Organizational Performance for their comments.

References

Abowd, J. and Kaplan, D. 1999: Executive compensation: Six questions that need answering. *Journal of Economic Perspectives*, 13, 145–168.

Abrahamson, E. 1996: Management fashion. *Academy of Management Review*, 21, 254–285.

Abrahamson, E. and Fairchild, G. 1999: Management fashion: Lifecycles, triggers, and collective learning processes. *Journal of Management Studies*, 44, 708–740.

Adelberg, S. and Batson, C. 1978: Accountability and helping: When needs exceed resources. *Journal of Personality and Social Psychology*, 36, 343–350.

Akerlof, G. 1970: The market for "lemons": Qualitative uncertainty and the market mechanism. *Quarterly Journal of Economics*, 84, 488–500.

Alchian, A. and Demsetz, H. 1972: Production, information costs and economic organization. *American Economic Review*, 62, 777–797.

Amram, M. and Kulatilaka, N. 1999: *Real Options*. Boston, MA: Harvard Business School Press.

Ashforth, B. and Gibbs, B. 1990: The double-edge of organizational legitimation. *Organization Science*, 1, 177–194.

Ashforth, B. and Lee, R. 1990: Defensive behavior in organizations: A preliminary model. *Human Relations*, 43, 621–648.

Bacharach, S. and Lawler, E. 1998: Political alignments in organizations: Contextualization, mobilization, and coordination. In R. Kramer and M. Neale (eds.), *Power and Influence in Organizations*. Thousand Oaks, CA: Sage, 67–88.

Barkema, H. and Gomez-Mejia, L. 1998: Managerial compensation and firm performance: A general research framework. *Academy of Management Journal*, 41, 135–145.

Berle, A. and Means, G. 1932/68: *The Modern Corporation and Private Property*. New York: Harcourt, Brace and World.

Bettman, J. and Weitz, B. 1983: Attributions in the board room: Causal reasoning in corporate annual reports. *Administrative Science Quarterly*, 28, 165–183.

Brockmann, E. and Anthony, W. 2002: Tacit knowledge and strategic decision making. *Group and Organization Management*, 27, 436–455.

Brockmann, E. and Simmonds, P. 1997: Strategic decision making: The influence of CEO experience and use of tacit knowledge. *Journal of Managerial Issues*, 9, 454–467.

Brown, C. 1999: "Do the right thing": Diverging effects of accountability in a managerial context. *Marketing Science*, 18, 230–246.

Bushee, B. 1998: The influence of institutional investors on myopic R&D investment behavior. *Accounting Review*, 73, 305–333.

Business Week 1992: 25 executives to watch. *Business Week*, 3259, 74–101.

Caldwell, D. and O'Reilly, C. 1982: Responses to failure: The effects of choice and responsibility on impression management. *Academy of Management Journal*, 25, 121–136.

Cohendet, P., Llerena, P., and Marengo, L. 1998: *Theory of the Firm in an Evolutionary Perspective: A Critical Assessment*. Paper presented at the DRUID Conference "Competences, Governance and Entreprenership," June 9–11, Bornholm.

Coles, J., Mcilliams, V., and Sen, N. 2001: An examination of the relationship of governance mechanisms to performance. *Journal of Management*, 27, 23–50.

Conyon, M. and Florou, A. 2002: Top executive dismissal, ownership and corporate performance. *Accounting and Business Research*, 32, 209–225.

Coughlan, A.T. and Sen, S.K. 1989: Salesforce compensation: Theory and managerial implications. *Marketing Science*, 8, 324–342.

Curley, S., Yates, J., and Abrams, R. 1986: Psychological sources of ambiguity avoidance. *Organizational Behavior and Human Decision Processes*, 35, 102–118.

Denis, D. 2001: Twenty-five years of corporate governance research . . . and counting. *Review of Financial Economics*, 10, 191–212.

Donaldson, G. 1984: *Managing Corporate Wealth: The Operation of a Comprehensive Financial Goals System*. New York: Praeger Publishers.

Eisenhardt, K. 1989: Agency theory: An assessment and review. *Academy of Management Review*, 14, 57–74.

Elsbach, K. and Elofson, G. 2000: How the packaging of decision explanations affects perceptions of trustworthiness. *Academy of Management Journal*, 43, 80–89.

Emerson, R. 1962: Power-dependence relations. *American Sociological Review*, 72, 31–40.

Fama, E. 1980: Agency problems and the theory of the firm. *Journal of Political Economy*, 88, 288–307.

Fehr, E. and Falk, A. 2001: Psychological foundations of incentives. *European Economic Review*, 46, 687–724.

Fransman, M. 1994: Information, knowledge, vision and the theories of the firm. *Industrial and Corporate Change*, 3, 147–191.

Granlund, M., Lukka, K., and Mouritsen, J. 1998: Institutionalised justification of corporate action: Internationalisation and the EU in corporate reports. *Scandinavian Journal of Management*, 14, 433–458.

Grant, R. 1998: *Contemporary Strategy Analysis*. Oxford, UK: Blackwell Business.

Hagafors, R. and Brehmer, B. 1983: Does having to justify one's judgement change the nature of the judgement process? *Organizational Behavior and Human Performance*, 31, 223–232.

Hammond, K., Hamm, R., Grassia. J., and Pearson, T. 1987: Direct comparison of the efficacy of intuitive and analytical cognition in expert judgement. *IEEE Transactions on Systems, Man, and Cybernetics*, 17, 753–770.

Hart, O. 1995: Corporate governance: Some theory and implications. *Economic Journal*, 105, 678–689.

Hastie, R. and Pennington, N. 2000: Explanation-based decision making. In T. Connolly, H. Arkes, and K. Hammond (eds.), *Judgement and Decision Making: An Interdisciplinary Reader*, Cambridge, UK: Cambridge University Press, 212–228.

Hawley, J. and Williams, A. 2000: *The Rise of Fiduciary Capitalism: How Institutional Investors Can Make Corporate America More Democratic*. Philadelphia, PA: University of Pennsylvania Press.

Hertwig, R. and Gigerenzer, G. 1999: The "conjunction fallacy" revisted: How intelligent inferences look like reasoning errors. *Journal of Behavioral Decison Making*, 12, 275–305.

Holmström, B. 1979: Moral hazard and observability. *Bell Journal of Economics*, 10, 74–91.

Huber, O. and Seiser, G. 2001: Accounting and convincing: The effect of two types of justification on the decision process. *Journal of Behavioral Decision Making*, 14, 69–85.

IRES. 2000: *Investor Relations Monitor*. Dusseldorf: Handelsblatt.

Jensen, M. 1993: The modern industrial revolution, exit and the failure of internal control systems. *The Journal of Finance*, 48, 831–880.

Jensen, M. and Meckling, W. 1976: Theory of the firm: Managerial behavior, agency costs and ownership structure. *Journal of Financial Economics*, 3, 305–360.

Jensen, M. and Murphy, K. 1990a: Performance pay and top management incentives. *Journal of Political Economy*, 98, 225–264.

Jensen, M. and Murphy, K. 1990b: CEO incentives – It's not how much you pay, but how. *Harvard Business Review*, 68, 138–149.

Koonce, L., Anderson, U., and Marchant, G. 1995: Justification of decisions in auditing. *Journal of Accounting Research*, 33, 369–384.

Krogh, G.V. and Grand, S. 2000: Justification in knowledge creation: Dominant logic in management discourses. In G.V. Krogh, I. Nonaka, and T. Nishiguchi (eds.), *Knowledge Creation: A Source of Value*. Basingstoke: Macmillan, 13–35.

Lerner, J. and Tetlock, P. 1999: Accounting for the effects of accountability. *Psychological Bulletin*, 125, 255–275.

Lord, A. 1992: Pressure: A methodological consideration for behavioral research in auditing. *Auditing*, 11, 90–108.

Mahajan, A. and Lummer, S. 1993: Shareholder wealth effects of management changes. *Journal of Business Finance and Accounting*, 20, 393–410.

McMackin, J. and Slovic, P. 2000: When does explicit justification impair decision making. *Applied Cognitive Psychology*, 14, 527–541.

Mellers, B., Schwartz, A., and Cooke, A. 1998: Judgement and decision making. *Annual Review of Psychology*, 49, 447–477.

Murphy, K.J. 1985. Corporate performance and managerial renumeration: An empirical analysis. *Journal of Accounting and Economics*, 11, 11–42.

Nippa, M. and Petzold, K. 2002: Function and roles of management consulting firms. In A. Buono (ed.), *Developing Knowledge and Value in Management Consulting: Research in Management Consulting, Volume 2.* Greenwich, CT: Information Age, 209–230.

Nonaka, I. and Takeuchi, H. 1996: A theory of organizational knowledge creation. *International Journal of Technology Management*, 11, 821–832.

Palliam, R. and Shalhoub, Z. 2002: Rationalizing corporate downsizing with longterm profitability – an empirical focus. *Management Decision*, 40, 436–447.

Payne, J., Bettman, J., and Johnson, E. 1993: *The Adaptive Decision Maker*. Cambridge, MA: Cambridge University Press.

Petzold, K. 2002: Institutionelle Investoren: Element eines innovationsförderlichen Corporate Governance Systems. In M. Nippa, K. Petzold, and W. Kürsten (eds.), *Corporate Governance: Herausforderungen und Lösungsansätze.* Heidelberg: Physica (Springer) Verlag, 149–172.

Pfeffer, J. 1981: Management as symbolic action. *Research in Organizational Behavior*, 3, 1–52.

Porter, M. 1992: Capital choices: Changing the way America invests in industry. *Journal of Applied Corporate Finance*, 5, 4–16.

Rao, H. and Sivakumar, K. 1999: Institutional sources of boundary spanning structures: The establishment of investor relations departments in the Fortune 500 Industrials. *Organization Science*, 10, 27–42.

Ryan, L. and Schneider, M. 2003: The antecedents of institutional investor activism. *Academy of Management Review*, 27, 554–573.

Schwenk, C. 1995: Strategic decision making. *Journal of Management*, 21, 471–493.

Schwenk, C. and Thomas, H. 1988: Effects of strategic decisions aids on problem solving: A laboratory experiment. In J. Grant (ed.), *Strategic Management Frontiers*. Greenwich: JAI Press, 400–413.

Shleifer, A. and Vishny, R. 1994: Takeovers in the 1960s and the 1980s: Evidence and implications. In R. Rumelt, D. Schendel, and D. Teece (eds.), *Fundamental Issues in Strategy – A Research Agenda.* Boston, MA: Harvard Business School, 403–418.

Shleifer, A. and Vishny, R. 1997: A survey of corporate governance. *Journal of Finance*, 52, 737–783.

Simmons, A. 1999: Justification and legitimacy. *Ethics*, 109, 739–771.

Simon, H. 1987: Making management decisions: The role of intuition and emotion. *Academy of Management Exectutive*, 2, 57–64.

Simonson, I. 1989: Choice based on reason: The case of attraction and compromise effects. *Journal of Consumer Research*, 16, 158–174.

Smircich, L. and Morgan, G. 1982: Leadership: The management of meaning. *The Journal of Applied Behavioral Sciences*, 18, 257–273.

Spender, J. 1996: Making knowledge the basis of a dynamic theory of the firm. *Strategic Management Journal*, 17, 45–62.

Staw, B., McKenchie, P., and Puffer, S. 1983: The justification of organizational performance. *Administrative Science Quarterly*, 28, 582–600.

Stern, J., Stewart, G., and Chew, D. 1996: EVA: An integrated financial management system. *European Financial Management*, 2, 223–245.

Taylor, K. 1995: Testing credit and blame attributions as explanation for choices under ambiguity. *Organizational Behavior and Human Decision Processes*, 64, 128–137.

Tetlock, P. 1985: Accountability: The neglected social context of judgement and choice. *Research in Organizational Behavior*, 7, 297–332.

Tetlock, P. 1998: Losing our religion: On the precariousness of precise normative standards in complex accountability systems. In R. Kramer and M. Neale (eds.), *Power and Influence in Organizations*, Thousand Oaks, CA: Sage, 121–144.

Tetlock, P. 1999: Accountability theory: Mixing properties of human agents with properties of social systems. In L. Thompson, J. Levine, and D. Messick (eds.), *Shared Cognition in Organizations: The Management of Knowledge*. London: Lawrence Erlbaum Associates, 117–161.

Tetlock, P. and Boettger, R. 1994: Accountability amplifies the status quo effect when change creates victims. *Journal of Behavioral Decision Making*, 7, 1–23.

Tirole, J. 2001: Corporate governance. *Econometrica*, 69, 1–35.

Tosi, H., Werner, S., Katz, J., and Gomez-Mejia, L. 2000: How much does performance matter? A meta-analysis of CEO pay studies. *Journal of Management*, 26, 301–339.

Trigeorgis, L. 1996: *Real Options: Managerial Flexibility and Strategy in Resource Allocation*. Cambridge, MA: MIT Press.

Tsang, E. 2002: Self-serving attributions in corporate annual reports: A replicated study. *Journal of Management Studies*, 39, 51–65.

Tsoukas, H. 1993: Analogical reasoning and knowledge generation in organization theory. *Organization Studies*, 14, 323–346.

Turnbull, S. 1997: Corporate governance: Its scope, concerns and theories. *Corporate Governance: An International Review*, 5, 180–205.

Turnbull, S. 2000: *Corporate Governance: Theories, Challenges and Paradigms*. SSRN Electronic Paper Collection, http://papers.ssrn.com/paper.taf?abstract_id = 221350. Maquarie University Graduate School of Management: Sidney.

Useem, M. 1993: *Executive Defense: Shareholder Power and Corporate Reorganization*. Cambridge, MA: Harvard University Press.

Weick, K. 1979: *The Social Psychology of Organizing* (2nd edn). Reading, MA: Addison-Wesley.

Wiersema, M. 2002: Holes at the top: Why CEO firings backfire. *Harvard Business Review*, 80, 70–77.

Williamson, O. 1985: *The Economic Institutions of Capitalism*. New York: Free Press.

Wood, W. and Kallgren, C. 1988: Communicator attributes and persuasion: Recipients access to attitude-relevant information in memory. *Personality and Social Psychology Bulletin*, 14, 172–182.

Yukl, G. 1981: *Leadership in Organizations*. Englewood Cliffs, NJ: Prentice Hall.

Zack, M. 1999: Managing codified knowledge. *Sloan Management Review*, 40, 45–58.

CHAPTER THIRTEEN

A New Approach to Improving Board Vigilance: Shift the Focus to Board Process

Ann C. Mooney and Sydney Finkelstein

Introduction

Research on boards of directors has been dominated by a concern for board structure and independence and their effects on the monitoring of CEO actions and effectiveness (Finkelstein and Hambrick, 1996). Following influential inductive work by Mace (1971), and spurred on by the rise of agency theory (Jensen and Meckling, 1976), academic research on boards over the last 25 years has been guided by the implicit assumption that boards are generally ineffective monitors of CEOs because they are not structured correctly. Support for this assumption comes from the "usual suspects" – boards with too many insiders (Main et al., 1994), directors with insufficient shareholdings (Johnson et al., 1993), boards that are too big (Zahra and Stanton, 1988), and boards where the CEO also holds the Chair position (CEO duality) (Daily and Dalton, 1992).

In response to this attention paid by researchers and shareholder activists, a dramatic shift has been taking place in corporate governance in the United States. According to the Korn/Ferry International Annual Board of Directors Study (2001), the average Fortune 1000 board now has nine outsiders and two insiders, and is compensated at least in part with stock 84 percent of the time. The primary role in appointment of new board members is evenly split between CEOs and independent board committees. Average board size has dropped from 16 to 11 since the 1980s (Spencer Stuart Board Index, 2000). However, even with these reforms, numerous boards still remain less than ideal monitors of CEOs. For example, the Enron board consisted of only 14 directors; 12 were outsiders; all 14 owned stock, and the CEO did not hold the Chair position; yet, it was still ineffective. In other words, the "usual suspects" may be necessary but not sufficient to ensure board effectiveness.

Recently some scholars have begun to examine board process rather than board structure as a determinant of its effectiveness (Finkelstein and Hambrick, 1996; Forbes and Milliken, 1999). Because a board of directors is comprised of individuals that form a group, how they interact may indeed influence their effectiveness in advising, counseling and monitoring CEOs. Yet, the understanding of such group processes as conflict, integration, and comprehensiveness as critical determinants of board effectiveness is only in its infancy. Thus, our aim in this chapter is to shift research attention to board process in the context of corporate governance today. Boards have embraced many, though by no means all, of the "usual suspects" of effective governance; yet, board effectiveness has not been fully "solved." Clearly a better understanding of the board process is warranted.

To help guide the development of our ideas on boards as groups, we combined insights from the group and top management team literatures with clinical data on how directors view their own interactions among themselves and the CEO. We conducted a series of 25 structured interviews with board members to better understand the nature of board processes as seen by the board members themselves. This grounded theory building based on combining multiple literatures and clinical data represents a new way to study boards of directors, and has the potential to yield important findings on the nature of board processes.

We begin our discussions by first reviewing previous research on the "usual suspects": the number of outside board directors, director shareholdings, board size, and CEO duality. We build on this research by stressing the importance of considering board process in our quest for better understanding the determinants of board effectiveness. Specifically, we identify five critical processes and discuss implications of each on board effectiveness.

The "Usual Suspects"

Boards of directors play multiple, critical roles in organizations. Boards are responsible for (1) providing advice, and counsel to CEOs, (2) monitoring and if necessary disciplining CEOs. Although the former role has not been researched as much as the latter, both share a key theme for effective corporate governance: the structure and independence of the board of directors (Finkelstein and Hambrick, 1996). Previous research on board structure and effectiveness has coalesced around identifying four main problems – few outside directors on the board (Main et al., 1994), insufficient share ownership by directors (Johnson et al., 1993), boards that are too big (Zahra and Stanton, 1988), and CEOs that also serve as the Chairman of the board (Daily and Dalton, 1992). While a focus on board structure and independence in research and practice has had some effect on improving our understanding of boards and encouraging board reform, it is not the whole story of what makes for a good board. Rather than providing the answer to corporate governance breakdowns, these "usual suspects" may well be distracting attention away from a messier, but more important, consideration – how board members interact as a group.

The recent spate of stories in the business press on boards that were "missing in action," "asleep at the wheel," or "rubber stamps" shows that attention to board structure and independence has failed to stem the tide of corporate governance failures. Many boards which adhere to the "usual suspects" prescriptions can still turn out to be fundamentally flawed in other ways. For example, the independent and well-structured Mattel board of directors still watched former CEO Jill Barad dramatically miss earnings targets for four consecutive quarters before finally forcing her resignation. Directors at Enron still consistently signed off on a catalog of questionable calls.

It is time to dig much deeper. The usual suspects, as measured by classic indicators, may in some cases make boards more effective. However, given these two high profile examples, they still do not ensure boards will be effective in serving the best interests of shareholders. As a result, each of the usual suspects requires further examination in where it may break down in achieving its intended objective.

Outside board members

No other attribute of board composition has likely garnered the same attention as the relative number of outside board members (Dalton et al., 1998). Outsiders are supposedly more vigilant than insiders; they are purportedly less dependent on the CEO, and are the formal representatives of shareholders (Walsh and Seward, 1990). They may seek to protect their reputations as directors, further enhancing their attention to management (Fama and Jensen, 1983). Indeed, there is evidence that an outsider-dominated board is more likely to dismiss the CEO following poor performance than a board with fewer outsiders (Boeker, 1992). In line with this dominant viewpoint, boards have been adding outsiders for years, to the point that the average board today only has two insiders, the CEO and another top executive (Korn/Ferry International, 2001).

Although this reform is promising, board composition is much more than a mere count of outsiders versus insiders. Simply being an "outsider" does not guarantee that a director can provide valuable counsel to a CEO – other, more substantive, attributes are much more important. For example, for John Cook,[1] CEO of Profit Recovery Group, outside board members' knowledge and skills should complement those of the CEO and top management, providing a richer consideration and resolution of strategic issues. Russell Lewis, President and CEO of the New York Times Company, said that he and his board try to get directors with "a diversity of professional backgrounds that pertain to our business and we also try to get a diversity of folks from a gender and ethnic point of view because we think that is important and mirrors what we are doing at the business level."

Furthermore, CEOs we interviewed said they preferred active executives, especially other CEOs, on their board. For example, D. R. Grimes, CEO and Chairman of NetBank told us:

> The NetBank board is a tough place to train a new board member because we are growing so fast and things move so fast. So, I look for experience in board members and that experience could be as a board member or a manager with significant responsibility. I really value people that have run a company before.

Finally, freshness of perspective is also important. Over time, CEOs tend to consolidate their power as they fill board seats with their own allies (Hambrick and

Fukutomi, 1991). Furthermore, the ability to monitor deteriorates as longer-serving board members become accustomed to working with the same CEO. Clearly, there is no reason to believe that outsiders are immune to these patterns. Indeed, if a company has changed dramatically over time, long-tenured directors may not have the required experience. Directors typically have terms of two or three years, but few boards have term limits (a recent survey pegged the number of companies with terms limits for board members at 10 percent) (Korn/Ferry International, 2001); directors are often re-elected at the end of their terms and serve for years. D. R. Grimes, the NetBank CEO, noted in one of our interviews that board turnover could be particularly important for high-growth firms:

> If you are a director of a company and the biggest company you ever worked for is X and then all of a sudden the company you were a director for is 10X – that may be a challenge. On the other hand, while it's growing to X, you may be able to make a tremendous contribution and even beyond that.

All of these attributes, complementary talents and experiences, diversity, active executives, and freshness of perspective, which define whether boards can provide the advice and counsel that is needed, count for much more than a simple assessment of whether a board has enough "outsiders."

Yet, even with these attributes, the ability of outsiders to effectively monitor a CEO may still be constrained. First, outsiders may not be sitting on the key board committees, such as auditing and nominations. Without direct participation on such influential committees, outsiders may find it difficult to influence board decisions. This observation is particularly true for the nominating committee, which has primary responsibility for selecting new board members. Yet, even with this level of participation, outsider influence may still be limited because CEOs tend to play a central role in director selection (Anderson and Anthony, 1986). They are likely to select friends or allies as board members (Lorsch, 1989) who are somewhat less vigilant in questioning top management decisions.

Second, often outsiders come to their positions with considerable baggage, which may not aid board independence and monitoring. For example, outsiders may still have considerable business with the company or are linked through a complex spider web of director interlocks (Pennings, 1980). For example, when James Robinson was CEO of American Express in the early 1990s, no fewer than nine outsiders sat on the same corporate or non-profit boards as did Robinson, and several board members were business partners of the company. Under these circumstances, the ability and willingness of outsiders to ask tough questions may be seriously curtailed. Indeed, in the case of American Express, one of the very few outsiders without any connection to Robinson led the well-documented insurrection that cost Robinson his job.

Finally, outsiders may not have the time or information to effectively monitor CEOs (Baysinger and Hoskisson, 1990). Board meetings are held, on average, six times a year. Korn/Ferry International study (2001) found that the average board member typically dedicated 156 hours per year to his or her duties. Yet, outsiders are often busy and distracted by their own, often CEO, responsibilities. Indeed, these nontrivial time demands of being a director will certainly take their toll. Hence, the expectation that outsiders will necessarily be vigilant monitors of CEOs seems rather illusory.

In sum, while outsiders bring some advantages to corporate boards, their ability to effectively advise and monitor CEOs has almost surely been overstated by the "usual suspects" crowd. Clearly, boards need more than just outsiders to be effective.

Director shareholdings

Director stock ownership is another common prescription for effective corporate governance (Johnson et al., 1993). Directors who own stock in the company may indeed pay closer attention to what goes on in that company. After all, with "skin in the game," directors represent not just the amorphous shareholders' interests, but their own as well. This argument has been made in the agency and management literatures for some time (e.g., Alchian and Demsetz, 1972; Finkelstein and D'Aveni, 1994; Shleifer and Vishny, 1986). Corporate governance experts are in agreement. For example, Nell Minnow, director of The Corporate Library, told us of a conversation she had with a director who remarked that he had never seen calculators whipped out more quickly during board meetings than when board members owned at least $1 million of the company's stock. We heard the same refrain in some of our interviews. Paul Fulchino, CEO of Avial, stated, "Any board member should receive equity in the company because the company has to visibly show him that he is a meaningful part of the company and he has to show the company that he has a meaningful stake in the company."

The principle of directors owning stock in the companies on whose boards they sit seems to be a good idea. In practice, however, problems arise. First, how much stock should a director own? Various rules of thumb have been suggested (e.g., Hambrick and Jackson, 2000), but stipulating a stock ownership threshold depends on the wealth of the particular board member. Charles Elson, director of Sunbeam, said "the key is that it's got to hurt you in the sense that if you lose the investment it's got to hurt you financially. I always jokingly say if you lose the investment it should make you want to throw up." Of the directors we interviewed, Elson was the only one who was required to own a specific value of stock ($100,000); half were required to own an indeterminate number of shares, and those that weren't required said they did so anyway. Yet, wealthy individuals, typically those who sit on boards, most likely do not own enough stock in any one company to dramatically change their level of engagement. For example, all board members of Worldcom owned stock in the company, yet there is convincing evidence that the board failed in their responsibility to critically question the actions of the CEO and senior management.

Secondly, how board members acquire stock in the companies they serve is also a relevant consideration. Many board members we interviewed received stock or stock options as part of their board compensation, whereas others were required to purchase stock before taking their seat on a board. One board member noted such a requirement may, in fact, limit the board's ability to select the directors they want. Potential board members such as public officials, academics, and non-profit executives may offer valuable insights but may not have the personal wealth needed to meet initial investment requirements expected of them.

Thirdly, there is growing evidence that stock ownership may not be as beneficial as originally suspected (Daily et al., 1999; Grossman and Hoskisson, 1998). Josh Weston,

Honorary Chairman and former Chairman and CEO of ADP, told us that stock ownership does not affect behavior but "it's good to have because it looks good on the proxy statement." Grossman and Hoskisson (1998) argue that stock ownership may actually threaten long-term competitiveness. With significant shareholdings, board members may use their own influence to pursue their individual interests, which may be in conflict with the interests of other shareholders with less significant shareholdings. For example, in 1995, Chairman Kun Hee Lee of Samsung, whose entire net worth was tied up in the company, decided that Samsung should enter the auto business, despite the existence of stiff competition in Asia, Europe, and North America, the weak state of the South Korean auto industry, and the huge capital investments required to make the idea work. Samsung invested approximately $5 billion in the venture, much of it lost as their sojourn in autos was spectacularly short-lived. Why did Chairman Lee insist on entering the auto business? Numerous reports have highlighted his love of cars as a driving force (Healy and Nakarmi, 1999; Lee, 1998). Stock ownership in this instance, and countless others – Rite Aid, Coors, Schwinn Bicycle Company, Levi's, and Barney's – actually prompted directors (who in each of these instances was dominated by family members who also had operating responsibilities) to undertake highly questionable actions that were extraordinarily costly.

In sum, the importance and effectiveness of requiring directors to own significant stock is not as clear-cut as it may appear. Even when board members do own considerable equity, corporate governance breakdowns occur, suggesting once again that our attention to the "usual suspects" provides only limited guidance on making boards more effective.

Board size

For many years, a typical corporate board consisted of 16 to 20 directors. These groups not only were too large to effectively govern (Zahra and Stanton, 1988), but they also included a considerable number of insiders. However, over the past 25 years, the average number has dropped significantly to 11 directors (Spencer Stuart Report, 2000). While the old charge of bloated boards has been removed, the effectiveness of corporate governance still continues to be a problem. Hence, it is difficult to continue to rely on this mechanism, the most straightforward of the "usual suspects," as an explanation for board malfunctions.

It may be possible that boards have become too small. The desire to construct a board with a mix of backgrounds, experiences, and strategically relevant experience does become more difficult in smaller boards. Furthermore, the opportunity for one or two directors, including the CEO, to dominate proceedings increases. Indeed, very small boards may present fewer challenges to CEOs, not just because of potential limitations in bench strength, but because it is easier for this high-prestige person to dominate a smaller group. Finally, board members may have a harder time observing potential CEO successors when the only insiders are the CEO and the corporate legal counsel. The best talent may well desire such an opportunity to interact with board members on a regular basis.

Optimal board size may indeed vary with the nature of the strategic challenges facing the company, but as a general rule somewhat smaller boards – even with their potential drawbacks – are probably more effective than very large boards. Nevertheless, no empirical evidence has shown that a secular reduction in board size has had any effect on board effectiveness. Once again, we need to dig deeper to better understand what it takes to improve board effectiveness.

CEO duality

The last of our "usual suspects," CEO duality, or whether the CEO also holds the Chairman of the board position, is perhaps the most controversial. The combination of positions consolidates power in one person, the CEO, who would not only control how the board is organized and what is on its agenda but would also have primary responsibility for fulfilling the board's mandate (Daily and Dalton, 1992; Lorsch, 1989). For example, CEOs who are also Chairs can control the quantity, quality, and timing of information relayed to the board, and hence, have an opportunity to tailor board interactions in the manner they wish. As Josh Weston of ADP, put it, "I have seen CEOs [who are Chairmen] in certain companies that like to manage the news; don't want anything rocking their boat; will try to unilaterally determine the agenda and everything that comes up." CEOs inclined to play this game can significantly reduce board independence.

As with the other "usual suspects," the separation of CEO and Chair positions seems like a good idea. Yet, upon closer examination, three alternative perspectives on CEO duality can be offered: (1) CEO duality actually doesn't make much of a difference for effective corporate governance, (2) even when CEO duality exists, there are ready mechanisms boards can employ to minimize potential downside, and (3) separation of CEO and Chair positions may actually be dysfunctional in many instances.

First, studies peg the prevalence of CEO duality in large American companies at 80 percent (Daily and Dalton, 1997). Furthermore, companies such as Morrison Knudsen and Enron had independent board Chairs, yet were still ineffective. It may well be that avoiding CEO duality is a simple solution to a more complex problem, a position for which we have considerable sympathy.

Secondly, alternatives do exist that might mitigate some of the risks that come from combining these two positions. Several of the board members we interviewed appointed a "lead director" who takes on more of a leadership role, even when the CEO is also the Chair. Lead directors can be formally or informally designated and are usually more senior board members. John Cook, Chairman and CEO of Profit Recovery Group, explained that lead directors emerge naturally – "anytime you have a group, you have certain personalities that are more or less leaders, and thus, have more influence over other members."

Josh Weston suggested that executive sessions without the CEO present are also helpful because directors get an opportunity to voice their concerns about the CEO's performance, or discuss issues without his influence. In fact, Weston insists that each board he joins has an executive session on every agenda. Institutionalizing executive sessions, Weston explains, "is desirable so if there's something to be discussed, you don't have to furtively run through the halls or set up secret conference calls."

Finally, there may be circumstances when CEO duality is more beneficial than separating the CEO and Chair positions. Alan Greenspan, Federal Reserve Board

Chairman, argues that splitting the CEO and Chairman positions could result in "competing power centers" gridlocking board decision making. Instead, CEO duality might contribute "to a unity of command at the top that helps ensure the existence or illusion of strong leadership" (Finkelstein and D'Aveni, 1994: 1099–100). Furthermore, boards may have a hard time attracting top quality CEOs when a sitting independent Chair is part of the package. For example, both Louis Gerstner at IBM and Larry Bossidy at Allied Signal insisted on the joint positions before accepting their offers (Dalton et al., 1998). Former CEOs who sit as Chairs may be particularly worrisome, especially for new outsider CEOs; they may block new initiatives that they see as implicit indictments of their own past actions. In summary, avoiding CEO duality is not a panacea for board independence and effectiveness, despite considerable academic research (Dalton et al., 1998), and concerted efforts among corporate governance experts (Biggs, 1995).

In summary, when one looks more closely at these "usual suspects" – board outsiders, director equity, board size, and CEO duality – it becomes apparent that they may not be sufficient, nor in some cases necessary to make corporate governance a success. We need to go beyond these "usual suspects" by better understanding board process or the actual interactions of the board directors. While board process will surely not be a panacea in its own right, to learn how boards really work and how to make them work better, is clearly the next step.

A Shift in Focus to Board Process

Scholars and corporate governance experts advocate that a board of directors provides active and careful oversight of management, engages the CEO in challenging debates to push his or her thinking on key strategic initiatives, adds value to strategic debates by relying on strategically relevant experience, designs incentive plans that offer both upside opportunity and downside risk, removes the CEO in a timely fashion when clearly warranted, and conducts a careful search when a new CEO is needed. Completing these tasks successfully effectively depends on the quality of the individuals who become directors and their ability to work as a group. In essence, board effectiveness is a much more complex outcome resulting from more than just objective indicators such as the proportion of outside directors.

We developed a model to capture the key determinants of effective board process based on two sources. First, the group and top management team literatures informed us on related topics since there was so little research conducted on board process. Secondly, our interviews of board members clarified the key attributes of board process and gave us a much deeper understanding of board dynamics. Wherever possible, we tried to understand not only what the key process characteristics of boards were, but also how directors and CEOs were managing those attributes to improve the practice of corporate governance in their firms. The common themes that emerged from this work, cognitive conflict, affective conflict, behavioral integration, decision involvement and decision comprehensiveness are depicted in Figure 13.1, and discussed in the following sections.

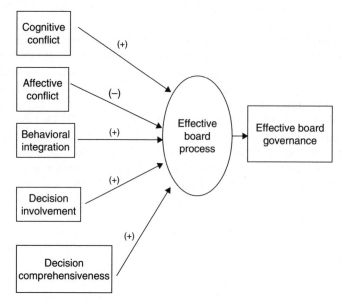

Figure 13.1   Board process: determinants and implications

Cognitive conflict: boards that can say no

Cognitive conflict occurs when participants in a group hold and debate diverse views about the task at hand (Amason, 1996; Jehn, 1994). Such exchanges help group members better understand issues surrounding the decision context and synthesize multiple perspectives into a decision that is often superior to any individual perspective (Schweiger et al., 1989). In other words, cognitive conflict can improve group decision-making and is an important determinant of group effectiveness.

Each of the 25 board members we interviewed commented on the importance of cognitive, or as many directors put it, "constructive" conflict. For example, Dave Wathen, an experienced director we interviewed, recounted how avoiding cognitive conflict led to continued management inaction. The top management in one of his outside boards did not want to recognize changes going on in the telecom industry and as a result, "they waited too long and we, the board, did not force them to act sooner. The lesson learned – and we learn this all the time – is be faster and more aggressive in dealing with management missteps. We didn't act quicker because we don't like conflict."

Robert Galvin, Sr, former CEO and Chairman of Motorola, provided the following example of cognitive conflict on the Motorola board:

> I proposed two acquisitions that I felt were very significant. The Board voted me down. We walked out of that Board meeting and you would never have known there had been a negative meeting ... that's what they are there for. They voted their point of view. It was different than mine. Too bad they weren't as smart as I was (laughed) ... we got along just fine. In our company if somebody wants to tell Chris [Galvin, Robert's son

and present CEO] that he's disappointed or doesn't think something in the company is not going right, they speak right up.

Paul Fulchino, CEO of Avial, suggested that the degree to which a board engages in cognitive conflict varies and that it often depends on the CEO. At one extreme, according to Fulchino, CEOs want a "bunch of rap dogs – guys that basically just say 'yes sir, yes sir'" and at the other extreme, CEOs can't make a decision on their own, so "every little thing that comes up he [the CEO] has to check it out with the board."

CEO comfort level and personal preferences for or against conflict were often brought up in our interviews. For example, one interviewee described how his father, a CEO, "wasn't really looking for input as much as he was looking for approval." By consulting with the board, he just wanted "to make sure he wasn't just so far off the wall that he had missed something significant."

Despite this CEO preference for or against cognitive conflict, we were still struck by the number of interviewees who told us how valuable cognitive conflict was for them. D.R. Grimes described an experience when he and NetBank management wanted to acquire another bank twice their size, but didn't because the acquiree's and their board were against it. While at the time Grimes was disappointed, he appreciated and respected the board's opinion.

The CEO of a consumer products company we interviewed described his board as having a great deal of cognitive conflict:

> Our board meetings are very lively with everyone voicing his or her opinion on the main issues that we bring to the board and there are typically two or three points of view; it works out well most of the time. Sometimes it's a little confusing because I leave the meeting thinking, "Well, some of the board members said yes and some of the board members said no . . ." (laughed).

The challenge then for a board of directors is to create the climate where cognitive conflict happens. Especially in the presence of a CEO who might see such board energy as a threat, individual directors must be, in the words of one director we interviewed, "forceful and outspoken, and not at all hesitant to voice their point of view on any subject."

First, cognitive conflict will more likely occur with more diverse opinions. Board members as talented and successful individuals are likely to have strong but not necessarily different options on the best course of action for a firm (Forbes and Milliken, 1999). Opinion diversity has probably increased in recent years as board membership has shifted to more outsiders including more women, minorities and those with strategically relevant work experience. Yet it is the varied mix of strategically relevant experience, which will lead to more cognitive conflict. Board members with "different positions see different environments" (Mitroff, 1982) based on their own set of "local perspectives" (Astley et al., 1982: 361) derived from a history of diverse experiences. This diversity would naturally induce cognitive conflict in board of directors' meetings.

Secondly, solutions such as appointing a lead outside director to facilitate board meetings in place of the CEO or setting aside time for outside directors to meet without the CEO present are also helpful in providing a more open climate. Yet, if their opinions or background are not much different cognitive conflict may not arise.

Finally, the onus is certainly on each director to take this high profile position of important responsibility more seriously than before. As one interviewee put it, "You are representing the shareholders and don't forget that. You can get pretty tight with management, but if you do, you have to realize that you may disagree with him at times."

Affective conflict: building chemistry on the board

While open and frank discussions have clear value, such task-oriented, cognitive debates may be taken more personally (Amason, 1996). Board members who are not used to being challenged might take umbrage or otherwise feel threatened when other directors challenge their ideas (Tjosvold, 1986). Thus, cognitive conflict can quickly spiral downwards.

Affective conflict occurs when group members differ on matters that are more personal, emotional, or relationship-oriented (Jehn, 1994). Affective conflict draws group members' attention away from issues relevant to the decision, making effective decision making more difficult. Hence, affective conflict tends to degrade group decision making, and interferes with group members' ability to perform their key roles.

Understanding the role of affective conflict in boards is particularly important as the few studies exploring board process tend to emphasize the positive role of cognitive conflict but do not consider the potentially debilitating consequences of affective conflict (e.g., Forbes and Milliken, 1999). It is not surprising that researchers have not studied affective conflict in boards; directors are often reluctant to share details about personal friction and tension in the boardroom. Surprisingly, however, quite a few of the directors we interviewed were rather candid.

Paul Foster, the former CEO of Tandy Industries, explained that the "dynamics of the board changed dramatically after the proxy fight when two dissident board members were added to the board membership. Prior to that, the personality of the board was one where there was a lot of open and free dialogue. When they came on board, it was clear they were working not with, but against, us."

Alan Maltz, CEO and founder of TSL, described an experience where other board members resented him when he joined the board of Brite Voice after Brite Voice acquired TSL. He explained that the "general consensus on the board was that the TSL acquisition wasn't smart and that they overpaid me for the company."

A computer company CEO we interviewed recalled an incident where there was personal tension among board members because one board member tended to emphasize issues of employee morale, which most others viewed as irrelevant. Another CEO remembered when his board would not permit him to bring in a new board member. He was considered too young and inexperienced. But ego was also involved. He was to take the place of a prestigious outside board member. The board and the outgoing board member wanted to replace the director with someone of equal stature, or as the CEO put it, "Jesus Christ himself."

Each of these examples illustrates the challenge boards face in embracing cognitive conflict without falling prey to the more personalized affective conflict that can accompany open discourse on boards. There are several steps that can be taken, however, to minimize the risk of affective conflict taking hold.

Since affective conflict often is a side effect of cognitive conflict, it is likely to occur in boards that push to be more demographically diverse. While there clearly are benefits of demographic diversity in groups (Bantel and Jackson, 1989), evidence suggests that less work-related and more visible diversity can promote affective conflict (Pelled et al., 1999). Thus a varied mix of directors but with strategically relevant work experience appears to be a step to achieve cognitive conflict while avoiding its negative side effect.

Furthermore, while strategically relevant experience should be the key criterion in new director selection, the oft-used phrase "chemistry" is also relevant. Many of our interviewees brought up this point. When asked to describe such a person, they replied with "somebody that was very optimistic and positive but not afraid to ask serious questions", and "somebody who is a good listener and has the patience to hear somebody else out." In other words, a good director is unafraid of cognitive conflict, but interpersonally astute enough to avoid affective conflict.

Yet, affective conflict may still appear when board members really don't know each other. Actively involving incumbent board members in selecting new directors has the salutary effect of enhancing their support for those individuals, creating an incentive for sitting board members to include them in the larger group. Boards can try to build in some social time to create better connections among directors outside the formal boardroom setting. Furthermore, it should be possible to manage board meetings (or offer off-line opportunities) to ensure that no directors are shut out of the debate. For example, board meetings filled with presentation after presentation end up being rushed such that time constraints start to dominate, where each minute of "airtime" becomes a scarce resource that is worth "fighting" over. These types of meetings would be particularly unhelpful in preventing affective conflict.

Behavioral integration: stimulating "teamness" on the board

Top management teams differ to the extent they work together in a cohesive and constructive manner. Such teamness, which Hambrick refers to as behavioral integration, includes three major elements – "(1) quantity and quality (richness, timeliness, accuracy) of information exchange, (2) collaborative behavior, and (3) joint decision-making" (1994: 189) – and has been found to improve decision making (Hambrick, 1998; Mooney, 2003) and performance (Li and Hambrick, 2003)

Behavioral integration characterizes board process. Since board members, like top management teams, are confronted with complex and ambiguous strategic decisions, they too are required to work together as a team by sharing information, resources, and decisions. In fact, promoting teamness may be even more valuable at the board level since directors meet so infrequently and have fewer opportunities to develop team norms.

Our interviews support the importance of behavioral integration or teamness in achieving board effectiveness. For example, one director noted how all his fellow board members felt very comfortable speaking up. "I feel very comfortable talking as much about something as I want and I think all of us do ... I don't feel any pressure that

I better not say this, or that if I say that it will be so controversial, I'll be thrown out of the room. I don't feel that at all, and I don't think any of the directors feel that way."

Yet, we found that the relative distribution of influence among board members also had a big impact on behavioral integration. As Paul Fulchino put it, "if you threw five dogs in a room they would be very clear about who the senior dog was and who the junior dogs were." This quote points out a wider insight. To our knowledge there are no academic studies on the distribution of power among individual board members[2] and its effect on such important outcomes as CEO hiring and firing, participation on board committees, and even corporate strategy. To avoid this potential problem of overly powerful board members, several suggestions by the interviewees were made.

Dave Wathen, who has sat on several corporate boards suggested that: "every one of us [board members] has a responsibility to help fix that problem of deferring to high-status people on the board and purposely turn to Bob and say, 'you haven't talked much. What do you think about this?' You've just got to do it once in a while."

A consumer products CEO we interviewed also tried to solicit feedback from quieter board members. In some circumstances, he might have even called or had lunch with such board members so that he could talk to them individually.

In addition to encouraging the contributions of everyone on the board, directors also remarked on the importance of assessing how they are working together as a team. For example, Bill Springer, former board member of Walgreen Co., provided the following advice:

> The board should act as a collegial body of experience. When factions arise within the board it's up to the board members to recognize the problem and try to break the factions so they can get back to acting as one. One thing a board can do and I think should do at least once a year and perhaps more often than that is meet in executive session as an independent group without the presence of the inside directors. They should examine their actions to assess how they are doing as a group, whether they are together or split.

Teamwork can be further enhanced when standard board practice involves asking each director to comment on major issues (thus reducing the opportunity for one or two directors to dominate). Furthermore, if the work of board committees is regularly disseminated to all directors the quality of information exchange is enhanced. Finally, when the entire board embraces teambuilding as a valued activity, such as periodic off-site facilitations, board effectiveness may be enhanced.

Behavioral integration, as with affective conflict, will be tested when new directors join a board. Indeed, the prospect of joining an already established group of high-powered board members is still daunting for new accomplishment-laden directors. As one interviewee told us, he will "stay quiet for a few board meetings. Some regrettably stay quiet for a long, long time." Thus, the suggestions offered to help avoid affective conflict – careful selection of new directors and taking steps to assimilate them into the board – also apply here to stimulating behavioral integration among board members.

Decision involvement: when does the board step in?

All boards vote on major strategic decisions. However, what one board deems as a "major" strategic decision may be very different than another board. Furthermore, some boards may get involved in more issues and decisions than just major strategic decisions. In short, "decision involvement" will vary often in ways that will not only affect how boards work as a group but also how boards perform.

Decision involvement is particularly important today as the expectations of boards are changing. The CEO of a financial services company told us that "today's director has to go further than just monitoring the CEO – they have to become deeply involved in understanding what the company is doing. There is just too much liability for directors that don't pay any attention to what's actually going on in the company." This extra responsibility presents a dilemma, as described by D.R. Grimes, Chairman and CEO of NetBank:

> I would say that there is a little bit of a philosophical change here – the outside world is beginning to hold directors more accountable and directors do have day jobs. That's becoming a tougher and tougher problem. Where do you cross that line between oversight and micro-management of the company? Where's the balance between management and the board?

Indeed, many of the board members we interviewed stressed that boards should not be involved in every decision. As Josh Weston of ADP said, "I don't think it should be for every board member to be an internal busybody." The CEO of a consumer products company put it this way: "Some boards take some liberties and encroach upon management's role [by saying things like] 'here's whom you should hire, here's whom you should use, here's a decision you should make.'"

Finding that balance between micro-managing and rubber stamping is difficult. A CEO of a major fashion company explained to us the level of decision involvement he believes is appropriate: "I think the board should approve the strategies of the company – I don't mean that in any passive reactive way – it should be engaged in the process and I think it ought to hold the CEO and the management accountable for results." D.R. Grimes, Chairman and CEO of NetBank, stated he had some success setting aside quarterly board meetings that deal with strategic planning and monthly meetings that deal with the bank's operating results. "Otherwise, it's just really demanding on the board members."

Indeed, being a board member can be difficult, and not all are up for the challenge. Some board members feel they do not have the expertise to contribute to the decisions with which the board is involved. For example, Robert Galvin, Sr, former Chairman and CEO of Motorola was blunt:

> The reason I have not gone on other Boards was that I never felt knowing what I knew about Motorola – and I was very hands on – that I could ever know enough about the other company to be relevant in my advice to the Chief Executive Officer. If you want to talk generalizations, fine, call me and we'll have a drink together and I'll do that every couple of years."

The board's involvement in decision making will also depend on the situation a firm and its board find themselves in. For example, the last thing a board wants to do is get overly involved in the activities of a newly hired CEO, and few do. CEOs need some time to establish their vision and priorities, and excessive board pressure could lead to a revolving door at the top. On the other hand, the noose must be tightened when the outlook turns downward; CEOs who are over their heads tend to make less effective decisions by neglecting new or varied sources of information (Staw et al., 1981). The biggest challenge for boards is to identify early warning signs and then act on them. While other aspects of effective board process such as vigorous cognitive conflict and real behavioral integration will help, a board's biggest challenge is to know when to take charge. The experience of boards in companies such as Enron, K-Mart, Global Crossing, and WorldCom suggests that the burden of proof may well have shifted toward ever-closer board involvement.

Decision comprehensiveness: drilling down to understand more

Decision comprehensiveness refers to the depth and breadth of issues a group explores surrounding a particular decision in which it is involved. Decision comprehensiveness comprises the degree to which a group searches for information, seeks out help from experts, and explores and evaluates decision alternatives (Fredrickson and Mitchell, 1984). Just as top management teams address decisions with varying levels of comprehensiveness (Fredrickson, 1985), so too do boards.

How comprehensive boards are delving into a decision depends on numerous considerations. However, the company's financial condition and the risks involved appear to be the most salient. For example, the Mattel board was heavily criticized after they allowed then CEO Jill Barad to continue missing earnings targets quarter after quarter because they did not understand why earnings were deteriorating so quickly. Clearly, when the margin for error is small because of a firm's weakened financial state, greater scrutiny is called for. Similarly, the actions of the Enron board are going down as textbook examples of what not to do – board approval for a myriad of risky off-balance sheet partnerships and other arrangements with only the most cursory of investigations.

Such high profile board mistakes as Mattel and Enron have made others more deeply appreciate the value of decision comprehensiveness. This theme certainly came up in our own interviews. For example, one director told us, "Most boards are not as inquiring as they should be. Either they don't know that much about the subject even though they should have done more homework, or they feel shy challenging the CEO."

Other boards are more inquisitive and involved in issues. For example, several of the board members we interviewed noted that their involvement in decisions extends beyond just the scheduled board meetings. Specifically, one board member noted that he and other directors would occasionally call the CEO outside of board meetings. He said,

> If I see something in the paper or I'm curious about a competitor I'll often call him [the CEO] and chat with him about it, what's going on with this guy and how about this, some strategic, M&A thing that is going on with one of the competitors, have they moved into another business or discontinued a business.

The value of comprehensiveness is also apparent to board Chairmen who are also CEOs. John Cook of Profit Recovery Group talks with his board members about once a week. He said which board member he talks to "depends on the issue – if there would be some sort of a financial issue, I would talk to the head of our audit committee. If it's an investment or Wall Street issue, I often take the advice of one of the managing partners of Berkshire Funds, a very successful investment management firm." Cook also says it is not uncommon for the entire board to have telephone meetings in-between their scheduled quarterly board meetings.

To help ensure decisions are addressed comprehensively, three major areas should be emphasized. First, and perhaps the most important, is the priority boards should place on gathering the information they need to understand a decision or issue. Relevant information sources abound. The board should insist on the opportunity to occasionally interact with senior managers other than the CEO; information packets directors receive should have sufficient detail to make them useful, and unsanitized accounts of how the company is really doing should be sought. For example, at Home Depot, board members are required to visit dozens of stores a year, bringing rich interactions to directors that could not be replicated by sitting in the boardroom. It is also increasingly common for boards to seek outside experts, such as lawyers or investment bankers, to help them better understand an issue. Paul Fulchino, Chairman and CEO of Avial, explained that he regularly brings in experts to help boards understand a decision that they need to vote on. Fulchino also makes it a practice to bring in consultants about once a year to help his board members understand and contribute to Avial's strategic plan.

Secondly, information is not as helpful as it could be if directors do not rigorously prepare for board meetings, or lack sufficient time to fully digest the information. Part of the responsibility for developing a culture of rigor rests with the CEO who should encourage board participation and demonstrate to directors that their input is valued and helpful. Yet in the tougher world of corporate governance that exists today few boards can afford to stay on the sidelines anymore. As one director said, "the more preparation people can put into board meetings, the more productive they would be; it's like teaching a class – if you showed up and didn't prep for it, you would get through it but it probably wouldn't be as good as if you prepared for it." The quality of board preparation is also naturally enhanced when board members come to their positions with strategically relevant experience, another reason to emphasize this criterion in director selection.

Finally, board members need more time to do their jobs better. As one director lamented, "We get a packet and typically people haven't read them before board meetings. They just glance at it; they don't have the time; it's a time issue." It is thus critical that directors receive detailed information before board meetings with sufficient time to carefully study the key issues. However, when the average director is on four other boards, and many on considerably more, there will never be enough time. Almost a quarter of the companies in the Korn/Ferry International survey (2001) now actually place limits on the number of other board seats their directors can take on, a trend that may well accelerate in the future.

In summary, decision comprehensiveness, like the other key determinants of board process, is at the heart of what it takes to make effective board process and successful corporate governance happen. Boards of directors are indeed groups. The implications that come from this realization offer subtle and compelling insights, and enrich what we already know about boards.

Conclusions and Implications for Research and Practice

Researchers and shareholder activists have long argued that greater director independence and improved board structure results in board effectiveness. They have spent considerable time and effort focusing on four key areas, or "usual suspects," to improve board structure – the number of outside board directors, director shareholdings, board size, and CEO duality. However, researchers and shareholder activists need to go beyond the "usual suspects" and embrace a more complex but realistic perspective. Simple structural solutions to the corporate governance problems appear to have reached a point of diminishing returns – boards are more "independent" and better structured than at any time; yet corporate governance breakdowns still occur.

In this chapter we have tried to make three points: (1) reliance on the "usual suspects" to improve board effectiveness is limited; (2) board process, while messier and more complex, is in the end a more valuable approach to understanding boards; (3) the attributes of board process are potential levers that directors and CEOs can use to improve the practice of corporate governance in their companies.

Four major implications for research and practice come out of this study. First, further research is needed on how each of the process attributes affects the effectiveness of boards of directors' activities. The implications of our discussion are clear. As shown in Figure 13.1, cognitive conflict, behavioral integration, decision involvement, and decision comprehensiveness are expected to improve, and affective conflict worsen, board process and, in turn, board effectiveness. Yet, there have been no large-scale empirical studies to date that have directly tested these attributes in the context of boards of directors. The challenge in such work would be to measure the key constructs appropriately. While constructs for each of the board process characteristics have been empirically studied in group and/or top management team literatures, few studies have come up with a board effectiveness measure. Expert panels and careful survey work may be helpful in this regard. In the end, such studies could better inform boards not only on which process attributes may have the most impact on board effectiveness, but also on the actions that could affect these attributes.

Indeed, a closer examination of what affects the five process determinants identified in this study is needed. Since these five process determinants affect board effectiveness, it is important that we understand the actions that affect them. For example, if cognitive conflict makes boards more effective, then what factors or conditions help or hinder a team's ability to engage in cognitive conflict? Indeed, the "usual suspects" may play a strong role. For example, a greater number of outsiders may enable a board to engage in cognitive conflict and address decisions more comprehensively, but may hinder the board's ability to exhibit behavioral integration and know the right level of strategic involvement. However, we also suspect that a number of other factors besides the "usual suspects" likely affect the five determinants: the way board meetings are run; the nature and timeliness of the information provided to directors prior to board meetings, and the personality and career background of outside directors, etc.

Thirdly, board process needs to be included in corporate governance and agency theory. Not only have the traditional measures of board structure and independence been problematic, but board effectiveness has also been viewed only in terms of vigilance and involvement rather than than the fulfillment of key activities and ultimately firm performance. These differences have fundamental implications for how we do research on boards of directors. Rather than seeing board structure and independence as the most important determinants of vigilance, we should also be studying how board process affects vigilance. For example, boards characterized by cognitive conflict and comprehensiveness would be expected to do a much more thorough job evaluating key strategic decisions advocated by management than boards without such attributes. These key board processes may also be inter-related, presenting another interesting research opportunity. For example, affective conflict may make it difficult for boards to generate the consensus needed to engage in decision comprehensiveness.

Finally, board process may have an important impact on overall board effectiveness and even firm performance. While more empirical work on these relationships is called for, we can make some preliminary assertions based on the extensive interview data we collected. Board members readily acknowledge the importance of process when asked how boards really operate. They see process issues as central not just to how they function as a group, but to their ability to act independently of the CEO. Board independence is thus less an objective set of indicators based on composition and structure, and more a function of how board members themselves can effectively operate as a group to fulfill their roles. Efforts to improve how boards manage their cognitive and affective conflict, engender greater behavioral integration, prioritize what they pay attention to, and build comprehensiveness are needed. This study, by bringing together the academic literature and qualitative data from interviews with 25 directors is but one step in our evolving understanding of how boards work, and how they can be made to work better.

Notes

1. Where interviewees gave us permission, we include their names and titles to provide context for what they told us.
2. There is a large research literature on the distribution of power between boards and CEOs, but not on how power differentials among board members affects board processes or outcomes.

References

Alchian, A. and Demsetz, H. 1972: Production, information costs and economic organization. *American Economic Review*, 62, 777–795.

Amason, A. 1996: Distinguishing the effects of functional and dysfunctional conflict on strategic decision making: Resolving a paradox for top management teams. *Academy of Management Journal*, 39, 123–148.

Anderson, C. and Anthony, R. 1986: *The New Corporate Directors: Insights for Board Members and Executives.* New York: Wiley.

Astley, G., Axelsson, R., Butler, J., Hickson, D., and Wilson, D. 1982: Complexity and cleavage: Dual explanations of strategic decision making. *Journal of Management Studies*, 10, 357–375.

Bantel, K. and Jackson, S. 1989: Top management and innovations in banking: Does the composition of the top team make a difference? *Strategic Management Journal*, 10, 107–124.

Baysinger, B. and Hoskisson, R. 1990: The composition of the board of directors and strategic control: Effects of corporate strategy. *Academy of Management Review*, 15, 72–87.

Biggs, J. 1995: Why TIAA-CREF is active in corporate governance. *The Participant*, p. 2.

Boeker, W. 1992: Power and managerial dismissal: Scapegoating at the top. *Administrative Science Quarterly*, 27, 538–547.

Daily, C. and Dalton, D. 1992: The relationship between governance structure and corporate performance in entrepreneurial firms. *Journal of Business Venturing*, 7, 375–386.

Daily, C. and Dalton, D. 1997: CEO and board chair roles held jointly or separately: Much ado about nothing? *Academy of Management Executive*, 11, 11–20.

Daily, C., Certo, S., and Dalton, D. 1999: Pay directors in stock? No. It's supposed to align them with stockholder interests, but it's an idea full of traps and snares. *Across the Board*, 10, 47–50.

Dalton, D., Daily, C., Ellstrand, A., and Johnson, J. 1998: Meta-analytic reviews of board composition, leadership structure, and financial performance. *Strategic Management Journal*, 19, 269–290.

Fama, E. and Jensen, M. 1983: Separation of ownership and control. *Journal of Law and Economics*, 26, 301–325.

Finkelstein, S. and D'Aveni, R. 1994: CEO duality as a double-edged sword: How boards of directors balance entrenchment avoidance and unity of command. *Academy of Management Journal*, 37, 1079–1108.

Finkelstein, S. and Hambrick, D. 1996: *Strategic Leadership: Top Executives and their Effects on Organizations* (in West's Strategic Management Series). Minneapolis, MN: West.

Forbes, D. and Milliken, F. 1999: Cognition and corporate governance: Understanding boards of directors as strategic decision-making groups. *Academy of Management Review*, 24, 489–505.

Frederickson, J. 1985: Effects of decision motive and organizational performance level on strategic decision processes. *Academy of Management Journal*, 28, 821–843.

Fredrickson, J. and Mitchell, T. 1984: Strategic decision processes: Comprehensiveness and performance in an industry with an unstable environment. *Academy of Management Journal*, 27, 399–423.

Grossman, W. and Hoskisson, R. 1998: CEO pay at the crossroads of Wall Street and Main: Toward the strategic design of executive compensation. *The Academy of Management Executive*, 12, 43–57.

Hambrick, D. 1994: Top management groups: A conceptual integration and reconsideration of the "team" label. In B. Staw and L. Cummings (eds.), *Research in Organizational Behavior*. Greenwich, CT: JAI Press, 171–214.

Hambrick, D.C. 1998: Corporate coherence and the top management group. In D.C. Hambrick, A. Nadler, and M. Tushman (eds.), *Navigating Change: How CEOs, Top Groups, and Boards Steer Transformation*. Boston, MA: Harvard Business School Press, 123–140.

Hambrick, D. and Fukutomi, G. 1991: The seasons of a CEO's tenure. *Academy of Management Review*, 16, 719–42.

Hambrick, D. and Jackson, E. 2000: Outside directors with a stake: The linchpin in improving governance. *California Management Review*, 42, 108–127.

Healy, T. and Nakarmi, L. 1999: The big squeeze. Asiaweek.com. November 12.

Jehn, K. 1994: Enhancing effectiveness: An investigation of advantages and disadvantages of value-based intra-group conflict. *International Journal of Conflict Management*, 5, 223–228.

Jensen, M. and Meckling, W. 1976: Theory of the firm: Managerial behavior, agency costs, and ownership structure. *Journal of Financial Economics*, 3, 305–360.

Johnson, J., Daily, C., and Ellstrand, A. 1996: Board of directors: A review and research agenda. *Journal of Management*, 22, 409–438.

Johnson, R., Hoskisson, R., and Hitt, M. 1993: Board of director involvement in restructuring: The effects of board versus managerial controls and characteristics. *Strategic Management Journal*, 14, 33–50.

Korn/Ferry International 2001: 28th Annual Board of Directors Study.

Lee, C.S. 1998: Collision course. *Far Eastern Economic Review*, 51–52.

Li, J. and Hambrick, D. 2003: Demographic gaps and disintegration in factional groups: The case of joint venture management teams. Working Paper, Hong Kong University of Science and Technology.

Lorsch, J. 1989: *Pawns or Potentates: The Reality of America's Boards*. Boston, MA: Harvard Business School Press.

Mace, M. 1971: *Directors: Myth and Reality*. Boston, MA: Harvard University Press.

Main, B., O'Reilly, C., and Wade, J. 1994: The CEO, the board of directors and executive compensation: Economic and psychological perspectives. *Industrial and Corporate Change*, 4, 293–332.

Mitroff, I. 1982: Talking past one's colleagues in matters of policy. *Strategic Management Journal*, 10, 125–141.

Mooney, A. 2003: What makes a top management group a top management team? An examination of the determinants of behavioral integration. Presentation at the Academy of Management, Seattle.

Mooney, A. and Sonnenfeld, J. 2001: Exploring antecedents to conflict during strategic decision making: The importance of behavioral integration. Best Paper Proceedings of the Academy of Management, Washington, DC.

Pelled, L., Eisenhardt, K., and Xin, K. 1999: Exploring the black box: An analysis of work group diversity, conflict, and performance. *Administrative Science Quarterly*, 44, 1–28.

Pennings, J. 1980: *Interlocking Directorates*. Washington, DC: Jossey-Bass.

Schweiger, D., Sanberg, W., and Rechner, P. 1989: Experiential effects of dialectical inquiry, devil's advocacy, and consensus approaches to strategic decision making. *Academy of Management Journal*, 32, 745–772.

Shleifer, A. and Vishny, R. 1986: Large shareholders and corporate control. *Journal of Political Economy*, 94, 461–484.

Staw, B., Sandelands, L., and Dutton, J. 1981: Threat-rigidity effects in organizational behavior: A multi-level analysis. *Administrative Science Quarterly*, 26, 501–524.

Tjosvold, D. 1986: Constructive controversy: A key strategy for groups. *Personnel*, 63, 39–44.

Walsh, J. and Seward, J. 1990: On the efficiency of internal and external corporate control mechanisms. *Academy of Management Review*, 15, 421–458.

Zahra, S. and Stanton, W. 1988: The implications of board of directors' composition for corporate strategy and performance. *International Journal of Management*, 5, 229–236.

Index

Note: "n." after a page reference indicates the number of a note on that page.